Subjectivities, Knowledges, and Feminist Geographies

Subjectivities, Knowledges, and Feminist Geographies

The Subjects and Ethics of Social Research

Liz Bondi, Hannah Avis, Ruth Bankey, Amanda Bingley, Joyce Davidson, Rosaleen Duffy, Victoria Ingrid Einagel, Anja-Maaike Green, Lynda Johnston, Susan Lilley, Carina Listerborn, Shonagh McEwan, Mona Marshy, Niamh O'Connor, Gillian Rose, Bella Vivat, and Nichola Wood

ROWMAN & LITTLEFIELD PUBLISHERS, INC.
Lanham • Boulder • New York • Oxford

ROWMAN & LITTLEFIELD PUBLISHERS, INC.

Published in the United States of America
by Rowman & Littlefield Publishers, Inc.
An Imprint of the Rowman & Littlefield Publishing Group
4720 Boston Way, Lanham, Maryland 20706
www.rowmanlittlefield.com

12 Hid's Copse Road
Cumnor Hill, Oxford OX2 9JJ, England

British Library Cataloguing in Publication Information Available

Library of Congress Cataloging-in-Publication Data
Subjectivities, knowledges, and feminist geographies: the subjects and ethics
of social research / Liz Bondi . . . [et al.].
    p. cm.
Includes bibliographical references (p.   ) and index.
    ISBN 0-7425-1561-3 (cloth : alk. paper) — 0-7425-1562-1 (pbk. : alk. paper)
    1. Feminist theory. 2. Feminist geography. 3. Spatial behavior. 4.
Subjectivity. I. Bondi, L. (Liz)
    HQ1190 .S82 2002
    305.42'01—dc21
                                                            2002001880

Printed in the United States of America

♾™ The paper used in this publication meets the minimum requirements of
American National Standard for Information Sciences—Permanence of Paper
for Printed Library Materials, ANSI/NISO Z39.48-1992.

Contents

Acknowledgments

Many individuals and organizations have provided invaluable assistance in the production of this book. Several chapters draw on conversations with people who have agreed to talk to one or more of us in the course of our various research projects. We are deeply indebted to all of them. A number of colleagues have offered feedback on drafts of individual chapters and we would like to thank Charles Withers and Katarina Nylund for their comments on chapter 2, Jan Penrose and Susan Smith for their comments on chapter 4, Robyn Longhurst and Robin Peace for their comments on chapter 5, and John Holmwood and Charles Withers for their comments on chapter 9. We would also like to thank Melanie Wall for the generous part that she played in the development of this book.

Among us we have also benefited enormously from the financial support provided by two organizations. The Economic and Social Research Council provided support through grant number R000222825 for research drawn on for chapter 7, and through grant numbers L320253245 and R000223013 for the projects informing chapter 11, and through postgraduate studentships for research projects on which chapters 1, 7, 11, 13, and 15 draw. The University of Edinburgh provided support through postgraduate studentships for the research on which chapters 3, 4, 8, 9, 10, and 12 are based. We would also like to thank the Department of Geography at the University of Edinburgh for financial assistance toward the costs of the workshop at which first drafts of the majority of chapters were discussed.

Finally, we are very grateful for the encouragement and support of our publishers and most especially for the patient guidance shown by Brenda Hadenfeldt without whom this project could not have been brought to fruition.

Introduction

Liz Bondi

As feminists have long argued, the Western academy has been, and continues to be, dominated by a particular group—namely white, heterosexual, nondisabled men. This state of affairs is reflected in the form and content of the knowledge produced by those constituting the Western academy (Antony and Witt 1993; Lloyd 1984). Over the past thirty years feminist academics of varying disciplinary backgrounds and political persuasions have challenged this by bringing a wide range of feminist ideas and aspirations to bear on the production of academic knowledge, with a view to identifying and redressing its manifold gender biases. Closely, if not inextricably, intertwined within these efforts have been the twin concerns of transforming the character of knowledge produced, and transforming the academy itself, especially its openness to, and treatment of, the people it has traditionally excluded. Feminist geographers have, of course, played a part in this. Thus, in the United States for example, feminists in the Association of American Geographers lobbied for and created two bodies, namely the Geographic Perspectives on Women Specialty Group, which is dedicated to supporting the production of new kinds of knowledges, and the Committee on the Status of Women, which seeks to secure equal treatment for women and men. Feminists in the United Kingdom, where the project from which this book emerged was based, have pursued similar objectives through a single organization, founding the Women and Geography Study Group to encourage feminist research and its dissemination (via teaching as well as other means), and as a network within which issues about equality and access could be discussed (Peake 1989).

Engaging with long-established and powerful institutions in these ways has proven to be fraught with contradiction (Aisenberg and Harrington 1988; Morley and Walsh 1996). Feminist academics have repeatedly confronted and struggled with profound tensions between different strategies for challenging gender biases,

1

variously depicted in terms of equality and difference, liberalism and radicalism, and so on. A central and oft-revisited dilemma concerns tensions between efforts to secure fair treatment for all and attempts to instigate or foster more radical changes (Bondi 2001). The goal of fair treatment is essential to enable those who do not belong to the dominant group to enter and influence academic institutions. But such efforts tacitly accept and endorse the value systems of, and the boundaries around, the institutions concerned. So feminists also work to expose and challenge underlying values and boundaries, but in so doing they run the risk of undermining rationales for goals like equal access. Such issues are brought sharply into focus when judgments are made about the academic "standard" of feminist work: to what extent must feminist students and feminist academics perform within the existing "rules of the game" in order to articulate their claims to knowledge, and to what extent must those "rules" be challenged in order to change them (Gallop 1995)? Put another way, to what extent is the adoption of "authoritative," "masculine" ways of knowing necessary and inevitable, and to what extent is it possible to "perform" academic knowledge in other ways (Bondi 1997; Rose 1996)?

Dilemmas of this kind are the stuff of academic labor: each day we negotiate them, whether in routine, microlevel decisions about our interactions with others, or in more major ways that may have a decisive bearing on the lives of those within or beyond the academy. Consequently, feminist engagements with the academy change those who labor in this way as much as their labor changes the production and relations of knowledge. Indeed, feminism within and beyond the academy has been as much about finding new ways of being women (and men) as about changing the conditions within which lives are led. In other words, the subject of feminism is neither external to, nor identical with, the student of feminism. Rather, feminism has always entailed questioning its subject in multiple ways.

This book is an expression of such questioning. It emerges directly from the day-to-day struggles of its authors (all of whom are women)[1] to create and sustain places for ourselves within, or in relation to, the academy. At the same time its substance contributes to feminist theorizations of subjectivity, and especially to the spatiality of subjectivities, through research that engages with people in ways designed to create and sustain other kinds of places, whether for grassroots activism or for ways of being that contradict dominant discourses. That I choose the metaphor of place to describe this project is no coincidence. Although we do not all define ourselves as geographers, we came together as a group because of our shared connections to a department of geography, whether as graduate students, research workers, or lecturing staff. Our intellectual engagements with questions of subjectivity take place at or near points of convergence between feminist and geographical arguments that knowledge always bears the impress of the contexts within which "knowers" produce it (Haraway 1988; Kirby 1996; Jones, Nast, and Roberts 1997; Livingstone 1992; Rose 1993).

Our work elaborates a plural understanding of feminist perspectives in that we draw on a variety of theoretical resources to develop our arguments. We contest attempts to limit the application of feminist ideas to questions of gender and instead illustrate the wider relevance of feminist insights. In so doing we seek to move beyond boundaries that often circumscribe the field of "feminist geography." Our work is, nevertheless, bounded in particular ways, for we write within, or at least close to, dominant conventions of academic publication.

Introductions to books conventionally provide overviews of their contents, and this is especially the case in coauthored volumes or edited collections. To embark on such a task assumes the capacity to view the whole from a place apart from, or "above," the main body of the text, thus enacting traditional forms of academic authority in which the writer of the introduction takes up a position supposedly offering a "commanding view" (compare Rose 1993; also see Bondi 1990). Introductions of this kind are often very useful to readers in a manner analogous to maps used for tasks like route finding. However, as geographers have elaborated, neither map making nor map use are ever neutral: both are deeply imbued with cultural meanings. It is because these cultural specificities typically remain tacit that particular kinds of maps (or representations or ways of knowing) acquire exceptional prestige, authority, and power, primarily through their claims to accuracy and objectivity (on maps, see Harley 1992). Even if such claims are disavowed within textual introductions, they are simultaneously invoked by the genre. Moreover, as I have said, readers often find such introductions very useful. This introduction therefore expresses a pervasive tension within feminist scholarship: while I seek to work against the grain of traditional forms of academic authority, I am also bound to (re)enact them (Bondi 1997). My choice in this case is one of many possible compromises. I begin by briefly discussing some of the processes by which this book came into being before outlining the key themes addressed by each of its main sections. My intention is to insinuate consideration of the contexts of the book's production into my representation of its contents.

FROM READING GROUP TO COAUTHORSHIP

Issues about authorship present feminist academics with particular difficulties and nowhere more so than in writing about subjectivities and knowledges. The convention of attributing authorship to named individuals is a product of culturally specific ways of representing both knowers and knowledges (compare Hawkesworth 1988). We may insist that academic writing is always dependent on the context of its production and is always dependent upon interactions among people, which authors conventionally represent through acknowledgments and citations, but the naming of individuals as authors powerfully personalizes and individualizes research and scholarship. Notwithstanding exhortations to "collaborate" in the development of research, the academy operates in ways that intensify processes of personalization and individuation. Consider, for example, how institutions examine for, and award, degrees, and how appointments and promotions are determined. In all such processes individuals are judged on individual records, however prominent collaborative work may be within those records. Moreover, the more directly we address, collaborate

with, or make our work available to the people about whom we write, the less our
efforts "count" within the currency of academic prestige. If feminists want to survive
within academic institutions they must submit to, and participate in, these
processes. Consequently, it is not surprising that published work almost invariably
names one or more individual authors, one of the rare exceptions being the first
book coauthored by the Women and Geography Study Group (1984). In the years
since then, the institutional pressures toward the personalization of authorship have
certainly not lessened. While *Subjectivities, Knowledges, and Feminist Geographies* was,
to a considerable extent, inspired by the pleasures of meeting together and talking
face-to-face in a reading group, it is equally informed by the needs of individuals to
claim credit for (possession of) "their" work through publication. While we signal
the collaborative character of our work through collective authorship of the volume
as a whole, we also attribute individual chapters to individual authors (compare
Women and Geography Study Group 1997). Moreover, except for this introduction
and the conclusion, all the chapters draw on substantive research projects designed
and implemented in the course of undergraduate, masters, or doctoral degrees or externally funded research, for which the named authors carried major responsibilities
as individuals.

A group of us (overlapping with but not identical to the authors of this book) have
written elsewhere about a key element of the practice through which this book was
created, namely a three-day workshop at which first drafts of most of the chapters
were presented (Feminist Geography Reading Group 2000). As coordinator of this
volume I take this opportunity to explore other aspects of the process of its creation,
the selection of which reflects my particular preoccupations, arising at least in part
from my particular position among the group of coauthors.

For some fifteen years I have considered myself to be part of a community of feminist geographers. In recent years I have been very fortunate to have the opportunity
to participate in such a community not only at a distance but also locally in the Department of Geography at the University of Edinburgh, specifically at the university
through the presence of several feminist colleagues and graduate students. Many of
those who make up this local community knew their participation would be temporary, whether as visitors, students, or on limited-term contracts as teachers or researchers. Others have chosen to move on. But a sense of community has nevertheless been sustained, principally through the regular meetings of a feminist geography
reading group, membership of which has changed year by year as well as meeting
by meeting. For several years our meetings were organized primarily around articles
or books that members of the group were interested in reading and discussing, and
the process of exchanging ideas proved to be stimulating and rewarding. Frequently
we reflected on what we had read in relation to our own research, and in the course
of this gradually came to new insights about our shared interests. So what began as
a shared commitment to feminist practices and a shared interest in feminist scholarship in the social sciences evolved into an awareness of more profound interconnections between our ways of thinking about the various projects in which we were
and are involved. To some extent this was a result of our various conversations: we

were influencing one another not so much through explicit attempts to do so but through conversing with one another. We were therefore illustrating some of the ways in which context or situation are inscribed within knowledge production. But we also became increasingly aware that we all engage closely with particular issues arising from the various ways in which critiques of universal knowledge claims render problematic the subjects about whom, through whom, and in relation to whom knowledge is produced.

Before discussing these concerns in more detail, I comment briefly on the process of writing. The decision to write a book changed our working practices within and beyond the reading group. We needed to think of ourselves as a different kind of collectivity from what we had been so far, positioned in new ways relative to others, and especially relative to other writing. Instead of coming together as an audience for other people's work, we came together with a vision of making our ideas available to circulate textually through other audiences. We had to take new kinds of risks with one another by engaging more closely and more critically with one another's work. We did this not simply as one colleague to another but as members of a group who communicated intensively throughout the writing of this book. Chapters were subject to multiple readings. The order of chapters and the main sections of the book emerged from this process and generated further readings of our work. At this stage some of us met face-to-face while others participated at a distance having left Edinburgh since work on the book began.

Acknowledging the coauthorship of our work did not transform the intensely private qualities of writing: most of us spent considerable periods of time "alone" in order to produce the text that makes up this book. But we did not write as isolated individual authors; rather our writing emerged in what might be thought of as in between times and spaces. These times and spaces existed between exchanges among the coauthors, between other activities, between writers and texts (including their own and others), and between writers and imagined others (compare Metcalfe 1999). They existed between Edinburgh and the other places from which participants came and to which they went; they existed in the interplay between face-to-face and electronic forms of communication. Several chapters in this volume problematize such in-between times and spaces, drawing on a range of theoretical resources to do so. In such ways this book sustains a complex interweaving of subjects and subjectivities: its production (as well as its consumption) was and is profoundly intersubjective.

While I have emphasized our coauthorship and my own immersion within the processes through which this book was written, my position was also unique. As the book's coordinator I drew extensively on conventional forms of authority, such as setting deadlines, assuming the right to determine boundaries around authorship, and, to varying degrees, editing text supplied by coauthors. As its coordinator I assumed the right and the responsibility to introduce the key themes of the chapters that follow. I do so under the headings that structure the book as a whole, which represent our common concern with, and commitment to, feminist reshapings of academic knowledge.

EMBODIMENT, EMOTIONS, AND SUBJECTIVITIES

A central tension for feminists concerns the relationship between gender and a binary distinction between rationality and irrationality. An association between rationality and masculinity on the one hand and between irrationality and femininity on the other has long been used to undermine the value and validity of women's knowledge. Women have often sought to decouple gender from the opposition between rationality and irrationality in order to take up positions as knowledgeable actors; indeed, women's presence within academia has depended and continues to depend at least in part upon women's capacity to perform rationality within this framework (see for example Richards 1980). But alongside such performances many feminists have also sought to challenge the binary formulation that differentiates rationality from its irrational "other." One influential way of approaching this task has been via critiques of the enormously influential legacy of Descartes' philosophy on Western thought. As several feminist philosophers have argued, Descartes' treatment of mind and body as basic and mutually exclusive categories set in train the liberal humanist differentiation of rational, independent, self-directing agents from the emotional, irrational, messy materiality of bodies, together with the gendered connotations of these oppositions (Alcoff and Potter 1993; Battersby 1998; Lloyd 1984; Hekman 1992). Such critiques begin the task of opening up spaces for the articulation of different versions of subjectivity, which do not invoke or depend upon a radical and absolute separation between "self" (mind) and "other" (body), and enable relationships between "selves," "bodies," and "spaces" to be rethought (Ainley 1998; Butler and Parr 1999; Carter, Donald, and Squire 1993; Duncan 1996a; Kirby 1996; Nast and Pile 1998a; Pile and Thrift 1995; Rose 1993; Teather 1999). It is to these critiques that the first part of this volume contributes. Focusing on particular aspects of emotional life, the chapters individually and together offer distinctive post-Cartesian perspectives on the human subject. In contrast to the rational, self-knowing subject, these chapters illustrate how subjects are always embodied and how subjectivity is always fractured and multiple. The chapters thus seek to unsettle and move beyond the denial and neglect of emotion and corporeality characteristic of most social research.

Through a study of self-help resources aimed at sufferers of agoraphobia, chapter 1 shows how notions of the rational, self-knowing subject are both extremely pervasive and seriously at odds with subjective accounts. Joyce Davidson illustrates ways in which agoraphobic women contest these accounts of selfhood, and so opens up questions about exactly what *kind* of self is presupposed by self-help texts. By critiquing the Cartesian notion of self that such texts propound, and by questioning what self-help resources of a more inclusive hue might look like, she offers an account of subjectivity in which embodiment is central. Chapter 1 also illustrates how, despite their enormous influence, efforts to enforce a radical separation between cognition and emotion, or between the rational and the irrational, are in practice doomed.

Chapter 2 develops this line of analysis through an examination of geographies of fear. Carina Listerborn shows how existing conceptualizations tend to reproduce an unhelpful distinction between the social and the spatial as potential sources or causes of fear. Rejecting such separations, she draws on Henri Lefebvre's discussion of the social production of space to propose an understanding of fear in which the spatiality of subjectivity is fully acknowledged.

In the context of this interpretation of the geography of women's fear, chapter 3 draws attention to significant misrepresentations of agoraphobia, foregrounding the more complex spatiality of the person vulnerable to panic attacks. Through her analysis of sufferers' accounts, Ruth Bankey shows how panic attacks render boundaries between bodies and environments highly unstable (compare Longhurst 2001). The microgeographies elaborated by sufferers help to illuminate often taken-for-granted qualities of everyday space and therefore illuminate more fully the intrinsic spatiality of subjectivities.

Chapters 1, 2, and 3 each emphasize the centrality of emotional life in the production of subjectivity from the starting point of fear. Chapter 4 approaches emotions and embodiment from another angle, exploring their significance in geographies of music. Through this study Nichola Wood shows how consideration of emotional aspects of everyday life has the capacity to transform our understandings and representations of cultural phenomena. By focusing on what are generally pleasurable forms of cultural consumption, the chapter also provides a rather different illustration of the inseparability of embodiment, emotion, and thought from those emerging from the earlier chapters' concern with fear and panic (also see Williams 1998).

DUALISMS, BODIES, AND SUBJECTIVITIES

The chapters constituting the first part of this book highlight some of the limitations of dualistic concepts of the subject and of knowledge, for example in the form of the Cartesian split between mind and body. The second part explores the construction and persistence of dualisms more closely, highlighting in particular the spatial constitution of subject positions and subjectivities that derive from dichotomous distinctions between self and other. Such distinctions posit stable and impermeable boundaries capable of containing and individuating subjects. Each chapter in this part identifies the status of such boundaries as both fictional and powerful. These analyses help to identify points of rupture in dominant understandings of subjectivity at the same time as acknowledging their resilience.

Chapter 5 considers the significance of corporeal borders in the production of subjectivities through a case study of two of the gay pride parades that have become commonplace in Western cities since the New York Stonewall riots began on the night of June 27, 1969, when police raided a gay bar called the Stonewall Inn, in Greenwich Village. The parades in question are simultaneously forms of tourist entertainment and political protests. In this context Lynda Johnston attempts to upset the corporeal borders that exist between tourists and parade participants drawing on Julia Kristeva's notion of "abjection." She shows how the embodied transgressions of paraders can be viewed as both disrupting and reproducing binary distinctions between gay and straight, male and female, self and other.

The influence and the limitations of dualisms deriving from the Cartesian concept of subjectivity also informs chapter 6, this time in the context of the gendered spaces and bodies produced in the sport of golf. As Shonagh McEwan shows, golf continues to be dominated by men and particular forms of masculinity and can be understood to "accommodate" women by creating distinctly gendered spaces and boundaries. These gendered dichotomies do not go unchallenged or unmodified, and the case study elaborates an understanding of subjectivity as embodied, multiple, fractured, and highly contradictory, albeit within the context of persistent and powerful binary framings.

Chapter 7 is a study of the production of knowledges and knowers in an implementation of geographical information systems (GIS). Using interview material from users new to these technologies, Susan Lilley maps the emergence of competing knowledge claims and subjectivities. Exploring the various discourses users rely upon and reproduce, from the rationality of science, to magic and spectacle, she illustrates the complex interplay between subject positions and speaking subjects. Like the other chapters in this part of the book, her analysis highlights the simultaneous persistence and transgression of dualistic concepts, which insist, for example, on a radical separation between "objective" science and "irrational" magic. But whereas chapters 5 and 6 emphasize the inescapability of dualistic formulations, chapter 7 shifts the emphasis to the impossibility of containing subjectivities within such framings. In so doing this chapter paves the way for part III.

KNOWLEDGES AND SUBJECTIVITIES

The chapters making up parts I and II illustrate how particular kinds of knowledge claims are associated with particular conceptualizations of subjectivity. While universal knowledge claims presuppose rational subjects capable of transcending the materiality and particularity of embodiment, post-Cartesian notions of subjectivity generate partial and situated claims to knowledge (Haraway 1988). Part III explores this situatedness. Through four chapters rooted in research projects undertaken in a wide range of geographical and social settings, we consider the politics of claims to knowledge in relation to understandings of subjectivity as multiple, fractured, embodied, and situated.

Chapter 8 explores efforts to create spaces within which subjectivities that are denied, repressed, or potentially unrepresentable might emerge. By examining the performances and narratives of three artists of Palestinian origin living in Canada, Mona Marshy shows how particular artistic forms serve to articulate and define social distinctions and to delineate or reimagine boundaries of nation, subject, and identity (compare Hall and du Gay 1996). But, as the artists themselves observe, the knowledges they produce and perform are contingent on the contexts of their production and performance. Always vulnerable to cultural colonization through which dichotomies between self and other are reproduced, their artworks seek to clear spaces for identifications of more complex, in between, kinds. Mona Marshy's sensitive interpretation of their work contributes to the task of rethinking subjectivities and reshaping knowledges in more inclusive ways.

Chapter 9 is also concerned with the cultural politics of art, but shifts the focus from artistic production to the subject-forming practices of British arts policy. Anja-Maaike Green examines debates about the development of new audiences for publicly subsidized art, paying particular attention to tensions between the anti-popularism embedded in the arts world and representations of those described as "non-attenders." She shows how knowledges (about art) and subjectivities (through which potential audiences are defined) are mutually constituted within particular political contexts. While arts workers and arts policies tend to limit the range of subject positions available, by disclosing their discursive tactics her analysis suggests points of resistance.

Chapter 10 examines the production of subjectivity in another arena of British public policy, namely that of welfare reform. Niamh O'Connor contrasts dominant political discourse about the supposed "dependency culture" of those claiming welfare benefits in the United Kingdom with claimants' accounts of their lived experiences. In so doing she challenges key ideas informing current policies, particularly the dichotomous categories of "paid workers" and "benefit claimants," which are used to differentiate between citizens for political ends. By illuminating the discursive work through which such categories are produced and sustained, and by highlighting their lack of correspondence with the lives of those they other, she begins to undo their effects. Like several preceding chapters, Niamh O'Connor effectively clears discursive spaces for the articulation of subjectivities excluded, disavowed, and marginalized in the domain of formal politics.

Turning from policy documents to gossip and rumor, chapter 11 considers practices that are often represented and denigrated as peculiarly feminine. Drawing on fieldwork conducted in Zimbabwe and in Belize, Rosaleen Duffy illustrates how both relatively powerful and powerless interest groups use rumor and gossip in their efforts to influence political processes in the conservation sector. In so doing she illustrates the complex interrelationship between structures of power and the production of knowledges. Her analysis shows how knowledges are constituted in, and constitutive of, political networks as well as political subjectivities. This chapter thus draws attention to the intersubjective production of knowledges, on which the next part of the volume focuses.

INTERSUBJECTIVITIES IN RESEARCH PRACTICE

The knowledges produced through the practices of research depend upon relationships between researchers and those they research. These practices illustrate how knowledges are produced intersubjectively. Feminists have paid a good deal of attention to the relations of research, focusing especially on questions of power (Maynard and Purvis 1994; Nielsen 1990). The chapters making up the first three parts of this volume are all informed by such work. In the final part we focus directly on research practice and explore the mutual production of (inter)subjectivities in research encounters. We work with complex and critical understandings of reflexivity and self, opening up explorations of nonrational and noncognitive dimensions of research relationships and attending to both the need for and the limits to self-awareness in the conduct of research.

In chapter 12 Hannah Avis retraces her steps, or rather her speaking, through a series of pilot interviews conducted as part of her doctoral research. She discusses her struggle to find a way of learning to do interviews and to be an interviewer, acknowledging the subtle influence of the conventions of detachment as well as the sometimes overwhelming complexity of feminist accounts of research practice. She interweaves a reading of feminist debates on methodology with reflections on and excerpts from her interviews, (re)tracing a journey from the character of the "old-style" detached researcher she knew she didn't really want to be, to the deeply connected and immersed researcher that she eventually heard.

Personal connection and immersion in fieldwork are not without dangers. In chapter 13 Amanda Bingley addresses the ethical issues involved in working with people who participate in research designed to elicit childhood and unconscious experiences. She explores the advantages of, and the potential problems associated with, using a working knowledge of psychotherapeutic practice in qualitative research. She argues that psychotherapeutic supervision is essential in research of this kind in order to ensure the availability of spaces within which researchers can process the emotional impact of their work and so sustain ethical practice in relation to their research participants. In this way the chapter provides a fresh perspective on the conduct of fieldwork and on the nature of research relationships.

The personal demands entailed in qualitative research are discussed further in chapter 14 by Victoria Ingrid Einagel who explores how identities forged through dislocation, disjuncture, and loss, which she encountered during fieldwork in a post-war environment, were echoed in her own subjective experience. The chapter takes as its starting point a sense of unease, uncertainty, and helplessness the author experienced on returning to the environment of the academy after seven months in post-war Sarajevo. Conveying to others the struggle of Sarajevans to make sense of their lives in the context of transformed discourses of (ethnic) identities was both painful and urgent, challenging the author's own sense of her self and her place in the world. Tracing these parallels she offers a powerful account of the challenges of ethnographic fieldwork.

Feminist philosophers have approached ethical questions in a variety of ways, and in chapter 15 Bella Vivat draws on some of this work to examine how knowledge, subjectivity, agency, and morality are interwoven. She places Carol Gilligan's (1993) distinction between an ethics of care and an ethics of justice in this broader context before considering the implications of researching spiritual aspects of care for her own research practice. Outlining the issues that arose for her as a personally involved and concerned researcher conducting ethnographic research in a hospice, she discusses the difficulties of managing her own multiple personal loyalties and attachments in writing about opposing perspectives, while caring for the people involved and attempting to represent their multiple subjectivities and differing perceptions of ethical behavior.

CONCLUSION

This book concludes by revisiting conceptualizations of space running through the text. By exploring the ways in which theorizations of subjectivity invoke and produce different spatialities, Gillian Rose reworks the connections between the preceding chapters. She offers an account of some of the tensions with which feminist scholars engage when they conduct research in avowedly situated ways. In this context she explores issues in the politics of research implicit in the various contributions to the book and foregrounds the difficulties inherent in the processes through which the book came into being.

Among the boundaries problematized by feminist research are those around academia and academic knowledges. These are boundaries we straddle in our everyday lives. Our research is profoundly influenced by our experiences of negotiating such boundaries, whether through our choice of topic or our research methods or in other ways. As feminist academics we are acutely aware of the dangers of colonizing the experiences and knowledges of those on whom our research focuses. But we are also committed to increasing the permeability of the boundaries around academic knowledge, and in so doing we seek to unsettle the prestige it assumes. The chapters that result therefore engage with knowledges produced in a wide array of settings, from self-help texts, through policy documents, oral networks, artistic performances, to numerous conversations entered into in the course of research. By working with these various knowledges we seek to elaborate ways of thinking about subjectivity that expand the horizons of possibility available within and beyond the academy.

NOTE

1. The absence of men among the authors of the book has a complex history. It is not the result of an explicit decision. However, neither did we seek out men to join our group. It is probably the case that tacit assumptions circulated locally, which discouraged men from participating. That we made few, if any, efforts to challenge such assumptions may itself be viewed as a tactic for creating a women-only space within a male-dominated institution.

I

EMBODIMENT, EMOTIONS, AND SUBJECTIVITIES

1

All in the Mind?: Women, Agoraphobia, and the Subject of Self-Help

Joyce Davidson

> I think they try to fob us off, I don't think, um, they really take us, very seriously. I think they think probably because its mostly women that go to them with these problems that they think we're, a bit neurotic, maybe just a bit weak, an . . . don't want to cope with, maybe everyday life.
>
> —Kathy, agoraphobia sufferer and contributor to self-help video "A"

In its most extreme manifestation, agoraphobia will render its subject completely incapable of leaving home. Indeed many agoraphobic women—and around 85 percent of sufferers are women[1]—perceive the outside world to be so utterly terrifying that merely to contemplate crossing this threshold between safe and unsafe space is enough to initiate an episode of severe and debilitating anxiety. Their prior experience of panic in the face of social space[2] has served to infuse the very fabric of their (previous) life-worlds with an aversive aura so strong that they remain housebound for months, or even years.

That it is "peopled" rather than "open" spaces that agoraphobics fear and avoid runs contrary to both popular opinion and dictionary definitions of the disorder (Davidson 2000a, 2000b). This confusion about the very nature of agoraphobia is indicative of the lack of understanding surrounding the disorder. This, combined with sufferers' own reclusiveness, makes their condition extraordinarily isolating, both physically and emotionally. Sufferers may be reluctant to discuss or even admit to having difficulties they themselves don't understand, even with close friends and family. Should they eventually decide to seek help from health care professionals, it is, as Kathy's comments above make plain, by no means guaranteed that help or even understanding will be forthcoming. In circumstances such as these, self-help resources may seem to be the only source of information and support available, and it is therefore important to understand their character and role.

15

Self-help resources in general are, as Robin Allwood remarks (1996: 19), "*aimed primarily at women*" and mostly concerned with what are (stereo)typically considered to be "women's problems"—those related to depression, weight, and anxiety. Such texts would therefore seem to be an important focus for feminist researchers' attention, and I want to consider what a feminist interpretation of self-help resources aimed at agoraphobic women might reveal. Perhaps the most immediately obvious focus for such an analysis relates to the ambiguity inherent in the very name of the genre. The term "self-help" can either be read in the (common) sense of "help yourself," or in the alternative, more complex sense of "help *for* the self." The difference here lies between what is straightforwardly self-service, and what is a kind of therapy for the treatment of *selves*. Both senses clearly harbor implicit definitions, but the latter in particular begs specific questions regarding the nature of assumptions underlying this definition. Given that there are contested notions of what a self is or can be, *whose* idea of self is being invoked here? To exactly *what kind* of self is help being offered?

Feminists in particular have highlighted the predominance, and implications for women, of a particular (masculine) conception of the self within the history of Western thought (Battersby 1998; Bordo 1993; Butler 1990, 1993; Irigaray 1985). While the precise nature of these feminist critiques differ, they all seek to subvert the hegemony of a paradigmatic self defined as rational, autonomous, and bounded. Following Descartes, this dominant notion of the self is also regarded as being composed of two distinct elements: the mind (*res cogitans*) and the body (*res extensa*). I will argue that it is precisely this unitary, and yet internally divided, masculinist and Cartesian version of self that informs the self-help resources in question, which the representation of agoraphobic selves on offer is set *against*, while dependent upon, a myth of normal (masculine) identity.

Maintaining the hegemony of this particular conceptualization involves the denigration and suppression of alternative discourses, those associated with the wrong (read feminine) side of a familiar set of hierarchic dichotomies: of the body (as opposed to mind); of nature (held against culture); and emotion (as always subservient to reason). (See Bondi 1992; Plumwood 1993.)[3] I argue that these dualistic discourses are instrumental in positioning the subject(s) of agoraphobia and have an intrinsically normative role and rationale.

The audiences of these self-help texts are subjected to the pervasive notion that there is a particular version of self, *a* form of normality to which they should aspire. This mythical model is, I will argue, inextricably bound with an interlocking set of masculinist discourses and is overly, if not overtly, reliant on an individualist, yet dualistic, liberal humanist model of the self. One of my aims here is to demonstrate the hegemonic operation of this very particular and potentially damaging model in self-help resources.

My ultimate aim in this chapter is to show that this limited and limiting "ideal" cannot contain or account for, and thus excludes, the embodied experiences of agoraphobic women. One need not, however, necessarily respond to this situation by positioning the agoraphobic as pathological, by representing her in terms of an aberration of an assumed normal self, and one that requires remolding within masculine terms. One might rather question the validity and adequacy of the masculine model itself. Perhaps sympathetic analysis of sufferers' relations with their environment might offer a challenge, a possibility for subverting a model incapable of recognizing this alternative (and largely gender-specific) experience, elements of which, I contend, are common to nonphobic women as well.[4]

One outcome of pursuing this line of thinking is the suggestion that self-help resources drawing on dualistic discourses are of limited effectiveness for sufferers from agoraphobia. This conclusion begs the question of what self-help of a more inclusive hue (informed by feminist critiques) might look like. I thus intend to close this chapter, but obviously not the problematic, by gesturing toward possible alternatives.

METHODOLOGY: APPROACHING THE SUBJECT OF SELF-HELP

The texts I will analyze in this chapter are two very different self-help videos.[5] *Not All in the Mind* is an amateur production, collaboratively made by eight members of an Edinburgh-based self-help group (video A). It is twenty minutes long, and just over two minutes of that time is given over to "expert" opinion. This is in marked contrast with the second video, which continually intersperses two sufferers' accounts with the opinions of two health care professionals. *Fight or Flight* (video P) was professionally produced in Australia by Monkey See Productions and is forty-eight minutes long. Before considering the videos in more detail, I will first outline the methods of data collection, interpretation, and analysis that will be used in the discussion: How does one attempt to investigate and analyze underlying presumptions about the nature of self in any given text(s)?

I watched these videos with a small group of women members of an agoraphobia self-help group in central Scotland with whom I had previously conducted a series of in-depth group interviews (Davidson 2001a).[6] Prior to the showing, I explained that my intention was not to "teach" them anything about their disorder, but that I was asking them to evaluate the usefulness of these texts and to remark on the truthfulness of their representations of agoraphobia. To this end, respondents were encouraged to comment on or stop the videos at any time. The viewings, and the discussions that took place afterward, were audio taped with respondents' permission, and the recordings have been transcribed verbatim. The transcripts have been used to inform and supplement my analysis of the self-help texts in question.[7]

My approach to the analysis of these videos draws principally on the methodological model developed by critical discourse analyst Norman Fairclough (1992, 1995).[8] He situates "text" within the realm of "discourse practice" (text production and consumption), which is in turn situated within the realm of "sociocultural practice." His depiction of the relations between these elements is intended to convey their interdependency. It suggests that we must look wider afield than the environment immediately surrounding the text if we are to appreciate the complexities of its role and uncover its unacknowledged relations with wider sociocultural and political factors.

Fairclough (1992: 12) describes the critical aspect that distinguishes his approach as being concerned with "not just describing discursive practices, but also showing how discourse is shaped by relations of power and ideologies, and the constructive effects discourse has upon social identities, social relations and systems of knowledge and belief." More recently, Fairclough (1995) has tended to focus on the analysis of "communicative events," such as newspaper editorials and television documentaries. With respect to their representations of the world, Fairclough (1995: 103–104) states that "media texts do not merely 'mirror realities' as is sometimes naively assumed; they constitute versions of reality in ways which depend on the social positions and interests and objectives of those who produce them." Various, but unacknowledged choices will have been made, and it is the task of the analyst to bring these choices to light, to reveal "what is included and what is excluded, what is made explicit or left implicit, what is foregrounded and what is backgrounded, what is thematized and what is unthematized [and] what process types and categories are drawn upon to represent events" (Fairclough 1995: 104; cited in Duley 1997: 42[9]). Fairclough's contextual approach suits the purposes of this chapter. As I have indicated above, the excluded, implicit, backgrounded, or unthematized elements I am concerned to bring to light in this analysis relate to notions of selfhood, and in particular, the ways in which selves are conceptualized in dualistic and gendered terms. Fairclough's method enables a sociophilosophical, or, I would suggest, a geographical reading that can unearth the unacknowledged discourses of self that underpin self-help resources.

Self-help texts are curiously situated, in that they occupy an unstable position between lay and professional territory, in terms both of their production and consumption. In relation to the former, although they tend to be produced largely by those from a medical background and thus with the professional authority to present the information and advice that ensues, self-help texts often incorporate experiential accounts from sufferers, who are positioned as "experts" because of their personal knowledge. As for their consumption, self-help resources may be used in the training of health care professionals, as well as by sufferers, and by interested friends and family members. The "discourse practice" surrounding the text, to use Fairclough's terminology, is then diversely constituted, and its heterogeneity provides a variety of interesting connections with the wider realm of "sociocultural practice." The complex positioning of the self-help text suggests that it is constituted by, and constitutive of, an unusually large and diverse range of discourses. One might then expect representations of agoraphobic and nonphobic selves to reflect this diversity, and that the texts could thus have a mediatory role, filtering information between distant subject positions. However, I will argue that what we do in fact find is a singular version of self that is presumed very strongly indeed. The self in question will be shown to be atomistic and autonomous, rational, and self-knowing. It is a firmly bounded individual, defined in terms of its separation from others, and yet essentially, internally dualistic. It is precisely this Cartesian self whom the viewer-subject is encouraged and helped to be.

The decision to focus on video recordings, rather than audio or printed literature, requires some explanation. Books and pamphlets especially are perhaps more commonly used than any other self-help resource, and they certainly tend to be more accessible in terms of both availability and cost. The main factor influencing me not to use these alternatives is that video material is the most amenable to a shared and participatory reading. We could watch and comment on these texts together. An additional reason for favoring the visual medium is that sufferers had frequently commented on the difficulty of articulating the appalling horror of the panic attack, the experience that sows the seeds of agoraphobic avoidance. Respondents have drawn on a wide range of metaphors in the attempt to verbalize the experience, likening it, for example, to such diverse phenomena as drowning or receiving electric shocks. I have repeatedly been told that unless you experience it yourself you cannot begin to grasp what it feels like (though one respondent qualified this by saying she wouldn't wish it "on her worst enemy"); "its like trying to explain red to a blind person" (Moira). Given such barriers to communicating the experience, I was interested to see how the producers of these videos might attempt to represent panic visually and whether or not the outcome would be meaningful for agoraphobic viewers.

As for my selection of these particular products, video A seemed an obvious choice, for reasons such as familiarity of location and accent to members of the group. Additionally, I rightly suspected that the group would be keen to engage with a text produced by individuals described by one member of the audience as "people like us" (Ruth). Video P was chosen because it came most highly recommended of those currently available by a recent newsletter produced by *No Panic*, the UK-wide self-help organization for panic sufferers. It advocates a form of cognitive behavioral therapy (CBT), which, I argue, sits firmly within, and does not problematize, the Cartesian tradition of selfhood. Additionally, and significantly, both videos opt to locate their portrayals of panic in shopping spaces, a central focus of both my own research and of many sufferers' personal narratives of agoraphobic experience (Davidson 2001b, 2001c).

REPRESENTING PANIC

I start this discussion of the self-help texts by examining their portrayals of the experience of panic. The shopping scenes will be described in some detail, and I will develop an interpretation that suggests their primary purpose is to depict the agoraphobic subject as out of control, a state of being-in-the-world that is, arguably, uncontainable within the dominant dualistic discourses outlined above. An empathetic interpretation of agoraphobic panic thus initiates a reconceptualization of the subject as deeply embodied and dynamically in touch with his or her environment.

That both these videos choose shopping spaces to represent panic is neither arbitrary nor coincidental. Social spaces of this particular kind often present sufferers with the greatest difficulties (Davidson 2000a). The name given to the disorder actually incorporates the Greek *agora*, meaning marketplace, a term applicable to the locale depicted in the opening scene of video A: Prince's Street in Edinburgh is among the largest and better known shopping sites in the city center. This text begins by positioning the viewer around the halfway point of this street, looking down a stretch of pavement along which crowds of people move, at various speeds, in both directions. In the center of our view, a woman walks toward us, clutching her bag tightly in front of her. Her eyes dart around nervously, then she stops and stands with her hands pressed to the sides of her head, covering her ears; she appears desperately uncomfortable. A steady, rhythmic, pulsing sound can be heard, increasingly loudly, in the background, and seems to simulate ultra-awareness of a rapidly beating heart. During these opening seconds, the following three accounts of panic are overlaid.

1. I feel faint, sick and dizzy, and I come out in a cold sweat.
2. My heart starts hammering, my chest feels tight, I can't breathe, and I feel as if I'm having a heart attack. The noise of the traffic seems to get louder and louder, and I feel more and more frantic.
3. I begin to feel absolutely rooted to the spot, and I just can't move at all. I feel as if there's an iron band tightening round my head.

The scene then changes to an aisle in a supermarket. It is brightly lit, even gaudy, and the light pulses in time with the repetitive beating sound. As we move forward, slowly and unsteadily, the aisle appears increasingly tunnel-like and never quite comes into focus. Objects on the shelves become closer, then move away, but their outlines remain blurred. Our perspective then alters, unexpectedly and quickly, as the camera pans upward, toward the light, then lurches down. The ground beneath us glares, blindingly, and our view slowly and shakily lifts to eye level. The effect is one of disorientation, and this is clearly the intent. We hear Sheila's voice:

Going to the supermarket is an everyday experience for most people, but to an agoraphobic, it is a *real* trauma. The stimulus is just too much for the eyes to cope with, and the fluorescent lighting, bouncing off the already tiled floor, causes a feeling of anxiety, if not *extreme* panic.

The shopping scene in video P opens with Sharon, seated outdoors among greenery, in what is presumably her garden. Her account begins:

And then I was in a shopping center, with my sister, the one day, and I think that's when I really got a full-blown, out-of-control, panic attack, where I was standing in the shop with her, and just, all of a sudden, my world just . . . the world started spinning, and I just thought I was going totally out of control. [The scene changes to the inside of a shopping mall. The camera is out of focus, and moves with a rapid freeze frame action in a circular motion. Sharon's voice continues throughout.] My legs started going weak, um, I couldn't focus on anything, um, I really started shaking, almost . . . hot and cold chills going down me, um, rapid heart beat, and I just actually thought I was going to collapse right there. Terrible nausea, and um, I remember my sister looking at me and saying, you know, you are absolutely white as a ghost!

This scene is accompanied by dissonant, drawn-out notes played, perhaps, on an organ. It begins erratically, then alternately ascends and descends an atonal scale, which is obtusely reminiscent of an alarm, or siren. The sound connotes confusion, disorientation, and the irregular interval between each note is suggestive of strangeness, unfamiliarity. What we actually see is an excess of bright lights and reflective surfaces, a predominance of glimmering whiteness that is decidedly not easy on the eyes. The camera moves in on signs, perhaps advertisements, which shift in and out of focus and are impossible to read. People, too, move in and out of focus, and the scene appears disjointed, unpredictable. The viewer's perspective appears odd, and changes without warning; side-to-side movement creates a sense of being off balance, and there is a jerky quality to the camera movement, suggesting a lack of continuity. The place looks thoroughly menacing, and the viewer has no control over the way visual information is gathered and presented.

Perhaps the first thing one would note about the shopping scenes would be the striking similarities between the visual portrayals of panic by both videos. Although it is apparent, and predictable, that there is greater technical expertise available to the producers of video P, clearly both are aiming to produce similar effects. Both intend to create a sense of disorientation, confusion, lack of focus, and of the overwhelming fear that accompanies the loss of control over one's senses, one's relations with the environment, and, ultimately, of one's self.[10] This element of "loss of control" can be seen to constitute the central theme of both portrayals; all aspects of these scenes, visual, verbal, and otherwise, are primarily geared toward communicating this state of being to the audience. Panic, the viewer learns, entails loss of control to a terrifying degree, not only over oneself, but crucially, also in relation to the environment.

It is my contention that this portrayal supports the interpretation of agoraphobic anxiety as a "boundary crisis."[11] The loss of *self*-control relates to a breakdown in the normally taken-for-granted relation between, not mind and body, but self and space, a subjective experience for which the Cartesian worldview does not allow. To warrant this interpretation, first consider the images in isolation. The presentation of visual information in both shopping scenes is strongly suggestive of lack of agency on the part of the protagonist. Think of the scene in video A where the supermarket aisle closes in on the subject, or where the ground lurches upward. In video P objects are shown to move rapidly closer or to become unexpectedly bright. One could interpret these images as suggesting that the balance of power in the relation between person and place has shifted from the former to the latter. This is to say that, for the agoraphobic, the environment itself takes on a kind of agency. It loses its static, predictable "thingness," and this lack of assumed continuity renders it threatening and dangerous. How can you feel secure in a place where the visual information it presents you with virtually *assaults* your sense of sight, and thus, your sense of self?

The notion that the self is under threat is supported by the linguistic accounts that accompany these images, as is the earlier suggestion that we can identify a central theme. In video P, Sharon characterizes her first panic attack as "full blown, *out of control*" and describes her environs thus; "my world just . . . *the world started spinning*." The effect of this sensation? "I just thought *I was going totally out of control.*" Sharon moves between descriptions of apparently "internal" and "external" happenings with manifest ease. It is "the world" that spins, but she herself that is "out of control," and I take this to be indicative of ambiguity, fluidity, in the boundary between the two. Her characterization suggests that her sense of her self is inseparable from her sense of her environment and is thus in tune with the relational construction of subjectivity put forward by feminist and post-structuralist theorists such as Judith Butler (1990, 1993).[12] What Sharon goes on to say, however, seems to focus entirely on *internal* bodily sensations, implying more stability of boundaries, more autonomy than my interpretation suggests. By her own account, these things are happening *to*, rather than around, her.

If, however, we take post-structuralist feminist approaches seriously, the sensations Sharon describes need not be understood so exclusively, as definitively within or without, the limits of the flesh, as an attribute of either subject or object. Theorists who are critical of dualistic conceptions of subjectivity, rather than those with a Cartesian perspective, can thus help articulate the experience of agoraphobic panic, which exceeds bodily limitations and corrodes the security one's boundaries afford. Consider, for example, the embodied experience of shakiness, nausea, hot and cold chills: these phenomena are symptomatic of a perceived disruption in the barrier between internal and external space. They are the subjective sensations of corporeal breaches, (im)mediate signs of permeability that are anathema to the stable subject of modernity.

In video A, participants present experiential accounts that are similarly suggestive of a confusion in self/space relations. While some of the sensations described are apparently internal—"my heart starts hammering," some apparently external—"the noise of the traffic seems to get louder and louder," others are concerned with the interactions *between* internal and external realms. To be "rooted to the spot," for example, and to "have an iron band tight round my head" is to make use of metaphors arising from person/place relations. Other seemingly straightforward descriptions also turn out to be more ambiguous on closer inspection. The statement, "*I come out* in a cold sweat" clearly implies a breach of the internal/external barrier, and Kathy's choice of words suggests that she her*self* is exposed in the process. Similarly, to be "faint, sick and dizzy" are all symptoms that disrupt the felt boundaries of the self. Lucy Yardley has paid particularly close attention to experiential accounts similar to these in developing her "ecological-constructionist" analysis of disorientation and dizziness. Yardley's analysis is, arguably, also applicable to agoraphobic anxiety. Here, the subject also experiences disorientating phenomena and doubts their ability to respond appropriately to their environment (Yardley 1997: 117), to maintain *self*-control.

The importance of Yardley's account for agoraphobia lies mainly with its focus on boundaries and its refusal to work within reductionist frameworks dominant in contemporary discourses of health and illness.[13] In her own words:

> [T]he ecological account characterises disorientation as arising at the interface between the individual and their environment [it places] the emphasis on dynamic relations rather than essential causes. . . . This is no simple pyscho-somatic or somato-psychic re-

lationship, but a profound and intricate interactive bond between the material and discursive aspects of disorientation, which creates and reproduces the condition and preconditions, meaning and implications of disorientation. (Yardley 1994: 118–119)

An ecological-constructionist view presents us with a means of understanding the subject in context. And, as the shopping scenes clearly demonstrate, context is intrinsic to understanding the nature of agoraphobic experience.

The women with whom I watched these scenes were clearly impressed by the faithfulness of their representations. The following exchange came immediately after the shopping scene in video P, which we viewed first.

Betty: That's what it feels like to me, that is what it feels like . . . but it feels like that to me out in the street as well.
Jane: Like things go out of focus.
Joyce: So d'you think that would be quite a useful thing, if I was to show that to people, and say that's what a panic attack's like . . . is that fair?
Ruth: Oh aye, that *is* what a panic attack's like.

Their response to the scene in video A is similarly enthusiastic, with comments like "that's what a panic attack's like, like a switch getting turned on" (Jane), and "that's the truth, that's how it really happens" (Ruth). It is reasonable to claim that for these sufferers at least, the shopping scenes managed to capture and communicate something of their experience. Inevitably the portrayals are particular and partial in that they try to give visual sense to sufferers' (as opposed to medical practitioners') descriptions of anxious experience. It is perhaps for this reason that the representation is felt to be authentic, that it is somehow faithful to the spirit of panic, whose picture it attempts to paint. There is, as of yet, no attempt in the texts to explain, or draw conclusions about these phenomena, and the face of panic remains recognizable to those who suffer its presence in their lives.

So far I have argued that there is a dominant theme shaping both of these shopping scenes, namely, the severe loss of control suffered by the agoraphobic subject. I have further suggested that this loss of control can be most constructively understood in (nondualistic) terms of a breakdown in the relations between person and place. I now want to consider the format of the texts as a whole, in order to place these portrayals of agoraphobic selves in relation to the Cartesian, masculine ideal of normality against which they are set.

(AB)NORMAL NARRATIVES

The remainder of video A consists largely of eight narrative accounts of agoraphobia that are presented by the sufferers in their own homes. All are introduced by first names, and all but one are women. The pieces are edited from interviews/discussions with Sheila, who is herself a sufferer and was the organizer of the self-help group at the time the video was made. Sheila narrates throughout, occasionally commenting on sufferers' accounts, or asking encouraging questions. It is Sheila who introduces the sole nonphobic respondent, whose contribution will be assessed below.

Video P begins with a male voice describing his first panic attack and his subsequent fear of driving. The scene switches between Wayne in his living room and footage of a night driving scene, while he describes how panic would "take over" and how he thought he "might die." Enough information is given by this sufferer for us to deduce that he was employed as a driver, though his first name is the only written text to appear on the screen. Wayne's piece lasts for around ninety seconds and is followed by the forty-second piece involving Sharon, which is described above. Immediately afterward the scene changes to the office of Dr. Lisa Lampe, who, the caption informs us, is a consultant psychiatrist. Lampe proceeds to reorganize and reiterate much of what Sharon has said, listing the symptoms of panic in an orderly manner. Professor Ron Rapee takes a similar role when he appears on screen around thirty seconds later. Rapee, a professor of psychology, offers another dispassionate account of panic episodes and concludes definitively, "if a person starts to associate those panic attacks with certain areas, and because of that they start to avoid doing certain things, or going to certain places, then we would call that agoraphobia."

The four characters involved in video P have all been introduced within the first few minutes of the video. As we will see, the layout of their introductory pieces sets the tone for the rest of the video. Sharon and Wayne alternately describe their experiences, and the professionals interject to retell their stories in an authoritative fashion, supplementing them with additional, technical language and information. In *translating* individual accounts in this way, Lampe and Rapee could be said to undermine the phobic contributors' authority. They also move beyond the particularity of the personal narrative, toward a more generalized account, arguably a metanarrative, of agoraphobia.

The authoritative identities of Lampe and Rapee are maintained throughout the text in a number of ways. First, both are introduced with their full professional titles, which has the effect of foregrounding their institutional, rather than personal, roles from the outset. This effect is perpetuated by presenting both as entirely static throughout the video. That they remain seated in what are presumably their own offices creates the impression of professional consultation in an institutional context. Additionally, both are presented in formal dress; Lampe and Rapee are seen in smart office attire, as opposed to Wayne's T-shirt, jeans, and overalls and Sharon's loose, patterned dresses. The manner and style of their delivery are also contributive. Both use calm, measured tones, and their use of language tends to be authoritative. The use of medical and semitechnical terms serves to enhance the impression of expertise, as does the occasional use of statistics—"as many as thirty-five or more, percent of the population will have a panic attack, at some point in their lives." The style of the professionals' delivery is then largely pedagogical.

In these various ways, the impression is created that Lampe and Rapee are providing unbiased information for the enlightenment of their audience. This information is never presented as opinion, and we are given little encouragement to doubt the veracity of their accounts. Neither Sharon nor Wayne questions the authority of any statement, and so an impression of consensus is created. Lampe and Rapee are also clearly at a distance from the subject(s) they are discussing (quite literally— "professionals" and "sufferers" never appear on screen at the same time). They are never *at pains* to communicate the reality of the disorder, so their contributions are less emphatic, less intense, even incompatible with those of Sharon and Wayne. There is none of the immediacy that often characterizes sufferers' accounts; rather, the professionals' approach to agoraphobia is objective and rational, directed toward bringing an unruly body under control. This approach privileges and reemphasizes the dominant (masculine) side of the hierarchic dichotomies referred to above.

For the producers of the amateur as well as the professional production, there is a specifiable, physical explanation for agoraphobics' "abnormal" loss of control. Video A posits a balance dysfunction as the root cause of sufferers' disorientation and anxiety. Their inability to maintain a normal level of self-control is, consequently, *not their fault*. This physical, rather than mental, attribution of the problem is an important point since, as Yardley emphasizes, there are "moral implications" to this far from neutral issue. "[D]eviations from normal behaviour for which no somatic explanation is provided inevitably carry a social penalty, since psychological problems are considered less 'real' and more blameworthy than physical defects" (Yardley 1997: 115). It is then, very much in the sufferers' interests to demonstrate that their "abnormal" behavior is a reasonable response to a physical problem. While adopting this viewpoint, the manner of sufferers' representation of rational (masculine), biologistic medical discourse arguably demonstrates resistance to its hegemony.

In video A, Dr. David Weeks is presented in a manner that foregrounds his institutional identity, using largely similar methods to those of video P. However, the surrounding contributions from nonprofessional participants serve to contextualize his expertise. He is introduced as someone who is conducting research on sufferers' behalf and is called upon to present findings that concur with the group's view of agoraphobia's links to problems with balance. Weeks is being used to verify and give the stamp of authority to what the sufferers' themselves already knew. He begins, "we discovered that agoraphobic balance problems are genuine and real . . . this condition is not purely psychological, there's a heavy, physical, biological, neurological component to it, that has been only marginally suspected in the past, but never actually proven. Now its been proven."

This contribution is clearly intended to be authoritative, but we can see that the agoraphobic women in control of this text have opted to include the professional's account in order to add credence to their own theories about their disorder. They have put themselves in the position of being able to choose who to include and who to exclude, in order to construct their own version of agoraphobia, perhaps realizing that "discourse is the power which is to be seized" (Foucault 1984: 110).

I have already suggested that the privileging of the masculine constitutes a recognizable theme in self-help discourses. In the following section I want to explore the (implicit and explicit) depictions of gender in more detail, focusing particularly on the implied association between masculinity and endurance, femininity and fear.

FRAMING FEAR AS FEMININE

> If it happens to you first of all when you're in your teens and you go to see the doc-
> tor, the doctor will say, "it's your age, it's adolescence. When you're a bit older,
> you'll get over that problem." When you're in your twenties, they say "once you're
> married, and have children, and have plenty to do, you'll forget all about that silly
> business." And then, you get to the menopause, and they say "once the menopause
> is over, you'll be much better." What happens then? What do you wait for then, 'til
> you die, will you be better then?
>
> —Sheila agoraphobia sufferer and contributor to self-help video "A"

This quotation, which brings video A to a close, suggests that some sufferers are
more than familiar with the practice of attributing their fearful condition to their sex
and/or expected gender role behavior. For many, agoraphobia is a woman's problem,
or even a "housewife's disease" (da Costa Meyer 1996: 150), and (thus?) an irrational
and thoroughly "silly" affair.

The women with whom I watched this video responded with much hilarity to
these closing remarks, although their cognizant laughter was perhaps tinged with
the *bitterness* of remembrance. They too had experiences of this kind of dismissal
and a refusal to take their "trivial," womanly problems seriously.

The assumption that agoraphobia is a feminine affair is often largely unspoken. It
is Bill, the sole male agoraphobic contributor to video A, who comments explicitly
on this gendered aspect of the disorder. He states:

> Quite frankly, in twenty-five years of suffering from agoraphobia, I have never met an-
> other male who has said that he is agoraphobic, and yet, I am told, that there are a num-
> ber of men, who do suffer, and um, I feel that most . . . that probably says a lot. Men
> have to think about their image, the macho image [so its difficult] to admit to suffering
> from something which a lot of people simply see as being a weakness.

Bill suggests that men are more likely to resist the agoraphobic appellation than
women, but *not* that they are less likely to have the same anxious experiences. While
his claim is clearly contentious, that a sufferer perceives this to be the case is in itself significant.[14] Bill highlights the notion that agoraphobia is widely perceived to
be a peculiarly feminine weakness. Given the male-stream Western tendency to be-
little all that is not masculine, men may well be reluctant to associate themselves
with this denigrated state of being-in-the-world. Bill's comments on his solitary experience as a male agoraphobic reveal what he sees as identifiable, understandable
reasons why men will refuse this particular subject positioning.

Wayne, commenting on his own disorder in video P, points to personal difficulties he encountered in admitting he was agoraphobic, difficulties we can perhaps relate to Bill's notion of the male "macho image"; "at first, my pride wouldn't let me do
it. . . . I'm not in that basket, if you know what I mean [laughs], that's not what's
wrong with me at all" (although Sharon expressed similar hesitancy, suggesting it is
not only men who would wish to distance themselves from "feminine" characteris-

tics). Overall, however, video P creates an entirely different impression of the gendered distribution of agoraphobia from video A. The inclusion of one male and one female sufferer suggests a gender balance, and there is no mention that this is not in fact representative of the actual gendered distribution of agoraphobia. One might then wonder if the producers were concerned *not* to represent agoraphobia and panic attacks as "women's problems," perhaps even to disrupt conceptions of fear as stereotypically feminine.

This notion can be supported by the fact that the text's portrayal of Wayne is often framed in terms of traditional constructions of masculinity. For example, his role is often active, and he is repeatedly seen performing tasks associated with paid employment outside the home. Wayne works on an outdoor pool, files papers and answers the telephone in his office, and attends to the mechanics of his racing car (apparently his main hobby) in his garage. These performances are markedly different from those of Sharon, who behaves "similarly" only to the extent that she too conforms to her gender-role stereotype.

Sharon is shown standing over a kitchen sink, looking out of the window, or peering through a door that she is holding slightly ajar, while her voiceover describes her inability to leave home. When we do see Sharon outdoors, she is driving her car to collect her children from school, standing in a queue in a post office, and entering a shopping center, all activities associated in some way with domesticity. It is thus Sharon's role as a housewife that is foregrounded by this text, and this clearly has implications for the way her contribution will be received by different audiences.

The visual representations of gender in video P might then be seen to challenge assumptions about the feminine nature of fear, by associating it with displays of masculine, even *macho*, imagery (racing car mechanics, do-it-yourself activities, and so on) and not simply with (feminine-coded) domestic chores. However, the potential power of this association is undermined by the text's consistent refusal to trouble gendered dichotomies in any other way, a tactic that effectively amounts to complicity in their hegemony. A greater degree of authority and credibility will thus continue to be associated with a male rather than female voice.

In video P, it is in fact Wayne's voice that opens and closes the text, and it is Wayne who is given the task, along with the professionals, of conveying information about new self-help techniques and demonstrating how they are to be carried out. These factors strengthen the sense of authority created by his "manly" activities, adding the weight of cultural capital to his masterly, masculine presence. Although it is Sharon who is experientially best placed to speak to agoraphobia sufferers, her contribution is denigrated, designated *less* than that of the male by framing it in terms of culturally undervalued domestic work. Whether deliberate or not, the gendered selves represented by this text are echoes of those masculinist stereotypes predominant in media discourse and the wider sociocultural realm of text production. The portrayal of gender is always the Same, and agoraphobic fear is still largely a "feminine" affair. Even if there are occasional aberrant males displaying similar symptoms, they must have the self-same ideal. In line with the privileging of masculinity we find throughout the texts, the advocated response to "aberration" is *aspiration*—striving to be yet *more*-of-the-Same; more manly, more in control, and above all, more rational.[15]

FROM EMOTIONAL WOMAN TO RATIONAL MAN

At various stages throughout video P, sufferers are advised to "rationalize their thoughts" and to *practice* "rational thinking." Agoraphobic fears are, on this account, physical in origin, and nothing that a good dose of rationality won't cure. They arise when subjects respond irrationally to physical symptoms and can be brought within their conscious control.[16]

> What happens with people with panic attacks is they get these feelings, these physical feelings, that, that begin their anxious feeling. They then start to think of these feelings as being something terrible. They've learnt across their lives that these physical feelings are bad, "I shouldn't have them," so they immediately start to be anxious. . . . The important thing for people with panic attacks to learn is that these are two separate things. There're physical feelings, and then there's your interpretation, your emotional response to those things. [. . . To] see them much more objectively [sufferers need to separate the physical from their feelings of anxiety].

It is important to be clear about the content of this statement. It contains the definition of panic and is presented as an entirely factual account. And yet this account is contentious, to say the least. Rapee effectively states that fear is a *response* to adrenaline, by no means an obvious or "common sense" conclusion, and one that many sufferers would dispute (see below). What we have here is an account that constructs the agoraphobic as exhibiting an irrational loss of control in the face of an unruly body. There is an assumption that nothing can be done to prevent the physical occurrences, that the body is beyond hope or restraint. However, one can learn, be taught, to control one's *responses* to its behavior, thereby reestablishing the body in its proper place in the mind's dominion.

Given that this dualistic model informs the professional view of the agoraphobic subject, we can begin to see the origin of what I term the "bureaucratic" approach to her treatment, one that is quite literally a case of mind over matter. Lampe and Rapee effectively advocate the development of a good management strategy, to enact their positivistic and quantitative approach to "treatment." First and foremost, the subject must accept her or his designation and be fully interpellated into the agoraphobic subject position. Wayne himself makes this point clear; "until such time . . . as you are diagnosed, and *you accept, that that's what's wrong with you* . . . you won't start getting better" (emphasis added). He then adds, in terms one might describe as "macho," that it is also necessary to "have the fight or the will to beat it." Having satisfied these conditions, the subject can embark on a program of "cognitive restructuring," in which "self monitoring" plays a crucial role. This process, the monitoring of the self, is aided by the provision of specially designed forms that are to be carried about the person at all times. This tactic enables panic symptoms to be recorded accurately and efficiently, and thus be objectified, "as soon as they've finished having an attack" (Rapee). In the appropriate boxes, sufferers should note details such as the time and the duration of the panic, as well as the intensity, "on a 0–8 scale." Gathering "evidence" about and quantifying symptoms are intended to encourage the development of less "extreme," more "realistic" thoughts. In addition, sufferers should "learn the right rate" for breathing, which is held to be "three seconds in, three seconds out," though appropriate adjustments can be made (with the aid of a second hand on a watch or alarm) if this is not found to be satisfactory.

Until now, I have clearly chosen to focus on vocabulary that emphasizes the scientific nature of the regulatory discourse. However, much of this terminology is actually couched in more "ordinary," colloquial phrases and delivered in a conversational style. For example, Rapee describes the self-monitoring form as "very nice as it comes as a little pocket-sized [form], so that people can always carry a bunch" with them. The effect of this "conversationalization" is, as Fairclough (1995: 10) argues, to naturalize the content of the speech, to suggest that these are run-of-the-mill, commonsense notions shared by all of "us." In fact, Rapee is often more explicit in his attempts to normalize his normative views; he describes the treatments he advocates as "practical common sense ones." He further attempts to naturalize biologistic aspects of his model of the self. For example, Rapee suggests that when a panic episode begins, the sufferer should try thinking "that's a good thing that my heart's pumping blood round my body, and helps me get ready to fight. It's something very natural and normal, its simply happening at the wrong time." One should, then, accept that the body is behaving "naturally," but only insofar as we can use this information to enculturate our volatility (knowledge is power after all). Our bodies can be civilized by the reach of the mind, and rational, realistic thinking should be practiced until it becomes, ironically, "almost second nature" (Wayne). Sharon too advocates the power of mind over body, reason over emotion; "I still, to this day, have to do um, rational thinking, and I'll probably have to do it maybe for the rest of my life."

The women with whom I watched video P were not always convinced by its "common sense" characterization of agoraphobia. (Although I ought to admit that they could have picked up on the fact that I personally was more favorably disposed toward the amateur production.) Besides this however, it is difficult to foster a sense of sharing a life-world with the characters involved, not least because of the strangeness of their surroundings. On a winter's day in a Scottish housing estate, it's difficult to empathize with someone basking in the Australian sunshine by the side of their outdoor pool. There may well be other mitigating factors, but it remains significant that members of this audience were critical of some of the assumptions underlying this version of agoraphobia, and that they drew on their own experiences to validate these criticisms.

Iris, for example, commented on the nature of panic thus: "I think sometimes the physical feelings are the result, that it's the other way round . . . the emotional feelings that you have leads to the physical things." Jane tentatively agrees, then states, "I mean . . . the effect's there, the whole thing, before I start thinking, my fingers are tingling, or my heart's starting to beat a bit fast, or I feel dizzy. It's . . . the whole lot comes . . . phwoooh [this is accompanied by hand gestures, to simulate something rushing toward her face], without any reason."

Sufferers' accounts suggest that they simply do not experience this distinction between physical and mental symptoms in the way the above examples from professional discourse suggest. Their vocabulary and metaphors of panic point rather to a concern with the relationship between themselves (as deeply embodied) and their surroundings; that is to say, with their immediate psycho-corporeal geographies. As one would expect, Cartesian conceptualizations of subjectivity are not adequate to the task of articulating the experience of dynamically constituted subjects. "The reduction of disorientation [or agoraphobic anxiety] to purely physical or wholly psychological factors presents many individuals with an artificial forced choice between the somatic and psychic models, with the result that important aspects of their experience remain unexplained and untreated" (Yardley 1997: 114). Moreover, sufferers' difficulties are compounded by this impossibility of fully articulating their experience. "[T]hey are forced to resort to the unsatisfactory discourses available to them in order to (mis)represent their problem to themselves and others" (Yardley 1997: 115). This does not, however, mean that the therapies reliant on such "unsatisfactory discourses" are completely without merit.

Clearly, it must be acknowledged that the CBT being advocated here does in fact "work" for some agoraphobia sufferers, in the crucial sense of giving them a hold on their disorder, and thus making their everyday lives more tolerable, less infused with panic. Despite my obviously critical analysis of the ideological underpinnings of CBT, such apparently academic matters need not necessarily be a concern for the subject of self-help whose anxiety can be partially soothed and steadied, slowed down by counting, controlling measures.

However, I want now to draw attention to potentially substantial problems associated with an overreliance on this particular model of the self. I have suggested that the supposed "universality" of the self represented in these texts is challenged by the embodied experience of agoraphobic women, thus revealing a gap between (at least) two contesting conceptions of self. However, despite the texts' representation of agoraphobic women as problematizing the Cartesian view of the self, the professionals' response to their experience is to continue to privilege and reemphasize this Same (masculine) notion of self. The superiority of this model is uncritically assumed, and sufferers are left in no doubt that they ought to (com)press themselves into an ill-fitting Cartesian mold, a restrictive mold, which, I would tentatively suggest, may be partially responsible for their dreadful difficulties in the first place.

CONCLUSION

This chapter has initiated a feminist interpretation of self-help texts for agoraphobia sufferers, stressing the importance of rendering underlying assumptions about the nature of selves explicit. I have argued that it is a Cartesian notion of self that is uncritically assumed by the texts in question and that this has important implications for the treatment of agoraphobic women. The point to be emphasized is that therapies constructed around notions of self to which agoraphobic women cannot easily relate will have limited effectiveness. Sufferers most likely do not feel, may never have felt, autonomous, rational, or firmly bounded as subjects, surrounded by, yet separate from, a world of isolable objects. Within dualistic discourse, however, there is little room for alternatives, and the agoraphobic woman can be seen only as somehow lacking and inadequate; like, but less than, the rational (male) ideal. As Rose points out, "[d]ualisms maintain order by offering only two positions, both of which are constituted around a single term—the masculine Same" (Rose 1993: 82). There is as of yet no conceptual position to comfortably house the excessive experience, the (to borrow from Irigaray 1985: 112) *exorbitant* bodies and voices of agoraphobic women.

My intention is not, however, to argue that we should or even could ever entirely reject this Cartesian model or the dualisms at its heart. Dualistic thinking is obviously firmly entrenched within our language and worldviews, utterly pervasive throughout all aspects of society. That it can operate to stabilize troubled identities, more or less temporarily, is not in doubt. And in fact, rather than celebrating their "difference," the person who is "ill" will most likely want nothing more than to "fit in," to conform with their society's expectations of normality and rationality. Yet this is not to say that dualisms should not be problematized, that we should not question exactly what kind of society, what kind of selves, they are helping to produce and maintain.

This discussion has shown that unquestioning and uncritical approaches to subjectivities are severely limited, incapable of conceptualizing or containing the full extent of agoraphobic being-in-the-world, and that in fact, the results are always the Same. I want to suggest that by analytically probing predominant conceptions of normality we might create potential spaces for alternative models of self to arise, models that allow difference in terms other than deviation, and to which "*ill*-defined" women could more comfortably relate.[17]

I am not suggesting that such strategies could somehow alter the phenomenology of fear, that the experience of panic and anxiety could be rendered more tolerable; rather, that the troubled identities of agoraphobic women are not *so* far removed from an acceptable (feminist) "ideal" of normality that they should be beyond representation. We initially require a vocabulary with which to articulate such experience, and this must be the practical goal of a strategy to make discursive space for integrated corporeal and conceptual involvement with the world. This strategy would also be utopian, however, in that it reaches out toward the "no-place" beyond dualistic thinking, speaking, and writing.

It has long been the contention of many feminists that language matters, and one's ability to mobilize discourse to communicate with others is of fundamental importance for innumerable aspects of our lives, not least for our mental health. As I have shown, the personal narratives composed by agoraphobic women draw on metaphoric language in particular ways, to communicate how their experience consumes and confuses their senses.[18] They are "drowned" or "suffocated," "shaken" and "shocked," "frozen" in both time and space. Their experience is deeply embodied, but in a way that blasts through dualist borders.

I want to suggest that the language used by these women to express their experience is at times an attempt to transcend the dualisms implied by, and inherent to, our specular symbolic order (Irigaray 1985). Consequently, it may not always be helpful therapeutically to (op)press this experience back into dualistic discourse, to interpret it strictly, for example, in terms *either* of mind *or* of body.[19]

Perhaps, then, feminist theorists and therapists should acknowledge and encourage the use of spatial and other metaphors to *ground* such boundless and fearful exposure, to create a platform of sorts on which it can be articulated and, therefore, granted legitimate existence. We might constructively develop existing elements of our vocabulary that do not insist on the mind/body split and that therefore resist complicity with masculinist, dualistic thought. Boundary-breaking speech acts can be literally transgressive. By developing feminist and therapeutic language games[20] with a more integrated, holistic approach to selves and space, we may be more adequately equipped to faithfully represent agoraphobic, and perhaps *Other*, experiences, to provide alternative self-help.

NOTES

1. Clum and Knowles (1991) review twelve different agoraphobia studies and put the figure as high as 89 percent. See also Brehony (1983), Chambless and Mason (1986), Marks (1987), and Tian, Wanstall, and Evans (1990). For *non*clinical accounts of agoraphobia relating to sex difference, see Bankey (2001) and chapter 3 in this volume, Bordo, Klein, and Silverman (1998), da Costa Meyer (1996), and Capps and Ochs (1995).

2. I use the term "social" rather than "public" when referring to experientially difficult spaces to avoid invoking the problematic distinction between public and private space. (No space can ever be *wholly* private. See for example, Dowling [1998], Duncan [1996b], and Pateman [1989]). I would suggest that agoraphobic difficulties arise in relation to differing intensities in social *interaction* rather than in response to "public" space. See also chapter 3 in this volume.

3. Val Plumwood (1993: 41) characterizes dualistic thinking and its place in Western philosophy in terms of a "logic of colonization," describing the concept of dualism as "the construction of a devalued and sharply demarcated sphere of otherness [which] results from a certain kind of *denied dependency* on a subordinated other" (emphasis added).

4. Social psychologist Lucy Yardley's (1994) work on "disorientation and dizziness" is drawn on to support these claims.

5. For examples of self-help *books* for agoraphobics, see Savage (1987), Marks (1980), and Vines (1987).

6. Some members of the group have since been interviewed individually in their own homes.

7. On the occasion we watched the videos, there were five members present, all of whom were women over the age of thirty-five, who have been given pseudonyms to protect their identity. All were married and had children. All identified themselves as agoraphobic and were

long-term sufferers, "coping" with their disorder well enough to attend group meetings fairly regularly. The women had varied backgrounds and life histories. None were employed outside their homes. My methodological approach has been influenced by, among others, Devault (1990), Longhurst (1996), and Parr (1998).

8. See Burman and Parker (1993) for an overview and discussion of alternative approaches to discourse analysis, and of associated problems.

9. Duley (1997) has adopted Fairclough's method to provide an exemplary account of the construction of New Zealand national identity through analysis of a series of television broadcasts.

10. However, see Yardley (1997: 123) for a discussion of cultural or drug-induced alternatives, where "loss of control" is positively welcomed. She writes that "there are clearly important differences between disorientation which is deliberately self-induced, whether by dance, drugs or dazzling displays, and sudden attacks of vertigo and dizziness which were neither anticipated nor desired."

11. The term "boundary crisis" is also used by Kathleen Kirby (1996) in her partially autobiographical account of "post-traumatic vertigo."

12. See also, for example, Lorraine's (1999) exploration of Irigaray and Deleuze on subjectivity, and Battersby (1998).

13. See Lupton (1994) and the collection edited by Jones and Porter (1998), especially contributions by Armstrong, Osborne, and Rose.

14. Dianne Chambless (1982: 5) has presented research findings that may be taken to support Bill's claim, suggesting that agoraphobia in men may often be masked by substance abuse. She writes, "[g]iven the prevalence of alcohol in Western society, it may be expected, then, that large numbers of male agoraphobics are to be found, not in phobia societies and psychiatric clinics for phobia treatment, but in bars, Alcoholics Anonymous, and alcoholism treatment centers." However, her findings have yet to be replicated, and the vast majority of research on agoraphobia continues to point to a significant sex difference in distribution (Marks 1987; McNally 1994).

15. Gillian Rose (1993: 75) provides a useful account of the phallocentric nature of dualistic thought. In her words, the two sides of dualisms "are not two discrete alternatives, because the feminized side is defined in relation to the masculine. The two sides are not oppositions between two unrelated terms. . . . Rather, this is a field of knowledge divided between two related terms. Woman is described in terms of Man, as the Other of the Same." This "field of the Same" "cannot admit radical difference from itself." According to this masculine symbolic order, women are both *partially* Other and the Same, but *fully* neither. They are thus always already unstable.

16. For discussion of feminist critiques of rationality, see Hekman (1992).

17. For alternative criticism of "normal" conceptions of embodiment, see Dyck (1995) and Park, Radford, and Vickers (1998).

18. See Kearns (1997) for discussion of narrative and metaphor in relation to health and illness.

19. Where such dualistic splits are desirable and helpful, we need, at the very least, to explicitly recognize that they are being employed for strategic purposes, and acknowledge that the split may not seem to accord with individuals' embodied experience of the world. It is not a naturally occurring boundary, but rather *a* particular way of conceptualizing identity, and one that will have both positive and negative effects. There are other possibilities.

20. For a feminist interpretation of the Wittgensteinian concept of language games, see Davidson and Smith (1999).

2

Understanding the Geography of Women's Fear: Toward a Reconceptualization of Fear and Space

Carina Listerborn

The intensified demand for security, safety, and crime prevention is creating a growing industry and generating business all over the world. This demand for safety is taking place as a response to the increased number of people who are expressing feelings of insecurity in society and who regard violence and other forms of crime in public space as a serious problem. Whether this fear is a reaction to actual increases in crime rates, or if it should instead be understood as social anxiety or a response to a growing fear of the "other"—of strangers—is debatable (Sennett 1994; Ellin 1997). We might also wonder whether these safety and crime prevention projects are aimed at the people who are most exposed to crime and violence, or whether safety has become a luxury for those who can afford it.

Governments all over the world are trying to gain control over the problem of crime and fear and have adopted "safer cities" projects or crime prevention programs to alleviate the fears of their citizens. During the 1980s the built environment became an important aspect of safety and crime prevention as part of an approach that involved a broad spectrum of crime-preventing agencies, including planners, architects, and community groups, as well as the police force. Crime prevention thus became an issue for all citizens and not just for governments. Today the form of the built environment is regarded as an important part of dealing with crime, and crime prevention can therefore be said to be having a considerable impact on urban development (Crawford 1998).

In planning practice, human bodies are often regarded as neutral, and differences between them are not often taken into account. Feminist critics have argued that such differences are crucial in understanding the consequences of planning decisions (for example Booth, Darke, and Yeandle 1996). In this context, and in parallel with the development of crime prevention and safety discourses, women's fear of (male) violence has been made visible, mostly by women's grassroots groups and feminist researchers. The importance of fear was acknowledged in feminist social sciences before geographers took an interest in the issue (Pain 1991), but in the past two decades the geography of women's fear has attracted a good deal of attention within feminist geography, drawing on existing geographical work on fear of crime as well as feminist work on women's fear of violence.

Although space and place are emphasized in this literature on the geography of women's fear, these concepts are seldom defined explicitly. This lack of definition is problematic because fear of crime is related to space and place in many ways, and these relations need to be analyzed if their implications for planning are to be addressed appropriately. Thus, I agree with Herbert (1989: 11) who writes "as a 'geography of crime' develops so the need to examine its conceptual bases acquires increasing significance." This chapter examines the conceptualization of space in research on women's fear and proposes a new approach to the interconnections between space and fear. To develop my argument I discuss the influence of feminist analyses about research on geographies of fear and crime, then I consider the concepts of space and place implicit in this work, before advancing a framework that draws on Lefebvre's (1990) differentiation between perceived, conceived, and lived space.

FEMINIST PERSPECTIVES ON THE GEOGRAPHY OF FEAR

Fear is a subjective and ambivalent feeling. Sometimes we experience fear intentionally (for example when we choose to see a "scary" movie), and sometimes the feeling is the result of a threat to our lives. Fear may lead to positive change, for example when prompting concern and action on environmental issues, but it can also be an obstacle to our everyday lives, for example when manifest as agoraphobia as discussed in chapters 1 and 3. The fear discussed in this chapter is fear of crime, more specifically the fear of violent crime committed in "public" space in urban milieus.

Fear is the subject of research in several disciplines, including ethnology, criminology, sociology, and psychology. Susan Smith (1987) has distinguished between a psychology of fear, a sociology of fear, and a geography of fear in relation to crime, and geographers claim to add an important spatial dimension neglected by others (Herbert 1989). Likewise Rachel Pain (1991: 415–416) argues that "women's fear of crime merited separate attention in geography" because "it differs in its extent, its nature, its relation to actual risks, its effects and its potential for structural analysis." But a spatial perspective is not confined to the discipline of geography: for example, ethnologist Jochum Stattin (1990) acknowledges that fear could be related to borders or thresholds, and criminologist Eva Tiby (1991) points out that environmental features are important in relation to fear. There has also been a growing interest in fear from an architectural perspective, from which the concept of an "architecture of fear" has emerged (Ellin 1997). Thus, research on the geography of fear blurs boundaries between disciplines and is often interdisciplinary.

Fear of crime was first acknowledged in the late 1960s and early 1970s when national crime surveys were undertaken in the United States, followed by the United Kingdom and other countries. These surveys were primarily concerned with the impact of crime on the quality of life of ordinary citizens and therefore focused on crimes affecting the day-to-day lives of citizens, including property crimes and crimes against the person (Smith 1987). Importance was attached to the emotional consequences of people's experiences of danger and anxiety, which were understood to generate a sense of malaise. Feelings of anxiety and perceptions of danger were often presumed to be most intense in larger urban areas, prompting the majority of the survey work to be conducted in these environments.

Large-scale surveys have generated similar results in different countries, including systematic mismatches between the experience of crime and fear of crime. These surveys show that young men are most at risk of becoming victims of violent crime, and that violent sexual crimes against women are very rare. But in terms of fear of crime, women and elderly people are the most afraid, while young men are least afraid despite being most exposed to violence (Smith 1987; Painter 1992; Tiby 1991; Malm 1997, 1999; Koskela 1999). There is also a spatial dimension to this mismatch: women are most fearful about "public" urban spaces, especially lonely, dark, and unsurveilled spaces, while they are much less fearful about "private" or domestic spaces, such as their homes. But women are at greater risk of violence from men they know within domestic spaces than from unknown strangers in "public" spaces. These mismatches led to claims about women's fear of crime being irrational or disproportionate.

It was several years before feminist researchers began to challenge such claims, but when feminist research in this area did emerge, fierce criticisms began to be articulated. Kate Painter (1992) for example, is very critical of the common "finding" of large-scale crime surveys that young men are most at risk of violent crime. She argues that since men go out more they are more likely to be exposed to crimes, but that if women went out as much as men do they would be just as likely to be victims as men. She also argues that national crime surveys in particular relied far too heavily on police statistics and paid far too little attention to what people reported about their own experiences. Her views are echoed by Rachel Pain (1991: 421) who draws attention to that fact that a great deal of the sexual harassment and sexual abuse endured by women never shows up in crime statistics, and she argues that if women were able to define sexual violence in terms of their own experiences, the incidence of such crimes would rise very significantly. Thus, feminists argued that women's fears reflect the reality of their experiences and should not be dismissed as "irrational."

Authors like Painter (1992) and Pain (1991) find crime surveys useful for providing evidence about broad trends in reported crime, but argue for the use of rather different methodologies in order to understand people's experiences of (the impacts of) crime, favoring local surveys that collect evidence about people's own accounts of what they fear and why, together with in-depth interviews. Contradicting national crime surveys, local surveys show that women are more likely to be the victims of crime (whether reported or not) than men, that women experience a wider spectrum of crime and threat of crime than men, and that women are the focus of particular kinds of crimes and threats, notably those with a sexual dimension. In this context it is no surprise that for women "rape is feared more than any other offence" (Warr 1985: 241). Local surveys also show that people who have been directly affected by crime are often haunted by the experience for a long time. This is especially true for women and elderly people. Overall, regardless of victimization rates presented in large-scale surveys, it is elderly people who suffer most from the *effects* of crime in that fear of crime is most likely to shape their social and emotional lives in particularly significant ways (Smith 1987).

Perceptions of risk are also influenced by media reporting, which inevitably heightens public awareness of crime (Smith 1989). Whether the mass media exaggerate the extent of crime and how they view their role in the formation of public opinion about crime are contentious and debated issues. Daly and Chasteen (1997) argue that the crimes that are least likely to happen are the ones most exposed in the media, and that for women the fear of rape is strongly associated with its representation in the media.

In-depth interviews provide evidence of the deeper experiential causes and consequences of fear (Burgess 1998). In her path-breaking study of the geography of women's fear, Gill Valentine's (1989) use of this method reveals intense fears of sexual violence, together with the internalization of a culture of blaming victims for behaving in "dangerous" or "inappropriate" ways, by virtue of being in particular places or dressing in particular ways. In response to their fears, which are often regarded as "normal" and "appropriate," women develop "coping strategies" by avoiding "dangerous" places at "dangerous" times (usually at night), sometimes by following lengthy and circuitous routes. Thus, women develop "mental maps" according to their fears and perceptions of danger and impose corresponding restrictions on their mobility. If they feel "at home" in an area they are likely to feel safer in it than in unfamiliar places. However, the character and meaning of spaces changes through the day and Valentine (1989) observes that most women become more vigilant at night, paying detailed attention to microdesign features of the environment in which they move and intensifying their listening and looking for signs of danger.

One of the key contributions of feminist work on the geography of fear concerns its analysis of power relations. Valentine's (1989) interviews show that women often fear male strangers, whose behavior or potential behavior is experienced as aggressive, intimidating, and threatening. Women, therefore, perceive urban space differently from men, often sensing it to be hostile and masculine, and feeling alienated and excluded from many places. In this way the power relations of gender are expressed spatially. Notwithstanding such things as career success and economic independence, fear of male violence deters the majority of women from being socially independent of men. Valentine (1989: 389) suggests that this "robs them [women] of their confidence" and contributes to the maintenance and perpetuation of patriarchal power relations. Painter (1992: 177) advances a similar argument observing that:

> the women surveyed, do not fear crime, they fear men and it is a real fear; fear which limits their freedom of movement, where they can go, when they can go, how they can go and with whom they can go. Fear which alters their perceptions of space and the built environment . . . ; fear which reminds them that men dominate public space and control access to it.

The emphasis on power relations to which feminist researchers have drawn attention is relevant to differences in fearfulness other than those of gender. For example, large-scale surveys show that elderly people experience high levels of fear, and the same is true of disabled people. Feelings of physical vulnerability and powerlessness contribute to such fears and may be fostered not only by frailty or limitations on mobility but also by feelings of isolation and loneliness. This points to the need to consider factors such as social (and spatial) exclusion in interpreting variations in, and causes of, fearfulness. Evidence of high levels of fear among gay men and lesbians corresponds to vulnerability to attack and harassment, including "hate crimes," with debates about the extent to which issues of sexuality or of gender are at stake in violence and threats of violence against sexual minorities (Namaste 1996; Pain 1991; Valentine 1998; Tiby 1999). Power relations are also useful in understanding why quantitative research on links between fear, race, and class is inconclusive. In some circumstances a relative lack of power may intensify fearfulness, but in other contexts, where disadvantaged groups feel a high degree of support within their own communities, levels of fear may be lessened. Indeed, although poor people living in poor neighborhoods suffer high levels of crime, they tend to be less fearful of burglaries than people living in wealthy neighborhoods (Herbert and Darwood 1992; Painter 1992; Smith 1987). This suggests that there is not one universal solution, and that safety always is focused on certain issues and certain groups of people, from whom some are excluded and some are included.

In early work on the geography of fear quantitative approaches were dominant. As I have argued, one of the influences of feminist work was to introduce the use of qualitative methods into this field. Some feminists have argued for greater use of ethnographic methods and for qualitative approaches to fear among previously neglected groups, such as children (Pain 2000). But more prominent in recent work is a shift of another kind, namely, toward an emphasis on the discourses in which ideas about fear circulate and the subjectivities invoked in such discourses. From this perspective, a focus on experiences of fear may serve to foster fearfulness, or to perpetuate stereotypes about the fearfulness of particular groups and the dangerousness of particular places. For example, J. K. Gibson-Graham (1997a: 310) argues that research on women's fear too often uses concepts that "portray women's bodies and female sexuality in spatial terms as an empty space waiting to be invaded/taken/formed," thereby reinforcing stereotypes of women's passivity.

Examining fear in terms of discursive constructs can contest such views. Hille Koskela (1997), for example, examines how women talk about their responses to fear and points especially to notions of bravery and boldness, arguing that this is a more effective discourse for contesting the power relations that generate fear. In their research on university students' responses to questions about fear and safety, Anna Mehta and Liz Bondi (1999) analyze the ways in which particular gendered subject positions are mobilized by their respondents through their use of particular discursive resources. They conclude that the negotiation of danger can also be understood as the negotiation of power.

Thus, some feminists, such as Elizabeth Wilson (1991) contest the idea that urban spaces are dangerous for women, and argue that cities have always been important sites for women's empowerment. The notion of the city as an unnatural place for the body is also challenged by Elizabeth Grosz (1992: 250), who writes "there is nothing intrinsically alienating or unnatural about the city . . . each environment or context contains its own powers, perils, dangers, and advantages." There are continuities between this perspective and Jane Jacobs's (1961) classic work on urban life: these studies all reinscribe cities as places in which strangers can coexist to their mutual enrichment rather than as "others" to be feared (also see Young 1990). Their argument suggests that it is possible to be both "pro-women" and "pro-cities."

In summary, feminist researchers have influenced approaches to the geography of fear in a variety of ways. They accord women's subjective, embodied, and emotional experience status as important knowledge about fear of crime, and their analyses reveal the fallacious character of claims that women's fear is "irrational" or "disproportionate." By attending to power relations they help to explain variations in levels of fear within and between a wide variety of social groups. They also open up questions about the subjectivities and knowledges deployed in the circulation of ideas about fear, including ideas produced by research in this field. In a variety of ways, feminist research has also highlighted the relevance of time and space to understanding fear of crime, and it is to this issue that I now turn.

CONCEPTUALIZING SPACE IN GEOGRAPHIES OF FEAR

In research on the geography of women's fear one important dimension of debate concerns the relative importance of social processes and the physical environment. Feminist research on fear of crime shows how it is men and male power that women fear. This discussion has focused mainly on either social power relations or physical issues, but other researchers, such as Rachel Pain (2000: 372), argue that relations of power operate through the symbolic connotations of places and spaces, with the physical environment itself being of little importance:

> Evidence is increasing, then, that particular features of the built environment play a
> minor role in the constitution of fear of crime. Rather, fear is expressed in particular

environments, as their social associations may bring existing fears to the surface. Women's fear of men will not be easily unsettled by correcting environmental flaws.

Developing this argument, Hille Koskela and Rachel Pain (2000: 270) suggest "that the built environment has received far more attention from academics and policy makers concerned with fear of crime than it warrants, at the expense of the social causes of fear." They insist that fear cannot be "designed out," and that feminists who propose that the built environment is a product of gender relations could be regarded as "naive" (271). Moreover, commenting on the relative importance of physical and social causes, they argue that "women rarely mention one (physical) without the other (social), and the social often offers the explanation as to why some physical places are especially frightening." They infer that "women's routine avoidance of particular places is largely underpinned not by fear of concrete structures but by fear of unknown men" (275).

While Koskela and Pain (2000) are undoubtedly correct in their criticism of much architectural work for being overly deterministic, they set up an unduly polarized distinction between the physical environment and social processes, and risk leaving the "geography" out of "the geography of fear." It is also difficult to understand what they mean by symbolic connotations, since these include both physical and social dimensions. To leave out the material dimension is not useful when talking about fear in public spaces.

Other contributors to this field construe the relative importance of social and environmental dimensions of fear rather differently. Indeed, elsewhere Hille Koskela (1999) offers a historiography in which she identifies three main traditions concerned with crime by region, places of fear, and the production of space, respectively. The first tradition works on a macrolevel and draws on survey evidence to map crime and fear, for example using geographical information systems. Koskela argues that this tradition conceptualizes space as a surface. The second approach focuses on the local level by studying a particular place and typically combines in-depth interviews with quantitative methods (Pain 1997). Koskela considers that this approach recognizes physical and social dimensions of space, including the symbolic associations of particular spaces and places. The third approach, which Koskela prefers, develops an understanding of space in which physical and social dimensions of space are intertwined, and in which fear of crime is not seen as either an individual or a private problem. Rather, space is understood as being produced by power relations in social practices. An example of the "production of space" approach is the work on agoraphobia, where perceived fear is analyzed within its spatial and social contexts, with feminist theory being drawn upon to trace the influence of power relations in the production of fearful spaces (Davidson 2000b; Gardner 1994; and also chapters 1 and 3 in this volume).

Painter (1992) argues that the question is not so much *if* as *how best* to use the concepts of "spatial" and "social" to analyze crime, fear, and crime prevention. As she observes, little attention has been paid to the interactions between the social and the space-time dimensions of crime, and she argues that we need to conceptualize the ways in which individuals' lives are constructed within historical processes (including time historical and time present) and the ways in which these connect to their risks and fears of crime . . . [and to understand] how space and time and social characteristics are mutually modifying, interacting dimensions, which profoundly affect the nature, shape, impact and prevention of crime in urban areas. (Painter 1992: 165. Also see Bottoms and Wiles 1992)

Her analysis echoes the work of feminist architects such as the Matrix Collective (1984) who criticized male architects and planners for neglecting gender and showed how built environments have incorporated oppressive gender relations and therefore contributed to restrictions on women's mobility (also see the Women and Geography Study Group of the IBG 1984). According to Painter (1992) relations of power are, literally, built in to the physical fabric of the ("man-made") environment, which is understood to have an important impact on levels of fear (also see Valentine 1989; Smith 1989).

While I am in broad agreement with this approach to the relationship between the social and the spatial, it remains rather vague about the concepts of "space" and "place." Doreen Massey's work provides a way of beginning to clarify these ideas. Massey (1994: 120) defines social space "in terms of the articulation of social relations which necessarily have a spatial form in their interactions with one another." Places, according to Massey (120), can be described as "particular moments in such intersecting social relations, nets of which have over time been constructed, laid down, interacted with one another, decayed and renewed." Some of those relations stretch into wider relationships and processes, outside their locality. Experiences of everyday life, including fears, are related, through social relations, to time, spaces, and places (Nylund 2000). Thus, Massey (1993: 68) emphasizes that "sense of place, an understanding of 'its character,' can only be constructed by linking that place to places beyond":

> The uniqueness of a place, or a locality, in other words is constructed out of particular interactions and mutual articulations of social relations, social processes, experiences and understandings, in a situation of co-presence, but where a large proportion of those relations, experiences and understandings are actually constructed on a far larger scale than what we happen to define for that moment as the place itself, whether that be a street, a region or even a continent. Instead then, of thinking of places as areas with boundaries around, they can be imagined as articulated moments in networks of social relations and understandings. (66)

Places, therefore, are best understood as processes (places are not static), as always linked to other places, as full of internal differences and conflicts, and as continually reproduced.

Massey's account of space and place is a useful start, but like most theories of space it tends to focus more on social relations than on subjective experiences or meanings of space. Bill Hillier (1996) argues that space and spatial configurations are not just abstract ideas with which we engage at a conscious level, but also constitute the media, or "fabric," through which thinking occurs. This may be one reason why it is difficult to "grasp" space: it is so inseparable from how we experience and think about the world that it is exceedingly difficult to conceptualize in its own right. We react to and interact with the physical environments we inhabit, which both provide the context for, and constitute, our social relations and personal experiences. Relations of power not only configure spaces and places in particular ways but are also constituted spatially.

Henri Lefebvre's (1990) threefold conceptualization of social space—involving perceived, conceived, and lived aspects—goes some way toward incorporating such ideas. In his formulation *perceived space* refers to the spatial practices of everyday life, which constitute people's perceptions of space; *conceived space* refers to representations of space produced by planners, architects, and so on in their design of urban and other spaces; and *lived space* refers to the representational spaces through which space is directly experienced, imagined, and symbolized by its inhabitants and users in particular cultural contexts (Lefebvre 1990: 38). Applying Lefebvre's conceptual framework to the relationship between space and fear, three levels or aspects can be identified, namely, perceptions of fear and space; social relations through which fear and spaces are conceived; and the lived experiences of fear and spaces. At one level, fear is about how spaces and places are imagined or represented subjectively. This aspect of fear draws on perceptions of spaces and places, which are influenced by rumors, ideas about built environments, previous experiences, personal relationships, and so on. This fear could be described as a *fear of space*. At this level, fear is a subjective experience that draws on the discourses that shape our thinking. At the second level, fear is about the social relations of power. This aspect of fear draws on dominant ways of representing spaces, including what individuals represent within the urban landscape, for example the mobilization of representations of women as passive victims and men as active aggressors. This fear could be described as *fear of what space represents*. At the third level fear and space are directly experienced. In this context fear (and other emotions), spaces, and physical structures are "felt" as inseparable. This fear could be described as *fear in space*.

Lefebvre focuses primarily on psychological and phenomenological dimensions of space, to which he accords primacy relative to the physicality of space. However, the notion of "lived space," together with what I have called "fear in space," provides an indication of the importance of the materiality of urban environments. In this context the example of a child bouncing a ball against a wall provides an apt illustration. The ball moves between the child and the built environment, creating a relation, something that affects both, and creating an invisible entity, or "room,"[1] between them. This accords closely with Grosz's (1992: 248) description of the relation between the body and the city:

> [T]here is a two-way linkage which could be defined as an *interface*, perhaps even a cobuilding. What I am suggesting is a model of the relations between the bodies and the cities which sees them, not as megalithic total entities, distinct identities, but as assemblages or collections of parts. . . . I am suggesting a fundamentally disunified series of

systems and interconnections, a series of disparate flows, energies, events or entities, and spaces, brought together or drawn apart in more or less temporary alignments.

I would suggest that the notion of "frame" achieves something similar in thinking about space (Dovey 1999). "Frame" refers to the materiality of space and to the dynamic interaction between the social and the spatial: people both use and produce the "frames" in (relation to) which they live. I would argue that we cannot talk about space, especially not in relation to fear, without taking into account its configuration or physical "framing," whether in an urban milieu, a built environment, or a park area (Burgess 1998).

How might ideas such as these inform urban planning? The first thing to note is that planning is, by definition, a practice committed to rational discourses and technological approaches. It tends to assume a straightforward relationship between how space is conceived by planners, and how it is perceived and experienced by users, which underpins claims about the scope to "design out" problems like fear, vandalism, and so on. However, it is increasingly recognized that environments cannot be fully planned or created as "ready-made" because people need to shape and produce their own spaces. There is also increasing recognition of the fact that "master" plans are exceedingly problematic because they fail to attend to differences between people and within and between different places.

The case of fear of crime highlights the diversity and complexity of everyday urban life. Fear is a complex emotional, cultural, social, and situated phenomenon. Whether planning measures such as better lighting, improved bus networks, monitoring cameras, fences, and so on might help to reduce levels of fear among particular people in particular places depends upon a wide array of factors. They may be welcomed by some groups but opposed and experienced as oppressive by others. The conceptualization of fear and space I have outlined here may help to explain why some measures might be effective for some people in some places but counterproductive in other contexts.

NOTE

1. In the Swedish language the word for space and room is the same: *rum*, which suggests a space for living in a similar way to the German word *lebensraum*. *Rum* can therefore be seen both as an abstract concept, as in "space," and in a more concrete way as in "room."

3

Embodying Agoraphobia: Rethinking Geographies of Women's Fear

Ruth Bankey

There is a growing literature within feminist geography concerned with the "geographies of women's fear," a phrase first used by Gill Valentine (1989: 385) to describe how fear of male violence has resulted in women's inhibited use of space and constitutes a spatial expression of patriarchy. Most contributions to this literature have focused on the form and consequences of women's fear of male violence whether in public or private spheres and how these fears are linked to patriarchy more broadly (Day 1999; Pain 1991, 1997). While this work has been very useful in illustrating the spatial effects of women's fear, several feminists have argued that it also tends to reproduce representations of the feminine subject as a weak and passive victim (Hester, Kelly, and Radford 1996). Extending this critique, this chapter argues for an approach to the geography of women's fear that problematizes the object and location of women's fear of violence. I contend that the focus on fear of male violence, and its treatment as exemplary of more general gender relations, has resulted in an unduly narrow approach to how geographies of fear are created and maintained within women's lives. More problematically, the focus on fear of (male) others has perpetuated assumptions about women's experience of fear and what fear means, which implies a far greater degree of homogeneity than is warranted. Women who avoid particular spaces do not necessarily do so for fear of "stranger danger" or for fear of being attacked or harassed by (male) others.

Ironically, while efforts have been made to examine in detail the wide array of *geographies* that result from violence against women, little attention has been paid to the wide array of *fears* and, therefore, how specific experiences of fear create specific geographies of fear. There has been correspondingly more of a focus on the structural and geographic parameters of violence directed toward women and much less of a focus on the highly personal and embodied meanings of fear. In order to address this gap, I explore how the embodied experience of fear is linked to the production

44

of fearful subjectivities and geographies of fear. To do so I will elaborate how women with agoraphobia negotiate their somatic (bodily) and spatial boundaries in the context of their experience of panic. I show how the embodied experience of a panic attack produces an agoraphobic self and agoraphobic geography. In this way I argue that geographies of fear are created not only by the fear of violence from others, but also by fear of one's own body and its sensations, which results in a fear of being "othered."

As illustrated in chapter 1, women with agoraphobia often describe their spatial movements as curtailed by the debilitating sensations of panic attacks and by fears of having panic attacks. In this chapter I examine accounts of panic attacks more closely, showing how they mobilize powerful images of violence to, and emanating from, the self. The violence of a panic attack is not only inherent in the horrific physical and emotional sensations of panic itself, but also in the way it triggers feelings of self-doubt, self-loathing, and self-alienation. These feelings generate a sense of being "other than" oneself and transform people's understandings and perceptions of themselves and their environments. Using such evidence I explore how fears of this kind might deepen feminist understandings of the geographies of fear, and how they might contribute to the development of more adequately embodied, as well as spatialized, understandings of feminine subjectivities. Throughout this chapter I do not suggest that people suffering panic attacks and agoraphobia are "abnormal," but, on the contrary, I argue that their experiences shed important light on how we think about the geographies of fear and on the importance of self-presentation and body "image." In so doing I seek to advance feminist geography's capacity to theorize subjectivities.

Given the lack of attention to first-person accounts of panic attacks or of agoraphobia (Bordo, Klein, and Silverman, 1998; Davidson 2000a, 2000b), I focus in depth on sufferers' descriptions. I draw on material gathered in the Ottawa area through semistructured interviews with ten women conducted between 1997 and 1999.[1] Most of these women were contacted through the Anxiety Disorders Association of Ontario (ADAO), though some heard of the research by word of mouth. All of those I interviewed had received a clinical diagnosis of panic disorder with agoraphobia. While they all emphasized the importance of panic in their experiences and uses of space, all resisted the label "disorder." In this chapter I respect their objections to this label. I foreground their accounts of panic but sometimes use "agoraphobia" as a shorthand for a condition to which panic is central. I do so with reservations, however, not only because the significance of panic attacks is overlooked in much of the nonclinical discussions of agoraphobia, but also because of widespread misunderstandings and misinformed assumptions about what agoraphobia is, as well as what panic is (Bankey 1999). My hope is that this chapter, like chapter 1, will contribute to the development of both clinical and nonclinical understandings of agoraphobia more sensitive to the subjective experiences of sufferers.

Various studies indicate that upward of 70 percent of those *diagnosed* with panic disorder with agoraphobia are women (American Psychiatric Association 1994; Health Canada 1996). In common with ailments such as anorexia, bulimia, and hysteria, agoraphobia is often written about as a female condition, linking issues of the feminine to ill bodies (Symonds 1973; Chambless and Goldstein 1982, 1992; Brehony 1983; Seidenburg and Decrow 1983; Brown 1987; Bordo 1992, 1993). However, it should be noted that most of those I interviewed did not think of agoraphobia as a problem specific to women. Some argued that the predominance of women among those diagnosed reflects the consequences of social assumptions about gender rather than the incidence of the condition. For example, one interviewee stated that "women are far more likely to report their conditions to others because women are socialized to talk about their problems, and admit to their vulnerabilities and weaknesses much more so than men." My decision to focus on women is strategic in that it enables me to link my analysis to feminist debates about gendering of subjectivity without attempting to disentangle the complicated gender variations in experiences and meanings of panic.

Before analyzing accounts of agoraphobia, I discuss existing studies of the geographies of women's fear, drawing out some of the implicit assumptions and exclusions of this literature. In the sections that follow I discuss sensations of panic and explore the associated interconnections between bodies, subjectivities, and geographies.

GEOGRAPHIES OF WOMEN'S FEAR

Geographical work on women's fear of violence has drawn on and developed the work of sociologists, criminologists, and others. Although perceptions of, and responses to, violence and crime vary along all major axes of social differentiation, including those of age, class, "race," and so on, gender differences emerge so strongly that they have generated a great deal of attention. Not surprisingly feminist work has focused particularly on women's fears of violence, especially sexual violence (Hanmer and Maynard 1987). Evidence of gender differences in levels of fear prompt widely varying responses from feminists, some emphasizing the significance of (a continuum of) violence against women as a clear evidence of dominant heteropatriarchal structures and arguing that analyzing and challenging such violence should therefore be central to, and a unifying theme for, feminist politics (Kelly 1988). But others are wary of this emphasis because of its tendency to portray and objectify women as passive victims, underplaying their own capacity for violence, and because of its neglect of violence perpetrated against men (Hester, Kelly, and Radford 1996).

As argued in chapter 2, within geography the former view has been the more influential and feminist geographers have examined spatial dimensions of women's fears together with the consequences for their mobility and their experiences of space (Mooney 1997; Pain 1991). Despite the greater incidence of violence in domestic spaces, this work has focused primarily on the geographies of women's fear within the "public" sphere, especially outdoor spaces, in part because women's spatial patterns are much more obviously restricted in such contexts (Valentine 1989;

Pain 1991; Gardener 1994; Mehta and Bondi 1999; Koskela 1997; Stanko 1990). But this work has also addressed some of the factors generating such fear, especially the influence of the media (Valentine 1989, 1992), crime prevention advice (Gardener 1996; Stanko 1990) and parental and other forms of authority (Kosekla 1997), which have all been shown to encourage women to believe that it is normal or commonsensical to fear unknown strangers in a wide variety of "public" spaces and places, especially in hours of darkness.

The locations in which women tend to perceive high levels of risk of violence, together with other evidence about the geographical incidence of violence against women, are, of course, of enormous importance in understanding how violence affects women. But fear is a highly variable psychological and physiological phenomenon, which cannot be expected to relate simply and directly to objective measurements of risk. It is therefore important to recognize that the symbolic connotations or meanings attached to spaces women fear are at least as important as their location. As Pain (1991: 417) argues:

> For individual women the spatial separation of feelings of fear and safety may well be experienced as particular localities, or conversely there may be no clear physical boundaries to what is "safe" and "unsafe." It is of greater significance, though, to study on a broader scale how these experiences are constructed, what they represent and how cumulatively they might affect women's lives.

The landscapes of fear emerging from this literature on the geography of women's fear could be construed in terms of fear of the *agora*,[2] that is of public, market, or meeting spaces, which is the etymological and popular, nonclinical definition of agoraphobia. For example:

> When one woman out of every four in the United States is raped (or one every ten minutes), agoraphobia—the fear of *public* spaces—takes on different coloration altogether. In the case of rape victims, public space as such does not exist except as a topology of fear. And time not just space, is also a constituent element of agoraphobia: at night in most large cities, all women are agoraphobic. (da Costa Meyer 1996: 152–153)

However, the landscapes of fear experienced by agoraphobic women are rather different. What these women fear most frequently and pervasively are panic attacks. As I illustrate shortly, such fears are highly spatialized, hence the avoidance of particular spaces and places that is characteristic of agoraphobia. Davidson (2000a) argues it is largely peopled or social space rather than public space per se that is associated with these fears, and it often relates as much to people whom sufferers know as those they do not. But, as I will illustrate, the geography of fear of panic is further complicated by evidence that some sufferers actively seek particular kinds of social spaces to alleviate their fears. As I elaborate in the sections that follow, these varied agoraphobic behaviors can be understood in terms of a fear of being "othered" or being seen as abnormal, especially but not exclusively in "public" spaces. Several theorists of gender, from Simone de Beauvoir (1997) onward, have argued that "othering" is a defining feature of femininity. I will therefore go on to argue that the spatial experiences of women with agoraphobia provide important insights into larger societal norms about what it means to be a woman and about women's bodies and geographies in contemporary Western cultures.

BODIES IN PANIC: SHIFTING BODILY BOUNDARIES

Within both clinical and self-help literatures, panic is typically defined as a fear of fear itself, or a fear of fearful thoughts (American Psychiatric Association 1994; Anxiety Disorders Association of Ontario 1999). Panic attacks are a combination of bodily sensations and emotions, which are unexpected, that appear "out of the blue" and that include an overwhelming sense of fear and terror (ADAO 1999). Among the wide range of symptoms of panic, sufferers typically experience some or all of the following: erratic or increased heart rate, numbness, sweating, dizziness, faintness, hot or cold flashes, shaking or trembling, terror, fear of dying or losing control, and a sense that things either outside the body or within the body are "unreal" (American Psychiatric Association 1994). The ADAO (1999: 5) uses this example to describe the horrors of a panic attack to those who have not experienced one:

Imagine yourself in a car that has stopped directly over a train track. You twist the key on and off, on, off, but the car won't start. The more you try, the more worried and frustrated you become. Suddenly you hear the distant sound of a train whistle and at that moment you start to sweat and your heart begins to race. You pull on the door handle and its stuck. The sound of the train is getting louder. You're trapped and feeling completely out of control. The terror has begun. You move over to the passenger seat and desperately try to push it open. It won't budge! You jump into the back seat and continue to fight to get either door open. By now you're as white as snow and desperately trying to catch your breath. You don't know if you'll ever see your family again and you feel as though this is it, you're going to die!!!

The physical sensations of a panic attack often resemble those of a heart attack, and many of those I interviewed thought that their first panic attack was a heart attack. They described rushing to the hospital emergency room, where they were told that, in Lana's words, "there was nothing seriously wrong with them, and to go home."

In chapter 1 Joyce Davidson describes agoraphobia as a boundary crisis (also see Davidson 2000a). In order to understand the embodiment of panic in greater depth, it is worth teasing out the ways in which bodily boundaries are disrupted. In particular I distinguish between three interrelated features of panic, namely, what clinicians call depersonalization and derealization, together with a widely reported heightened awareness of sensory stimuli that disrupts the sufferer's sense of bodily boundaries and blurs distinctions between internal and external environments.

Depersonalization refers to sensations in which the boundary between the body and its environment dissolves from the inside, leaving a person feeling as if she or he is disassociated or detached from her or his body. McDowell and Sharp (1997: 3) argue that the body is not simply a "surface to be mapped or inscribed, a boundary between the individual subject and that which is other to it, a container of individual identity, but fundamentally a boundary which is permeable and penetrable." During depersonalization this boundary is not just permeable—it collapses. The body is perceived by the sufferer to be absent and so he or she becomes a "no-body." Catherine described the sensation thus:

> Do you remember ever having a feeling, you look in the mirror and you think about leaving yourself and it's scary, like you were fading out. . . . I seem unreal to myself? 'Cause when I'm on the phone and suddenly I start having a panic attack and I look down at the receiver. I look at my hand but, to me it's not really my hand. It's essentially the same, it's like stepping away from my own conversation.

Depersonalization is often described by sufferers as a feeling of being two-dimensional and of being unable to exert control over one's body. For example, another interviewee described feeling "like my body has a mind of its own and I don't feel connected, and I panic, it's like it decides for itself what it is going to do." Not surprisingly these sensations leave the sufferer "feeling vulnerable."

Unlike depersonalization, where the individual feels that his or her body has faded away, or is foggy, disconnected, and "unreal," derealization involves sensations in which the sufferer's external environment is felt to be unreal and "slipping away." Lisa, who began to have panic attacks in her late teens after leaving home for university, described one such experience:

> As I was approaching the building, I suddenly felt as if I was, the buildings were no longer there. The streets became blurred, I felt dizzy and yet I know that I wasn't falling down or walking strangely. I wasn't happy. . . . I was moving at a different speed I was just going by, I couldn't focus on myself anymore, and the space was no longer even there. I felt as if I was moving at a slow motion pace, that everything around me was faster and more intense. I felt as if I was no longer there, it was just speed and space.

During panic attacks heightened awareness of sensory stimuli, including sights, sounds, smells, tastes, and touch, disrupts the sufferer's sense of bodily boundaries and renders boundaries between the embodied self and the environment highly unstable. Distinctions between inside and outside often lose meaning because sensations are experienced as coming simultaneously from within the body and from the external environment. This often generates an overwhelming sense of no longer being a bounded individual (Health Canada 1996; Davidson 2000a). Nancy, for example, described numerous experiences in which she lost any sense of bodily boundaries capable of separating where her body boundaries began and ended:

> I leave my body and somehow I actually am worked into the noise of my body and the outside, and its overwhelming the noises and the sounds. I know it's not a right feeling and I couldn't walk if I had to during the panic, it's strange. Voices and sounds are heightened and I slide into a feeling that I'm no longer connected to myself. I don't know why it happens and it happens everywhere.

The "bodyscape" of panic is therefore one in which the sounds and sensations of bodily processes and external stimuli become deeply enmeshed within one another. It is therefore not surprising that fear of having a panic attack becomes associated as strongly with particular spaces and places as with bodily sensations (compare Kirby 1996).

AGORAPHOBIC SUBJECTIVITIES

The women I interviewed all hold strong beliefs about how their bodies and behaviors are seen by others. All of them were aware that panic attacks produce relatively limited visible changes, notably sweating, breathing problems, flushed skin color, and increased pupil dilation. Nevertheless, they all offered accounts that included a powerful sense that at some point during the course of a panic attack others must be able to see that something was terribly wrong. Their descriptions portray their bodies as screens onto which the sensations of panic are projected and therefore made visible to others. This perceived visibility intensifies their terror of panic attacks. Thus, the women "pictured" their psychic and bodily sensations of panic using very negative terms and imagery, as the following quotations illustrate.

> When I go through an attack I go through the process, no I should say, I used to, at first, I was thinking I'm going crazy and I'm going to faint, or die or embarrass myself, I'm going to collapse right here and people will think I'm crazy. I know that people can't see, in fact that really makes it worse. . . . But I think that I used to think people would see a woman, me, collapse, big dramatic crash, because that's what I felt like doing. (Lisa)

> When I first started having attacks I thought everyone must know that I'm about to collapse. I felt like I was swaying back and forth and that people could see me unsteady, like I was going to faint at any second, collapse on the pavement, big scene, I never did you know, I was frozen to my spot. . . . I feel like I need to burst out and scream. . . . I can't I'm helpless, but I think that people must see my fear, big eyes, going crazy, a madwoman screaming and crying. . . . I imagine that picture, "The Scream," but it's me with big hair, screaming, crying, moving my arms all over having a great big fit. (Elizabeth)

As I have argued elsewhere (Bankey 2001), the fear that sensations of panic are visible to others is based on a belief that madness or deviance can be seen on and through the body, within a "logic of visibility" (Chow 1992). According to Sander Gilman (1993, 1995) this belief is steeped in a long-standing medical tradition of representing deviance, abnormality, and madness as a surface presentation of the body: a "disorder" that could be both classified and treated if it were made visible to the physician. The disordered body was thus constructed as a weak or unpredictable "other," which physicians often identified or labeled as feminine or female in nature (Showalter 1985, 1997). My interviewees' descriptions of their sensations of panic highlight how agoraphobia is experienced not only as a loss of control over one's bodily and environmental boundaries, but also as intense fearfulness of images of the self as inadequately bounded and violently disrupted. Being seen by others is central to such experiences, and these women draw on culturally pervasive ideas about women's bodies and women's identities in which close scrutiny and measures of "self-control" are used (contradictorily) to define, delimit, and pathologize femininity.

The women I interviewed had several ways of identifying themselves and several different visions of themselves during panic. These visions included images of women who are out of control, either passively (for example, fainting or collapsing) or aggressively (for example, exaggerated movements and facial expressions), which represent different aspects of feminine behavior and femininity within Western cultures. They show the variability with which negative feminine characteristics and markers have been incorporated into the memories, subjectivities, and bodily sensations of those I interviewed and the malleability of those images. Many of the women identified their fears as stemming from a fear of being labeled as abnormal, deviant, or crazy. The images on which they drew indicate that they are afraid of being thought of as irrational, incapacitated women, or as hyperfeminine.

Fears about how one is seen during panic is liable to increase the likelihood of suffering panic attacks, creating a vicious circle. As Fiona put it, "this is not normal, and now that someone else knows and I'm going to be found out, I have more to worry about, and a better reason to panic." Agoraphobic women often describe avoiding places in which they have previously experienced a panic attack, but because of this circle of fear and panic, agoraphobic spatialities are equally the result of attempts to avoid being seen and judged. Crucial here is avoidance of the gaze of other people, particularly, but not exclusively, the gaze of strangers, and therefore of spaces in which the agoraphobic might be (at risk of being) stared at: these women want to avoid the scrutiny of others. Thus, agoraphobic subjectivities illustrate the very close connection between fear of others and fear of being "othered," that is, defined as "abnormal."

Because agoraphobic women are acutely aware of themselves, and especially that other people will see their panic and judge them negatively, they become very concerned about self-presentation. Sometimes this prompts an urge to hide from everyone, described by one woman thus: "the person who might be there while you panic is just too terrifying so you avoid everyone as much as possible." However, the representation of agoraphobic women as withdrawing from others and from public spaces greatly oversimplifies the situation. Many of the women I interviewed feared isolation and invisibility, as well as being seen.

Many of those interviewed linked agoraphobia to feelings of isolation and loneliness. In part this reflected a fear of being shunned or abandoned because of perceived abnormality: "My fear is that I'm going to be judged and I'm not going to have friends because I got angry or said nasty things. Or if I have a panic attack they'll think I'm losing control, I'm not a good person to be around, or a good friend" (Pat). Such fears prompt a need for affirmation and validation and, therefore, desire for sociability and interaction with other people. For agoraphobic women the company of others has the potential to *alleviate* anxiety:

> The only reason I seek out people is because it makes me feel less anxious. I don't seek them, I mean, if they are walking by, it's just because it helps me feel less alone, the idea of not having friends, being abandoned. . . . Basically it makes me feel less panicky. (Pat)

More generally, my interviewees longed to be, and to be seen as, "normal." But because they did not feel "normal" they also felt very much at risk of being misunderstood or rendered "invisible" in the sense that their experiences were belittled, dismissed, or denied, or they were accused of "acting up" or misbehaving. They drew attention to two contexts in which this was particularly likely to happen: in primary health care and at work.

Several of the women I interviewed described how, after performing a routine examination, their general practitioners assured them that no physical problem could be detected, and that therefore there was *nothing* wrong with them. The women who reported this sort of experience were left feeling that their doctors had not taken their complaints seriously, thereby compounding their sense of frustration and confusion because their experiences did not matter, and were not "real." As Edward Shorter argues:

> By defining certain symptoms as illegitimate a culture strongly encourages patients not to develop them or to risk being thought "undeserving" individuals with no real medical problems. Accordingly there is great pressure on the unconscious mind to produce only legitimate symptoms. (cited in Showalter 1997: 15)

All of the women that I interviewed were afraid of the repercussions of their agoraphobia within the workplace, where they often felt defined as "undeserving." They faced acute dilemmas in this context, having to choose between struggling to conceal their difficulties or exposing themselves to the risk of highly critical judgment. Some spoke of how employers and coworkers did not believe them when they tried to explain their fear of panic attacks because they looked "perfectly healthy." Most also expressed anxieties about being seen as weak and incompetent in front of their colleagues and especially their employers. And they were very concerned about the stigma associated with a problem that might be labeled as a "mental" disorder. For example, Jennifer took a leave of absence from her job for a time when her symptoms were particularly debilitating and felt stigmatized as a result:

> The repercussions for my work . . . the company viewed me as being weak psychologically. . . . I had to defend my stability and the fact that I was mentally competent and so on and forth. . . . I think they were doubting my confidence because of the time off . . . there was that seed of doubt planted by the time off, that wasn't forgiven and was always something that raised caution.

In common with several others she drew on notions of "stress" to emphasize connections between her difficulties and those of other workers, but she also described a work environment in which any sign of vulnerability was liable to be exploited:

> I mean I think there were lots of people who felt a lot of stress. I don't know anyone else who discussed it. First of all people don't discuss these problems in this environment because if you do you're labeled. I do know a number of colleagues who took time off because they were stressed, overworked but no body ever talked about it. If you want to stay home and hide under the bed you just couldn't cope. It's not spoken of, you have to be completely competent at all times. You have to be allowed not to be, not fully competent at all times. You are not allowed any natural feelings you have, to keep it steady you have to be straight.

As well as taking leaves of absence, interviewees reported quitting their jobs entirely and seeking paid work that could be done at home or relying on their spouses to supply the family income.

Many of the concerns expressed by my interviewees are shared by women with other debilitating health conditions including multiple sclerosis (Dyck 1999), myaligic encephalitis, or chronic fatigue syndrome (Moss 1999; Moss and Dyck 1999), and anorexia (Malson 1997). In all cases sufferers feel intensely vulnerable because they fear the consequences of both disclosing and not disclosing their illnesses to others. If they choose not to tell others in their workplaces they live with the ever-present threat of "discovery" if their work performance is impaired in any way. And if they inform colleagues or employers, with a view to securing the flexibility they need to fulfill the demands of their work without further impairing their health, they fear stigmatization and discrimination. In many workplaces the performance of a particular kind of workplace identity, which is always necessarily an embodied performance, operates as a powerful if unspoken assumption, stimulating intense anxieties about (bodies) being marked out as "hysterical," or as weak, or out of control. The fears experienced by agoraphobic women are by no means unique but serve to highlight much more widespread anxieties.

GEOGRAPHIES OF AGORAPHOBIA

The geographies resulting from (the fear of having) panic attacks are as varied as experiences of fear. Consequently, the avoidant behaviors of women with agoraphobia are diverse, varying not only between individuals but for each individual over daily and longer timescales. So although some spaces are avoided most of the time by most agoraphobic women, there are also many spaces that might be accessible to one person one day but inaccessible on another day. Further, while some sufferers are completely housebound for long periods of time, the majority have rather more complicated geographies. Moreover, as the preceding discussion indicates, agoraphobics do not respond to spaces as fixed givens but experience space in terms of the interrelationship between their bodies and environment, which may become radically destabilized by the sensations of panic. They therefore adopt a wide range of strategies for transforming the experiential character of particular spaces. For example, they utilize a wide range of tactics to avert the gaze of others or to conceal what they assume are visible signs of panic. For example, many of those interviewed found being with a companion "protected" them from (the fear of) being watched or "othered." And many found that items such as jackets, umbrellas, or newspapers provided the means by which to conceal their bodies and facial gestures (Gardener 1994; Davidson 2000b).

Because of the dynamic interplay between bodies and environments associated with panic, particular issues arise for sufferers in relation to movement across space. Many of the women I interviewed expressed strong preferences in relation to different modes of transportation. Forms of public transportation such as buses were greatly disliked because interviewees had no control over the driving of the vehicle or over the (intrusive) presence of others. Most were particularly afraid of being stared at on the bus, or that some "lonely man" would approach them for conversation or gaze at them for the duration of their bus ride. Walking was another panic-provoking form of mobility because it is experienced as slow, thereby limiting opportunities for escaping a stressful situation quickly. The presence of other people who might, for example, ask for directions was also described as a problem. Car driving was the preferred mode of transportation for most, because it provided a protective shield against visibility and conversation and it allowed the driver to go wherever she wanted at the speed she desired. Driving allowed these women to reclaim some sense of control over their environments and to move through the city while still remaining anonymous, becoming a kind of a mobile "home" (Davidson 2000a, 2000b). In the context of subjectivities shaped by fear of being othered, these preferences are readily understandable. They may also shed new light on more general preferences for car driving and against public transport.

Existing studies of the geography of women's fear point to a very strong link between fear and dark, concealed or lonely spaces, but agoraphobic women's geographies of fear tend to be very different. While women are often presumed to find safety where other people tend to congregate, agoraphobic women typically avoid such spaces. Likewise, while women are often presumed to dislike paths concealed from view and may even be advised to avoid them, agoraphobic women often navigate their way across space by seeking out such routes. And while conventional safety instructions discourage women from walking alone at night, for agoraphobic women the fear of being seen and scrutinized often seems to outweigh fear of attack. For example, Elizabeth said: "I like night because nobody can see me, I feel more anonymous. . . . I just feel safer it's like a blanket protecting me. If I do get into danger there will be fewer people to help me, but I don't think of it that way."

Although avoiding places where they would be exposed to the gaze of others is common among agoraphobic women, individuals devise a range of other tactics for moving through space without attracting unwanted attention. Fiona described a microgeography that enabled her to move about more easily:

I prefer street lamps so I can see where I'm going, but in a way where people in apartment buildings or in cars can't necessarily spot me. Because, I feel people are judging me . . . I kind of imagine people and their minds picking me to pieces. It drives me crazy. I prefer not being with somebody, in the dark.

CONCLUSION

The public realm is regulated by banishing from sight behaviors that are considered repugnant, such as madness or deviance (Duncan 1996a). As Tim Cresswell (1996: 22) notes, "it is difficult to get people to recognise normative geographies until these are transgressed . . . the occurrence of out of place phenomena leads people to question behaviour and define what is and what is not appropriate for a setting." Endorsing this statement, the public sphere is seen by those I interviewed as a place of discipline and scrutiny, in which the exposure of panic and anxiety results in being characterized as abnormal, deviant, or transgressive. And while in contemporary Western society failing to enter into "public" spaces, including workplaces, is considered abnormal and unhealthy, abnormal or deviant bodies in such spaces are considered equally if not more unhealthy. My interviewees were therefore faced with a dilemma: remaining in seclusion and isolation, which are unhealthy activities they must strive against; or exposing themselves to the gaze of people who might view their bodies and actions as mad or abnormal, something they must also avoid. Their responses to this dilemma entail geographical forms of self-discipline and self-punishment through the imposition of precisely defined walls and boundaries that constitute the avoidant behaviors of agoraphobia (compare Foucault 1970). Walls and other barriers to being "seen" enable agoraphobics to conceal themselves and so avoid the possibility of becoming a "spectacle." These barriers therefore become "crutches" and create local havens, but because they also isolate sufferers within their agoraphobic worlds they serve simultaneously as prison and salvation. And through the circle of fear of panic I have described, these prisons help to shape and (re)construct agoraphobic subjectivities and spatialities that are connected to a history of creating "feminine" spaces and subjectivities.

Agoraphobia is sometimes used as a metaphor for women's geographies of fear (da Costa Meyer 1996). In this chapter I have shown that such usage misconstrues the experiences and geographies of women diagnosed with agoraphobia, and in so doing I have highlighted some of the limits and exclusions of much of the literature on geographies of women's fear. By examining the embodied spatiality of panic I have illuminated the character of agoraphobic subjectivities and geographies. Moreover, my analysis of the fears of a particular group of women illustrates pervasive features of constructions of femininity in Western urban societies. While most of the time most women negotiate these constructs without experiencing panic attacks and without recourse to complex avoidant behaviors, there are many similarities between agoraphobic subjectivities and feminine subjectivities more generally. In particular I would argue that fear of others is in many cases better understood as fear of being othered. Furthermore, by attending to the specificities of women's fear, I have illustrated the intrinsic spatiality of embodied subjectivities. While this chapter has focused exclusively on a small group of women, the dynamic interplay between bodies (and bodily sensations) and environments is undoubtedly relevant to understand other kinds of subjectivity.

NOTES

1. Because of a lack of information about the lived experiences of sufferers, I felt that it was important for my research to be directly informed by persons who had experienced, or were still experiencing, agoraphobia. The research is based on ten individual tape recorded semistructured interviews, thirty "informal" interviews, where notes were taken but the conversations were not taped, and five focus group interviews, where, again, notes were taken but the conversations were not taped. All of the women who participated in the taped interviews had lived in the Ottawa area for the majority of their lives and had been diagnosed by a practitioner in the Ottawa area. They all identified themselves as white, but varied in terms of marital status, socioeconomic position, and employment status. An introductory meeting was arranged for these interviewees, at which time the women gave their consent to the tape recorded interviews that followed. Follow-up interviews were conducted at a later date, and these focused specifically on the question of whether or not agoraphobia could be thought of in terms of fear of being seen in a state of panic, that is as a fear of the image of the hysterical woman. In the interest of maintaining the women's anonymity the names used are pseudonyms and details of their contexts are limited.

2. The *agora* was a public market space within the Greek city. In addition to being a center of trade and commerce within the Greek city, it was also a place of public assembly.

4

"Once More with Feeling": Putting Emotion into Geographies of Music

Nichola Wood

When I started my doctoral research I knew that I wanted to explore the emotive power of national identities. However, I was unsure of exactly how and what I was going to study in order to gain a greater understanding of national identities as emotive phenomena. It soon became clear that studying live musical performances could offer an interesting route into exploring the emotional attachments that people have to a nation and their national identity. This decision was inspired, in part, by the works of a number of scholars writing within studies of nations and nationalism, who recognized that music is often "used" by a variety of actors to encourage nationalistic sentiments (Connor 1994; Penrose 1994).

My decision to study musical performances was also influenced by a strong belief that while there appear to be a number of ways in which people can form an attachment to a nation, music seems to be an especially emotive medium through which ideas of national belonging and nationalistic sentiments can be experienced and expressed. Here the examples of the expression of nationalistic songs in international sporting fixtures and the nationalistic rhetoric surrounding the Last Night of the Proms are illustrative.

The Last Night of the Proms is the annual finale of a series of summer promenade concerts that were first organized in 1895 to widen access to classical music.[1] The Proms are known for their informal nature; "prommers" are given the option of either standing or sitting at concerts, and tickets are usually very inexpensive. Over time the "Last Night" has become something of a fun celebration of British tradition. Traditionally many members of the audience attend wearing Union Jack costumes,[2] join in the singing, and blow whistles and air-horns during the final four pieces of the performance. These are Elgar's Pomp and Circumstance March no. 1 ("Land of Hope and Glory" sometimes thought of as an alternative British national anthem), "Rule, Britannia!," "Jerusalem," and Sir Henry Wood's "Fantasia on British Sea-Songs." These four pieces of music *appear* to elicit nationalistic sentiments in the audience as they are sung with great passion and fervor and are accompanied with enthusiastic flag waving. Sitting at home watching these performances on the television I have often been moved by feelings of national belonging and community. These are pieces of music that I recognize as being significant to ideas of Britishness (although perhaps ideas of Englishness may be more accurate here) and seeing and hearing them performed in such passionate ways strikes a chord within me.[3] If it is acknowledged then that music has emotive properties, and that performances can be used in various ways by a number of actors to produce nationalistic sentiments, then it appears that there are good political reasons for exploring the emotive capacity of music as a medium of communication. Indeed, I would argue here that I believe that any expression of nationalistic sentiments, whether musical or not, are potentially dangerous, because the concept of nation and the ideology of nationalism are inherently exclusionary. Therefore, while musical performances such as the Last Night of the Proms may provide an occasion for people to "celebrate" their British (or English) identity, they simultaneously aid the construction of particular, exclusionary ideas of nationhood, in this case, a nationhood that is white, cultured in "high arts," and so forth.

While the Last Night of the Proms is only one representation of Britishness, questions should be asked about the effect that this event, and others like it, have on people's ideas of national distinctiveness and national belonging. People may express, in what may seem like harmless ways, ideas of national identity. However, what is being expressed is an identity that is ultimately exclusionary. Here the complexities of belonging to a national community are exposed. There is nothing wrong per se with wanting to belong to a community of people with whom you feel some kind of affinity. However, problems occur when a community is constructed along strict social and/or cultural criteria that limit membership and then, in turn, restrict access to certain rights and resources. In addition, if musical expressions and experiences of national identities are emotive, then one also has to consider the potential that musical performances have for inciting hatred and prejudice against those who are not considered part of the imagined national community. Here the examples of the use of music in Nazi Germany and contemporary European neo-Nazi groups are illustrative (Wicke 1985; Hockenos 1993). It is for this reason that I think it is important that we gain a better understanding of what it is about music and the social, cultural, and political contexts in which it is performed and experienced that makes it potentially so emotive.

Recently, a number of works have been published that are termed aural or sonic geographies. This rapidly growing subdiscipline is potentially relevant to my interest in the links between the experience of musical performances and the formation of national identities and communities (Kong 1995; Leyshon, Matless, and Revill 1995; Revill 2000; Smith 1997, 2000; Valentine 1995). However, while a number of authors recognize that music is emotive, few of them discuss what it is about music, as a medium of communication, that makes it so powerful.[4] Indeed, despite geography's recent interest in the ways in which sound and music[5] inform the production and experience of space, place, and social processes (such as the formation of identities and communities), little is said about the ways in which the emotive properties of music influence these phenomena.

In some respects it is not surprising that this issue is rarely addressed, because it is extremely difficult to conceive of and articulate the emotive properties of music. As a form of communication, music is often used to express those feelings and emotions that cannot be expressed as easily through other media, such as writing or painting. Indeed, Smith (1997: 504) argues that "[w]riting about music is like dancing about architecture, listening to a ballet or feeling the texture of a painting—it might be helpful, but it is not the best, most direct or most appropriate way of illustrating the power of the art." However, a further reason why consideration of emotions has been omitted from geographies of music may be found in the way in which geographers (and musicologists) have conceptualized music. As the next section of this chapter will illustrate, traditionally geographers have treated music, almost exclusively, as a cultural product. In recent years, though, geographers have begun to reconceptualize music, recognizing that it is not just a cultural product, but perhaps more importantly, it is a medium of experience (Frith 1996) and a way of understanding the world (Attali 1985).

Building on these developments, this chapter investigates the reasons why an exploration and consideration of emotions is crucial to such a reconceptualization of music *and* aural geographies. I argue that an omission of the emotive qualities of music creates a missed opportunity for exploring the power of music as a medium of experience and exchange. In addition, this chapter considers the more general impacts that an exploration of emotions may have for geographical inquiry as a whole, and I argue that absenting emotions from geographical scholarship prevents a consideration of the ways in which individuals potentially experience and interact with their social, cultural, and physical environments in emotionally intensive ways. Such an omission of emotion limits our understanding not only of the ways in which people experience space and place emotionally but, perhaps more important, it neglects the potential importance of emotional experiences in processes of subjectivity formation.

I develop these arguments by first exploring in greater depth the ways in which music has been conceptualized and utilized in geographical inquiry. I then discuss the notion of music as an emotive medium of experience through an examination of the work of Douglas Pocock (1989) and Anthony Storr (1992). I go on to develop the debates arising from these studies through an exploration of some of the factors that may, in part, explain how music has emotive power. I argue that it is not just the performance or consumption of music per se that enables the experience of emotional reactions; rather there are a number of temporal, spatial, social, and cultural factors that potentially influence the ways in which a person emotionally experiences music.

MUSIC AND GEOGRAPHY

Recent developments in cultural geography have highlighted the visual bias within the discipline and, more generally, within the social sciences (Leyshon, Matless, and

Revill 1995; Pocock 1989, 1993; Rodaway 1994; Smith 1994), and call for a more multisensory approach to social research. Out of these debates has arisen an awareness that privileging visual forms of empirical evidence has limited geography's and geographers' understanding of the ways in which people experience sensory stimuli in their everyday experiences of space and place. In addition, *how* these sensory stimuli influence social processes such as identity formation and the production and experience of space and place has also been neglected.

In an effort to counter this omission a number of geographers have begun to incorporate nonvisual experiences into geographical thinking (Pocock 1993; Porteous 1985; Rodaway 1994; Smith 1994). In particular, there has been a strong emphasis on the significance of the aural or sonic world, including recognition of the importance of sound and music in people's *experience* of, and in the *production* of, both "real" and "imaginary" spaces and places (Kong 1995; Leyshon, Matless, and Revill 1995; Pocock 1989; Rodaway 1994; Smith 1997; Valentine 1995).

Despite the significance of these works, it is surprising how few authors discuss *why* and *how* music influences people's perceptions of space and place. It appears that while music is being incorporated into geographical knowledges, it is treated primarily as a cultural product, rather than as an experience that is dynamic and can be "felt" and "embodied." By the notion of *feeling* music, I refer to two things. The first is the notion of feeling as emotion. For example a person may experience feelings of happiness or sadness when listening to particular pieces of music. Second, feeling music refers to the idea that the vibration of music (and sound) causes a tactile sensation. Think, for example, of how strong bass lines or loud noises can be felt to resonate through the body. Indeed the success of the deaf percussionist Evelyn Glennie is illustrative of this.

By using the term embodied I refer to the ways in which the experience of musical performances influences the formation of subjectivities. Here I allude to the ways in which music enables the (mental *and* physical) expression and experience of emotions, which, in order to be understood, require life experiences to be drawn upon, while simultaneously aiding the creation of *new* understandings of knowing and being.

This omission of emotions from sonic geographies inquiry is interesting for a number of reasons (Widdowfield 2000). Although contemporary commentators have not studied the ways in which music influences the emotions, this does not mean that these phenomena have not been studied in the past. As Meyer (1956) and Storr (1992) remind us, classical scholars recognized that music, as a form of communication, had a distinctive intimacy that could shape people's characters. For example, Plato argued that "musical training is a more potent instrument than any other, because rhythm and harmony find their way into the inward places of the soul, on which they mightily fasten, imparting grace, and making the soul of him [sic] who is rightly educated graceful, or of him [sic] who is uneducated ungraceful" (cited in Jowett 1892: 665). Plato's work is valuable because it illustrates that during the classical era scholars described links between music and emotion and, what is more, recognized that music could be influential in the construction of identities. This raises the question of why scholars ceased to explore the emotive qualities of music.

One answer—and I am aware that it perhaps only partially addresses the issue—is to be found in the influence on academic thinking of the modern (Cartesian) notion of sight as the most important of the senses. Indeed, as Jay (1993) illustrates with the example of the invention of the telescope and the microscope, seeing was assumed to be the equivalent of knowing. Out of this ocular-centrism arose the rational/irrational dualism that has influenced the way in which social science has been conducted for many years. It was assumed that anything that could be seen could be explored and examined in a "rational" way (Shepherd 1991). However, phenomena that could not be seen or explained through visual methodologies were deemed irrational and, therefore, somehow unworthy of inclusion in academic pursuits. It is for this reason that visual methodologies have dominated social science research for so long and have influenced people's conceptualization and perception of the world so heavily.

It therefore appears, as Smith (1997) argues, that the omission of the aural from academic inquiry is at least in part an outcome of the dominance of the visual ideology. For modern social scientists the use of the nonvisual, and more important, the inclusion of emotional experiences in social science research, was regarded as irrational (Lupton 1998). In the contemporary era, however, conventional notions of truth and rationality have been disrupted so that many social scientists now believe there is no one rational or irrational way of experiencing the world; rather people and their experiences are complex, multiple, and fractured.

This disruption is due mainly to the works of a number of feminist scholars (Alcoff 1996; Harding 1994; Stanley and Wise 1993), including feminist geographers (Gibson-Graham 1994; McDowell 1995a; Rose 1993) who have critiqued the idea of singular notions of truth and rationality. Indeed, these feminist scholars have successfully illustrated that a pursuit of truth through the utilization of rational, objective scholarship is erroneous, because the gendered (as well as classed, racialized, and sexualized) subjectivities of scholars necessarily influences the design, conduct, and interpretation of academic research.[6] Feminist scholars have also questioned what constitutes "proper" academic knowledge and have called for an inclusion of what were once deemed irrational forms of knowledge, such as those ideas and conceptions thought to belong to the feminized realm of emotions (Lupton 1998).

While these ideas support the view that aural experiences of the world are as valid as visual experiences, the reluctance of social scientists to use aural experiences and to develop new methodologies that allow for a better exploration of the aural world is illustrative of two further points. The first is that visual methodologies have had a profound influence on patterns of thought. As Smith (2000) argues, it appears that many people have enormous difficulty in conceptualizing a world in which the visual is not central to experiences of space and place, and in which nonvisual experiences are not placed in a visual/nonvisual dichotomy. The tendency of scholars to treat music as a cultural product that can be studied in an abstract manner (via the study of musical scores, or lyrics), rather than exploring the potential importance of the practice of *performance*, is illustrative of this.

Second, reluctance to use aural experiences illustrates concerns arising from the dominance of modern notions of rationality. Despite feminist challenges to conventional notions of truth and rationality, the reluctance of social scientists to engage in explorations of emotions suggests that scholars continue to find the incorporation of "irrational" concepts into their research problematic. However, as Connor (1994) argues in his work on ethnonationalism, it is important that scholars address what were once regarded as irrational phenomena (such as emotions), because it is here that the power of nationalism is to be found. Connor (204) problematizes the rational/irrational dualism by arguing that some phenomena, such as the notion of the existence of national bonds between people, can be explained neither rationally nor irrationally, because they are what he terms *nonrational*: they "can be analysed, but not explained rationally." What is more, Connor argues that an exploration of music is one way in which the nonrational core can be reached and triggered. Thus, there are excellent grounds for social scientists to explore aural experiences as a route to studying nonrational phenomena such as emotions.

MUSICAL EXPERIENCE AND EMOTIONAL RESPONSES

It has been acknowledged since classical times that music can evoke emotional responses (Meyer 1956; Storr 1992). Pocock (1989) argues that hearing is the most primitive of the senses: fetuses as young as five months old can respond to sound, and hearing is the last sense to be "lost" when people are given anesthesia. He also argues that music holds a special key to interiority, emphasizing that "sound not only surrounds but can penetrate the very core of the sentient." He states "[t]he primitive power of music, which bypasses the cerebral and directly addresses the heart, elicits an emotional response: we are 'moved' perhaps elated, perhaps disturbed" (194).

While Pocock's emphasis on the way music is felt accords with my argument, his separation of "the cerebral" and "the heart" is problematic for two reasons. First it is impossible to separate mental and physical ways of experiencing music. To do so simply reinstates the Cartesian dichotomy between the rational and the irrational. Second, incorporating a consideration of "the cerebral" into our *overall* understanding of people's experience of music is extremely important. As Susan McClary (1991: 21) argues, the ways in which people experience music is influenced by a number of social, political, and cultural factors:

> Most members of a given social group succeed in internalising the norms of their chosen music and are quite sophisticated in their abilities to respond appropriately. They know how to detect even minor stylistic infractions and to respond variously with delight or indignation, depending upon how they identify themselves with respect to the style at hand.

McClary's argument that people's emotional reactions to music are socially, culturally, and politically conditioned is supported by Deborah Lupton's observation that emotions are "shaped, experienced and interpreted through social and cultural phenomena" (1998: 2). It seems then that there are good reasons for challenging Pocock's description of how music elicits emotive responses, and to explore alternative explanations, such as those proposed by the psychiatrist Anthony Storr.

In his book *Music and the Mind*, Storr (1992: 4) investigates why "the art of music and the reality of human emotion" are closely linked. He articulates these links through the concept of arousal, which he describes as:

> a condition of heightened alertness, awareness, interest and excitement: a generally enhanced state of being. This is at its minimum in sleep and at its maximum when human beings are experiencing powerful emotions like intense grief, rage, or sexual excitement. (24–25)

Storr argues that a number of physical and psychological reactions to arousal can be measured. For example, tests using an electroencephalogram (which records changes in the amplitude and frequency of brain waves) show that during arousal the electrical resistance of the skin is diminished; the pupil of the eye dilates; and respiratory rates may change speed.[7] In addition there are also increases in blood pressure, heart rate, and muscle tone (which may be accompanied by increases in restlessness). Storr likens these changes to those experienced by animals preparing for action, whether it be fight, flight, or mating.

This evidence suggests that there are multiple physical and psychological responses to music, but Storr argues that these are the conditions of arousal and not of specific emotions. Although it is difficult to separate the arousal and specific emotions because arousal is a necessary part of the process of emotional reaction, Storr's distinction is important because the two "parts" of the process have very different social and cultural implications. In other words, while most people may identify with processes of arousal such as increases in heart rate, they may not necessarily experience identical emotions that accompany such states. This challenges the assumption that music elicits the same emotional experiences in people and is significant for interpersonal relationships that are built upon the shared experience of a musical performance (whether these relations are between an individual listener and a performer, or between members of the same audience).

Contradicting Storr's (1992) account, a number of authors (Cohen 1995; Valentine 1995) argue that the concept of "shared emotions" provides a possible explanation of why people often find music to be a source of comfort and support as well as crucial to the formation of communities. Cohen (1995) for example, explores how social practices involving the production and experience of music drew the immigrant Jews of Brownlow Hill in Liverpool together. One of her interviewees, an eighty-eight-year-old, second-generation Polish immigrant, Jack, described how his mother and aunts used to sit and listen to gramophone recordings of Yiddish songs, and Cohen (1995: 437) argues that:

> The Yiddish music provoked and structured particular emotions in Jack's female relatives, through which they expressed their feelings about their country of origin and the

relations and practices that they had left behind. The music brought them together and symbolised their collective identity.

According to Storr (1992) emotions are not shared in this way, and all that is shared is the experience of arousal. So how can the experiences described by Jack be understood and explained? Rom Harré (1986) offers a useful account, arguing that physiological responses such as increased heartbeat and swollen tear ducts become irrelevant to the study of emotions when one considers how the local social world, by way of its linguistic practices defines emotional encounters. Indeed Harré (5) argues that examining the social practices that surround the construction of emotions presents the possibility that "many emotions can exist only in the reciprocal exchanges of a social encounter" (compare Lupton 1998). In other words, people may undergo processes of arousal (as Storr illustrates), but they only experience emotions through social interactions or discourses. In Cohen's (1995) example Jack described his relatives' emotions (and not just processes of arousal) as experienced through the discourse of song.

Harré's argument offers a useful explanation of the ways in which emotions are socially constructed. However, I would argue that it is not just the social world and its linguistic practices that influence the construction of emotions. Rather, it is equally important to consider the spatial and temporal contexts in which emotional reactions to music are experienced. This is particularly important when thinking about the ways in which musical performances provide opportunities for the emotional experience of national identity.

MUSIC AS AN EXPERIENCE OF TIME, SPACE, AND PLACE

I have argued that the temporal and spatial contexts in which people experience music may affect the emotional ways in which music is experienced. I now want to discuss what some of these temporal and spatial factors might be. The purpose of this section is not to produce a definitive list of temporal and spatial influences. Instead, by drawing primarily on my own experience of music, I demonstrate that the temporal and spatial settings of music are important for understanding how music "works" as an emotive medium of experience and exchange. I illustrate that music is not simply a cultural product, as many aural or sonic geographers would have us believe, but that the spatial and temporal settings in which music is performed and experienced is what makes the experience of music dynamic, exciting, and unpredictable.

Cultural Considerations

There are a number of cultural conventions that both performers and audiences adhere to when experiencing performances of music. The way in which one listens and "participates" during a performance is dependent not only on the type of musical performance attended, but also on the cultural context within which the music is experienced. For example, there are "acceptable" types of behavior that are normally expected when attending a classical music performance.[8] Once seated, for instance, it is not acceptable to walk around the auditorium, just as it would be thought highly inappropriate to sing along to your favorite aria at the opera.[9] In contrast, the experience of listening to a pop or rock concert may be very much more informal. Depending on the venue, the audience is not always seated and audience participation such as singing and dancing is regularly encouraged by the performers rather than frowned upon.

At a classical music concert, a range of emotions from sadness and despair to joy and excitement can be experienced, but they are seldom expressed outwardly. Consequently, when looking around the audience it is rare to see anybody moving or showing any physical expression of emotion, except perhaps through the exchange of glances and smiles with neighboring audience members. For me, at least, the emotions that I experience are expressed on a very intimate level, such as tears gently rolling down my face, hair rising on the back of my neck, or getting a "lump" in my throat, which is caused by the suppression of an emotional response. However, at the rock concerts, I express emotions much more openly through clapping, cheering, singing, and dancing.

Such cultural conventions are also dependent on the geographical location of the performance. In a recent article in the music magazine *Q*, journalist Alexis Petridis (1999: 72) described the audiences who attended the Swedish rock group The Cardigans' "sell-out" Japanese tour as "almost comically reserved, applauding politely after each song then lapsing into a disconcerting pin-drop silence." This observation was echoed by the group's lead singer, Nina Persson, in an interview with Petridis (72):

> Even when we played the Budokan,[10] it's dead quiet. . . . In the beginning it was scary, because we thought we were really popular, we were like "What are we doing wrong?" We've sold a million albums in this country and no one seems to know the songs. Someone told us·they just wanted to listen, they didn't want to interrupt.

Both Petridis and Persson interpret the reactions of the Japanese audience as something unusual, and both rely on the stereotypical understanding of the Japanese as a socially reserved society. As well as raising a number of questions about understandings of and interactions with other cultures, these comments highlight the fact that there are multiple, culturally specific ways in which music can be experienced emotionally.

A Shared Experience?

In addition to the influence of cultural conventions, who people share (or don't share) their experience of musical performances with also merits consideration. Indeed, part of the emotional power of musical performance comes from the experience of being surrounded by other members of the audience. The bonds that are formed through sharing musical experiences in this way operate on a number of different social and spatial scales. On a smaller or more intimate level, music can be one of the bases and/or accompaniments to friendships and relationships. Through sharing musical experiences with other people and through using music to relay one's feelings to another person, music can be an important medium of communication. For example, music may arouse feelings of closeness and intimacy with friends and lovers. What is more, this can be done through the creation of certain spaces that allow for the expression of feelings and emotions at temporally specific times.

On an individual level, music can be important in the provision of a space and time for reflection for the listener or performer. People often seem to find solace and strength in either listening to or performing certain pieces of music that resonate with their own personal feelings. In addition, music can act as the "trigger" for memories that an individual may experience as pleasurable or painful. Thus experiencing music alone can be an emotionally intense experience. Indeed, for some people, being alone may enable them to express emotions more freely and fully than when sharing musical experience with others, for example by crying or playing the "air guitar."

Although I have separated personal from shared listening, my own experience suggests that it may be possible for an individual to experience all of these phenomena simultaneously. This multilayered quality explains, at least in part, the complexity and the richness of people's experiences of musical performances. However, what may be of equal importance to the ways in which people experience music is the role of "the personal."

In common with all human experience, the musical is personal. When individuals attend a musical performance of any type they take with them a lifetime's worth of emotional experiences that may, or may not, allow them to extract personal meanings from the music. Particular melodies, rhythms, or lyrics may provoke thoughts and feelings of past events and experiences, but the process of linking emotional meanings to music may not happen consciously on the part of performers or listeners. In noncognitive or nonconscious ways, emotions may be evoked that depend on past feelings and experiences (whether "real" or imagined) as well as on the present emotional state and mood of the listener.

On the surface it would seem that the ways in which music elicits emotional experiences are highly personalized. Some people's emotional reactions are triggered by particular melodies, bass-lines, or beats, while for others particular lyrics may be more influential. People develop their own personal, dynamic musical tastes. The music that gives pleasure and joy to one person may incite boredom or irritation in others.

Further exploration of the musical triggers that incite particular emotional experiences would allow us to identify commonalities and to understand more fully the potential music has to accommodate the sharing of emotional experiences. Colin McLeay's (1997) work is suggestive. He argues that there is a reciprocal relationship between the power of social and cultural discourses and people's personal experiences of music, with specific reference to expressions of national identity. He highlights the contradictory meanings attributed to Bruce Springsteen's song "Born in the USA," showing how some social groups regard it as a celebration of the achievements of the United States, while others interpret it as a lament for a past "golden era." McLeay's work reminds us that even though people may have "personal" music tastes, these will be influenced by social, economic, cultural, and political factors, just as the personal and the self are constructed through these contexts.

The Importance of Intermediaries

It may also be important to think about how intermediaries between producers and consumers of music use genre to encourage particular kinds of emotional responses. In Western European and North American societies people are culturally conditioned to experience upbeat pieces in major keys as connoting emotions such as happiness or pride, whereas slower pieces in minor keys typically elicit more somber emotional experiences.[11] However, it is not just the key and tempo of the music that influence people's emotional experience of music: I would argue that listening to an upbeat piece of classical music may elicit different emotional responses than listening to techno, and while the influence of genre may be highly personalized, I would suggest that people's age, gender, race, sexuality, and class may also affect their experience of particular genres of music.

Through genre, music has the potential to be "used" as a medium of communication, as its producers are well aware. For example, the film industry has long used music (even during the era of silent movies, where pianists and organists added musical accompaniments) to enhance the emotional impact of selected scenes, and consider the impact that music has on love scenes or in heightening the drama of action movies. Such power has been recognized by a number of commentators, most notably Theodore Adorno. Writing in the 1940s, Adorno argued that the soporific effect of popular music was used as a tool of control as it distracted people from thinking about social consciousness and their role in the world (Adorno 1990, 1991; Negus 1996). This, he argued, was because the popular music required little effort with regard to listening. Indeed the audience, according to Adorno (1991), was encouraged to listen to the most obvious sections of a melody, and not to listen in a critical manner.

Perhaps the most interesting aspect of Adorno's work, for my own purposes, is his emphasis on the role that intermediate actors in the music industry, such as record producers, advertisers, and disk jockeys, have on *how* people listen to music, and further, how this influences people's experience of music. For example, Cohen (1994) has highlighted the way in which a "Liverpool sound" has been developed at least partially as a marketing strategy. Similarly, Lehr (1983) and Shuker and Pickering (1994) have emphasized the importance that compulsory "national music" quotas can, or could potentially, have in Canada and New Zealand, respectively. Thus, intermediaries intervene to encourage people to respond to music in particular, necessarily emotional ways (compare Cohen 1994).

Spatial and Temporal Influences

As my comments so far suggest, spatial and temporal contexts are crucial to people's experience of music, and I now turn to these factors in a little more depth. Music accompanies people's daily lives in a whole range of contexts from private spaces like the home to public spaces such as shopping malls and concert halls. Experiences of music take place in specific spatial and temporal settings, but music is not simply performed or listened to in particular settings: it also actively "creates" and "constructs" space. Musical practices can physically structure space through, for example, the segregation of performers and audience members, and can influence people's experience of spaces through, for example, "piped" music in supermarkets (DeNora 2000).

In public places listeners often have very little control over the music that they experience, although jukeboxes are a partial exception to this. In home spaces people have greater freedom to determine the type of music that is played and where and when it can be heard. Given this, people can tailor their experience of music and can create personal soundscapes. Where people listen to music also affects with whom they share their musical experiences. The idea that music can forge social and cultural communities has been explored by a number of commentators.[12] Valentine's (1995) discussion of the use of the music of k. d. lang in producing queer space is illustrative. She argues that lang's music helps form not only queer space, but aids the construction of a lesbian community. However, Valentine emphasizes that the sense of community created at a concert is only a temporary, "imagined" community. Anderson (1991) argued that the notion of an imagined community rests on the idea that people perceive bonds between themselves and others, often regardless of their knowledge about the perceptions of others. This bond is imagined to be strong enough to overcome significant social and cultural differences that could otherwise divide the community. While I agree with Valentine (1995) that the "communities" formed by music are in one sense temporary, it is worth considering whether the experience of comradeship and belonging that she highlights might influence people's lives beyond the performance space.

To explore this further, I draw on some of my own experiences of live performances. I heard Crowded House's song "Weather with You" at one of the band's concerts some years ago. This song had significant success in the United Kingdom in 1992 (it reached number seven in the UK charts) and is especially well liked among fans. When it was performed at the concert that I attended, the crowd (predictably) began to sing along. The feeling of being in a space with hundreds of fans singing along was exhilarating, especially when the band stopped singing the melody and provided an accompaniment to "our" performance. The feelings of excitement, elation, and communion left a lasting impression on me to the extent that whenever I hear that piece of music I remember the performance and all the emotions that went with it. I wonder whether this is a common occurrence and if so, is there the potential for music to influence a more lasting notion of community (on the grounds of race, sexuality, or nationality, for example) through the notion of a shared emotional experience? In other words, can the sense of community experienced through musical performances influence people's experience of self and the more permanent notions of community they experience in everyday life, or are musical experiences and people's recollections of them temporally bounded?

Although I have some great memories from the Crowded House concert, there are plenty of other examples of experiences that I either haven't enjoyed or that I can't remember in any detail. There is no way that an experience of a musical performance can be predicted. Arguably, this is what makes performing and experiencing live music so exciting and enjoyable. At certain times all the elements of experiencing music "click together" to produce something that is incredibly powerful and memorable.

CONCLUSION

Throughout this chapter I have tried to illustrate the importance of studying music as an *emotive* medium of experience and communication. Past commentators have argued that music is important for a number of social processes such as the construction of communities (McLeay 1997; Valentine 1995), and the production of both real and imagined places and spaces (Cohen 1994; Leyshon, Matless, and Revill 1995; Smith 1997). These contributions imply that music is a powerful medium of experience and communication. However, the majority of these commentators have neglected to explore *why* music is powerful in these ways. I have addressed this omission by arguing that it is the emotive capacity of music, which is in part created through the social, cultural, spatial, and temporal contexts in which music is performed and heard, that makes it such a powerful medium of experience.

While some commentators (Pocock 1989) have emphasized the "natural" tendency for people to have emotional reactions to music, I have argued that this alone is not the reason why people may experience music in emotive ways. Indeed, I have outlined a number of contextual factors that have the potential to affect people's experiences of music. I have also argued that in order to gain a greater understanding of the communicative and emotive power of music, scholars need to explore these factors in more depth.

Recognizing the emotional power of forms of communication and experience, including music, opens up new approaches to understanding social and cultural processes. I would argue that exploration of the role of music in social processes, such as the formation of national identities, *without* consideration of its emotional potential, presents music as an abstract and distanced cultural product, rather than as a phenomenon that is experienced intimately, immediately, and sometimes in nonrational ways.

Putting emotions into geographies of music not only challenges visually biased and overly "rational" approaches, but also prompts a reconceptualization of music as a "living," dynamic phenomenon that people encounter *simultaneously* as a cultural product and as an emotive medium of communication and expression. Incorporating the emotional into geographies of music encourages a more holistic approach, whereby music retains the dynamism and power that is often lost when it is regarded as a cultural product. This consideration of emotions in geographical inquiry is vital to understanding such phenomena as nationalistic sentiments and other forms of mass affiliation. Think, for example, of how campaign managers deliberate over which pieces of music to play during election campaigns[13] or how the opening of new state buildings is staged. If music is "used" in these ways by powerful agents, then scholars need to conceptualize it not just as a (signifying) product, but also as a tool for inciting particular emotions.

Developing a methodology that allows music to be studied as a dynamic and emotive phenomenon is by no means easy. I close by acknowledging two important methodological issues. The first is that the language available to describe emotional phenomena is often inadequate. Words regularly fail to communicate the experiences and emotions created through music. Given such difficulties, the second is that researchers may have to rely to an usually great extent on their own experiences of music as a reference point in understanding other people's experiences. Such a self-reflexive approach to research may be beneficial in some ways, but is problematic because it is clear that people's emotional experiences of music are highly personal, as well as socially and culturally specific. Therefore, how can one truly know what someone is experiencing? But the difficulties of studying people's emotional experiences of music do not constitute an excuse for ignoring them. On the contrary, what is needed is creative and sensitive experimentation with empirical methods (Duffy, Smith, and Wood 2001; also see part IV of this volume) through which to gain a greater understanding of the ways in which emotions, mediated through phenomena such as music, affect our experiences of the world in which we live and how, in turn, these experiences affect the formation of subjectivities.

NOTES

1. Since 1927 the Proms have been organized by the BBC. A comprehensive history and virtual tour of the Proms can, at the time of writing, be found at <http://bbc.co.uk/radio3/proms/lastnight/index.shtml>.

2. The Union Jack is the British national flag.

3. It is worth noting that although I am moved by the music, my experience of it is complex. While, for me, it undoubtedly triggers feelings of national belonging, these pieces of music are, in many ways, controversial in that they celebrate Britain's imperial and colonial past. Therefore, I experience these pieces of music in a complex and highly contradictory manner. I am moved by the *notion* of sharing a history and a set of meanings and understandings with a community of people; however, I am uncomfortable with a lot of what that *particular* "British" history involves. Indeed, for many people (both British and non-British) the music's emphasis on Britain's imperial past may incite feelings of anger and rage.

4. Some authors such as Thrift (2000) and Smith (2000) have argued that studies of performance arts allow for powerful "alternative" ways of knowing and being which, until recently, have been ignored by geographers. It is for this reason that Thrift and Smith both ad-

vocate the development of nonrepresentational styles of geographical inquiry. This is a style of research that attempts to gain a better understanding of the *practices* that sustain and inform the social world, rather than emphasizing the representations that are created through performance. Both of these authors have argued that there is a need for us to reconceptualize the role and function of performing arts, so that we gain a better understanding of how they work as mediums of expression and experience. However, even though the role of emotions is acknowledged in their work, little is said about how or why they are influential in people's experience of place, space, and social relations.

5. By "sound" I refer to what is, or may be heard. By "music" I refer to culturally specific products, which, while possessing aesthetic qualities, can also express and arouse emotions and feelings. This is not to imply that nonmusical sounds cannot or do not have similar qualities, rather it refers to the notion that the expression or communication of emotions is primary in music (Storr 1992). It should be noted that this definition itself is culturally specific to a Western European context.

6. It should be noted that all feminists do not share this view. Feminist empiricists would argue that objectivity is desirable in academic research because it eradicates androcentrism.

7. It is interesting that in order to argue that music can stimulate arousal Storr (1992) returns to technologies that allow him to measure stimulation visually. This illustrates further the significance "the visual" has on modern academic research.

8. Although, as Johnson's (1995) work demonstrates, these conventions are a relatively recent phenomenon.

9. Although some classical performances such as the Last Night of the Proms encourage the partial transgression of such codes of conduct, the audience's participation is still quite tightly regulated by cultural and historical conventions. For example it is permissible to sing during "Rule Britannia," but not during the more formal solo operatic performances.

10. The Budokan is an 8,000 capacity venue in Tokyo.

11. Indeed, during my childhood music lessons I was taught to recognize major and minor keys by learning to identify music as either "happy" or "sad."

12. It should be remembered though that just as music can aid the creation of communities it can also divide and separate social and cultural groups.

13. The example of D. Ream's "Things Can Only Get Better" as part of "New Labour's" 1997 UK election campaign is illustrative.

II

DUALISMS, BODIES, AND SUBJECTIVITIES

5

Borderline Bodies

Lynda Johnston

This chapter is about borders that are made and broken at gay pride parades. Specifically, I examine the discursive and material borders maintained in tourism discourse. Binary oppositions such as self/other, straight/gay, and tourist/host provide a focus for this chapter. I am interested in where these borders wear thin and threaten to break and disrupt social order. I explore the bodies of gay pride parades because it is bodies such as these that threaten the borders of corporeal acceptability.

Bodies on display for tourism depend on particular commodifiable experiences. Within a context of gay pride parades, a tension and contradiction is maintained between parading bodies, as tourism commodities, and political displays of pride. It is within this contradiction that I situate this chapter. Parading bodies become borderline bodies—bordering on politics, streets, and tourism practices.

I begin by drawing on empirical data from two specific gay pride parades: the Auckland, Aotearoa/New Zealand HERO[1] parade and the Sydney, Australian Gay and Lesbian Mardi Gras parade.[2] These parades are simultaneously forms of tourist entertainment, as well as political protests. I discuss the spatial constitution of symbolic resistance through the lens of the carnivalization of society. Streets can be queered and, as a result, heterosexuality becomes denaturalized—made obvious—during gay pride parades. Another effect of parading bodies in streets can be understood as making queer bodies seem *queerer*.

I develop my argument by suggesting that queer parading bodies can arouse feelings of abjection, which plays a crucial role in the popularity of the parades. I use the notion of abjection because it is useful to theoretical and political strategies. Abject bodies on parade trouble borders at the same time as the Cartesian subject tries to redraw them. I focus on the urge to separate self/other and straight/gay, and the mobility of subject positions that this urge creates. My intention for this chapter, therefore, is to examine the notion of fixed subjectivities by examining embodied contradictions.

cf. liminal spaces - Turner 75

Lynda Johnston

SPECTACULAR CARNIVAL EVENTS

Gay pride parades have become commonplace in Western cities since the New York Stonewall riots began on the night of June 27, 1969, when police raided a gay bar called the Stonewall Inn, in Greenwich Village, New York. Three days of rioting became an emblem of defiance against normative heterosexuality and officially established the beginning of the gay liberation movement. Born of these riots, gay pride parades made public the previously private bodies of gays and lesbians. Under the public gaze, certain urban, cultural, and social geographies emerged.

    HERO and Sydney Mardi Gras parades can be understood as socially contested events whose political significance is inscribed in the landscape. The presentation of marginalized peoples in public places can be seen as a subversion and transgression of what is usually termed "high" and "low" values. This presentation, however, is more than a site of hierarchical social inversion. It is worth noting that HERO and Sydney Mardi Gras are parades of the "South" and are very different from comparable events of the "North," which tend not to be structured around entertainment and difference. In this chapter I elaborate on the place and political specificities of gay pride parades down under.

    Claire Lewis and Steve Pile (1996: 39) state that "In certain places and in certain times, carnival may be a ritualised resistance, or it may be a contested territory, or it may be a site of hybrid ambivalences, or it may be an opiate to the people." Carnival has been attributed with providing an opportunity for self-expression among marginalized groups, as can be seen in the Notting Hill Carnival in London (Cohen 1980, 1982; Manning 1989), and there have been several studies of the construction of gender and race at carnival events (Jackson 1988, 1992; Lewis and Pile 1996; Spooner 1996). The idea of carnival as reversal establishes the dominant social order as something that is static and "allowed" to be temporarily punctured. Carnival is understood as "a *licensed* affair in every sense, a permissible rupture of hegemony, a contained popular blow-off as disturbing and relatively ineffectual as a revolutionary work of art" (Eagleton 1981: 148, emphasis in original).

    Carnival, therefore, can be seen as a form of ritualistic value display that redefines the meaning of urban spaces. These displays have often been discussed in terms of urban economic gain versus possible civic disruption, which tend to place city governments in a double bind. On the one hand they are interested in events that make the city attractive to large numbers of people, because money spent at events indirectly feeds tax revenue. On the other hand, they perceive such events as threats to the establishment because they are often spatially unstructured and involve large groups in playful activities (Bonnemaison 1990; Hall 1992). The political impact of the Sydney Mardi Gras affects many areas of public and civil functions, from, for example, political consciousness and organizational ability for lesbian and gay communities, to major political centers and the state (Marsh and Galbraith 1995).

    The representation of carnival as the reverse of static, everyday normality has been an important starting point in a focus on the spectacular. Attention needs to be paid, however, to the contradictions of carnival bodies as constituted by and within the spaces in which such events take place. HERO and Mardi Gras parades are also contained within dominant discourses of tourism and entertainment, which tend to create binaries of self/other or tourist/host. Furthermore, Sydney Mardi Gras and HERO parades are not just street parades. Their meanings are constructed from a month-long festival of events that involve, for example, art exhibitions, theater, film festivals, health programs, and tourism.

REDEFINING URBAN SPACE ·

Gay pride parades do not simply (and uncontestedly) inscribe streets as queer, they actively produce queer streets (Bell and Valentine 1995). Parades can be read as deconstructive spatial tactics, a queering of the street. Nancy Duncan (1996b: 139) states, "Gay pride parades, public protests, performance art and street theatre as well as overtly homosexual behaviour such as kissing in public" upset unarticulated norms. Sally Munt (1995: 124, emphasis in original) argues that such behaviors produce a "politics of *dislocation*." Duncan (1996b) believes that lesbian and gay practices, if they are made explicit, have the potential to disturb the taken-for-granted heterosexuality of public places. The street tactics of gay pride parades are also "crisis points in the normal functioning of 'everyday' experiences" (Cresswell 1996, cited in Duncan 1996b: 139). Gill Valentine (1996: 152) argues that "Pride marches also achieve much more than just visibility, they also challenge the production of everyday spaces as heterosexual."

Discussions of the vitality and controversy of pride parades do not usually focus on the role of tourists and tourism industries in such controversial displays in public space. But I would argue that when gay bodies are on parade they are clearly marked as "different," their bodies constitute an "extraordinary" tourist attraction. This is because, as John Urry (1990: 11) argues, "tourism results from a basic binary division between the ordinary-everyday and the extraordinary." The dichotomies of tourists and hosts, or self and other, however, are not inherent or "natural" binary divisions. They are produced, for example, when bodies become gendered/sexed and sexualized at gay pride parades. Away from the parade, the tourist event, queer bodies may seem ordinary, everyday, and even normal. During parades, however, the border or binary division becomes visible and accentuated between paraders and spectators.

The creation of such oppositions provides a spectacle of queer bodies to the dominant culture. That the majority of tourists at HERO and at the Sydney Mardi Gras are heterosexual is strongly suggested by a questionnaire survey I conducted among spectators on the night of the 1996 HERO parade: of the 118 people returning questionnaires, 90 (76 percent) identified themselves as heterosexual.[3] The popularity of gay pride parades for heterosexual spectators, particularly the Sydney Mardi Gras, has been noted elsewhere. David Bell and Gill Valentine (1995: 26, emphasis in original) claim:

It seems that the construction of Pride marches for a straight [tourist] spectator audience is becoming a very important issue for marches in the US and, judging by some footage of Mardi Gras shown on British TV recently, in Australia too (look at who's *watching* the parade).

HERO, according to the HERO project director, has always been constructed for the "straight" tourist spectator:

> Well the parade is basically put on for the straight community when it comes down to it. Like a hundred thousand people there, I don't know, 5000 would be gay? . . . Ah, so it's for straights and that's fine. I don't think we should have a problem with that at all. We should encourage it. (individual interview, September 22, 1995)

Another indicator of the construction of HERO for the "straight" public is that in 1997 and 1998 the full parade was presented in primetime on national television. The HERO parade as public "product" is now sold to television production companies and can be purchased as a video cassette. The Sydney Mardi Gras is also televised in Australia and marketed in video cassette form. Such products are advertised as tourist souvenirs in Sydney, along with T-shirts, tea towels, key rings, and so forth.

To summarize my discussion so far, gay pride parades have the potential to queer the "everyday" or "ordinary" streets of cities (Johnston 1997, 2001; Bricknell 2000). They also tend to be caught up in discourses that construct queer bodies as others and tourists as self. The spectacle of the HERO parade is constituted through binaries of tourist/host and straight/gay. Tourism literature suggests that these events can be theorized as the powerful producer of the exotic (Rossel 1988) and a commodifier of cultures (Greenwood 1989) that constructs "others." Next, I argue that this contradiction troubles the spaces and bodies at gay pride parades.

PLACING BORDERS

HERO and Sydney Mardi Gras are intensely structured spatial events. Clearly marked borders between paraders and tourists is maintained at the roadside through the use of road markings, road barriers or barricades, parade officials and police, as well as self-policing[4] by tourists. This may be one of the reasons that the HERO parade and the Sydney Mardi Gras are so popular among "straight" tourists, because tourists are physically separated from the gay bodies on parade. When spatial segregation is maintained, there can be no confusion between heterosexual and homosexual bodies. The threat of sexualized transgression is, at one level, controlled. The dominant group (heterosexual tourists) can keep its distance from the "other."

At the parades that I attended, road barriers were erected along the sides of the streets. The barriers created a wide space in the middle of the streets that tourists could not access. At the 1996 Sydney Mardi Gras the barriers were extensive and formidable (see figure 5.1). Metal frame crowd control barriers, which were approximately one meter high, stretched the entire length of the parade route. The barriers were supplied by the Sydney City Council and were fixed into place several hours before the parade started. Streets were closed to traffic from approximately 3 P.M., five hours before the start of the parade.

Figure 5.1   Road barriers at the Sydney Mardi Gras parade
Photographs by Lynda Johnston, 5 March 1996

SAFETY FIRST

The *Sydney Star Observer's* guide to the 1996 Mardi Gras festival, parade, and party, reported that:

> The Parade begins at around 8 PM at the corner of Liverpool and Elizabeth Street, moves up to Oxford Street, turns right into Flinders Street and then left into Moore Park Road. As vantage points in Oxford Street are usually the first taken, try Flinders Street or Moore Park Road. Remember that after 7 PM it gets very difficult to get a good possie anywhere.

The attention paid to parade crowds and to places from which to view the parades and getting a "good possie" are imbued with discourses of safety. The numbers attending the Sydney Mardi Gras have increased dramatically since the parade's beginnings. The *Sydney Star Observer's* guide reports on some of the historical changes:

> But how things have changed! From 1981 . . . Sydney summer and Mardi Gras energy have seen crowd numbers and float numbers grow. Some of us remember when there were no barricades between the crowd and the Parade and you could jump in and out of the marching thong at will. Don't try that now. It's—after all—safety before spontaneity these days. Crowds in 1994 topped 600,000. . . . The float count should be well over 100, there'll be several thousand participants, and more than 800 officials of various kinds.

The "800 officials of various kinds" are usually volunteers who wear uniforms that distinguish them from spectators and paraders. The parade officials carry radio-telephones, hand-held megaphones, and whistles. In 1996 I waited for three hours behind the barriers at Oxford Street before the parade began, and during this time, I noted several things about safety procedures. If tourists wished to cross the street they had to ask the officials to let them through the barricades and over the street. During the parade there were no opportunities to step out from behind the barricades and cross the street. If spectators attempted this, they were stopped and encouraged to remain behind the barricades.

Similarly, at the 1996 HERO parade the crowd was encouraged to stay behind the erected street barriers. Auckland crowds were disciplined before and during the parade. One of my duties, when I worked at the HERO parade workshop in January and February 1996, was to find thirty volunteers who could be placed on streets that intersected with Ponsonby Road. Each volunteer had a "marshal" T-shirt, reflector vest, and distress flares. In addition to these marshals, each parade entry had to provide two of their own marshals to walk beside their float and to maintain an "appropriate" distance between paraders and tourists where there were gaps in the road barriers. Marshals were briefed at a pre-parade safety meeting with the organizers and police. The use of road barriers at the HERO parade has increased each year with the size of the attending crowd.

The 1997 and 1998 HERO parade organizers made use of the Auckland City Council's road barriers. These are large plastic container-type barricades, which, once in place, were filled with water (see figure 5.2). These barricades were wide and approximately waist height. Marshals and police kept the crowd behind these barricades. Tourists' bodies, for the most part, become disciplined, controlled, and carefully separated from the homosexual bodies on parade. By extension, paraders' bodies were also disciplined, controlled, and contained within the barricades.

There are several implications of this attention to crowd safety. In making the parade site safe and controlled, a distinction is created between paraders as spectacle and heterosexual tourists as watchers. When safety is well publicized and barriers are erected and maintained by barricades, marshals, and police, more people are attracted to the parade site. Of course one could argue that the barriers *really* are there for safety, to stop the crowd from being crushed by a large truck, or spectators run over by motorcycles. However, my experience, from attending both barriered and nonbarriered parades, is that the barriers tend to increase risk of physical injury. The barriers concentrate large numbers of people in small spaces, and because people cannot move away from the roadside barriers they become dangerous obstacles.

At the 1996 HERO parade, I was elated to see the final parade "product," which I had helped to create. I was also video recording the parade and hence did not form part of the main crowd at the side of the road. I walked with the parade at times. Carrying a video recording camera marked me as different from the other spectators. At the 1997 HERO parade, however, when I observed the parade from behind the barricades as a lesbian tourist, surrounded by mostly heterosexual tourists, I felt uneasy. I was physically "trapped" and I became caught up in the feelings of those around me. In field notes made after the parade, I reflected on my feelings of being a tourist at the 1997 HERO parade and I documented some of the comments that were made while I watched:

> One woman said to the man who was watching the parade with her: "There are some *normal* people in the parade, there are some *normal* people in the parade, you know, *straight* people. It's not all gay."
> "Oh—*what?*—that's sexually dysfunctional" (said a man as he watched a float containing a lesbian sadomasochistic performance).

These comments can be interpreted as (heterosexual) tourists' attempts to reconstruct gay bodies as deviant and "other" and establish their own "normalcy." Despite the physical barriers that maintained some distance between parading bodies and tourists, some heterosexuals employed other measures to preserve the border between self and other. For example, I observed the "coupling" of heterosexuals at both HERO and Sydney Mardi Gras parades: men draped their arms around their female partners; women and men held hands; and, even more provocatively, some engaged in kissing and other sexual behavior in the street. Stereotypical jokes were made by heterosexual men about "keeping their backs to the wall." I asked a white heterosexual man: "Why did you come to the parade tonight?" He responded: "Because cute women hang out with gay boys." Such a response serves to maintain distance between the self and the other, the tourists and the hosts.

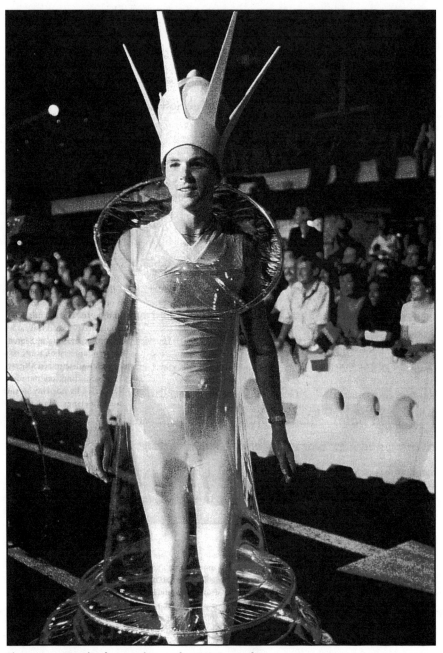

Figure 5.2   Barricades, tourists, and a HERO parader
Photograph by Ann Shelton. Reproduced with permission of Australian Consolidated Press, publishers for *Metro* (Crawshaw 1998, 33).

GAY ENCLAVES

The majority of tourists at HERO and at the Sydney Mardi Gras are, as I have already noted, heterosexual. There are, however, also gay, lesbian, bisexual, and transgendered tourists behind the barriers. At the 1996 HERO parade I was aware that the spaces occupied by gay tourists were quite different from the spaces occupied by heterosexual tourists. I began distributing questionnaires a while before the parade was due to start. Doing this on Ponsonby Road, which has many gay-owned and operated restaurants and bars, I became aware that many of the people eating at the tables lining the street were gay. They were very willing to fill in my questionnaire, talk to me about my research, and openly identify as gay (the majority were gay men). They had positioned themselves in the restaurant seats by the road, as well as upstairs in restaurant and bar windows, and had come to watch the parade and engage in associated activities ("find a man," "check out talent," "watch the 'girls'"). In areas like this, gay tourists maintained spatial enclaves away from the large number of heterosexual tourists. Gay guides to viewing the Sydney Mardi Gras suggested that people could rent rooms in hotels, guesthouses, and restaurants from which to view the parade.

The pleasure obtained by these gay tourists provokes a reconceptualization of the definition of "tourist." On the one hand, gay tourists can be positioned as hosts and part of the gay pride parade spectacle for heterosexual tourists. Gays and lesbians watching the parade, eating at restaurants, drinking at gay bars, and "picking up" partners on Ponsonby Road are in their "authentic" or home location. On the other hand, some gay tourists position themselves as "normal" or "ordinary and everyday" (self), and position the gay paraders as exotic and extraordinary (other). These binaries of self/other, straight/gay, and tourist/host are subject to contestation and never remain stable or static.

Tiered seating behind a fenced-off area created another bordered area at the 1998 HERO parade. This was a fundraising initiative by HIV/AIDS organizations with pre-sold tickets at $45, which could be considered expensive given that many spectators are attracted to the parade because it is free. The area included a bar where drinks could be bought and there were toilets. I bought a seat in this area for the 1998 parade. The majority of people in the tiered seat section were queer. Couples could visibly "be" together, hold hands, and so forth. I could not hear any comments that may have been made by heterosexual tourists that "othered" and degraded the bodies on parade.

While I had thought this space would be a "gay spectator enclave," it also contained a complex mix of VIPs such as National Party member Jenny Shipley, the then prime minister of Aotearoa/New Zealand (accompanied by her husband), other (Opposition) politicians and media representatives. The VIPs were in an area demarcated with a white picket fence, with gay tourists sitting on the tiered seats beyond. The white picket fence seemed to act like a sanitized border that kept the "extraordinary" people and the "ordinary" queers separated. I saw a spare table in the VIP area where I sat. In this area "we"—gays, straight and gay politicians, queer entertainers and television celebrities—became another part of the tourist entertainment. Television cameras focused on the prime minister's reaction to each float. People from outside the area watched us. I found *myself* watching for the prime minister's reactions as floats passed by her. My roles as researcher and gay/lesbian activist were overshadowed by the allure of celebrity watching! Behind "us," in the tiered seating, gay men made sexual comments about the prime minister's husband. Thus, discursive and material borders between straight/gay, self/other, tourist/host shifted constantly.

The physical, or material, borders that operate at HERO and the Sydney Mardi Gras are predicated on discursive borders between paraders and tourists. In the next section I consider psychoanalytic theory on abjection (Kristeva 1982; Grosz 1989, 1990, 1994; Young 1990) as a way of understanding further some of the reasons why HERO and Mardi Gras have become such popular tourist events.

BORDERING ON ABJECTION

Young (1990) uses the concept of cultural imperialism to examine general forms of group oppression and violence. Cultural imperialism works to keep a group invisible at the same time as it is marked and stereotyped. The most visible "others," for example, women, blacks, and disabled people, are clearly marked as different from the dominant white, male subject. However, a border anxiety is present when the other is least visible. Young (1990: 146) argues that "homophobia is one of the deepest fears of difference precisely because the border between gay and straight is constructed as the most permeable; anyone at all can become gay." The border is most threatening when the gay body cannot be distinguished from the straight body. Only when gay bodies are clearly marked as different, as in gay pride parades, does this border become visible and therefore less threatening to the dominant culture.

This corporeal border was illustrated in many questionnaire responses. At the roadside (behind the barrier) one respondent (male, white, and heterosexual) had come to the HERO parade to "have a look" and defined the HERO parade as a tourist event because "It's strange, a freak show and a laugh if you're straight." This response can be read not only as an attempt to mark the parade participants as different from the dominant white, heterosexual subject, but also to mark the parade bodies as "freaks." Several responses from heterosexual tourists (including men and women of differing ages and backgrounds) illustrated a desire to maintain a border between straight and gay:

"Alternos deserve to have their lifestyles exposed a bit—makes us more comfortable."
"To watch the strange people."
"To perve."
"Have a look, entertainment."
"Out of curiosity."
"Have a look, to see it firsthand."

There were many floats that directly emphasized the threat that queerness poses to social order. For example, the "Demon Float" and "Salon Kitty" (which is a bondage and sadomasochistic float described as "Rubber/Latex fetish: Dressing for pleasure") both challenged the heteronormative notions of acceptable sexual desire and pleasure through their displays of sadomasochism; the "New Zealand Prostitutes Collective" bought the bodies of illicit sex workers into public view; the "TransPride" float challenged the authenticity of rhetoric about two genders/sexes; "Miss Kitty and Friends," which consisted of a six-foot-six tall drag queen with two men on dog leads dressed as poodles, provided an animated debate about sexuality, bestiality, and gender/sex roles; the "Safe Sex: No Ifs, No Butts" float, which consisted of a large revolving polystyrene penis and eight dancing men and two women whipping each other, exposed the penis/phallus in a public place; and finally, the "Body Positive" (an HIV/AIDS organization) and the Herne Bay House floats brought defiled, diseased bodies into view. Such bodies do not constitute proper social bodies (Grosz 1994). They threaten to disrupt order and purity, but, and at the same time, they reinforce societal order by remaining in the parade and not spilling into the watching tourists. Thus, these parade entries, which tend to be perceived as some of the most risqué, also tend to reinforce a dichotomy between heterosexual and homosexual.

Julia Kristeva's (1982) notion of abjection is very useful in understanding the ways tourists at gay pride parades combine fascination in, with revulsion against, queer bodies. According to Kristeva the feeling of abjection is one of disgust, often evoking nausea, and it is

> an extremely strong feeling which is at once somatic and symbolic, and which is above all a revolt of the person against an external menace from which one has the impression that it is not only an external menace but that it may menace us from the inside. So it is a desire for separation, for becoming autonomous and also the feeling of impossibility of doing so. (Kristeva 1982: 135)

That which is abject is something so repulsive that it both attracts and repels; it is both fascinating and disgusting. The abject exists on the border, but does not respect the border. It is "ambiguous," "in between," "composite" (Kristeva 1982: 4). The abject is what threatens identity. It is neither good nor evil, subject nor object, but something that threatens the distinctions themselves. Kelly Oliver (1993: 56) claims: "Every society is founded on the abject—constructing boundaries and jettisoning the antisocial—every society may have its own abject." Kristeva (1982) maintains that the impure can never be completely removed. Abjection's ambiguity means that while releasing a hold, it does not radically cut off the subject from what threatens it; on the contrary, abjection acknowledges it to be in perpetual danger.

David Sibley (1995: 8) adopts Kristeva's notion of abjection to argue that "the urge to make separations, between clean and dirty, ordered and disordered, 'us' and 'them,' that is, to expel the abject, is encouraged in western cultures, creating feelings of anxiety because such separations can never be finally achieved." The urge to maintain the distinction between "us-tourists" and "them-gays" at the HERO parade and the Sydney Mardi Gras can be understood as abjection, but the separation between tourists and hosts, self and other, mind and body can never be achieved. Abjection "is a desire for separation, for becoming autonomous and also the feeling of impossibility of doing so" (Kristeva 1982: 135), and Kristeva argues that the abject provokes fear and loathing because it exposes the borders between self and other as fragile and threatens to dissolve the subject by dissolving the border.

Drawing on Kristeva's work, Grosz (1994: 193) differentiates between types of abjections: "abjection towards food and thus toward bodily incorporation; abjection toward bodily waste, which reaches its extreme in the horror of the corpse; and abjection towards signs of sexual difference." Different floats in the HERO parade can be viewed as illustrative of each of these categories. The first category, abjection toward food and bodily incorporation, can be linked to paraders who reject the notions that

> A slim, fit body is for some a source of pride to be paraded in public places, spelling discipline, success and conformity, whereas fat is seen as a sign of moral and physical decay. Fat people are stereotyped as undisciplined, self-indulgent, unhealthy, lazy, untrustworthy, unwilling and non-conforming. . . . Unlike the disciplined slim body the fat body is not welcome in everyday places. (Bell and Valentine 1997: 35–36)

Few lesbian bodies on parade represent existing norms of "feeding regimes." Many of the lesbian bodies on display are large. Paraders, such as "Dykes on Bikes," "Marching Girls," and the lesbian float called "Lassoo," tend to ignore disciplinary regimes that aim at making a slim body. Instead there is often pride associated with being large. Tourists' abject reactions to large lesbians are evident in some of their comments. For example, two men exchanged the following comment about a large "Dyke on a Bike": "Oh, God, did you see her? She's *huge* (. . .) nice bike though."

The second category of abjection, bodily waste and horror of the corpse, is integral to many floats at the HERO parade and Mardi Gras. Both parades are organized to raise funds for HIV/AIDS organizations, and in resting on gay male bodies, they also rest on the notion of abjection. "Sexuality has become reinvested with notions of contagion and death, of danger and purity, as a consequence of the AIDS crisis" (Grosz 1994: 193). Gay male sex is understood (by "straight" society) to be predicated on oral penetration and fecal contamination and this carries an unspeakable connection to excremental pollution. Kristeva (1982: 71) argues: "Excrement and its equivalents (decay, infection, disease, corpse, etc.) stand for the danger to identity that which comes from without: the ego threatened by the non-ego, society threatened by its outside, life by death." Several floats in the HERO parade can be connected to this understanding of abjection. Specifically, floats that represent HIV/AIDS organizations, such as the "Safe Sex" float, Herne Bay House float (residential care for people living with HIV/AIDs), "Body Positive" float, and the "Remembrance" float, intensify the abject thoughts that disease is picked up off rectal walls and that death follows from this disease.

Gay pride parades are also significant sites for analyses of sexual difference, the third category of abjection. There are many HERO floats that fit this category. In particular, the following floats and paraders most obviously focused on sexual difference: "Drag Queens," "Te Waka Awhina" (a waka—canoe—with gay and transgender Māori), "Mika" (singer/entertainer in a queer Māori temple), "Sisters of Perpetual Indulgence" (gay men as nuns), "TransPride" (various people from the transgender community), "Lost Grannies" (men dressed as "grannies"), and "Surrender Dorothy" (a large shoe and yellow brick road with drag queens). These paraders disrupted and subverted conventional and hegemonic notions of sexual difference. I conducted a focus group with five people who constructed the "TransPride" float for the 1996 HERO parade, the theme of which was "Heavenly," their objective being to upset the construction of transgenders as, what Young (1990: 123) terms "ugly bodies." Aroha[5] began with a description of their float:

Aroha: All the, the costumes on the float, the majority on the float are pastel colours and gold.
Lynda: Great.
Aroha: We wanted to create a heavenly (//)
Chris: (//) yeah yeah.
Aroha: approach.
Janet: Cos we can be pure just like anybody else . . . why are we, why are we suddenly, why are we suddenly, considered dirty? (Yeah) because we want to cross a borderline sexually. You know and um, why should we look like sluts when we don't feel like sluts?
Chris: Yeah, get rid of the typecast.
Lynda: Yeah, take away the stereotype.
Janet: Most people think transgender is a mockery.
Aroha: They do.
Janet: You know sort of taking off something.
Aroha: But then when you look at it, a lot of it, public attention is focused on girls on the street. (Mmm). They're the ones they see, but it's not always the case.
Lynda: No.
Janet: And a lot of the girls on the street are just making a living, there's nothing else they can do.
Aroha: And there is an awful lot of talent within the transgendered community.

Aroha, Janet, and Chris wanted to challenge the dominant discourses that degrade and debase transgenders as "dirty" and as "sluts." They wanted to do this by invoking the opposite of being defined as ugly, hence their float had a very feminine and pure theme. It was constructed around traditional markers of femininity in terms of colors (pastels and gold), costumes, and other props, in an attempt to offer a transgendered subjectivity other than that of "working girls on the street." It could be argued that transgenders represent a type of intolerable sexual ambiguity (Kristeva

1982). The heterosexual (cultural imperialist) tourist constructs a conceptual limit of human subjectivity. Categorizations of subjects as "freaks," "ugly," and "dirty sluts" are attempts to reposition the border between the self and the other.

CONCLUSION

Although the HERO and Sydney Mardi Gras parades contest the everyday construction of streets as heterosexual, territorial strategies of containment and control of homosexuality are fundamental to the success of the parades. They therefore provide important sites from which to discuss power relations involved in tourism processes. At these parades, borders are maintained between tourists and hosts, which are crucial to their success as spectacular events. The physical or material borders keep the (largely heterosexual) crowd separated from the queer bodies on parade, and, for the watching heterosexual tourists, this physical separation takes some of the "threat" out of homosexual bodies. Simultaneously, a conceptual border separates those who are perceived to represent the body from those who are perceived to represent the mind. This mind/body dichotomy becomes aligned with heterosexual tourists/homosexual hosts.

Young's (1990) theory of cultural imperialism adds weight to my argument that queer bodies on parade become "othered" by the heterosexual tourists. Straight tourists, or "cultural imperialists," culturally inscribe homosexual bodies as deviant, freaks, and as ugly, by which they are both fascinated and repelled in ways consistent with Kristeva's notion of the abject.

My discussion has involved theoretical and political tensions surrounding notions of liberalism, group identity, and difference and therefore inserts "political struggle" into tourism studies. Gay pride parades provide an opportunity to deconstruct acts of tourism, pleasure, and politics as these are lived through the bodies involved. This discussion of the HERO parade and the Sydney Mardi Gras and relationships between heterosexual tourists and gay hosts shows that such tourist events are both complicit with dualistic mechanisms of Western thought, and, at the same time, they contest hierarchical dualisms through a disruption of the cultural imperialist position as "normal" and neutral. Boundaries are central to Western conceptual frameworks of space and bodies. However, as my account has shown, it is possible to mobilize dualisms and to produce contradictory readings and experiences of gay pride parades.

NOTES

1. The HERO parade is part of the HERO project. The project was initially run, in 1994, to help raise funds for gay men living with HIV/AIDS. The name HERO validates the courage people have while living with HIV/AIDS. The name also incorporates both male and female genders (see <http://www.hero.org.nz/>).

2. The abbreviated title, the Sydney Mardi Gras parade, is used from this point in the chapter.

3. Of the remaining responses 18 (of 118) identified as gay male, 3 identified as lesbian, 3 identified as bisexual, and 4 did not specify their sexuality.

4. I am referring to general social control and regulation of communities that is carried out by all of its members. Individuals also engage in self-surveillance, self-control, and self-disciplining regimes (Foucault 1970).

5. In my choice of pseudonyms I have attempted to mirror the "racial" markers of each participant's real name. For example, if a participant has a Māori, I use a Māori name.

6

Crossing Boundaries: Gendered Spaces and Bodies in Golf

Shonagh McEwan

In recent decades women have made significant advances in several fields tradition-ally dominated by men, including several occupations, professions, and leisure ac-tivities. Such advancements have been accompanied by debates about the extent to which women's progression has depended upon working within dominant dis-courses rather than completely dismantling them. In this context particular studies (McDowell and Court 1994) consider the extent to which women are required to conform to a "male norm" in order to "succeed" and the extent to which such norms are (or can be) challenged. These debates open discussions about the gendering of subjectivity and highlight the complex and often contradictory ways in which women (and men) navigate their way around dominant discourses of gender.

Many academics, including geographers (Butler and Parr 1999; Duncan 1996a; Longhurst 1997, 2001; Nast and Pile 1998a; Rose 1993), work with feminist theo-ries to demonstrate the persistence and consequences of a Cartesian concept of sub-jectivity, which insists upon the separation of mind and body. Feminists have argued that in Western thought, the mind has traditionally been associated with masculin-ity, reason, and rationality, and that this has been conceived as separate from, and su-perior to, the body that has traditionally been aligned with femininity, irrationality, and, thus, rendered incapable of reason (Rose 1993; Longhurst 1997; Grosz 1993; Young 1990). In this chapter I engage with critiques of the Cartesian subject to pres-ent an analysis of women's experiences of golf, which problematizes these gendered binaries and points toward an alternative account of subjectivity. Golf is of particu-lar interest in relation to the negotiation of gendered binaries for several reasons, in-cluding its powerful and distinctive engagement with the binary opposition between mind and body.

In the United Kingdom, the United States, and other countries the game of golf constitutes a popular leisure activity and a professional, competitive sport that attracts large audiences. However, at the beginning of the twenty-first century, golf continues to be dominated by men and particular forms of masculinity. Stark gender inequalities persist: for example, at many private members' golf clubs across Scotland restrictions and constraints are placed upon female golfers, limiting their participation in terms of playing rights, voting rights, committee representation, and access to clubhouse facilities (Crosset 1995; George 1997). Many female golfers, myself included, experience gendered boundaries that restrict where they can go and determine where they should be. Overall, women's golf and female golfers are positioned as inferior to men's golf and male golfers and on the margins of the sport.

My experience of golf has been complex and contradictory in that I have been treated in different ways in different places at different times. Exclusion because of my gender has been a prominent theme: for example, I have been restricted from certain rooms of certain golf clubhouses, particular bars, lounge or pool rooms; excluded from playing on golf courses or entering some clubhouses at all; or forced to enter certain golf clubhouses through a side door as opposed to the "main" entrance. On some occasions, however, I have been "allowed" to enter some traditionally "male-only" spaces and cross these gendered boundaries: when participating in national women's golf tournaments at "male" courses I have been permitted to enter those spaces of the golf clubhouses normally barred to women.

This chapter is based, then, on a collection of narratives: personal narratives, discursive constructions of golf and participants' narratives. Empirical evidence was gathered for the purposes of my undergraduate dissertation using three key qualitative methods: participant observation through the summer months of the golf season (June through to September); in-depth interviews with four female golfers, including two coaches, and with four male golfers; and analysis of media representations of golf articles, including visual images, in a popular women's golf magazine, *Women & Golf*. The next section discusses the practice of golf and I explore how contradictory tensions exist in the supposedly coherent dualisms of mind/body and masculinity/femininity. I then analyze the spaces of golf, showing how gendered boundaries are claimed, controlled, and maintained in golf. Yet within this picture of oppression, some golfers (especially female golfers) resist and fracture these boundaries. This examination of gendered spaces and bodies in golf, therefore, presents a notion of subjectivity as necessarily embodied, fractured, multiple, and highly contradictory.

THE PRACTICE OF GOLF

A great golf shot. It's all in the head.

—Advertisement for Callaway Golf

The masculinist separation of minds from bodies and the privileging of minds over bodies remain dominant in constructions of gender and golf. Great emphasis is placed upon characteristics such as concentration, rational thinking, and reason, and the mind/body dichotomy is mobilized in representations of the golfing body as

needing to be controlled or "mastered." The "ideal" golfer is the cool, calm, and focused player who does not display signs of frustration or other apparently "negative"
emotions. On the golf course, people are conditioned to remain still and silent to allow those undertaking a golf shot to concentrate.

This mind/body spilt is encapsulated in an advertisement for Callaway golf equipment (see figure 6.1), which states: "A great golf shot. It's all in the head." The word
"head" refers to both the golfer's mind and the titanium head of the golf club being
advertised. Next to this caption is a male golfer who appears to be focusing on a golf
shot. The golf club is named Hawk Eye, associating it with a bird of prey noted for
its killer instincts. This advertisement deploys discourses of "objective" science to
lend an authoritative "disembodied" perspective on the performance of this equipment. A computer-generated image of the golf club head is shown alongside the text.
The privileging of the mind over the body is reinforced in the closing paragraph of
the text that states that, "Hawk Eye Titanium Drivers and Fairway Woods are designed to help you *think* you're going to strike a great golf shot every time you stand
over the ball" (emphasis added). The final sentence asserts: "in the game of golf,
that's always the best thought to have in your head."

Despite these hegemonic constructions of golf that separate the mind from the
body, the gendered mind/body dualism is upset in the practice of golf. This becomes
particularly clear in relation to coaching, as the following quotations illustrate:

> [W]omen have to be explained exactly why things have got to happen and they will
> change, but if you just say to them, "no you're gonna do this, this and this" and leave it
> at that, then it won't work. Whereas the guys will say "okay I'll do that" without even
> questioning it sometimes. Y'know women will question things. (Isla)[1]

> A woman has to know . . . the logic behind what she's doing. She has to have an un-
> derstanding of what she's doing whereas some of the guys will just do it naturally . . .
> they don't even want to know the logic behind what they're doing. They only come back
> for the logic if it starts not to work. It's as simple as that. (Morag)

These female coaches construct female golfers as rational thinkers who need to be
given the reasoning and the explanation as to why their technique should be
changed. The interconnected binaries of mind/body, rational/irrational, reason/
nonreason are reversed as the first part of the dualism becomes related to female and
the second part of the dualism to male. Thus, it is women golfers who are constructed as rational thinkers based on logical reasoning. The quotations also illustrate that mind and body are firmly and intimately connected in golf coaching. Golf
coaches constantly negotiate hegemonic constructions of golf that attempt to separate the mind from body.

While both respondents quoted above construct women as rational thinkers, they
also represent women as emotional:

> [W]e can't take a tellin' off—women will cry. [Isla puts on a "sobbing" face while saying
> this.] Whereas the boys will go, "fuck you, I'm gonnae be better this time. I'll show you."

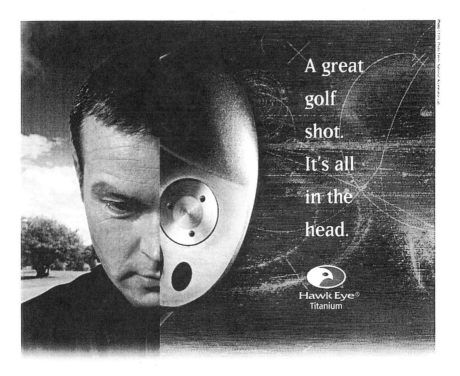

New Callaway® Hawk Eye® Titanium Drivers and Fairway Woods
with the unique Tungsten Gravity Screw.

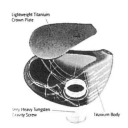

Lightweight Titanium
Crown Plate

Very Heavy Tungsten
Gravity Screw
Titanium Body

Callaway,® Hawk Eye® and 'How Golf Should Feel'™ are trademarks of Callaway Golf Company

The new Hawk Eye Titanium Woods have been designed with one objective – improving your enjoyment of the game of golf.

With this in mind, we have brought together two very special metals: light, super strong titanium and the very dense metal tungsten.

It's a combination that allows us to make an innovative clubhead with a deep forgiving clubface which has 65% of its hitting area above the centre of gravity. This helps to produce more forgiveness, an ideal trajectory and less back spin for optimum roll and distance. This increase in performance is due to the remarkable Tungsten Gravity Screw which is machine-fit into the sole of each club. In the three

wood for instance, the heavy Tungsten Gravity Screw represents less than 2% of the volume of the clubhead but almost 25% of the weight, creating our lowest ever centre of gravity. And that contributes to superb shot-making.

Whether you're on the tee or the fairway, Hawk Eye Titanium Drivers and Fairway Woods are designed to help you think you're going to strike a great shot every time you stand over the ball.

And in the game of golf, that's always the best thought to have in your head.

GOLF
How Golf Should Feel™

Figure 6.1 The mind is privileged over the body in golf
Source: *Women & Golf,* vol. 8, no. 7, 1999. Reproduced with permission of Callaway Golf.

Whereas the girls will go, "he jist did this and I cannae cope" [Isla acted this out pretending to be sobbing and crying. I laugh at her acting.] (Isla)

[W]omen are far . . . deeper thinkers and they're also, in a sense, more easily offended.
. . . I find at elite level, especially under pressure, um the men are easier to handle because you know exactly how they're thinking and you know . . . if they have a disagreement within the team, we can maybe have a red hot ten minutes and the language and the air's pretty tense as everybody sorts it out, but after that it's finished. It's dealt with. . . . Women are different. The same thing just wouldn't happen. You might think you've got the air cleared, six months later the whole thing rears its head again and that you know . . . they're emotionally harder to deal with. (Morag)

Although female golfers may be constructed as rational thinkers who demand reason when being taught, this cannot be separated from their emotions and feelings. These two coaches have to negotiate this connection between mind and body in their teaching environments. This suggests a more complicated notion of subjectivity than a Cartesian concept of the subject allows.

GOLFING BODIES

While I have illustrated the inadequacy of the Cartesian concept of subjectivity, it remains highly influential. It seems that women cannot be the right kind of golfer because they have neither the right *minds* nor the right *bodies*. The "inferior" status of female golfers is justified by mobilizing essentialist constructions of embodiment that emphasize inherent physical differences between men and women's capabilities reliant on a fixed biological understanding of the sexed body. In dominant constructions of golf, power and strength are desirable characteristics in a golfer. This form of hegemonic masculinity is exemplified in an advertisement for golf balls, which reads: "Not only have we got more muscle. We've got more balls" (*Women & Golf* 8, no. 7, 1999). A lack of physical strength is attributed to female golfers and constructed as inferior in golf. The work of feminist philosopher Iris Marion Young (1990) draws attention to the importance of bodily distinctions used to differentiate between superior and inferior groups. She suggests (1990: 123) that members of the inferior group are "imprisoned in their bodies." This is clearly illustrated in the following quotations:

[N]ow in all sports you can't really—there's no point in forcing people, men and women, to compete on level terms—and whether it's tennis or golf . . . the men are probably physically stronger than women and they're gonna hit the ball further. It's no good saying to women, "okay well . . . play in . . . all the events, . . . men and women . . . got to play off the same tees." That would spoil golf for everyone. (Duncan)

[W]hether it'll, it will change that you'll have to have mixed competitions. I mean, I don't think ladies can compete against the men—we don't have the strength. . . . I mean even if you—sticking you against a bloke off one, y'know, he's gonna out drive you. So it's not a question of being [able] to compete on a level playing field. (Emma)

As the second of these quotations illustrates, the body of my own person did not escape these hegemonic discursive constructions of golfing bodies: my female golfing body was marked in this particular interview as weaker, less capable, and inferior to those of my male golfing counterparts. My corporeal surface was inscribed differently to male golfing bodies who were considered by Emma to be stronger and more capable (compare Grosz 1997). In this way, essentialist discourses that make reference to the biological body are used in golf to reinforce patriarchal notions of sexual difference and to portray female golfers as incapable of competing at the same level as their male golfing counterparts (Haig-Muir 1998). These pervasive discourses of gender are highly constraining for both men and women in many sports (Cahn 1994; Connell 1995; Hargreaves 1994; Jackson 1991). However, binary oppositions between masculinity and femininity do not go unchallenged or unmodified. Female golfers in particular demonstrate that gender can be performed and experienced in far more variegated ways, as I elaborate through three points concerned with clothing, strength, and competitiveness.

Golf Clothing

The following quotation points to the notion that if female golfers look too masculine then their bodies become "threatening"—they threaten to upset the binaries of masculine/feminine and mind/body:

> I never considered myself girlie at all. I don't consider myself masculine either, but the way I dress people just automatically assume I'm more on the masculine side anyway because of the sport. I feel comfortable in golf gear, I don't wear anything else because I'm always in golf. So I suppose that can be a problem, you can be labeled. You watch the lassies on the telly, they dinnae do themselves any favors by the way they dress . . . whereas in [the] American Tour I think because it's always warm they've got shorts and stuff like that, so they can still wear shorts and still be very feminine and sell themselves that way. (Isla)

Some women golfers (myself included) refuse to buy and wear golf clothing that reinforces stereotypical constructions of "woman" and "femininity"—mostly flowery patterns, checked trousers, pastel shades, usually unsuitable for playing golf in as they are designed only to look "good." One interviewee observed that golf clothing manufacturers in the United Kingdom design their clothes with "little lady golfers" embroidered on the front of the T-shirt in a limited range of colors—"you've either got to buy pale blue or pink." The same golfer added that she ends up purchasing men's golf clothing:

> [S]o I ended up [with] one [slipover] that was meant for a guy, but it looks okay, it's quite feminine really . . . it's jist, you know, you end up lookin' like a bit of a bloke, you know, and it's not very glamorous. (Kath)

This reinscribes the female body with masculine characteristics and further disrupts the notion of a true gender identity (Butler 1990: 137; Bell et al. 1994).

An intersection between gender and sexuality is implicit in some of the interviewees comments. Female golfers who tend to dress "mannishly," along with the other masculine characteristics they display—such as power, strength, and competitiveness—are often considered to be lesbians in hegemonic discourses of sexualities (Cahn 1994; Haig-Muir 1998). For example, Isla said that because of the way that she dresses—that is, in "masculine" clothing—this can "be a problem, you can be labeled." This assumed link between the masculine appearance of a female and lesbianism has been problematized in at least one discussion of performing sexualities (Bell et al. 1994). While golfers like Isla and Kath actively disrupt the association of female with feminine and male with masculine, however, they remain concerned about and disavow any disruption of ideas about sexuality.

Female Golfers with Strength and Power

Female golfers who display strength and power when playing golf also disrupt the masculine/feminine binary. These characteristics are "out of place" on a female golfing body, so much so that female golfers such as Laura Davies (see figure 6.2) become a focus of fascination:

> Um, the thing about Laura Davies is, I mean she done so much good, but again it's a sort of freak thing. It's like oh my God, she hits the ball, you know, as far as so and so on the European Tour or the US Tour, [the men's tours and therefore likening her hitting the ball "like a man"] let's go an' see what she looks like . . . it's almost like she's a kinda freak because she's so good. (Kath)

This quotation points to the notion that women's embodiment is contradictory. While a female golfer such as Laura Davies disrupts binary thinking by occupying both sides of the binary of masculine/feminine, other people position her back into binary logic.

Competitive Female Golfers

Women who achieve a high level in the game of golf, nevertheless, provide a greater threat to upsetting the binary discourses in golf, because of their involvement in tournament golf. Competing in golf tournaments, thus displaying competitiveness and a will to win, is a gendered characteristic principally associated with hegemonic masculinity. One respondent noted how two golfers actively resisted and challenged stereotypical images of women golfers through a golf tournament set up for businesses:

> They have been having a bit of fun at the expense of the men because they have a [name of organization] Team[2] in and it's been Karen and Debbie and Colin MacKenzie, who's plays off about seven or eight [whereas Karen and Debbie are both far lower handicaps

Figure 6.2   Professional female golfer, Laura Davies
Source: *Women & Golf* vol. 8, no. 6, 1999. Reproduced with permission of Action Images.

than that and both have represented Scotland]. . . . And Debbie's been 'phoning up you know to play these other teams and they've been very patronizing, you know, [saying to Karen and Debbie] "you'll be allowed to play off the ladies' tees" and all this sort of stuff and of course Karen and Debbie had turned up and been out-hitting the men they were playing against and I think thoroughly enjoying themselves [laughter]. (Morag)

Morag illustrated how, through competing in a corporate golf competition where they displayed "masculine" traits, such as being competitive and hitting the ball powerfully, these two female golfers subverted traditional constructions of women golfers as weak and passive.

In this section I have explored the practice of golf. I have demonstrated that there are productive tensions to be unpacked within the supposedly coherent dualisms of mind/body and masculine/feminine. I now consider the spaces of golf.

THE SPACES OF GOLF

Claiming Space in the Clubhouse

Many (but by no means all) golf clubs in the United Kingdom segregate clubhouse spaces into men-only or women-only rooms. These are private members' clubs, which are not covered by the Sex Discrimination Act of 1975. This segregation extends beyond toilets and changing areas to social spaces such as bars, poolrooms, and lounges. Many such clubs have a men's bar, or a men's lounge, and facilities such as television and pool tables are usually located in these male zones. The women-only areas usually consist of a separate ladies' lounge, often without bar access or facilities such as pool tables, and the ladies' locker rooms. Golf can therefore be understood to accommodate women by creating distinctly gendered spaces and boundaries with important implications for women's and men's experience of golfing landscapes.

This separation of private clubhouse rooms into male-only or female-only is illustrated in the following observation noted during a women-only golf competition. There was a major football match live on television that a group of female golfers wanted to watch while waiting for the other competitors to finish. One of them asked an organizer of the competition where the television was situated, but before he could finish his sentence she retorted: "But that will be in the *men's bar*" (original emphasis). From past experience, she seemed well aware of gendered spaces within golf clubs. Adding to this she expressed her viewpoint: "that really *pisses* me off. It's so bloody sexist it's a *joke*" (emphasis in original). Within this particular golf club, female golfers are excluded from a social space that has facilities some of them wish to use. This observation also demonstrates that golf clubhouses are used as a site of social interaction of all kinds, and some golf clubs (especially prestigious golf clubs and the new "corporate" type of golf courses) can be considered to be places at which to "network." The exclusion of women from these spaces not only limits them from participating fully in golf club life, but may further exclude them from social networks that extend beyond the golf club itself.

These boundaries based on sexual difference can be analyzed further using the work of Elizabeth Grosz (1992), who argues that the body cannot be understood outside place. Building on Grosz's ideas, Lynda Johnston (1996: 328) analyses the mutually constitutive relationship between the built bodies of female body-builders and their training environments, arguing that "Sexual difference creates feminine and masculine spaces, and these sexed spaces help to create feminine and masculine bodies." Similar processes are evident in golf clubs. For example, referring to a golf club of which she had once been a member, Emma drew attention to a room in the clubhouse from which women were excluded, namely "a *dirty* bar, a spike bar which *ladies* weren't allowed in" (emphasis added), which can be understood as constitutive of sexual difference. A "dirty bar" is a social space in a golf club where golfers do not have to change out of their golf clothing, often including spiked golf shoes, which had been worn on the golf course. These bars are usually designated for men only and are typically considered "inappropriate" spaces for "lady" golfers to enter because of codings of gender behavior and bodies. Apart from being allowed to remain in the same clothes that are worn on the golf course, "dirty" also refers to the language (such as swearing) and behavior (sometimes drunken) that is allowed to take place in such rooms. This masculine space is very different from mixed lounges in golf clubs where more formal dress codes are often enforced—for example jackets and ties for men, and skirts for women—and different discourses that construct appropriate notions of how women and men should behave. More specifically, gender is performed in these spaces through the repetition of a specific corporeal style regulated by formal rules concerning dress codes (Butler 1990: 139–140; see also McDowell 1995b). Such dress codes and standards of acceptable behavior impose the masculine/feminine binary on male and female golfers and are thereby active in creating particular types of bodies that can be considered to "fit" particular spaces. Thus, as Heidi Nast and Steve Pile (1998b: 4) observe, "Bodies and places are woven together through intricate webs of social and spatial relations that are made by, and make, embodied subjects."

Not all women are excluded from entering men-only spaces of golf clubs such as dirty bars or men-only bars. Class and gender roles are significant in this context. Some women cross the gendered boundaries because they are employed in golf clubhouses, for example as cleaners and bar staff. A recent experience at a Scottish golf club illustrates the point. I was meeting my partner at the clubhouse and on arrival saw him in the bar. As I entered I checked the door to see if it was designated as a space for men only, but there was no notice to that effect. In the bar, I chatted with some of the (male) golfers about the outcome of their competition and was offered a drink by one of them. Soon after, I was told to leave by the bar-*woman*. I asked her: "Why?" She replied: "Because it is for *men-only.*" I retorted: "Well how come *you're* in here then!" She laughed, explaining that the rules were "daft" and that she did not make them. I refused to leave but I was soon forcibly ejected by one of the male members. Some of the men I had been chatting with left with me, to signal their own disgust at how I was treated. This experience demonstrates how these spaces are claimed in ways that permit some women to enter, but only in highly scripted roles. It also illustrates that not all men necessarily wish to claim space in golf clubhouses in this way.

CONTROLLING BOUNDARIES

Being ejected from a clubhouse space claimed by male golfers suggests how the gendered boundaries I have described are controlled and enforced, but it also suggests how they may be disrupted and crossed. In this section I discuss four ways in which gendered boundaries in golf are maintained: by using informal actions and comments; through formal rules and regulations; by mobilizing the gendered distinction between public and private; and through the dominance of men and masculinism in decision-making processes within golf clubs.

Policing the borders of gendered spaces through informal actions and remarks is an effective way of making people feel either "in place" or "out of place," as noted by Robyn Longhurst (1995) in relation to pregnant women's participation in sport. During a prestigious event for women amateur golfers last year, I noted my experience of a room in the clubhouse that had recently been designated a mixed lounge. The room contained a television, pool table, and access to the main bar, and, until recently had had a sign on the door stating "Men's Bar." In order to qualify for funding through a major British source, the club had to allow both sexes access to this space. The new sign on the door read "Small Lounge." My experience of this space suggests that it is still treated and maintained as a male zone. When entering to play a game of pool with another female golfer, my friend asked the four men already in this room watching the television "Is it okay for us to be in here?" One of them replied, "Yes," but added (jokingly?) that we should "feel privileged." The following morning I was watching television in this room with three other female golfers. There was also a group of men, and another man entered the room and began talking to them, expressing his annoyance at not being able to have a game of golf all week. Looking in our direction, he said that this was, "because of all these bitches." Antagonistic behaviors of this kind made me feel uncomfortable and very much out of place in this room. Through remarks such as these, the border of this space is policed in a way that continues to marginalize and exclude female golfers.

Second, gendered boundaries are also maintained through formal rules and regulations as the following quotations illustrate:

The main entrance [to the golf club], no women are allowed in . . . women have to walk *round* and go in, sort of, the far entrance. (Steven, emphasis added)

You cannot, a lady cannot go into Royal Troon Clubhouse . . . the only way you can go in is if you're going in for dinner with a member [which has to be a man because it's a male-only club] and you can go in a *particular* door. You can't go in the *main* entrance, I don't think. [Shonagh thinks to herself: "No you can't, I tried that once!"] You go in a *side* entrance into the dining room. (Ross, emphasis added)

Both of these quotations highlight the existence of golf club rules that restrict women from entering the clubhouse through the main entrance. The designation of the main entrance and hallway as for men only constructs women golfers as inferior to men golfers since the women may only enter an area of the clubhouse through a *side* entrance. This interpretation parallels Daphne Spain's (1992) assertion that the creation of gendered spaces is connected to status differences between women and men.

A third way in which gendered boundaries are preserved in golf is through the gendered dichotomy between public and private (compare Duncan 1996b). The public arena has been traditionally associated with men and masculinity, along with social, economic, and political power, while the private sphere aligned with women, middle-class domesticity, femininity, and dependence (Bondi 1998). Gendered divisions in golf, including the ones described so far, are imbued with the notion of separate spheres for men and women inflected with notions of public and private, respectively. One interviewee reported comments from male golfers that locate female golfers in the domestic sphere rather than on the golf course, which is considered to be a male domain:

> I still get comments here about, "should you be at home cooking the supper" . . . they [some male golfers] were saying that the girls should be at home cooking. (Emma)

Such remarks reinforce a traditional notion that a woman's place is in the home, and therefore the private sphere.

This ideological distinction between public and private influences the organization of golf and the operation of golf clubs and brings me to my fourth point about the means whereby gendered boundaries are maintained in golf. Men and masculinism dominate in the decision-making processes of golf clubs, and this can be linked to the stereotypical perceptions that men are disembodied, objective, and rational thinkers while women are irrational and, therefore, incapable of undertaking major decisions involving the running of a golf club. Female golfers are restricted in the public sphere of (private) golf club politics because they may not be allowed to attend or vote at meetings such as the annual general meeting or they may not be entitled to sit on club committees. The following quotations highlight the patriarchal organization of golf clubs of which the interviewees are members:

> [T]he men will decide and they'll say, "Here we are ladies, this is what we're going to do." (Kenny)

> [A] lot of the ladies have husbands playing in the *main* club—note the choice of words! [I laugh] You know, the ladies' section is a little off-shoot of it . . . the ladies have their own committee, but it has no power as such. I mean . . . the ladies committee really decides . . . how the ladies section is going to run itself. But for any big decisions to do with, you know, Newbattle golf course or the clubhouse or something like that, the ladies committee have to go back to the men all the time [and] clear it through the men's council. (Morag, original emphasis)

These quotations demonstrate that male golfers are constructed as the "master subjects" (Rose 1993, drawing on Haraway 1985). Morag's comment in particular highlights that the men's golf club is considered the "main" club and the ladies' section—"a little off-shoot"—is defined by the male members (master subjects) only in relation to their positions of power.

Formal rules in golf clubs may allow female golfers only to play in the daytime on weekdays and not at all on the weekends on the presumption that women do not work in full-time paid employment. Such formal rules and procedures are decided by golf club committees, and presumptions about women in the private sphere lead to prime times in golf being allocated to men only, with the restrictions that are placed upon female golfers hinging on the notion that women are free to play golf at any time, whereas the men work all week and therefore get priority on evenings during the week and Saturdays and Sundays.

These gendered assumptions can be challenged. For example, "business ladies" in golf clubs occupy a peculiar position in that they do not conform to the public/private dichotomy but disrupt traditional associations of women with the private, domestic sphere. Female golfers who are in full-time paid employment during the week are often only able to play golf on weekends:

> [T]he way of life now is not the wife at home looking after the kids waiting for the husband to come home and cook him supper at six o'clock at night. So many girls are working and Saturday and Sunday is the, sort of, prime time to play golf and that's normally where the ladies are restricted. Monday to Friday they're not restricted at all. (Emma)

> [T]hings have changed in golf. Many golf clubs where they had women members and men members, there used to be the idea that women sort of don't work, they stay at home and so they can play their golf throughout the week. And then at the weekends, the men come and play and so the women don't get on the course 'til late afternoon or something. Well that of course has all changed now. Women work just as much as men and in our view, most golf clubs have men and women as members, if they're working men and working women, then they should have the same opportunity to play golf at any time at the weekend, because there are a lot of men who retire earlier and they play golf throughout the week. (Duncan)

The circumstances of these female golfers raise two important issues. First, the public/private dichotomy cannot be straightforwardly mapped onto people's lives: "business ladies" resist such gendered dualisms. Second, assumptions about public and private spheres are not only gendered but classed, too. For women to occupy the private sphere and undertake domestic work is dependent upon the availability of financial resources to enable someone, "ideally" the woman, to stay at home performing domestic duties. But as Duncan suggests, in most middle-income households both women and men of working age are in paid employment.

FRACTURING BOUNDARIES

Since the decision-making processes at many golf clubs are dominated by men, the capacity for change is limited by what the male members decide:

Y'see I mean that all comes because they're all still run by, or the majority of them [golf clubs] are still run by men and they're the ones that are in control of changing . . . it's the men that are dictating who is goin' to be using the golf course on a Saturday and Sunday. I mean until you get sort of some of the ladies on the committees and going to the AGM to vote, you won't get change. I mean it's still being changed within the men's, what the men want. (Emma)

The gendered power relations in golf limit the possibility of implementing new rules and procedures that could overturn existing ones, those that currently segregate the use of clubhouse rooms and facilities, into male and female spaces. Indeed, the claiming and controlling of clubhouse spaces by male golfers and the existence of private members' clubs for men only demonstrate how certain golf clubs and club-houses are constructed as private places for men. These exclusionary practices are suggestive of the power that men retain in the claiming and controlling of spaces in golf, a power that female golfers cannot claim on the same scale. The crossing of boundaries in golf by women, therefore, are often, but not always, enabled by permission granted by men.

An autobiographical vignette illustrates how transgressions tend to take place only at certain times and on "special" occasions. I have had two very different experiences at Royal Liverpool Golf Club (Hoylake). My first experience was during the 1996 Ladies' British Open Amateur Matchplay tournament. I was able to access almost every single inch of the clubhouse, including the men's locker rooms, which all the female golfers were granted use of for the duration of the competition. I also experienced Hoylake during the Universities' Home Internationals tournament in May 1998, when I was limited to one room in the clubhouse—the mixed lounge—apart from the women's locker room. I was suddenly aware of the gendered boundaries within the clubhouse unnoticed on my previous visit. I was not allowed into the up-stairs lounge—because it was for men only; I was not allowed in the downstairs bar—because it was for men only.

The scope for some female golfers on certain occasions to cross gendered boundaries illustrates very clearly how these boundaries are not fixed, but are continually made and remade within the golfing environment. One interviewee reported a particular instance where a female golfer disrupted the gendered boundaries at a golf club and entered a male-only space within the clubhouse. It was a schools event in which there was only one girl competing. The prize-giving was held in the men's bar and the girl was "*invited*" into this space for the duration of the presentation. Similarly, for the purposes of the Curtis Cup, an amateur women's international team event between the United States and Great Britain and Northern Ireland, the players were *granted* access to clubhouse facilities, practice facilities, and the golf course by the extremely prestigious, male-only golf club, the Honourable Company of Edinburgh Golfers, which plays on Muirfield golf course:

Muirfield had the Curtis Cup . . . in [nineteen] eighty-four—so you know, they obviously opened it up to women then. (Isla)

Another respondent considered it impossible to adhere to rigidly gendered spaces because of her position as secretary of the golf club and the location of her office within the clubhouse. She has to travel through the men's bar and pool room area in order to access the main part of the clubhouse from the secretary's office. She chooses to *ignore* the construction of spaces as gendered:

> I can't take any notice of that, you know, I have to go through it [the men's bar] to get to the loo for a start. I'm not going outside every time I have to go to the loo and as I, I think most of them just take me as one of the boys now anyway as it were and they don't take any notice of what sex I am. (Emma)

At some amateur tournaments, such as the Ladies' British Open Amateur Stroke-play Championship and the British Open Amateur Matchplay Championship, be-cause there is a large number of entries and the men's facilities are usually consid-ered superior to the women's, the competitors may be given use of the men's locker rooms for the week of the tournament. This opens up situations where these female golfers are transgressing the boundaries that would "normally" exist and disrupting male/female spaces within the clubhouse, which is evidently a subversion of mascu-line space:

> [I]n terms of goin' to, you know, . . . the Britishes [British Matchplay and Strokeplay golf tournaments] an' things like that—I . . . know that sometimes they'll use the men's locker room and put plants in the urinals [laughter]. (Kath)

Attempts by the organizers to give these masculine spaces a "feminine" touch causes much hilarity among the competitors and draws attention to the point that female golfers are not supposed to be "in there." For the week of the tournament, the boundaries are redrawn and usually there are no restrictions on where the women golfers can or cannot access during the week.

These illustrations demonstrate that there are various ways in which gendered boundaries are transgressed and rigidly dichotomous "male" and "female" spaces are disrupted in golf. These points of disruption are not limited to particular events or levels of competition, but may take place in a wide range of contexts, including county school events, national tournaments, international team events, as well as at ordinary golf club level.

CONCLUSION

This chapter has examined how gendered spaces and bodies are produced in the game of golf and in so doing has illustrated both the influence and limitations of a Cartesian concept of subjectivity. I have demonstrated how discourses of golf mobi-lize the hierarchical dualisms of mind/body, male/female, masculine/feminine, and public/private. But these gendered dichotomies do not go unchallenged or unmod-ified, and I have shown how golf not only produces, but also disrupts, binary distinctions: at certain times and in certain places some golfers disrupt these distinctions and cross boundaries in a variety of ways. In particular, I have argued that female golfing bodies provide a basis for challenging gendered binaries such as mind/body and masculine/feminine, and I have suggested that female golfing bodies disrupt the association of female with feminine and the construction of particular spaces as "male." These contradictory tensions in golf suggest that gendered spaces and boundaries are neither rigidly maintained nor fully transgressed. The points of resistance to gendered binaries in the organization and practice of golf demonstrate that dichotomized spaces and boundaries can be contested and remade, but crucially this contestation and remaking occurs within the existing framework of dualistic thinking. Therefore, although there are resistances to gendered binaries in golf, it may be impossible to completely transcend dichotomous ways of thinking that shape male and female golfers' experiences of the golfing landscape. However, I have presented an account of subjectivity as necessarily embodied, multiple, fractured, and highly contradictory, which points to the possibility of conceptualizing practices such as golf in ways that "loosen up" assumptions about gendered binaries.

NOTES

1. Pseudonyms are used to protect the interviewees' anonymity. In these quotations I preserve, as far as possible, the interviewees' patterns of speech. A few words may need explanation, as follows: gonna = going to; cannae = can't; dinnae = don't; jist = just.

2. As well as changing the names of interviewees, I have removed the names of organizations.

7

Talking with the Magician's Apprentice: Fleshing Out GIS Users

Susan Lilley

This chapter explores the processes through which fluid subjectivities are (re)produced in the mutually productive relations between embodied users and the digital technologies they use. Drawing on accounts of geographical information system (GIS)[1] users gathered in in-depth interviews, I illustrate how the corporeal is central to their understandings and experience of this technology. Such empirical research is crucial in order to challenge the powerful Cartesian dualisms, which this technology both depends upon and reproduces. The notion that using computer technologies is a disembodied experience is prevalent in descriptions of how users might experience digital environments and in understandings of these applications as sites of knowledge production. Feminists have argued that the possibility that the computer user might "leave the meat" behind, allowing the disembodied, rational mind to transverse cyberspace, facilitates the notion that computer-generated outputs constitute impartial, objective truth. The empirical evidence gathered in this research contests the plausibility of these powerful dualistic structures that unproblematically separate mind from matter and subject from object. I will argue that, far from being discarded in the practice of technology, the corporeal is pivotal to users' understanding and use of GIS.

Feminist theorists of science and technology have long questioned the status of the body, cogently critiquing the binary separation between mind and flesh, which has been pivotal to the truth claims of Cartesian science (Bordo 1986; Lloyd 1984; Harding 1986, 1991; Haraway 1985, 1988, 1997). Rendering knowledge a "correspondence between rational minds and intelligible forms," this paradigm depends upon the "assumption that pure intellect cannot distort reality" (Lloyd 1984: 11). Such science, therefore, presents itself precisely as disembodied, where the autonomous rational mind anchors its claims to knowledge in its separation from a passionate, feminized body (Keller 1985; Haraway 1985; Longhurst 1997). Rose

(1993: 6–7), drawing on the work of Le Doeuff and Haraway, adopts the term masculinist to differentiate this paradigm from embodied male individuals. Rather, it is the "master subject," constituted through and contributing to potent hegemonic discourses, who occupies a position of power from which he can "see" things only in relation to himself. The disembodied masculinist mind has thus been associated with reason, logic, and objectivity, while the category "woman" has been exploited as a repository for that which rationality transcends or leaves behind.

Conversely, feminist scientists, including feminist geographers, have advocated the centrality of the corporeal realm (Cream 1995; Rose 1993; Haraway 1988; also see chapters 5 and 6 in this volume). They argue that as knowledge does not exist independently of the knower, it is impossible to transcend the perspective of any situated individual. The embodied experiences of the subject are therefore pivotal to the construction of knowledge. Feminists have also challenged the notion of a stable, corporeal realm, arguing instead that bodies do not preexist, but emerge from their iterative citation in discourse (Butler 1993; Stone 1995a; Steffensen 1996). Rejecting the concept that bodies are stable material artifacts, which can be reduced to biology, they argue that bodies and identities evolve through complex processes of social material inscription through the sites, situations, and narratives they help to constitute. That is, while the material body is dense and capable of resisting discursive interpretation, neither does it exist as a stable given. It can only be known through the discursive context in which it arises, to which it contributes, and by which it is shaped.

This chapter explores these processes with particular reference to the situated practice of one digital technology—GIS—in an attempt to disentangle the messy, "co-constructive" relations between bodies, technologies, and subjectivities. Haraway (1992) adopts the term "co-construction" to describe the processes by which artifacts come into being through the situated effects of numerous actors, both organic and nonorganic. Although Haraway is concerned in this instance with the construction of nature, this concept can equally be applied to the mutual (re)production of technological artifacts and their users, which are situated in social contexts, and which continuously (re)produce each other through rich actor networks. This implies that continuous and complex constructions leave artifacts, like discourses, in a state of flux, promoting fragmentation and inconsistency, as different supporting and conflicting discourses interact. In the following section, I explore the interrelations between GIS technologies and the embodied subjects who use them. Contesting masculinist conceptions of the body and identity as discrete and stable, I argue that both are fluid, open to dispute, lacking in stability, and mutually (re)productive. I then exemplify these processes by drawing on material gathered in in-depth interviews with GIS users, in order to explore the emergence of particular subjectivities as they evolve through the situated practice of this technology. The experiences of these users support the assertion that, far from the practice of technology being a disembodied experience, as masculinist accounts suggest, the corporeal is pivotal to the co-construction of embodied identities.

FLESHING OUT THEORY

Understandings of the body in masculinist science are marked by a contradiction, for while science relies upon the rationality of the disembodied mind, its truth claims are also supported by theories of one science and two sexes, which anchor the will for truth in the notion of a singular body (Hendershot 1992; Keller 1992). An understanding of the male subject as contained and coherent, embraced by a bounded, impermeable body, has been exploited in masculinist reason to support the concept of a neutral, coherent, and objective *Man of Reason* (Lloyd 1984). Arguing instead that technologies, bodies, and discourses (re)produce themselves and each other as multiple, fluid, and unstable, feminists have resisted the concept of both the unitary self and the male- and female-sexed bodies (Ferguson 1989; Fraser and Nicholson 1990; Proybn 1993). Concurrently, the bounded masculinist body has been attacked by feminists as a discursively situated method of social control, which produces a manageable and trackable form of identity (Lloyd 1984; Fuss 1990; Stone 1995b; Steffensen 1996). That is, the notion of the singular subject is supported by the myth of a single corporeal form, anchoring the individual in his or her own body.

Perhaps the most corporeal form of subjectivity to evolve in the intersection between body, discourse, and technology debates is that of Haraway's (1985) cyborg. Recognizing that the technology/body interface has been mobilized in masculinist discourses to solidify the discursively constructed distinction between manufactured artifacts and natural organisms, Haraway proposed the cyborg as one possible challenge to this dichotomy. For Haraway (1985: 66), the cyborg constitutes an "imaginative resource," which confuses dichotomous boundaries, whilst emphasizing the responsibilities inherent in constructing them. The cyborg figure thus both reproduces and transgresses technology/body distinctions. Asserting that notions of both the bodily and the technological mediate human experience of the world, cyborgs provide a multitude of monstrous hybrids who *can* be differently situated, for they blur the boundaries at which the body starts and ends (Whatmore 1997).

Haraway's intention was to exploit the instability of this boundary as a catalyst for social change, stimulating new uses of the body. The body from this perspective is more than just an organic body, and more than just a screen onto which cultural fantasies are projected (Steffensen 1996). Instead, cyborg monsters have a potential to provide a realm of possibility alternative to the fictions of "man" and "woman," since the amalgamation of machine and organism is suggestive of a new notion of self, where the concept of being human can no longer be taken for granted (Wolmark 1993). Haraway (1992: 298) proposes that bodies should be perceived as "material-semiotic generative nodes" because their boundaries materialize in social interaction, and thus the body itself cannot preexist. This is not an ontological claim, but merely reflects the embedded nature of discourse, for ultimately it is impossible to imagine an artifact outside its discursive meaning, that is, outside our discursively formed understanding of it (Grosz 1994). Equally, however, such a conception of the body allows for its inventive and multiple creation, for such flexibility allows there to be a disjuncture between lived bodily boundaries and the borders of the material body itself (Marsden 1996; Poster 1990).

The notion that bodies can be constructed, for example, as cyborgs or virtual selves, has led some feminists to adopt multiplicity as a point of departure: if embodiment is a process then opportunities exist for the active creation of bodies and of multiple identities. Turkle (1995) concludes from her studies of the Internet that the ability of the user to become author of both text and self allows for the construction of multiple parallel identities, where the boundaries of each are fuzzy and the self is fractured. But Turkle's analysis implies that the production of bodies is experienced cumulatively, and that each body and associated identity is discrete and perfectly formed. That is, Turkle's description suggests that each "incarnation" can be created, stored, and known, while she offers little explanation as to how these multiple facets interact to produce the fractured self. The notion of multiple, parallel bodies also echoes uncomfortably with the rather mechanistic concept of parts and wholes. Instead, the process of (re)producing the body and the subject might be better described as metabolic, where both, through a continuous process of self-constitution, exist in a constant state of flux. This seems consistent with the notion of performance that Butler (1990, 1993) advocates, where performance becomes an iterative act, constantly reaffirming meaning and power, though never being certain of reproducing the same thing. In this sense the body becomes a resource for the operation of power, burdened with the need to signify, heavy with signification (Rose 1999).

This suggests that in terms of the practice of digital technologies, embodiment emerges through performing the body. The centrality of the body serves to constantly influence the discursive construction of technology and the subject. So in cyberspace, users take deliberate measures to construct bodies for themselves and others as they perform elected identities. Correll's (1995) study of a lesbian online cafe, for example, details how socializing in this cyberspace is performed as a bodily experience, where cafe dwellers drink coffee or alcoholic beverages, depending on the time of day, sit in their favorite chairs, and leave together to have sex. Technologies, therefore, become a means through which the corporeal is negotiated and articulated, and because bodies can never be entirely malleable, they become instrumental in the production of technologies. The user becomes author of both text and self, and where the self is constructed through the interaction of bodies and technologies, the boundaries of each are messy (Turkle 1995).

The suggestion that bodies are culturally produced through performance does not imply that they lack materiality. Indeed, feminists have expressed concern that overemphasizing cultural interpretations of the body harbors the danger of both disregarding women's lived bodily experiences, while also giving the impression that the material body offers no material resistance (McNay 1992; Bordo 1993). Cyberfeminists have also been concerned by this growing tendency to shed the material form, as though the "meat" can be left behind when the disembodied rational mind enters cyberspace. That is, technology is presented as if it renders the body entirely malleable, open to any technically feasible construction. Thus, in an age of virtual reality, cyberspace, genetic engineering, and cosmetic surgery, the material seems to get in the way, and get put out of the way, and cyberspace becomes the ultimate phallic fantasy, where the mind apparently *replaces* the body, leaving the material form in suspended animation (Penny 1994; Morse 1994). Clearly, however, the body is not so easily silenced: as the user sits at her terminal, her back aches, her eyes grow tired, she thirsts and hungers for food or sex. Although technology can mediate embodiment, it does not create bodies that are not anchored to material forms, be it through the aching back of the operator, or the influence of lived experience, and so lived bodily boundaries form part of an intensive corporeal schema.

Some feminists have argued that the dissolution of these boundaries has potential for women, because in acknowledging that technology can invade the impermeable body, it disrupts a traditional site of male power, contesting a boundary from which women have historically wrought little benefit (Steffensen 1996). A distinct machine/human border and its connotations around the sanctity of life have traditionally been applied to male bodies. The distinction between man and technology (re)produced by hegemonic masculinist discourse functions as, and reflects, an extension of male freedom, dominance, and a will to power (Ross 1991); while, as with other binary constructions, such as nature/culture, animal/man, and woman/man, it functions to express the dominance of a masculinist *Man of Reason* and to champion the rights of the "master subject" over machines, animals, nature, and women. Clearly, however, challenging the oppositional relationship between bodies and machines, which has characterized masculinist thinking, contests the notion of a unitary self predicated on the stability of a singular body. The subjectivity of the user is thus not predicated on the essence of a material form, but stems from the practices that construct the user. Recognizing that the stability of material flesh is inadequate as a basis for the self, the subject becomes provisional, produced by contingent social practices, which form an embodied subject who is multiple, fluid, and possibly contradictory (Fuss 1990). The individual is rendered discursive and exists as a product of the discourses, to which it contributes and from which it is formed (Ormrod 1995). The illusion of a coherent and unitary identity is thus a function of discourse. For if subjectivity is predicated on the body, as it is performed and constructed through language, as computing systems manufacture embodied users, they also produce subjects. Technology thus contributes to subjectivity, and in this symbiotic relationship technology is an active constituent of the subject (Lupton 1995; Stone 1995b). Fluid, open to dispute, and always contingent, embodied subjects emerge from the situated practice of technology.

FLESHING OUT GIS USERS

In this section, I draw on interview material to explore how the inscription of bodies produces subject positions through the situated practice of one technology—GIS. This section relies on data collected in fifty-nine in-depth interviews with GIS users employed by a public sector organization. Scottish Natural Heritage (SNH) is a government body, whose purpose is to promote good management and enjoyment of the Scottish countryside, as well as to provide certain executive services to government. The interviewees comprised a range of staff employed at different grades, with various responsibilities, and included individuals ranging from those with limited GIS skills to highly qualified technicians. Six of the interviewees were identified for their GIS competencies, while the remainder were selected at random from two hundred SNH staff who had undertaken an intensive training course in ArcView,[2] a GIS software package. The interview data, which were audio taped and transcribed, were coded using HyperResearch software. These codes, developed with a view to uncovering the subjectivities that emerged in the user's accounts of interacting with the system, formed the basis of the analysis presented in this chapter.

Analysis of the interview material suggested that these emergent subjectivities can usefully be explored by examining notions of expertise. Degrees of competency emerged as an important factor to the GIS users who were interviewed, and it is clear that as users developed (or did not develop) GIS skills, the concept of expertise functioned both to structure their relationship to the technology, to themselves, and to other embodied users. Concurrently, the magical and mystical were repeatedly invoked by interviewees as they struggled to stabilize relations between the mysterious black box of the GIS, the seemingly magical powers of the competent operator, and themselves. These themes are explored in this section. This discussion is, however, not intended to suggest that the subjectivities described below are the only discernible ones that emerge from the practice of GIS at SNH. They are merely described here to exemplify the processes that occur. Although the subjectivities that emerge from these interactions are necessarily complex, three figures recur through the user's accounts: that of the expert, the developing novice, and, in opposition to these, the incompetent.

The figure of the expert was most actively constructed by those who identified themselves as lacking in competency. Often appearing daunted at the prospect of acquiring skills in this unfamiliar technology, it was common for SNH staff to rely on a more "advanced" colleague as a means of mediating their interaction with GIS. Novice users would routinely articulate their desire to have "an approachable expert technician at hand" (James),[3] while Laura admits that she would prefer to "turn to" her more experienced colleague than tackle the GIS herself, even though his only experience was the same training course as she had taken:

> I would probably turn to someone like Simon. . . . he's far more au fait with using computers . . . yes, tend to turn to him for anything I wanted put into a . . . project, or anything, or inputted into the system.

Such comments function to construct a sense of distance between the interviewee and the technology, while also differentiating between different users. The physical presence of both the interviewee and the expert user is apparent. Both are embodied as interviewees emphasize the physical proximity between them: they actively "turn to them" and "approach them." Conversely, while interviewees express their desire to interact bodily with their colleague, the technology is distanced. This has the effect of rendering the expert body touchable and approachable, while the technology is not.

The notion that the expert is more approachable than the GIS was supported in the interview data, for example by novice users' accounts of how a technician or more experienced colleague had assisted them with GIS-related tasks. These descriptions were frequently characterized by a lack of understanding about how the "expert" had interacted with the technology on their behalf. Sometimes this resulted from the "expert" undertaking all of the GIS component of a piece of casework without any assistance from the interviewee. This situation often inspired admiration for the technically adept colleague, even though the interviewee often admitted that they didn't actually know how difficult or easy it had been to produce the output. However, incidents where users had sought technical support from an "expert" colleague were equally marked by a lack of understanding. Joan, for example, who expressed considerable unease with a technology that she felt had been forced upon her by management, recounted her frustration at frequent system crashes, which resulted in her "never" being able to find what she had just been working on, but for "a couple of chaps in the office . . . who are very, very good on the computers and [who could] usually be prevailed upon to know what's hap . . . what's doing." The process of what the expert has done with the GIS is rendered mysterious, and often the interviewee does not comprehend the skills or functionality that have been employed to achieve a needed output.

In some cases the uncertainty surrounding the GIS and those who "understand" it seems to be translated into the almost mystical, as Rose illustrates in her description of the possibilities for exchanging data with other agencies: "Maybe it's an impossible dream, but these are GIS persons that . . . are telling Roy that this was possible . . . different languages or something conversions or something." Lacking understanding, for Rose the GIS loses substance, but exists instead like a "dream" beyond the bounds of touch or of a more corporeal, tangible reality. Drawing on the notion of "different languages," which are incomprehensible to her, and repeating the colloquial word "something" rather than the technical term, she juxtaposes their competency with her lack, discursively constructing notions of expertise. It is the subjectivity contained in this expert body that lends the dream substance, and thus the embodied expert functions to both create a material point of interaction and to solidify the concept of expertise within the flesh.

The relationship between the expert and the interviewee varied, depending partly on the type of interaction occurring, for example, whether the user was seeking support or relying on the expert to perform services. Generally, however, there appears to be a degree of admiration, even reverence, for the person who is attributed expert status. The position of the expert is constructed as one of dominance in relation to the inexpert user, so Joan suggests that she "prevailed upon" them, while countless other interviewees expressed unease about "impinging on people's time" and, significantly, about the need to have GIS support located in the same building as them. Thus, Pete, like many interviewees, emphasizes his "concern if all the sort of GIS experts went, went west." The body of the expert, itself a conceptually laden and evocative label, is positioned as central to his sense of ease with the technology. The spatial metaphor of going west reflects a need for physical proximity, the hope of touching the expert, of having them sit beside you as one interacts with the GIS, of ftf (face-to-face) contact. It is a need that is constantly reiterated by the interviewees. The reverence expressed by these interviewees stems from their need for the bodily presence of the expert. Physical closeness provides security, even if that relationship is complex, because it is also pervaded by concern about impinging on the important expert.

The expertise inscribed in the body differentiates it from others, making it both sought after and revered, and the bodily is clearly central to interviewees' negotiations with the GIS. It is, however, very particular types of bodies that are presented in these accounts. While frequently describing their need for the physical proximity of the GIS proficient, interviewees never complained about such things as their potential expert's body odor. Likewise, the status and power invested in GIS competence did not extend to rendering experts objects of sexual desire, although GIS and its outputs were often described in these terms: for example, I was invited to appreciate "this really sexy map" (Julian) or admire the new "mind blowing, sexy hardware" (Pete). Content to express at length their need for the bodies of the expert user, whether these bodies were fat, saggy, pimply, smelly, or hairy never arose in interviewee's accounts. Doubtless this reflects the professional context of the interviews. The sanitized version of the body in the workplace, particularly a professional environment, was preserved in the interviews. The bodies that emerged in these accounts thus arose from discourses around the body, the workplace, and technology. Yet although interviewees' accounts framed a particular, acceptable body, the *body* of the expert itself was never erased. It provides a medium through which users interact with the technology. It is both obtainable, providing a means through which the untouchable technology might be accessed, and potentially unobtainable, since the agency of the expert to refuse to help, or to physically leave, is latent.

Although the original GIS strategy pursued by SNH endeavored to give all of its two hundred ecological staff members GIS skills, and they all undertook the same intensive training course, it rapidly became apparent that only a handful of trainees were developing any proficiency with the system. The expression adopted to refer to this group by the SNH GIS Project Board was GIS "super-users." This label seems to exemplify the status afforded to those users who developed expertise and to differentiate these experts as a distinct group. Expertise thereby became a property of certain bodies, and while expertise itself was latent and manifest, these bodies signified it. That is, it does not appear externally to the bodies in which it is inscribed (Foucault 1977).

Embodying expertise through their ability to control the machine, these bodies developed as a focal point of wonder. This is aptly illustrated by an incident in the interview I conducted with Laura, who had made limited use of GIS herself. We were sitting, chatting comfortably in the SNH office library. Earlier in the interview, we had discussed the super-users. Most of their names were now familiar to me, since they were mentioned repeatedly by interviewees as the people who had helped them or provided services. The conversation had moved on, and we were discussing hardware provision, when a super-user happened to walk past the partition windows. Laura broke off and exclaimed "That's George Brown!" Our conversation halted, and we both sat mute while we followed his progress down the corridor. When he returned a few minutes later, we repeated the whole process again. His body seemed to provide a source of mutual fascination that is difficult to explain. It appears that the expertise embodied by him differentiates his body from others: he becomes a spectacle.

That bodies are inscribed with expertise and differentiated from those who lack it is apparent. However, an interesting aspect of this inscription is that such users do not inscribe their own bodies with expert status. Joe, selected for interview because he was identified by the GIS Project Board as a super-user, exemplifies this, as he describes his colleague's proficiency while denying his own:

> I wouldn't call myself a real expert in computers . . . people like Malcolm . . . he knows how to do [things], that nobody else here really knows how to do. . . . I'm learning some of those . . . tricks, but I'm not that sort of an expert.

Joe initiates the same distinction between experts and those who are not "au fait" with computers, but rejects his own body as a site of expertise. This viewpoint is far from inevitable. His justification for suggesting that Malcolm is a proper expert was revealed on further questioning to be based on Malcolm's skills with Microsoft Word. Although word-processing software was generally constructed as holding less status than GIS in the interviews, it was a package with which Joe was unfamiliar. Malcolm appears to be constructed as an expert for Joe, purely on the basis that he can perform operations that are beyond Joe's understanding. His expertise is predicated on the inexplicability of his skills, which are transformed from a rational technical competency to a mysterious "trick" in Joe's account. Joe invokes the magical, and Malcolm's inexplicable ability to produce amazing outcomes with the software becomes a performance.

Expertise, therefore, appears to be based on the ability of the expert to produce wonder and mystique, which is in turn predicated on an understanding of the technology itself as mysterious or mystical. For the interviewees in this study, the spectacular qualities of the GIS were based not only on its impressive functionality, but on the incomprehensible technology that made such outputs possible. GIS left users in awe, as tasks that would have taken hours manually were completed at the press of a few enigmatic keys by the GIS expert. For the interviewees, the analysis of results "seemed to appear on the screen like magic" (Joe). Slater (1995), in his study of early photography, suggests that the representationalist technologies of modernism are akin to magic, where pleasure is derived from the invisibility of the illusion. For the interviewees in this study, the GIS is certainly opaque. The plastic casing constitutes both a literal and metaphorical "black box," which is instrumental in forming the relationship between the user and the technology. Although it is not necessary to view the inner workings of the machine, the plastic casing becomes a metaphorical and literal boundary between the user and understanding the technology. Laura illustrates this:

> I wish I knew more about what goes on . . . inside the box. . . . You probably don't need to for my job, but I just feel that if I did, I might . . . not need to phone up the help line people quite so often.

The functioning of the machine remains hidden, and thus realism is used as a vehicle to transcend the real: to produce magic from what is known to be the accomplishment of science. The interviewees are aware that there is a rational explanation, but, nevertheless, are in awe of the illusion, their state of wonderment stemming from their inability to understand how it is done.

Similarly, the inexpert user reveres the expert, because they are unable to understand the process by which the proficient user has interacted with the machine. The wonder associated with the technology invests authority in the body of the expert, as the degree of fascination associated with the GIS is extended to its operator. Several years after GIS was introduced to SNH, one interviewee, a GIS technician, keen to champion the technology and encourage its uptake, told me, sighing, "if only we could persuade people that GIS was not some kind of hideous black art."

Whether GIS is embraced and revered or avoided and feared, whether it is white or black, it is certainly understood as magical. To expand the metaphor of magic adopted by many of the interviewees, it seems that expert bodies can be usefully thought of as magicians. Daunted by the complex system, which is beyond the comprehension of novice users, the technology is both magical and mystical, and it is the ability of the magician to operate it, to appear to control it, that imbues them with magical status. For the embodied user however, by definition their own actions are not shrouded by mystique. This does imply complete self-knowledge on the part of the user, but suggests that familiarity breeds contempt, that is, their own skills cease to amaze them, even if they continue to be in awe of the technology and its potential to produce sophisticated outputs.

These tensions are aptly exemplified by Terry's understanding of computing technologies. Terry had little formal computer training, but was exceedingly positive about the benefits of GIS and enjoyed using computers. After the ArcView course, he not only gained considerable skills in this package, but, under the informal instruction of a trained GIS technician, began to learn ArcInfo—the more complex command-driven GIS on which ArcView is based. In the context of an implementation where most trainees were not even using ArcView, this was astounding to his colleagues. However, Terry was keen to relate that such abilities had advantages and disadvantages by using Microsoft Office, rather than GIS, as an example:

> Powerpoint . . . EXCEL . . . I've come to know them like the back of my hand, and you can produce some really incredible stuff from what seems like a basic package . . . but the better you produce, the more people want you to do them, so you just kind of increase your work.

Terry's enthusiasm for GIS was predicated on a continuing element of wonder, and it seems plausible to suggest that he exploited Microsoft Office, which was now as familiar to him as "the back of his hand," in order to be able to describe it as a "basic package"—a description that would have been more difficult to apply to the GIS, of which he was still in awe. Introducing Microsoft Office to exemplify his account enabled him to maintain the tensions between the "basic package," the "incredible" outputs, and the impressed colleagues, who were making demands on his time. In doing so, Terry suggests that, although he both acknowledges the impressive nature of the outputs generated and understands the reactions of his colleagues, he continues to construct himself as someone using a familiar and basic tool, rather than as an expert. The competent are not a source of wonder to themselves.

Although expert users exploit the distinction between magicians and others, it becomes difficult to interpret themselves as magicians. Arguably this reflects discourses of masculinist science: magic produces pleasure and spectacle, which is discordant with the discourses of rationality and objectivity that are usually associated with GIS. Within the confines of the disembodied, rational scientist, there is no body upon which to inscribe pleasure or awe (Rose 1993). So while, like Joe, the users may admire the Magi and aspire to learn "some of those sorts of tricks," they can only ever self-identify as apprentice magicians. The magic of the machine rubs off on the magician, who is constructed from this process of othering. The beginners "feel just ever so slightly empowered, but they can't . . . [laughs]" (Colin). It seems difficult for interviewees to articulate exactly what can't be done, precisely because it is its inexplicability that creates the sense of power. It seems no one can hope to be a magician.

If the practice of GIS produces apprentice magicians, it also holds the possibility of creating the inept as a subjectivity oppositional to the revered magician. For if interviewees construct others as magicians, and sometimes self-identify as apprentice magicians, a subjectivity that relates to not using the technology is also evident.

One strategy employed by the interviewees who had not developed GIS skills, despite having undertaken the training course, was to assess the utility of GIS and to reject it on a "rationally" argued basis. Interviewees who had made limited use of the system routinely described GIS as a complex software, which for staff working in a pressurized environment is too intricate to learn: the time needed to acquire the skills cannot be justified. This arose because the skills are highly specialized, and staff did not feel that the effort entailed in learning the system would be repaid by their anticipated use of them, particularly because they felt that the spatial data management and analysis tasks they needed to do could be performed more effectively and efficiently by a "proper" expert, or by themselves using more traditional methods. Therefore, the "efficiency, time saving" rhetoric associated with GIS in the broader literature and reiterated in the SNH information technology strategy was not supported by these interviewees' experience.

This logical argument echoes uncomfortably with the potency of the magician subjectivity, in relation to which the inept emerges as a necessary other. For while interviewees suggest that some bodies are inherently magicians, others are rendered inept. Thus Joe, for example, identifies his colleague Malcolm as a person who he thinks would be good at GIS, even though he hasn't attended the training course, purely on the basis that "he's a bit of a computer whiz kid," while Kate, who described herself as someone who was daunted by computers in general, suggested:

> My brother's very interested in computers. I'm sure he'd love to have a go on a GIS thing, and it's just that . . . different people are interested in different things, and some people love what they can do on a computer, they love the way it—does things for them, don't you think?

As Malcolm and Kate's brother emerge as magicians from these comments, Joe and Kate contest the notion that expertise can be achieved through choice or practice. Thus, while interviewees continue to suggest that you need to take the course and use the system regularly to become competent in their rationalized accounts for rejecting their use of this tool, Joe is equally confident in his declaration that Malcolm could easily use the system if he wanted to, despite the fact that he has never been formally taught. Meanwhile, Kate constructs herself as inept. By suggesting her brother would "love to have a go on a GIS *thing*" (my emphasis), she seems to be producing herself as technically incompetent. By adding a clearly inappropriate word, which is actually completely unnecessary to her sentence, her unease with the technology juxtaposes and augments her brother's competence. She is excluded from the emotional and intense connection that her brother has with technology, where the deep emotive bond of "love" is invoked. She describes an intense and reciprocal relationship between the computer and her brother, based on his interaction with it and the things it does for him. This emotive description lies out with the bounds of a rational technical explanation. The body of the magician, whose relationship to the GIS is constructed as inherently different, creates the inept, who lacks access to this intimate interaction with the machine.

The construction of magicians therefore appears to produce the inept, even if embodied individuals do not self-identify in terms of this subjectivity. Rather there is a disjuncture between the rationally argued reasons that users expound to explain their lack of expertise and the emotive language used to distinguish the expert from the inept. Contradicting Western science's binary separation between passion and reason, these interviewees illustrate that logic and rationality is intimately bound with the emotional. It seems that although users who do not develop skills construct logical reasons to support their position, the mechanisms by which they relate and develop that position are more emotive and less logically argued. Certain people are just magicians, such as "this guy whose got a thing about computers, and he *always* can pick things up so quickly" (Sally, original emphasis), while others, like Rose, are inept: "do you really want to do it yourself, when you'll never be as good as that person, . . . they're bound to be able to do it in a better way than you are?" Expertise thus becomes a property of particular bodies, which serves to (re)produce embodied subjectivities.

The symbiotic relationship between the body and the subject is also supported as users describe their interactions with the system. In accounts of using GIS, interviewees frequently adopted imagery that suggested their bodies were situated inside the machine. References to "sticking their head in," spending time "in" the GIS (as opposed to on it, or using it), and "wading" or "stumbling through" the GIS data were a prevailing theme in the interview material. Users thus repeatedly invoked the bodily as a means of articulating their experience of using GIS. The type of body that users construct for themselves is, however, dependent on the type of relationship they have with the GIS. This is particularly apparent as users construct their own embodied, inept subjectivity, which is explored here to exemplify the processes through which the body, the subject, and situated practice co-constructively interact.

The corporeal is used consistently by users as a device to articulate their lack of expertise. Interviewees' accounts of their mistakes and the problems they encountered as they struggled to gain competency with the system frequently relied on a body that was "blundering about" or clumsy, "like baby elephants." Similarly they complained about "being in the dark" or "being completely lost." The body that inhabits the machine renders the user ineffectual, for the corporeal forms produced through this interaction with the GIS are incomplete and malformed: they are blind, they are disorientated, they lack dexterity. These users do not even possess control over themselves. Clearly, their accounts contest the notion that using technology is experienced as a disembodied act. These bodies serve to articulate and re(produce) the relationship between the powerful technology and the inadequate user, who is positioned as impotent, weak, and incomplete. It is a docile body, which reflects the prevailing discourses that construct technology as inevitable and dominant, and the body functions to reflect cultural values, rather than as a site for self-determination (Deveaux 1994). The body, as it interacts with the technology, is therefore central to the production of subjectivities. The revered corporeal magician emerges as a potent subjectivity, to counterpose the embodied instability and insecurity that is solidified in flesh, in the form of the clumsy inept.

The practice of GIS in this context produces three subjectivities associated with discourses of expertise: the magician, the apprentice, and the inept; however, none of these correspond consistently or exhibit stability in relation to particular embodied individuals. These subjectivities are fantasies, which are self-knowingly embodied by no one, except in a very temporary sense, because, although degrees of expertise are a property of bodies and do not exist externally to that inscription, the same embodied individuals mobilize different subjectivities to situate themselves in relation to the technology. These subjectivities operate in tension with the organizational categorization of users, and so while the term "super-users" applies to specific members of staff and contributes to the construction of magicians, magicians and super-users remain distinct. Thus, although there is a parallel in the binary distinction between the organizational categories of super-user and other (nonusers), and the subjectivities of magician and other (inept), the complexity of these subjectivities reflects and constitutes the messy relations between bodies and technologies. This supports the contention that multiplicity provides a point of departure for understanding both the body and the subject, where the self, formed through a continuous process of self-constitution, is al-

ways in flux (Butler 1990; Turkle 1995). The interviewees mobilize these different subjectivities as they articulate their relationship with GIS, and the tensions
between them produce both the subject and the body.

CONCLUSION

Feminist theorists have asserted the centrality of the body both to the production of
knowledge, and to the complex and (re)productive relations between bodies, technologies, and subjectivities (Bordo 1986; Haraway 1997; Rose 1993). Challenging
the masculinist dualisms between the rational mind and the passionate body, feminists have insisted that the illusion of corporeal stability and of a unitary subject is
merely a function of discourse (Fuss 1990; Stone 1995b). The accounts of GIS users
in this study support this claim, describing their use of GIS as inherently bodily experiences. This clearly challenges Cartesian science's claims to truth, which are
rooted in the pure objectivity of the disembodied rational mind. It is the body itself
that is the excess of this particular masculinist fantasy, for these users explicitly situate their understandings of GIS within an intensive corporeal schema. It is the embodied subject that is repeatedly invoked by them to articulate their experience of
this technology and that is central to their relationship with GIS. The productive effects of the body have implications for both their understandings of the system and
their experience of it.

The interviewees adopt embodied subjectivities, which reflect their position
within the complex network in which their practice of the technology is situated.
The potent subjectivities that arise from these interactions, or lack of interactions
with the technology, from revered magicians to clumsy apprentices, structure and reflect user's experience of the GIS and of each other. Constructing themselves tentatively as inept, they reject the technology, or identifying a potential magician, they
crave the ability to perform some of those sorts of "tricks." Their interpretations of
the GIS and their use of it, rooted in the corporeal, also challenge the masculinist binary between reason and emotion. While attempting to rely on rational arguments
to support their admiration for the magicians and the technology, or to make their
rejection of GIS explicable, the potent embodied subjectivities they construct betray
that emotion, spectacle, and passion are embedded in their understandings.

As feminist theorists of science and technology have argued, the production of
embodied subjects can usefully be envisaged as a dialogue between technologies,
bodies, discourses and their limits, where the boundaries between the body, the
subject, and the practice of technology are points of mutual construction, if they
can be considered discrete at all (Haraway 1985; Stone 1995b). The embodied
subjects revealed by the utterances of these users emerge from these processes as
multiple, fluid, and open to dispute. Self-knowingly embodied by no one, the subject positions of the magician, the apprentice, and the inept are fleetingly inscribed
in flesh. Predicated on contingent social practices, they form embodied subjects
who implicitly challenge the singular unitary body of masculinist Cartesian

thought. The practice of GIS at SNH can only be understood as a result of the (re)productive relations between embodied subjects and the technologies they use.

NOTES

1. GIS includes hardware and software that captures, manages, analyses, and displays specific types of spatially referenced data. For a more complete, straightforward definition of the technical configuration see Martin (1991).

2. ArcView was launched in the mid-1990s by its vendor ESRI as a "sister" product to the technically sophisticated ArcInfo, which was already established as a market leader. This strategy reflected a perceived need to provide a more user-friendly and accessible product to reach a wider user base. Unlike ArcInfo, which requires a mainframe and significant computing resources, ArcView can run on a desktop PC/laptop. Functionality in ArcView is limited in comparison to ArcInfo, and the package is far simpler to learn and does not require programming skills.

3. Pseudonyms have been used throughout.

III

KNOWLEDGES AND SUBJECTIVITIES

8

Performing Art and Identities: Artists of Palestinian Origin in Canada

Mona Marshy

Art represents attempts on the part of artists, as well as audiences, to engage with notions that are beyond words and, thereby, to create spaces for new subjectivities and identities. In this chapter I argue that works of art, performances, and exhibits are imbued with discursive meanings, representing rituals of inscribing borders and thematizing issues salient to particular communities and constitutive of differences within communities. Artistic productions and performances have a role to play in the constitution of narratives of the past and "ways of being" in relation to these narratives and discourses.

This chapter explores the musical performances and narratives of three artists of Palestinian origin living in Canada. All are musicians and singers and one is also a dancer. The aim is to examine the mutually constitutive form, content, and performance of art, together with the artists' narrative accounts of their work, identities, and attempts to create audiences. In so doing I illustrate the interweaving of their "memory work" and exile biographies, refracted through works and performances, in the context of the political and cultural transnational economies that shape sites of performance. Through this I aim to show how invention, memory, and transnational political geography articulate identities, subjectivities, communities of belonging, and artistic spaces. This is illustrated, in particular, through issues of language and "authenticity" that arise in each of the artists' performances.

The chapter is divided into three sections. The first conceptualizes exile and memory as constitutive of Palestinians' experience of loss and identity. The second section looks at three musicians of Palestinian origin living in Canada, in terms of the content, form, and performance of their works, their narratives of loss and belonging, and the multidimensionality of the performance sites in which they perform. The third section discusses the role of art in constructing spaces of subjectivity and oppositional narratives.

EXILE IDENTITY, MEMORY, AND CREATIVITY

Identity is always historically and spatially contingent, provisional, and hybrid. I use the term identification as well as identity to convey the individual's provisional self-positioning within multiple networks and discourses. There is a tendency to view identity as constructed by what are assumed to be homogenous national attributes. On the other hand, the very provisionality of identity is, for Palestinians, complicated by the historical condition of an unresolved national struggle, and unrecognized, "hidden transcripts" (Scott 1990) of national narratives. That is, Palestinians are dispersed throughout the world[1] and, since the signing of agreements between Israel and the Palestinian leadership in September 1993,[2] their national aspirations are largely negotiated within discourses and political economies of Western neo-imperialism.

The term "exile" is used by Palestinians of the two generations born since their dispossession and exile in 1948. Rupture from the physical and cultural "home" remains central to constructions of Palestinians' national identity because of their expulsion and dispersion to numerous countries around the world. Indeed, exile is the experience of all Palestinians, including those living in the West Bank and Gaza and within Israel.[3]

JanMohamed (1992: 101) describes exile as:

> [T]he absence of "home," of the cultural matrix that formed the individual subject; hence, it implies an involuntary or enforced rupture between the collective subject of the original culture and the individual subject.

A nostalgia for what is lost and an indifference to the values and characteristics of the host country also characterize the exile. The immigrant, on the other hand, has a voluntary directedness toward the host culture (JanMohamed 1992). While exile is associated with not being able to return to one's country, and migration with some degree of choice, the exile, I would contend, also actively engages with the new environment and is inducted through institutional processes and national discourses into what it means to be part of the national context in which he or she lives and engages with inter- and intracultural processes. As I will illustrate, this engagement produces new artistic forms and generates new positionings of the self and the collective.

Part of what reproduces Palestinian identity in exile is the taking on of the burden of memory. Jean Said Makdisi (1990: 32), a Palestinian writer living in Beirut, writes, "To have been born in Palestine means to be bound to a memory and to a sense of loss." Makdisi tells how her father's recounting of his childhood memories represented a passing on of the burden of identity: "in passing his memories on to me, he passed also the burden of memory, central to the Palestinian experience" (40). Memory is understood here as a response to and a symptom of a rupture or absence as well as "a substitute, surrogate, or consolation for something that is missing" (Bardenstein 1999: 148, citing Zemon Davis and Starn 1989). Memory and its representation are directly linked to questions of subjectivity, nationalism, power, and authority and to the consolidating or constructing of group or national identities (Said 1999a; Swedenberg 1995).

Edward Said (1999a: 13) elaborates this aspect of memory, noting that, far from inert or passive, memory is a "field of activity" that selects, reconstructs, maintains, modifies, and endows the past with political meaning. Further, "memories of the past invoke narratives of the nation's past, shaping notions of what 'we' and 'they' are" (5). Memory is a site of hegemonic struggle and, in the words of anthropologist Ted Swedenberg (1995: xxix), "a fluid ideological terrain where differences between dominant and subordinate are played out." This discussion is also informed by a conceptualization of memory as present and future oriented, enabling groups to define and recognize themselves through time and as directly linked to language and representation. Maurice Halbwachs (1992: 173) notes that "[w]e speak of our recollections before calling them to mind. It is language, and the whole system of social conventions attached to it, that allows us at every moment to reconstruct our past." Memory, then, is more than the content of what is remembered. Rather, it is integral to the fraught nature of representation (Said 1999a: 4) and to the constitution and contestation of predominant and oppositional narratives and discourses. And, finally, memory is transnational, which, as Swedenberg (1995) cautions, is largely ignored. This is particularly relevant to the Palestinian situation, for which memory is multidimensional, displaced, and articulating with local as well as global scales.

In the past five decades, Palestinian collective memory has been exalted more through oral than visual means. In the words of artist Kamal Boullata (1993: 68), the poet, more than the image maker, has the power to move "the Palestinian soul." Words, text, calligraphy, the sound and musicality of the language, and literary imagery have infused all forms of art by Palestinians. Artistic creations of the first generation of Palestinians who were displaced and dispossessed were a direct response to the loss of "home" as well as of "self."[4] Literary representations of "home" invoke the loss of connection to the physical and social environment, as well as the distance between past and present (Elmessiri and Elmessiri 1996: 18–19). The language itself can symbolize home as well as return.[5]

For Palestinians, dispossession and loss, representations of "home," and memory, including the "postmemory" of generations born after 1948, are intertwined and mutually constitutive. I borrow the term "postmemory" from Marianne Hirsch's (1998) reference to the separation and exile experienced by children of parents who have survived trauma. She notes that the children of Holocaust survivors, exiled from a world that has ceased to exist, have "a different desire, at once more powerful and more conflicted: the need not just to feel and to know [their parents' world before it was destroyed], but also to re-member, to re-build, to re-incarnate, to replace and to repair . . . memory is necessarily an act not only of recall, but also of mourning" (Hirsch 1998: 420). Palestinians born after the 1948 *necba*[6] or disaster attempt to "re-member" themselves to their pasts and future through their parents' traumatic rupture.

The postmemory or re-membering work of the artists discussed in this chapter is complicated by the fact that Palestinians, like other colonized peoples, have been denied a "remembered presence." As Said (1999b: 12) elaborates, "perhaps the greatest battle Palestinians have waged as a people has been over the right to a remembered presence, and with that presence, the right to possess and reclaim a collective historical reality." As the Palestinian national struggle becomes increasingly constricted by intensified military occupation and oppression,[7] the strategic importance of asserting narratives of Palestinian national identity increases.

The underlying political economy of Palestinian cultural productions and performance shapes the discursive context in which art is performed as well as the narrative space and vocabularies of art by artists of Palestinian origin. Art forms and performance can serve as sites for interjecting alternate readings of national (both Canadian and Palestinian) narratives. Further, artists' "play" with forms and sites of performance serves to dissipate several constructed binaries such as between "political" or "conceptual" art, and between "Palestinian" or "Canadian" enactments of identity. The following section looks more closely at the works and sites of performance of three musicians of Palestinian origin living in Canada.

SUBJECTIVITIES AND ART IN
THE PERFORMANCE OF IDENTITIES

While this section is structured around three musicians' "stories," a preexisting or static "Palestinian" identity on the part of the artists or their art is by no means assumed. On the other hand, as I show, each musician negotiates and embodies cultural and national trajectories of the historical Palestinian national struggle. The three artists[8] were born of parents who lived in historic Palestine; they themselves were born in the Arab world (two in Beirut, one in Kuwait). They are practicing musicians living in Canada and range in age from mid-twenties to mid-thirties. They all sing and compose music and lyrics, and one also incorporates dance into her band's performances.

Brief biographical sketches of the musicians are included. While I do not wish to privilege biography as an analytical tool, it is important to recognize the role of cultural performance and products in providing "immense opportunities for rewriting culture through our concerns and our journeys" (Rogoff 2000: 30). These journeys and concerns, artistic choices and performances, narrative searchings, and the multidimensional sites of performance all form part of what Said (1993: 20) refers to as "the map of interactions, the actual and often productive traffic occurring on a day-by-day, and even minute-by-minute basis among states, societies, groups, identities."

Interviews with artists were audio taped and segments of the transcripts are quoted at length to examine some of this "traffic" and to inquire "into what is hidden in language, what is deferred by signs, what is pointed to, what is repressed, implicit, or mediated" (Fischer 1986: 198). What might appear to be the individual's autobiographical searchings turn out to be, Fischer notes, "revelations of traditions, re-collections of disseminated identities . . . retrospection to gain a vision for the future. . . . The searches also turn out to be powerful critiques of several contemporary rhetorics of domination" (198).

My own renderings of the artists' works and their "re-collections" and searchings is informed by a certain "autobiographical reading." Hirsch (1998: 403) notes that "imaginative projection of the self onto another identity probably accompanies all reading of stories, and to that degree all reading can be considered autobiographical; but the strongest kind of autobiographical reading occurs when the reader's life story actually intersects in some significant way with the story she is reading." My half-Canadian, half-Palestinian origin perhaps fuels my own compelling interest in looking at Palestinian identity and, in particular, at the role of art and its performance as sites of negotiation and re-membering, or of ambiguity and regeneration.

Julian

Julian is "from" Nazareth. That is, his family fled Nazareth in 1948 and he was born and raised in Beirut. He left Lebanon in his teens to study music in Athens and Moscow and returned to live and work as a musician in Beirut during the civil war in Lebanon. Julian emigrated to Montreal in 1994, and four years later moved to Ottawa. He plays the *oud* and guitar, as well as the *bazouk*, an ancient instrument with only one string.

While he continues to give concerts, Julian stopped writing lyrics since the Oslo agreements were signed in 1993 between the Palestinian Liberation Organization and the Israeli government.[9] Like many of his musician friends in Beirut, he stopped writing songs because he felt he had nothing to say. He said:

Since 1980, we used to play music for a certain cause, for Palestine, for justice, for peace. But after Oslo . . . what are we going to say to the audience, to the people? That everything we were singing to you was a big lie? . . . I used to write about Palestine, about returning to Palestine, about refugees, about home, about Communism, about international solidarity. Now, I'm unable to write any lyrics about these issues. There's no communism. There's no cause for us as Palestinians. We lost our cause. . . . Songs and poems should talk about the future, not open up history. . . . So instead I'm writing music . . . and everybody has to imagine the lyrics. . . . we have nothing left to say.

The name of his forthcoming instrumental CD is *Yarayar*, an Arabic word meaning circles, and he explained that "you go around in circles and you don't reach anywhere."

Julian's sense of dissociation from the predominant framework of the Palestinian struggle is accompanied by a poignant alienation he feels in Canada:

I'm hoping to write [lyrics] but I'm unable to feel. . . . I believe this country took something from me from inside. I feel myself from inside very very cold . . . empty, without feelings. . . . If you want to write something you have to feel it first of all, you have to live what you are writing.

He uses memories in the production of his work to fashion a creative and perhaps emotional space to mitigate his sense of alienation in Canada: "For [composing] music, I'm depending now on my imagination, what happened, what I used to do, what I saw, the people I used to know, the people I love and am unable to see again." One particularly moving song Julian played for me was composed with the experience of his mother's labor and birth of him in his mind. The piece is instrumental, and, as I listened to it with Julian, he very movingly narrated the story of his relationship to his mother, with different segments of the song corresponding to his mother's labor, his birth, childhood, and adolescence. The piece was composed in Canada.

In moving from Beirut to Canada, the motivation behind his music shifted from singing for the return to Palestine toward exposing Canadians and Americans to Arabic culture. He feels that too little is known of Arabic music in the West, and said, "maybe they will understand us more, through this music." Julian plans a CD of songs with lyrics taken from English translations of poems by Mahmoud Darwish and Tawfiq Zayyad, two of the most prominent Palestinian poets. This music will be aimed at non-Arab North Americans. Julian said "so, I have in mind that if I want to sing again the audience will have to be non-Arabs. Non-Arabs have no idea about [Palestinian] history. Most of them don't have a clear idea."

Music, art, and culture, then, become conscious conduits of historical, Palestinian national memory. Through music, he will "go through their door, their wall" and have Western culture pay heed to his own Arabic culture. He plays Arabic scales on Western instruments and Western scales on Arabic instruments to attune audiences to Arabic music. He has played several concerts in Quebec and won first prize at the Montreal Jazz Festival in 1995 in a competition of thirty countries. He recounted to me in detail the scenario at the festival, which symbolizes to him the need to protect his heritage. At the event, a few performances before his own, a Jewish musician from Paris played a song by Said Darweish, a well-known Egyptian musician who is considered the father of modern Arabic music. Julian described the event in the following exchange:

Julian: She played the piece by Said Darweish and said that it's a Jewish traditional song. So I was shocked. I spoke with my friends, told them we have to do something. I said, "I'm going to play the same piece of music, we don't have to practice." We didn't practice. I wrote the notes in five minutes, then I told them "play the way you want to but what is important for me is to get the melody and I'm going to play the melody." I told the audience that I was very impressed because I'm playing with a Jewish musician in the same concert and her songs were very very beautiful. I said she played a song by Said Darweish, who died in 1923. Said Darweish . . . bla bla. I told them who he was. So I started to play this piece with Oriental instruments. She used a guitar. We started to play with the *oud* and *bazouka*.

Mona: And it was the very same piece of music that she'd played?

Julian: Yes, the same piece. But because she's French, she couldn't sing the *'orab*, something the Arabs have in their throat because of the language. So the audience was shocked because of the [power of the] music itself.

Before and after the performance, journalists attempted to have Julian and the Jewish musician shake hands for the cameras.[10] Julian relayed to me that she had refused to shake his hand following his performance, but that the president of the Canadian Jewish Congress had introduced himself to Julian after the performance and congratulated him. Julian replied, "Thank you, at least I protect my heritage." Julian's assertion of cultural integrity and "his heritage" is an attempt to counter the denial of Palestinian national peoplehood perceived to be affected in part by the theft of Palestinian cultural integrity and traditions.[11]

At the site of his performance, then, is a convergence of competing discourses of Palestinian and Jewish "peoplehood," media and public engagement in the "rivalry" of these discourses, underlying power relations in the Palestinian-Israeli conflict, and artists' attempts to engage the audience in a powerful and transcending way through music and performance. The artistic expression of memory remains a powerful avenue of engagement for artist and audience alike. Its power derives, perhaps, from the fact that only communally do we remember. As Maurice Halbwachs (1992: 52–53) argues, individual memory depends for its articulation on the social groups to which the memories belong. The overwhelmingly positive response by the audience to the beauty and power of his performance serves to reinforce Julian of his role as a conveyor of greater understanding. The songs performed by Julian provide avenues for shared emotional experience as markers of likeness and identification vis-à-vis the self and other. Asserting "his heritage" enables a re-membering of his sense of belonging and role within the Palestinian as well as Canadian lexicons.

Dalia

Dalia is an award-winning classical pianist turned aspiring popular rock singer.[12] Like Julian, Dalia was born in Beirut, but she grew up in Saudi Arabia and moved with her family to Canada when she was fifteen. Now in her twenties, she lives with her parents and two sisters in suburban Montreal. She plays guitar and is the singer in a four-piece band that is producing their first demo-tape.

Whereas Julian's identity was shaped within a highly charged context of civil war in Lebanon, Dalia grew up in Saudi Arabia, feeling disengaged from her culture and Palestinian identity. She went to an English-speaking British school in Saudi Arabia, does not read Arabic or listen to Arabic music, and was, in her words, "totally caught in the middle." She describes: "My parents lost their homes, their homeland . . . this forms who I am. My identity has also been shaped by being non-Saudi and non-Muslim." She is now consciously exploring her Palestinian cultural heritage by seeking out English translations of Palestinian national poets.

Dalia initially trained and excelled as a classical pianist, winning first place in a Quebec provincial competition, but decided to branch out into other forms of music. She recalled two incidents that had a bearing on switching musical genres from classical to pop:

> I remember one incident at a mall where I was doing a gig for the Alzheimer's Association. A woman in the audience asked me where I was from. When I said I was Palestinian, she said, "oh there are too many Arabs and Indians in Canada." Another incident, at McGill [University] served to shape what I would like to achieve through my music. A poster with my picture on it announcing a recital was sliced through with a razor. A friend and I taped it up again but it was soon after shredded up angrily and left on the wall. I put another one up to replace it and the same thing happened. This contributed to why I didn't continue to do a Masters in classical music.

She decided she wanted to reach the younger North American Arab public, explaining that, "there is a lot out there for young Jews, for young Italians where they can enjoy their culture. But with our culture, it's hard to separate out the politics." Wanting to reach Arab youth and provide some cultural referents for them, she began herself to "get in touch with my culture," but her link to her culture was problematic:

> I found my friends felt I wasn't really Arabic as I don't speak Arabic. I understand everything that is spoken to me but I respond in English and don't listen to Arabic music. Hence, to some of them, how could I be Arabic?

Not able to read Arabic "properly," she searched in the Middle East bookstore in Montreal and discovered the poetry of Mahmoud Darwish translated into English. She has put English translations of several Mahmoud Darwish poems to music.

Dalia's musical production is divided into two segments. First there are songs she writes herself and performs with her four-member band. The lyrics to these songs allude only very vaguely to the Palestinian cause. Second she performs songs, the lyrics of which are English translations of poetry by Mahmoud Darwish. She plays songs from both groups at gatherings of mostly Arab audience members, but at general student venues she plays songs only from the former group because "when I play for a generic audience, I feel I can't be too Arabic. I thought about changing my name so it wouldn't be so Arabic, and may still, but someone said that 'ethnic is in.' . . . It's hard to find a way of gaining credibility."

The contradiction embedded in this division in her work becomes apparent in her performance. Singing the latter, more political songs, she very powerfully captures audiences (according to my experience and my observation of other members of the audience). When I queried her about her ambivalence about performing the more political yet more moving pieces, she replied that "among Arabs there is a major fear that if anyone comes out and speaks they will be cut down. I don't want to be silenced before I can speak." She will "eventually work in a Middle Eastern influence" into her more popular songs, but has not yet decided how she will do this.

Dalia is now focusing on producing three "radio-friendly" songs. I was aware of an irony, after seeing her in concert a few times, that her desire to be "an Alanis Morriset" (that is, very famous on the basis of her embodiment of and appeal to a kind of raw energy) is being hampered by her anticipation of what she believes audiences are able to accept in terms of her Palestinian identification. She is keeping her more passionate performances and songs under wraps, so to speak, while the more "radio-friendly" songs may not have the raw energy and passion in them to "hook" an audience. When I suggested as much to her, she relayed that she is "chameleon-like" with her music, adapting it to her environment, "because that is what my life has been like. No real place is home."

One of Dalia's two main corporate sponsors stopped its support following a concert that was preceded by a screening of a film of Edward Said's return visit to his homeland. Shortly thereafter, Dalia expressed her resignation that she would subvert her "voice" to the proclivities of the music industry:

> I feel now I will have to find a way of distancing myself from the Palestinian cause and from identifying as Palestinian, which hurts me. The reason is financial, the sponsors, the business of music. The people who will be able to take my voice and put it out there have the general public to contend with.

She is still planning a CD of songs from Mahmoud Darwish poems but, because of the perceived career costs, she intends to produce it under an assumed name. Edward Said's (1993: 80) words are again brought to mind: "the 'what' and 'how' in the representation of 'things,' while allowing for considerable individual freedom, are circumscribed and socially regulated." Dalia's decisions and artistic production reflect the ongoing negotiation of social regulation through her own subjectivity, identity, and performances.

Rima

Rima is a dancer as well as a musician with two bands. One is a three-piece group that performs a kind of music called Mowashahat, consisting of Sufi devotional poetry put to music. The style was developed in Andalusia around the twelfth and thirteenth centuries in Moorish Spain (though some Mowashahs appeared in Egypt and Iraq as early as the ninth century). Rima and the band's other singer trained in Toronto and Aleppo, Syria, and are among a handful of musicians around the world who have begun to revive Mowashahat. The musical form necessitated a movement away from the old Arabic poetic forms and meters and toward new ones designed to be set to music. A revival of the style occurred in Aleppo in the nineteenth century and continues to be performed in parts of North Africa. The other band Rima plays in is an eleven-piece band that plays Greek, Arabic, and other music from various parts of the world.

For the purposes of this chapter, my focus is on Rima's musical and dance performance with the three-piece band. Its performances are passionate, and, in my experience, have a kind of hypnotic or mesmerizing effect on audiences. What is also remarkable is a striking playfulness interjected between and throughout pieces, which are performed with apparent love and devotion on the part of the band members.

Rima was born in Kuwait and, after the accidental death of her father when she was one month old, left with her mother to live in Amman, Jordan. When she was five years old, she settled with her mother, aunt, and grandmother in urban Toronto. After a personally difficult time in her twenties, she turned to dance and singing as a means of "grounding" herself. She had been living as a full-time artist for five years when I interviewed her. While she defines herself as a dancer primarily, Rima sings in both bands and has a background in theater and film, having appeared in several plays and in Canadian Armenian filmmaker Atom Egoyan's film *Calendar*. She also teaches classes that incorporate Middle Eastern dance and yoga, as well as creative movement and music to children.

Issues of language and authenticity arise in particular ways in Rima's work and narrative. Rima's band sings in Arabic, each of the members having come to the language late in life. She is very conscious of the musicality inherent in the language itself and of the moving effect of the music, but feels slightly removed from knowing precisely how the experience of hearing Arabic singing affects Arabic-speaking audiences. She says:

> All you have is a sense that there's importance here and you may not even know what it is in terms of how it emanates and affects the audiences or the people who come into contact with what you do. But you just have to follow the feeling that this matters, and that it is a gift from history that's come to you and that you have to honor it in how you present it within the context of who you are and your life and what's available to you.

Singing in Arabic connects them to, as well as differentiates them from, their Arabic-speaking audiences that "notice where we excel with the language and where we're deficient in the language." For Rima, the band's tackling of the language and music is a mutually constituting endeavor between the band members' Torontonian selves and their connection to the cultural heritage that Mowashahat music represents for them. She explains:

> We are in a position to take traditions associated with our cultural heritage and bring them across the borders that we've traveled across and I feel we are able to do that because we are so here and I feel like our taste artistically, our humor, our irony, all these things that develop from being downtown Torontonian people give us a perspective even in terms of making music more modern or bringing it across to the West . . . being able to send up where you come from but lovingly, or being able to celebrate and laugh at where you are because you're also there and you love it.

During the second of two sets of music performed by the band, Rima performs an Eastern dance, or belly dance, as it is known in the West. From my perspective in the audience of a performance in a small town in Quebec, Rima's dance seemed to take some people by surprise, and I felt a certain suspended atmosphere in the venue.[13] As I watched Rima, I was also uncomfortably conscious of

Hollywood images of the Arab belly dancer. I assumed that the audience, too, was viewing her dance through a similarly projected "veil" of Hollywood stereotypes, but realized that was not necessarily the case when a friend I sat with, who grew up in Canada and is of Egyptian origin and was making a concerted study of Rima's hand and foot movements, declared to me that her performance was not authentic.

When I interviewed Rima at the end of the evening in a nearby restaurant, I relayed my friend's comment and she responded:

> Oriental dance, the "belly-dance" is a hybrid form. It's borrowed. . . . It's definitely got Indo-Persian influence and African influence and other influences and my aesthetic is very influenced by court dance traditions and Indian dances and I know that. But I don't feel that it makes it less authentic. I feel that it's personal and also very connected to the music. Also, I study with the "authentic" people of belly dance as much as I can and I feel what stays with me and what comes out of me, especially when I improvise, is what's supposed to be there and what doesn't seem to latch onto my soul as part of my personal aesthetic other people can do it.

I also tried to get at the elusive subject of women's sexuality and provocative power that the dance form reflects and also constitutes:

Rima: Dance is a whole other mysterious thing in Arabic culture, how this icon of the dancer has survived and it's just incredible, and there's such a love-hate relationship with it.

Mona: Do you have a love-hate relationship with it yourself?

Rima: I do, for sure. I feel that in myself. . . . If I see a wonderful, beautiful woman who's got all this wonderful freedom and control in her body and who goes up and starts popping her boobs in some guy's face who's drinking Johnny Walker red or something, I don't care if what she's doing is harder than anyone in the room can do, for me I literally feel like I could start crying because it bothers me. And yet I kind of don't judge it because you know maybe this woman can handle that and for her it's celebratory. For me it bugs me. I can't go there. So I don't know, it's hard. . . . I mean there is tremendous passion and sensuality and tremendous cultural multiple personality going on among the Arabs. So women who come out and slap it on the table are saying part of the truth.

Said (1999b) notes that most of the belly dancers in the West seem to be non-Arab, lots of Russians, Americans, Ukrainians, Armenians, and French. He also suggests that belly dance (at least some performances of it, for example, those by legendary Egyptian belly dancer Tahia Carioca) is untranslatable and part of the "closed off areas" of Arab culture. Rima's performances, because she is perceived as embodying Arabic culture, serve to redefine the significance and space of the dance by some Arab audience members. Rima recounts one woman's reaction to her dance performance and the perceived need to keep it in a reputable space:

> I got this fantastic phone call from this Lebanese woman who told me a thousand times, "Rima whatever you are doing I don't know what you are doing but it's high art. You have to take this seriously, you must never do it where people are eating and drinking!" Maybe the bottom line was don't do it in the night clubs or something.

The issue of authenticity also arises with regard to Rima's self-identification. She says, of her Palestinian origin:

> I have a lot of strong emotions about it . . . and I feel an empathy for my family who is there and the people who are there but I feel like I'm such a diluted version of that struggle. . . . I can't begin to appreciate what it was like to live through the Intifada. I haven't made a big sweeping Palestinian statement in my art yet, and maybe I will in a way some day. I don't know how yet exactly. . . . I hope to find some way of expressing my Palestinianness in a way that's celebratory and humanizing and not just about presenting the political struggle. . . . It's always with me, though, I definitely feel that.

ART, EXILE, AND OPPOSITIONAL NARRATIVES

Musical and dance performance are means of articulating, regenerating, and redrawing subjectivities in relation to various cultural, social, and political lexicons. The musicians considered in this chapter reflect differing ways in which these lexicons are "played" artistically. The three artists rejoin experience and cultural expression in ways that highlight the complexities in lived subjectivities and performed identities.

Stokes (1994: 5) notes that music is socially meaningful "not entirely, but largely because it provides means by which people recognise identities and places, and the boundaries which separate them" (also see chapter 4 in this volume). Music and its performance both constitute as well as transgress boundaries, engaging the audience in the blurring of the sensual and the political. For example, Julian consciously takes on the burden of memory in order to "protect his heritage" and try to convey to audiences that Arab culture is "more than just belly-dancers." Alternatively, Rima pushes the boundaries of form in her belly dance, bypasses the stereotype by reinfusing into the dance various cultural influences and re-creating it (re-membering it to the audience) as an art form. Rima "stays true" to the mixing of influences that comprise the dance form to engage audiences on a human level, rather than a nationalist one. She says of her music and dance performance: "I feel like this is a humanizing experience and I feel like it is for the audience."

Liz Stanley and Sue Wise's (1993: 195) conceptualization of "self" is borne out in this study. That is, subjectivity is "historically, culturally and contextually specific and also subtly changing in different interactional circumstances." I would argue, nonetheless, that the evolving constitution of the self is shaped also by dualistic binaries. Bodies, for example, become invested with differences that are seen to be fundamental ontological differences (Gatens 1996: 73). Moreover, bodies are necessarily gendered. The role of women as reproducers of boundaries of ethnic and national groups (Walby 1996; Nash 1994; Yuval-Davis and Anthias 1989) and of delineating difference between East and West (Ahmed 1982; Kabbani 1986) renders Rima's performances potentially potent spaces of cultural signification and perception of difference between and within Arab and Canadian audiences. At the same time, Rima's concern with seeking her own way within the traditional forms of music and dance she performs enables her to find and articulate different balances between the universality of artistic appeal, the symbolic power of representations, and the specificity of her own "take" on forms of dance and music, including her renditions of the ever-evolving traditions and movements that constitute the dance form.

Pierre Nora (1989: 15) writes that "There are *lieux de mémoire,* sites of memory, because there are no longer *milieux de mémoire,* real environments of memory." Artists of Palestinian origin living in Canada live multiple exiles and are removed in multiple ways from the environments of memory that underlie their identification as Palestinian. Julian, for example, was exiled in Lebanon as a Palestinian refugee. Because of his activism he is unable to return to Lebanon. He is exiled in Canada from his Arabic culture, language, and communities. And, politically, since the signing of the Oslo agreements, which he does not support, he is living in exile from the Palestinian cause that infused his musical life in Lebanon. Nonetheless, through the "space-making" capacity of art and performance, spaces or "milieus" are indeed created that remember and regenerate subjectivities, identities, and artistic vocabularies of self and belonging.

Julian is attempting to create audiences that connect emotionally to Arabic culture and Palestinian cultural forms. Music communicates what cannot be spoken: referring to black music in the United States, Susan Smith (1997: 517) notes that its power "lies in its ability to go beyond the spoken word, expressing emotion, easing pain, sharing experience." The potential of music to function as a bridge of cultural experience and, by extension, to effect identifications beyond the emotional is partly what is at stake for artists like Julian, whose artistic and political commitments are closely tied. Through his performance, Julian attempts to create a space for a Palestinian narrative of loss. He consciously uses his music as a means of interjecting a narrative that is outside of the predominant historical knowledge and also distinct from some predominant Palestinian narratives. For Rima, emotional connection remains a powerful avenue through which to engage audiences with regard to apparently wider "humanizing experiences."

Art and performance enable ever new weavings of individual subjectivities with national narratives. A question that arises concerns how and when these weaves or, to use Said's (1993) term, "traffic" of cultural products and performances represent interjections of alternate narratives. Dalia's desire to change her name reveals how she continues, in Canada, to feel "caught in the middle." Her desire to integrate her Palestinianness into her music is at odds with what she sees as an Orientalist context of the music industry and her potential audience. Art and cultural production in the West takes place within the framework of universalizing discourses which, in Said's words, "assume the silence of the non-European world . . . and only infrequently acknowledges that colonized people should be heard from, their ideas known" (1993: 58). Dalia negotiates space for her Palestinian identity and subjectivity through the form and content of her art and through mechanisms of self-representation.

Dalia eventually changed the spelling of her last name (from a common Arab family name to one that has the same pronunciation but appears distinctly Irish), to render it "more friendly" to promoters and audiences. She also decided to limit her performances of her moving "Mahmoud Darwish songs." These decisions reflect her perception of the receptivity to her voice as a Palestinian in Canada.[14] Julian's hope that "maybe they [the West] will understand us more" is up against a proliferation of "world music" in the West that serves, according to Ted Swedenberg (1999), to "gut" Arabic music of its cultural or contextual meaning. "Arab World Music" is being marketed and consumed in such a way that an audience is being created for the sounds of the music at the expense of the cultural or contextual meaning behind the music. It is used in odd spots in film soundtracks, providing the aural backdrop as the space battle scene is set at the start of the American-made film *The Fifth Element*. Or Mowashahat music is played during terrorist attacks (Swedenberg 1999). Alongside this, the greater interest in belly dance in the West can be at least partly attributed to the creation of audiences and interest generated by "world music" and the "global music and art scene." Rima noted that:

> We're starting to get a certain kind of recognition and a certain kind of respect. And you know "world music" or the global music scene certainly helps a lot. I think the last time there was a wave of interest in belly dance was the "kitsch" phenomenon in the 1960s and 1970s. Now I think it's grounded in something that is taken much more seriously.

Borrowing James C. Scott's (1990) terms, the musicians' cultural narratives negotiate hegemonic "public transcripts" that reflect the wider context of their production. In Scott's wide-ranging study of resistance, "hidden transcripts are the 'infrapolitics of subordinate groups' since they register the defiance that the subordinate practice in secret, out of the view of the dominant power" (19). To offset cultural colonization, a means must be found for "a public declaration of the hidden transcript" (202). Indeed, with regard to art and musical performance, "hidden" and "public" transcripts coexist in complex interaction and articulate with and through embodied memory, personal histories, national narratives, transnational power relations, and art forms. The artists and art works looked at above serve to challenge binaries of "cultural" and "political," disturb the notion of a homogenized "other," further trajectories of the "question of Palestine," and suggest subjectivities and means of artistic engagement that are, potentially, spaces of resistance.

Artistic forms and performances of the artists discussed in this chapter are constituted through the artists' attempts to create audiences and widen vocabularies of artistic expression, the interplay of intracultural and artistic processes, various perceptions of denial of Palestinian aspirations, and national as well as transnational dimensions of power. Invention, memory, and transnational political geography, then, play out artistically to constitute identities, subjectivities, communities of belonging, and artistic expression.

NOTES

1. The war of 1948, which led to the creation of the State of Israel, resulted in the dispossession and expulsion of about 750,000 indigenous Palestinians (about 60 percent of the population) from 20 cities and about 400 villages. Of this population, about one-third fled to the West Bank, another third to the Gaza Strip, and the remainder to Jordan, Syria, Lebanon, and farther afield. In 1967, another 300,000 Palestinians fled from the West Bank and Gaza, to Jordan (200,000), Syria, Egypt, and elsewhere. Of these, about 180,000 were first-time refugees ("displaced persons"), while the remainder were 1948 refugees uprooted for the second time (Palestine Refugee ResearchNet). By 1982, 40.5 percent of Palestinians lived in historic Palestine, that is, within Israel and its occupied territories; 25.1 percent in Jordan; 10.4 percent in Lebanon; 6.4 percent in Kuwait; 4.8 percent in Syria; 7.3 percent in other Arab countries; 2.1 percent in the United States, and 3.0 percent in other non-Arab countries such as Canada, Australia, Germany, and Chile (Bowman 1994: 139). The Palestinian population is estimated at 6.6 million as of 1995 (Palestine Refugee ResearchNet). The average estimate by Canadian Arab organizations of the number of Palestinians living in Canada is about 70,000.

2. The Oslo Accords, also known as the Declaration of Principles signed August 20, 1993, came to the attention of the world on September 13 of that year when they were publicly signed by Palestinian and Israeli leaders on the White House lawn. Under great media attention, the agreement brought the Palestinian-Israeli conflict into the international arena at a time when American predominance was rising and the former Soviet Union's influence diminishing. The accord and its various successor agreements mention UN Security Council Resolutions 242 and 338 as the basis of negotiations, but the agreements have also served to precondition the attainment of Palestinian national aspirations (to self-determination and return of refugees to their homes) on the basis of negotiations between Israel, the occupying power and, vastly more powerful, the Palestinians, who remain under Israeli military occupation.

3. Palestinians in Israel are effectively living in exile. Anthropologist Glenn Bowman (1994: 139) notes that intense disruptions and dislocation, including the destruction of about 400 villages in 1948 alone, the mass relocation of populations, the destruction of agricultural communities that forced peasants into waged labor, the continuing and increasing expropriation of lands for military and settlement building, have led Palestinians "inside" (inside Israel), like those "outside," to perceive the territory that is the focus of their identity as mutilated and stolen. This view is held also by Palestinians living in their original homes within Israel who experience nonetheless a damaged connection to their history, language, culture, land, social relations and fabric, and Arab brethren in surrounding Arab countries.

4. The loss of "self" that accompanied dispossession for Palestinians was acute in the years following their uprooting. Anthropologist Rosemary Sayigh (1979: 107) writes: "The village—with its special arrangements of houses and orchards, its open meeting places, its burial

ground, its collective identity—was built into the personality of each individual villager to a degree that made separation like an obliteration of the self. In describing their first years as refugees, camp Palestinians use metaphors like 'death,' 'paralysis,' 'burial,' 'non-existence,' etc. . . . Thirty years after the uprooting, the older generation still mourns."

5. Referring to Palestinian writers in Israel, anthropologist Susan Slyomovics (1998: 172) notes that "Palestinian writing embraces the conviction that only the Arabic language, in either its classical or literary form, speaks the truth of the real inhabitants of the ancestral homeland." Further, many Palestinians who remained on the soil of historic Palestine seek consolation in the belief that the Israelis will never know or love the land as intimately as Palestinians or speak in accents appropriate to the place. Arab ruins, "carefully preserved by Palestinian Israeli artists, are 'faithful to their origins' even as they are inundated by a 'Babel of languages'" (172). This does not preclude the powerful use of the Hebrew language by Palestinian writers in Israel.

6. The term, literally meaning disaster, that is used by Palestinians to refer to the 1948 dispossession and dispersion.

7. While the interviews were conducted in 1999, at time of writing, the "second intifada" is entering its eighth month with devastating consequences and loss of life.

8. These interviews were conducted between March and September 1999, in Montreal, Ottawa, and Wakefield, Quebec, in the musicians' homes, studios, or near places of performance. They were loosely structured in order to draw out the musicians' own narratives and links between their work, their identifications, and aspirations. With the artists' permission, I am using their real names.

9. Like other Palestinian refugees, the fate of (approximately) 200,000 Palestinians in Lebanon, living in very cramped refugee camps with no political and very few civil rights, was not decided but left to be addressed in future negotiations.

10. In the years following the signing of the Oslo and subsequent agreements, it was typical of the media to attempt to depict displays of rapprochement between Israeli and Palestinian counterparts of any public event.

11. For example, this denial is witnessed in such events, since the creation of Israel, as fashions shows held in Israel and internationally that present Palestinian embroidered dresses as "Israeli traditional costume."

12. This description of Dalia's aspirations, while accurate, makes me acutely (and uncomfortably) aware of my selective depictions of the musicians as "stories within stories" and a fetish that is inevitable in any representation.

13. The venue is the Black Sheep Inn (or *le mouton noire*) in Wakefield, a town in rural Quebec, north of Ottawa. The audience consisted of local artists, professional Anglophones who live in town and commute to work in Ottawa or Hull, local rural and working-class people, as well as, typically for the venue, a good number of people who drove up from Ottawa.

14. Although it remains beyond the scope of this chapter, the "Canadian" context needs to be unpacked to properly examine ways in which performance spaces and identities are constituted. To mention but one aspect of this context, the discourse of official Canadian multiculturalism contributes to ways in which audiences and artists are mutually perceived. For example, critics contend that the concept of multiculturalism, which centers around the binary of a visible/invisible populace, has the effect of entrenching difference by racializing divisions between people. Further, possibilities of self-naming in the constitution of identities are rendered less efficacious with the (legally) entrenching of *visual* dif-

ference (Synnott and Howes 1996: 138). Multiculturalism as a discourse affects what one is allowed to assert of oneself (Bissoondath 1994: 31). The entrenching of difference *between* groups, I would argue, has the effect of effacing difference within groups and communities, making subtleties of individual contestations and performances of culture and identities less apparent or "readable."

9

Tasteful Visions: The Cultivation of "an" Audience for Art

Anja-Maaike Green

This chapter has its origins in a remark made by a participant in an arts group for people with mental health problems with which I was involved as a student of community education. After my flustered introduction, the man said to me, "Oh and I suppose we are the community." It was a defining moment for me professionally and a decisive intervention, which cut to the heart of public service and community development as a powerful system of identification and prescription. The incident underpins my concern with how publicly subsidized art is produced, managed, and distributed within institutional and professional frameworks that invest art and its audiences with particular meanings. In this chapter I examine how attitudes toward different audiences drive and shape the type of art provided for them. I am interested in the ways in which the audience—as defined and targeted by government and the arts profession—is evaluated, codified, named, and positioned. By examining the discourses through which audiences are objectified, I hope to extend the understanding of subject formation within institutional contexts and the ways in which perceptions of different audience communities drive cultural development. I draw on material gathered when working as a local government arts officer, and also through participant observation conducted during Ph.D. research on publicly funded visual art in Edinburgh.[1]

I argue that the construction of audiences for art must be understood as having evolved within a wider history of social, ideological, and aesthetic organization. The meaning given to audiences cannot be separated from the meanings given to "art" and "non-art." Audiences are defined by their association with particular cultural forms, and consequently, cultural affiliation is crucial to subject forming practices. To this end, I explore the parameters of subjective possibility operating within the Edinburgh art world by looking at a number of key discourses pertaining to those who do not attend the arts and the models of practice that emerge from these. I focus on nonattenders because attitudes toward potential audiences are particularly revealing of disputes about the relative value of fine art and popular culture, and also because the art world is currently under pressure from government to broaden its appeal to wider sections of the population. Noticeably missing from my account, however, are the voices of audiences themselves, ever rendered silent within the practices of their own identification.

Notwithstanding this, in their various exaggerated guises, as "cultural Philistine," "glutton," "intellectual inadequate," and "impulsive child," the unmediated presence of nonattenders continues to be regarded by government and the art world as a threat. I suggest that this understanding is in part upheld by the repeated linking of the art world with legitimate culture, and nonattenders with impoverished forms of expression; art with excellence and diversity; and popular or commercial cultures with homogenization. It is also part of ongoing struggles for legitimization between cultural and professional groups, a project that accentuates the importance of subjectivity and the capacity to name others in processes of government and systems of authority. Constructions of a public for art continue to evolve, however, and I also stress that there are other, more progressive stories about nonattenders that circulate within the art world.

SUBJECTIVITY WITHIN INSTITUTIONAL AND PROFESSIONAL CONTEXTS

In his description of "the reflexive project of the self," Anthony Giddens (1991) outlines a theory of "institutional reflexivity" in which institutions absorb knowledge about social life and adjust their operative frameworks accordingly. Following this observation, it is possible to see how sociological notions about audience identities are inscribed into institutional frameworks and models of practice: institutions and professional spheres provide discursive narratives that enable their members to construct stories about themselves and others (Moores 1995: 14). Arts workers[2] and institutions are thus engaged in processes of interchange, swapping, constructing, and consolidating stories about their own and other selves. Notions of "the" audience are thus constituted through institutional and professional discourses as well as through the cultures and perceptual frameworks of those involved in the production of art; indeed, the two are inextricably intertwined. As such, the cultures and attitudes of arts workers themselves shape and give meaning to different models of audience development.

Drawing on Benedict Anderson's (1991) work on "imagined communities," it is possible to see how arts workers are involved in the production of imagined audiences. Government arts policy and arts professionals invent and project particular ideals of audience subjectivity whose fictional character and cultural designation are disguised within the "objective" language of public arts policy and practice (Ang 1996). Diverse audiences are therefore named and ordered through epistemological and institutional devices, which enable professionals to impose their own representational order onto others. Institutional and professional authority thus give credence and legitimacy to individual and collective opinion, working to solidify inequalities established in everyday life within the workings of state institutions. Policy making in this sense is a deeply subjective and political experience, reflecting the opinions and cultures of arts professionals, politicians, and civil servants, as much as the seemingly objective processes of public management. Long-standing feminist assertions about the personal as political clearly facilitate this view of policy as a personal and cultural, as well as political, enterprise (Shore and Wright 1997).

Max Weber (1978) referred to "value-rational" frameworks when discussing the expressive, emotionally driven, moral and symbolic undercurrents that drive and shape actions. Similarly, an awareness of the multidimensional sources and mixed substance of knowledge-based rationales can help to humanize policy-making processes and "draw-in" professional inclinations, rather than "paint-out" the personal from the governmental or professional. Government and professional power are not then limited to instrumental calculation, but extend into, and are reflective of, those involved. Discourses about the public are created and then impressed upon those who are subject to professional and government actions, although this mediation is by no means unidirectional (Durkheim 1982: 47). My interest here is partly in the ways in which audience subjectivities are institutionally crystallized, to use a Foucaultian term (Foucault 1981: 92–93), but also in the types of subjective possibilities that are generated, promoted, or closed down.

I have therefore established as a platform for discussion the assumption that institutions and professional networks produce subjectivities, and that practitioners' individual cultures work in continuity with institutional cultures in the production of particular audience subjectivities. How then do discourses about audiences materialize and progress? Power, as Foucault (1981) proposed, operates in subtle ways; it is exercised through formal regulatory regimes as well as bodies of people; it is diffused through diverse institutional sites; and it is expressed in many different forms. Bruno Latour (1993, 1999) has developed Foucault's account by overturning the primacy of human agency within his discursive, technique, and practice-oriented argument, by refusing to discriminate between objects and subjects. Latour argues that if we are to understand scientific, and in my case audience, rationalities, we must consider the role of nonhuman actors within evolving networks of activity. Policy documents may be inanimate, but they are nevertheless compelling sources of influence, guiding actions and framing arts development. Views and opinions about audiences dwell within the pages of these documents, as much as within the imaginations of arts workers and the ideologies of the body politic. In this way, texts and signifying practices, institutional regimes, aesthetic conventions, and the variety of means through which audience subjectivities are instantiated should be considered as part of the same process.

These conditions—the personal and institutional, objective and subjective, human and nonhuman—cannot be separated, but rather, work in integrated ways to produce and assert particular visions of the ideal audience for art. My commitment to policy as personal/political, in combination with Latour's and Foucault's works, encourages sensitivity to the generative links between apparently separate spheres of operation. According to Latour (1993), modernity represents a doomed attempt to impose oppositional order and separations onto a world as much governed by hybrid states, anomalies, and in-between entities as it is by predictable structures and simplistic relations between factors. Opinions about audiences therefore do not resonate from one or two central or discernible points. Methodologically this calls for an integrated view of the research field involving movement between different sources of evidence, blending expressed opinion alongside statistical information, and material from arts strategies with observations about types of art practice.

The rationalities that underpin assembling systems, such as government policies, perceptual frameworks, and models of art practice, are often implemented in arbitrary and corrupted ways (Czarniawska-Joerges 1992) and contain internal contradictions that defy attempts to impose order. Assumptions about continuity of cause and effect can be minimized by remaining conscious of points of resistance, failure, and unanticipated consequences (Latour 1993). Apparent anomalies, restrictions of context, persuasive tactics, random and contrived elements are not simply rogue factors, but are as much part of the process of subject formation as more consistent trends and occurrences. Notwithstanding this, it is possible to detect broad strands of thought and points of principle that undercut and cross between disparate discursive positions. It is the broad discursive registers that are mobilized to mark out "the" audience as an object of interest with which I am concerned in this chapter.

ARTISTS AND THEIR AUDIENCES

In contrast to mass media and forms of commercial culture, such as the music industry, which operate in a competitive market, historically there has not been an economic imperative for public art to engage with broader audiences. In the nineteenth century direct forms of patronage from the European aristocracy, church, and the state largely disappeared, and so did their entitlement to be the principal audiences for art (Bätschmann 1997). This, combined with the rise of romanticism, effectively removed the obligation for artists to serve an identifiable constituency and instead allowed them to dedicate themselves to a new conception of the artist as "someone whose production cannot be rationally directed towards any particular audience" (Rosler 1999: 320). "Unconcern with audience," Rosler (311) argues, "has become a necessary feature of art producers' professed attitudes and a central element of the ruling ideology of Western art." Indeed, according to O'Docherty (1999: 76), hostility toward the audience is one of the key coordinates of modernism, and artists and audiences perform a semiotic ritual of hostility in which audiences suppress extreme anger and artists fulfill expectations by being obtuse and irresponsible in return.

While in the twentieth and early twenty-first centuries, public art is made without a conscious, explicit, or specific audience in mind, commercial products are strongly determined by audience preference. Artistic success is not formally defined in terms of meeting audience needs or satisfying an existing market, but by producing work that has its own integrity, often despite possible friction with public interests. Art is an essentially bourgeois institution. In Edinburgh, for example, 80 percent of the arts audience is currently made up of 20 percent of the population.[3] This fact is erased by appeals to the universal value of art, as well as through reference to "the" audience as an undifferentiated social and cultural group. This does not, however, mean that artists ignore particular audiences. Rather, it is to propose that the influence of key groups, notably critics, peers, and the art market, remains hidden in order to maintain the illusion that art is freely conceived, immune to mass public demands, economic considerations, and the professional ambitions of the artist. The dignity of art is in large part dependent on the apparent autonomy of creative intention and action. The nonprofessional, nonbuying, nonspecialist public is effectively rendered invisible within the formulation and production of art works. Within the art world the public's involvement is primarily perceived as an impediment to the full flow of creative impulses, restricting the essential freedom of the artistic imagination. The linking of "real" art to unfettered creative and operational freedom inhibits the potential for art to become more socially engaged and is the key point of tension between the art world and government in relation to audience development work.

Many arts professionals maintain that public subsidy is awarded precisely to protect artists from the demands of the free market, political and social restraints, and by implication the tastes of the general public. Artists strongly resist suggestions that they should focus or redirect their work toward the tastes and interests of specific audience groups, and as such, creative authenticity and integrity are closely interlinked with notions of marginality and insulation, at least from certain audiences. In this sense, popularity is viewed as fundamentally unartistic. A Glaswegian artist explained to me that:

> Transmission [a gallery] about five to eight years ago was really influential, everyone knew about it but you never saw anyone there. If lots of people had gone to the gallery it would have lost its reputation by becoming populist. You have to avoid being populist as this means your work becomes liked by the wrong people.

Commercial appeal is construed as compromising authenticity and, therefore, as transgressing the aesthetic codes of the contemporary art world.

Increasingly, however, there are pressing political incentives for engaging with new audiences and the broader public. While artists, critics, and a fairly narrow audience have held sanction over the artistic field, this authority is currently being questioned by the tastes, desires, and rights of the wider population. Engagement with the social, cultural, educational, welfare, and health needs of disadvantaged communities has become a political necessity in the arts, as in other areas of government in Britain, and is a primary means through which to gain public subsidy. In some senses, therefore, target audiences increasingly hold the key to institutional credibility, financial prosperity, and government approval. Under government insistence, invisible and untutored nonattenders are moving out of the shadows and are acquiring unprecedented power as public arts organizations are compelled to adopt the social inclusion agenda (Levitas 1998). Funding bodies insist that audiences are no longer an incidental outcome of putting on an arts event, but that their interests should be central to the production process itself. This is an important realignment of the relationship between artists and audiences, which has major implications for the concept of artistic practice as an autonomous self-propelled entity and for the representation of nontraditional audiences within the artistic field. Audience reaction can no longer be assumed or ignored, and it is not considered acceptable to play or exhibit only to the same repeat attenders. Essentially, long-established and faithful relationships with existing audiences are being questioned, and organizations are having to broaden the appeal of their work beyond relatively narrow professional, class, and cultural communities.

THE PRODUCTION OF TARGET AUDIENCES

The contemporary political impulse to devolve approved forms of cultural appreciation to wider audiences is in many ways similar to forms of enlightenment practiced in the nineteenth century. Indeed it is possible to trace the historic precedent for this reform to the early development of museums, in which the perceived needs of the poor shaped the purpose and application of aesthetic practices. Tony Bennett (1998: 128) suggests that the discursive coordinates governing nineteenth-century conceptions of the poor led to particular forms of administration designed to "induct the population into new, more prudential forms of conduct." He highlights the relationship between emerging forms of liberal government and the role accorded culture as a reforming resource. Aesthetic practices and the audiences they are designed to serve continue to be the object of government in a material, moral, and reforming sense, and the "community," both then and now, emerges as a construction of government effected through cultural policy. Although stripped of much of its overtly civilizing intent, current government rhetoric about the social value of the arts contains traces of similar forms of social manipulation. Arts professionals perform this wider history of engagement and use the past as a reservoir of accumulated cultural capital through which to direct current conventions (Bourdieu 1996; Gregson and Rose 2000). Nineteenth-century approaches to audience development are thus carried forth, admittedly in modified and fragmentary ways, and reconstituted into contemporary rationales.

Despite the emphasis currently placed on audience development, the notion of "an" audience remains largely unexamined. Working-class, ethnic, and disabled communities, as well as young people and the disadvantaged, are all targeted interchangeably as the focus for liberal forms of cultural engagement designed to bring them into closer contact with "valid" and rewarding cultural practices. Nonattenders tend to be defined in terms of target groups, with reference to their social and economic position and according to their relationship with the welfare state. In the

United Kingdom, arts funding (distributed by such bodies as the National Lottery, the arts councils, and local government) is increasingly tied to projects that target particular groups, such as ethnic minorities and those conceived to be socially excluded. Perceptions of target audiences thus primarily follow the contours of social and economic structures, reducing subjects to the personifications of positions within such structures (Morley 1989: 42). There is little appreciation of different audiences existing as individuals, or distinctive subcultural groups, or as moving between sociological categories. Arts policies thus gesture toward multiculturalism and diversity on the one hand, but on the other produce homogeneous notions of "an" audience or groups of audiences that deny individual diversity and the complexity of particular cultural groups. Such descriptions also operate internally within arts funding institutions, and I was told by a British arts officer of Indian origin that "as a black worker I was appointed with the idea that you know everything. I have a culture as an Indian and I'm not an expert on Chinese or Afro Caribbean Culture. Black culture isn't homogeneous." Definitions of subjectivity are therefore largely instrumental rather than descriptive, based on relative economic position or reductive notions of ethnicity, class, disability, sexuality, and age. Interestingly, gender seems to have lost favor as a target category within the arts, implying women are no longer regarded as socially excluded, which effectively silences gender as a form of subjectivity within government discourse.

The public, and more specifically the disadvantaged, is called upon to perform functions within grander schemes, such as the current UK government's social inclusion agenda, with which it has had no previous engagement or control. The more tightly defined funding criteria become, however, the more participants and their needs are required to fit into preconceived social and developmental categories. As one artist confessed, it is common for arts workers to go into the community in search of willing participants who fit their project's defined target group after they have secured the funding. Rarely are community and audience development projects initiated by members of the public themselves, and the perceived "needs" of communities are therefore framed by, and generated within, the professional rather than public realm.[4] Thus, arts development tends to be imposed on unsuspecting groups of people who have not actively expressed an interest in the arts. This echoes Ien Ang's work on television audiences, where she argues that audiences do not exist naturally but, in Dominic Strinati's (1995: 249–250) words, "are constructed by particular discourses which seek to know them in order to exert power over them," such that "elusive fields of reality are transformed into discrete objects to be known and controlled at the same time" (Ang 1991: 8–10). The processes I have highlighted involve the explicit objectification and subtle manipulation of sections of the public who are deemed to be in need of creative involvement. Flimsy empirical information and crude categories of identification are marshaled to justify funding for deficit-based audience development strategies. Assumptions about who nonattenders are produce a kind of truth about them that works to consolidate institutional interests in accordance with evolving political and professional priorities (Ang 1991).

Target audiences are constructed in circumscribed ways, their identities largely elaborated for them, and they have little power or opportunity to dispute the characteristics ascribed to them. Audience subjectivities are confined to a set of relationships with producers of the arts, which grants the art world power of definition and places audiences as recipients of fictions about who they are and what their cultures involve. In this way, audiences are denied an independent culture or identity of their own; they are molded as passive receivers and not producers of their own subject positions (Radway 1988: 361).

Bureaucratic and sociological categories lack explanatory power when individuals are artificially reduced to singular descriptions such as single mother, woman, or elderly person. Ang (1991: 8–10) argues that "the dispersed realities of audiencehood come to be known through the single, unitary concept of the 'television audience.'" As Raymond Williams (1995: 289) states, "there are no masses, just ways of seeing people as masses." Perceptions of order, in this instance, of audience subjectivities as knowable, are rendered tangible when policymakers, practitioners, or researchers write other people, their cultures, and systems into documents, models of practice, and so on. Not only do we "read" them as targets of our gaze, we also tend to divorce these readings from their locations within specific contexts (Barnes and Duncan 1992). Consequently, diverse audiences become disembodied, artificially extracted from localized frameworks of meaning (Gregory 1989). While the construction and use of sociological categories as a means of identification is problematic in itself, these shaky foundations are often further exacerbated by the specific models of practice designed for target audiences.

POPULAR CULTURE AND NONATTENDERS

Subject positions are not simply constructed through direct description of a given target group, but are also implied by comparisons between the cultural inclinations of the perceiver and those of the target group. Subjective processes thus work in both direct and indirect ways, and arts workers refine and reveal their own subjectivity as they construct the subjectivities of others. The distinction between art and popular culture, for instance, is one of the primary means through which those involved in the arts understand their own practice. In this section, I examine some of the underlying and privately expressed opinions about popular culture as opposed to art, and consider the ramifications of these attitudes for the construction of nonattenders. Despite increased integration between cultural fields, the art world's relationship with popular culture and its audiences remains highly ambiguous, riven by internal differences of opinion and latent assumptions about the integrity of mass cultural phenomena and its audiences. Hostility to popular aesthetics is frequently framed in terms of the threat of a brute cultural invasion, where visual art, apparently born of a more educated and delicate sensibility, is vulnerable to the frivolous excesses of commercial tastes. In the words of one gallery director: "[We] are facing times where there is a possibility of a take-over, the disneyfication, where the arts are moving into kitsch. . . . is this related to the fact that the arts aren't taken seriously enough in the education process?" To a great extent, artistic integrity is premised on social and professional exclusivity, which, in combination with discourses of aesthetic authority, maintain the elevated position of minority artistic concerns above the preferences of wider public cultures. Daniel Miller (1991: 16) has observed that "These global approaches almost always move from an attack on contemporary material culture as trivial and unauthentic to an implied (though rarely explicitly) denigration of the mass of the population whose culture this is." Aesthetic, economic, and cultural stratification collide to ensure the marginalization of some and the inclusion of others and enable sections of the art world to dismiss other forms of creativity and those engaged with them as being artless.

Notwithstanding this, attitudes toward "the" popular are by no means consistent. Popular culture has been both embraced and resisted, and it is at once a compelling source of fascination and abhorrence. As the director of a popular music festival exclaimed, "The [Scottish Arts Council] is supporting rock thirty years too late. It makes me laugh. All the art forms which are popular are sneered at." The integration of popular tastes into fine art aesthetics generates different degrees of support and resistance in different quarters. According to John Roberts (1996), younger artists do feel themselves to be part of a common popular culture and do not make a hierarchical distinction between its pleasures and the pleasures to be had from art. To some extent my own research endorses this crudely generational distinction, and for some young artists, mass culture has become a valid aesthetic resource. Just as the assumed cultures of non-arts publics are simultaneously celebrated and reviled, artists from working-class backgrounds often have a precarious status within the art world. One Glaswegian artist stated:

> I feel discriminated against in Edinburgh because of my accent and because I'm a working-class man from the West coast. . . . We all know art is exclusive, we just don't talk about it. It pretends to be classless and democratic and politically correct. Art is supposed to be like club cultures, classless and with everyone on the same level, all sharing. But in reality its not like that. . . . It isn't equal.

The Scottish artist and writer John Beagles (1997: 12–13) has pointed out that Glasgow is "ravaged" by a "deep schism between its art intelligentsia and the public," which curators respond to by staging "catch all theme shows" in order to assimilate populist clothing when they are accused of elitism. While class is clearly a compelling form of distinction within the arts, gender operates in less decisive terms. I encountered more female than male curators, gallery directors, and arts officers in a context where the numbers of female and male artists are roughly equal, which reinforces the impression of class rather than gender as the primary form of distinction and discrimination in the arts (Skeggs 1997).

Government pressure to popularize art, alongside a more internally driven interest in popular culture, has further animated exchanges between those in favor of distance from, and those seeking integration with, mass cultures. Where popular referents are present, however, these symbols are frequently executed with a self-consciousness or irony that seems to denote the objectification of popular cultures, rather than the easy familiarity that is likely to result from a more equal and integrated relationship. Incorporation is largely conducted within tightly confined aesthetic parameters, which renew rather than challenge the cultural authority of the art world. Commercial tastes are extracted from their original context, assigned different meanings, and appropriated by an increasingly voracious arts establishment eager to demonstrate its own progressiveness. The popular is thus transformed in order to become acceptable as art, while aesthetic authenticity and the category of art itself remain dependent on detachment from, rather than resonance with, non-arts cultures. In such a way, developments in art mirror the wider social and political means through which difference has become commodified by establishment interests. Nonattenders and their cultures are thus created and objectified within the artwork itself, as well as within arts policy documents and individual and institutional discourses.

Those involved in audience development work and popular cultures seem to be deeply implicated within an ongoing conflict between the different internal aesthetic interests of the art world and the cultural preferences of the general public. When studied more closely, the rhetoric of inclusion and cultural eclecticism does not necessarily translate into progressive audience development practices. These antagonisms, differences of opinion, and practices must be seen as part of the same operational whole. For example, outreach and education work is often begrudgingly tolerated within organizational structures. This was evident when I talked to a gallery education officer who was trying to hang photographs from a youth project in between water pipes behind the bookshop counter. He was very unhappy about the work being relegated to this space and complained that "you wouldn't believe the hassle I've had getting a place for them in the gallery at all." Exclusion in this instance takes on a spatial as well as a social dimension, with the maintenance of a physical distance between professional and community art preserving the purity of the gallery space for the former. Discursive authority and power over traditional nonattenders are expressed aesthetically and spatially, written into the very geography of arts and exhibition practices, a contention that echoes Gillian Rose's (1997a) research on the core/periphery relationship between community and professional arts in Edinburgh.

ART AND AUTHENTICITY

Unlike popular culture, art is valued because it is perceived to make audiences think and because it demands a greater intellectual commitment from the viewer than forms of mass entertainment. In contrast, mass media are often regarded as being uncultured, unreal, and unauthentic. One gallery director claimed that "Art galleries are not stuffy. People are discovering there is a real experience as opposed to TV experience, that there is another life as opposed to quite honestly the atrophying experience [of television]." In this instance, creative authenticity is seen to lie on the side of art gallery culture rather than televisual culture, which is viewed as an aberration of the creative imagination (Bragg 2001). Sport was also frequently depicted as the antithesis of all that art stands for, the negative shadow of what is uplifting and life-affirming about artistic endeavor. As a delegate at a Scottish Arts Council consultation event said, "I am sick of twelve pages in *The Herald* [a Scottish daily newspaper] on sport, where is the art?" Despite commanding enormous public support, the passion for sport is not regarded as equal to or as worthy of passion for art, and sport is denied the ability to legitimately move and inspire public consciousness. As one arts worker said:

> Every place needs to be sung about, written about, otherwise it doesn't exist. It's about whether it affects the imagination. This is the difference between art and sport, how we are feeding the imagination of the nation. Sports doesn't do this.

In the view of many arts workers, art alone has, or rather should have, a monopoly on the most eloquent expression of human experience. Sport and television are thus established as antagonistic to the arts, operating as compelling sources of distraction for a wayward public unable to rise to its full creative potential or to exercise finer cultural sensibilities. The similarities between the contemporary role of art and the original rationale for public museums as a powerful corrective to the temptations of the tavern and gin palace are evident. As Robert Hughes argued, however, "the idea that people are morally ennobled by contact with works of art is a pious fiction" (quoted in Weil 1997: 263–264).

Association with the arts is typically seen by arts workers to provide participants with moral as well as cultural authority and taste. This works to consolidate a moral economy as well as particular aesthetic preferences. Artistic judgments are thus involved in the making of audience subjectivities, generating statements about the moral and cultural integrity of those associated with different expressive practices. Discussions about other people's cultures continue to be deeply implicated within a wider framework of economic, moral, and social sanction and exclusion. The culture we produce is not separate from the people we are, and culture, in its objective (as conscious artifact, performance, product) and anthropological (lived) senses, is continually diffused. The cultural artifacts of others are viewed through the context of their lived cultures. Judgments about different forms of expression inevitably embody our preconceptions about those who engage them. By judging popular culture, arts workers also judge its audiences.

The embodied nature of cultural capital was apparent through repeated reference by arts professionals to the non-arts public in very visceral terms, as having decadent and narcissistic cultural and culinary tastes, greedily consuming fatty, processed food while indulging in lazy, mind-numbing pastimes. The following remarks were made by various arts practitioners and a voluntary sector worker at a Scottish Arts Council consultation meeting.

> Delegate 1. If [you] can eat crisps and stuff your faces in the theatre like [you] can do in the cinema, then people might make the effort to go there.
> Delegate 2. Cinema is easier than the theater.

Delegate 3. There needs [to be] a campaign to show there's a healthy diet of the arts in the same way there's a campaign for healthy eating. People eat expensive processed food rather than healthy cheap food.
Delegate 4. I agree, people eat . . .
Delegate 5. It's easier to eat chips and pies and turn on the TV to watch *Eastenders* rather than go to the theater.

In part condemned for an overindulgent pursuit of gratification and enjoyment, popular audiences are perceived to forsake constructive life-enhancing activities for a weak and uncontrolled appetite for pleasure (Huysmann 1988). The arts are perceived to offer a healthy alternative to the excesses of popular tastes, the creative equivalent of new potatoes to chips. What audiences consume and how they express themselves are conflated and interchanged, working in combination to define who they are and where they fit in to an implied cultural hierarchy. The mind and body of the non-arts audience are presented as being impaired, blindly consuming the harmful products of a commercial market that encourages easy, short-term indulgences over the more strenuous but ultimately rewarding opportunities offered by the arts. This basic distinction has built up through an essentially Kantian separation of sensory gratification from disinterested contemplation, facile expression from the interests of reason, profane from sacred culture, commercial from high art, and ultimately, "them" from "us" (see chapter 1). As Kant loftily surmised, "taste that requires an added element of charm and emotion for its delight . . . has not yet emerged from barbarism" (quoted in Bourdieu 1996: 42).

ART AND INTELLIGENCE

According to Bourdieu (1996: 12), "there is no way out of the game of culture," and we are all saturated with an aesthetic framework to which there is no outside. He qualifies this apparent universality by arguing that the degree of saturation is not equal for all people and suggests that the capacity for objectification and critical distance is highly class specific. Bourdieu claims that the *popular taste* of the working classes is not amenable to this kind of objectification. As I have suggested, the arts are generally expected to be intellectually stimulating and to encourage thoughtful responses from their audiences. Notions of passive and active audience subjectivities have generated compelling theoretical disputes within media and cultural studies disciplines (Frith 1991; Fisk 1987; Willis 1990; McQuail 1997; Ang 1996) and also surfaced as important distinguishing motifs within my own research, mobilized by arts practitioners to denote relative levels of critical engagement with art. One arts manager, for example, declared that "TV is passive and [in] the theatre people are actively engaged," implying a uniformity of content and value within both genres as well as a hierarchical disparity between them.

Aspects of Bourdieu's argument are reflected in the common assumption that working-class cultures are devoid of artistic ambition or pretension. Arts workers tend to valorize nonattenders for their past or lived authenticity, rather than for their current aesthetic or intellectual credibility, and a fashion has developed for celebratory forms of community festival together with uncritical explorations of ethnic and marginal identities. Community arts practice is primarily perceived in terms of its social function and its ability to unite troubled communities, and it is allocated a welfare role that would never be assumed appropriate of middle-class pursuits. As one artist said, "community art should be a division of social work . . . it's not about art, it's about regeneration." Government funding for the arts is increasingly framed around concepts of self-improvement, such as confidence-building, skills development, and combating crime. The less-well-off are expected to *do* art in an authentic, self-improving, and participatory manner, and the better-off are expected to *view* art in a more distant and thoughtful way. It is therefore rare to come across art appreciation classes within community development settings, where involvement is strongly associated with physical rather than intellectual participation, reanimating the slothful body, but not substantially engaging with the critical capacities of target communities.

According to Bennett (1998: 210), the aesthetic is "enlisted for reforming programs, which in varying ways" are designed to imbue "target populations with specific civic attributes," thus encouraging them to be self-civilizing. Bennett (1998) outlines how the reforming work of culture in the nineteenth century moved from exterior forms of behavioral management to encompass the internal psychology of the individual. This link between art and self-improvement still retains its potency today in relation to nonattenders. What has become known as governmentality literature (Foucault 1991; Gordon 1991; Rose 1992) further explains how government elicits "voluntary alliances" from subjects who actively participate in the making of their own selves. Internal and structural perspectives are integrated (A. Cohen 1994), and schemes of self-management and subjective transformation are aligned to the objectives of government (Garland 1997: 8). Large-scale processes of rule are thus linked into micropolitical and professional processes and individual self-governance. Individual subjectivity is not suppressed, but is cultivated and made up in the form of free subjects who actively align their choices with those of governing authorities. As we have seen, subjectivity involves constrained choices rather than free expression, which reflects Garland's (27) contention that within neo-liberal techniques of government, we are obliged to be choosers of particular services and ways of being. Jean-Jacques Rousseau's observation that "we can be forced to be free" is selectively applied, therefore, with some audiences granted greater freedoms than others.

According to Bourdieu (1996), bourgeois audiences also appreciate form, while popular audiences take refuge in function. In many ways, this association between the working classes and more "naturalized" and spontaneous aesthetic practices mirrors anthropological assertions about premodern people's apparent inability to separate subject from object and sign from thing (Latour 1993). Objectification and the ability to reflect consciously on one's own practices are therefore associated with a higher cultural state of being. The implication behind this analysis is that working-class people are rendered childlike and dependent by their socialization, and that they lack the ability to influence or direct their own choices and tastes.

The less-educated fractions of society are thus seen as immured in their own sub-jectivity and saturated by their own culture, possessing a certain spontaneous au-thenticity. For example, a Glaswegian filmmaker explained the current fashion for working-class films as a form of qualified access, the conditions of which demand realism as the only account of unredeemingly tortured lives. In contrast, the edu-cated are regarded as capable of objective reflection, free to escape themselves, not totally absorbed by who they are, and consequently able to construct an "artful" life for themselves. In short, the educated live *with* culture, while the working classes *are* culture. Thus a certain romanticism is attached to the lived cultures of nonattenders, but they are denied the capacity to translate or objectify these lived experiences into worthwhile cultural products. It is possible to see how this basic juxtaposition of object/subject and art/life translates into a series of common understandings about culture, how it operates, who engages in it, and ultimately what models of practice and policy recommendations are made on the basis of this logic. The result is a model of audience development that promotes physical participation over arts ap-preciation, community celebration over critical consciousness, self-improvement over arts education, group activities over individual endeavors, and amateur achieve-ments over professional standards.

AUDIENCE EDUCATION

Although many arts workers would genuinely like the field to be more widely sup-ported, debates about increasing the appeal of art to wider audiences invariably raise concerns about "debasing the product." The capacity for judgment and critical en-gagement is selectively allocated to different audiences, and many arts workers dis-trust the public's ability to make informed aesthetic judgments. The fear is that granting too much power to the masses will result in the erosion of ethical, aesthetic, and intellectual standards. In this sense, the public is regarded as potentially cor-rupting the purity of the artistic ideal (McQuail 1997: 12–13), and the exercising of its tastes, as well as its unmediated presence within galleries, is regarded as a threat to standards. The art world thus has a great investment in ensuring that contempo-rary art does not become democratically accountable, unless the public is schooled in an appropriate mode of appreciation. In other words, public involvement can only be contemplated when accompanied by an appropriate aesthetic education, which in part explains the strong emphasis placed on arts education.

Discussing preservation and what he terms the "cultural protectionist discourse" of art-writer and critic Robert Hughes, Craig Owens (1997: 19–21) notes that while museums claim to protect art works in the name of the public, they actually protect art works *from* the public. The majority of potential audiences for art are excluded as arbiters of taste, and aesthetic authority is reserved for those directly involved in the production of art. Indeed, not only does art need to be protected from the pub-lic, but the public has to be protected from its own cultural instincts. In this way, the public is considered to be the problem, the deficient factor, and its judgments are deemed essentially misguided. Consequently, the public, rather than the art world, has become the focus for reforming initiatives. As one senior civil servant explained, "the problem is more with people's perception of art than with the type of art which is offered; people's perception of it is the problem; [it] isn't that there isn't the right type of art in the right areas." There are those, however, who caution against this kind of didactic and deficit-based audience development model and who encourage more reciprocal practices that recognize the artistic sensibilities of target audiences. A delegate at a Scottish Arts Council seminar commented:

> Who are these communities? I've never met a person or community who haven't been artistic. [We] need to be careful not to patronize audiences when [we] talk about social inclusion, and be careful not to ruin a flower by telling people their culture isn't good enough.

Despite this, however, access for nonattenders is largely framed in terms of transforming their cultural sensibilities by lifting them into what one artist called an "enlightened sensibility," a position from which they can appropriately engage with and value art. Despite a rhetorical commitment to inclusion and audience development, one artist said in exasperation "Is it important people are converted?" The question assumes involvement is conducted as a form of conversion or missionary project, rather than as a renegotiation of existing practice into forms of expression that are mutually compatible. Audience development within this framework falls prey to problematic developmental concepts such as "empowerment," which assume power and powerlessness, knowledge and lack of knowledge, which can be demarcated and can have power/knowledge transferred from one group of people to another. James Clifford (1997: 193) discusses how nineteenth-century museums were, from the outset, deeply entangled in the colonial and imperial project through the collection and organization of objects from the colonial outposts of the metropolitan center. The spatial dynamic of this approach, which establishes a knowing, discerning metropolitan center in relation to a dependent marginal other, resonates with current audience development models. This spatial relationship has implications for the distribution of power as nonattenders, and their imagined cultures become a "site of discovery," objectified as exotic and/or dependent, within the conceptual terms and practices of the dominant, "gathering" institution. Just as the objects of museums are disciplined and ordered, so too audience development practices effectively tutor the public body into forms of engagement and attitudes of mind appropriate for the appreciation of "valid" cultural experiences.

The relationship between the art world and potential audiences has become one of unequal capital, knowledge, and power; of teacher to pupil, adult to child, the cultured to the uncultured. On this reading, nonattenders have everything to learn, and the art world has everything to teach them. The rhetoric of inclusion works to disguise a one-sided form of educational and cultural dispersal. Perceived differences in cultural taste and preference are mobilized to demarcate two apparently discrete social groups in opposition to each other, and correspondingly, to divide the educated from those in need of education, the actors from the acted upon. This form of subjectification is based on relations of "uneven reciprocity" between government, arts managers and artists, and potential audiences, and it formulates patterns of exclusion in relation to such publics (Clifford 1997: 193). In this sense, the arts sector promotes top-down development, which has long since been discredited within the voluntary sector, local government, and in international development.

Attitudes toward nonattenders and audience development practices tread a thin line between acceptance and intolerance, inclusion and reform. As one arts worker said, "Do you give them what you want or what they want?" Almost inevitably, education diminishes as much as it enhances, and equally, the artistic field condemns as it reaches out. How then does one encourage appreciation for the arts without simultaneously condemning existing cultures or the critical capacities of those engaged with them? I suggest that, along with existing outreach, education, and marketing initiatives, the profession should take into account the ways in which nonattenders are objectified, as well the ways in which the art world is structured, and should consider changes in programming, artistic content, and importantly, the class and cultural profile of the profession itself. Only by redirecting its gaze and acknowledging the need for mutual adjustment can the art world reconsider current assumptions about the intellectual and cultural imbalance between itself and nonparticipants. If audience development is to be undertaken seriously, art and not just audiences will have to change. This may be too much for many to contemplate.

CONCLUSION

Constructs of audiences are not coincidental, and even if their emergence is not entirely systematic, they are contrived within government and artistic fields to serve specific cultural, political, and professional purposes. In this sense, audiences are objectified as part of a wider process of governance that extends beyond the confines of public arts policy to embrace funding regimes, artistic practices, professional cultures, marketing initiatives, access programs, and so on. Nonattenders do have a presence within the arts network, but this is largely as objects to be acted upon. They are the objectified subjects of government and the arts profession, imagined into being and subsequently exposed to tenuous strategic and practical recommendations. Nonattenders are thus a fiction, a story told by the art world and by myself. Like a cubist painting with fractured angles and displaced elements, nonattenders have a shattered and momentarily real presence, creating an incoherent imprint on the mind's eye. Rather than bearing much similarity to the diverse realities of people's lives, these constructs of "audience," as well as of art and nonart, are variously manufactured in relation to changing institutional and professional interests (Harvey 1998). Knowledges about others are central to the governing process, being used to prescribe policy, frame recommendations for action, guide funding allocations, and ultimately manage lives. By exposing the construction of audience subjectivities, we can begin to unravel the ways in which authority is legitimized through association with different bodies of people and begin to understand how forms of stratification and/or equality are perpetuated in relation to them. While I have focused on the creation and management of audiences, it is evident that other types of public service provision are also shaped and driven by discourses based on particular visions of the "general public" (see chapter 10).

In a Latourian sense, aesthetic, intellectual, social, individual, professional and governmental, material and nonmaterial influences work in combination to create an integrated system of authoritative knowledge that names, positions, and judges those who do not attend the arts. Just as audience practices and experiences are indefinite, if not infinite (Ang 1996), so too are the means through which they are conceived. Different collections of individuals produce competing definitions of audience identity that cannot easily be reconciled. Through reference to a confusing number and combination of categories, arts workers carve an identity for themselves and others. Janice Radway (1988: 363) coined the term "complexities of determination," which defy neat conceptions of a communication circuit and encourage us to view "social formations and cultural practices in new ways, all of which confound a simple transmission model of cultural communication." It is this play of signifiers, sometimes deployed consciously, sometimes unconsciously, that, in sprawling totality, holds the keys to cultural identity, aesthetic disposition, and group identification. Faint traces of nonattenders' presences are to be found as words on pages, within artistic gestures, in the atmosphere at gallery openings, and in the minds of those through whom they are conceived. Bourdieu (1996) and Foucault (1981, 1991) would maintain that their world is held together by discrete discourses. Latour (1993, 1999), however, would also see their presence as brought into being through networks, which, like Ariadne's thread, weave together the myriad of "things" through which we live and act. What has emerged, therefore, is a precarious account of a necessarily incoherent field of subjective practices and projections.

There are, however, moments of clarity and systematic effect that endure within and between differences of opinion, and there are points of change and adjustment. It is these broad perceptions of the cultures and intellectual capacities of "the" nonattender that originally spurred my interest in audience subjectivity and that continue to make me feel uncomfortable today. Despite limitations in Bourdieu's framework, his work on cultural capital nevertheless compels us to recognize the systematic ways in which individual and communities of taste develop through prolonged participation in particular economic, class, and educational contexts. In such ways, cultural assets are vested in particular groups of people, highlighting the embodied nature of cultural capital and the dynamic circulating interrelationships between the economic, the cultural, and the social. The apparent completeness of this cultural saturation, or habitus, forewarns us of the naivety of current attempts to trace and overcome years of cultural accumulation and the deep-seated inclinations that both bind and separate us.

The developmental dilemmas faced by the arts profession reflect, and are part of wider disputes about, democracy and minority representation, freedom and censorship, coherence and diversity, and state protection/subsidy and global capital, which continue to animate Western societies and the liberal left in particular. We can see how apparently insignificant remarks from individual arts workers, policy statements, and localized practices work together as part of a wider network of moral, political, economic, and cultural activity. The awkward bits and pieces, as well as the comfortingly consistent aspects of a research project, all take on a resonance within this inclusive methodological approach. This search for the ties that bind, rather than the clean lines that separate, does not imply retreat into convenient generalizations. Instead it promotes a form of inquiry that refuses artificially to disconnect research material from the wider context in which it occurs and that seeks to understand the world as an integrated, evolving whole.

NOTES

1. The Scottish Executive (Scottish Parliament), City of Edinburgh Council, and Scottish Arts Council are the principal funders for the arts in Scotland. In combination with the UK government, their patronage far exceeds private donations in Britain.

2. When using the terms "arts workers," "arts practitioners," and "arts professionals," I refer to all those who work with publicly funded art, including managers, administrators, and artists, as well as local government and Scottish Arts Council officials.

3. This statement was made by the director of an audience research institution in Edinburgh, January 2001. Social classes AB and C1 (white-collar workers) make up 78 percent of those who frequently attend the arts in Edinburgh, and 57 percent of nonattenders consist of those from social classes C2 and DE (blue/pink-collar workers) (unpublished report by local audience research company, The Audience Business, Edinburgh, July 1999).

4. Although there is widespread commitment to public consultation within the public sector, its application in practice remains highly problematic, and consultative exercises are frequently unrepresentative of active "community" interests.

10

"Dependency": New Labour Welfare Reform Policy and the Production of the Passive, Dependent Benefit Claimant

Niamh O'Connor

> The greatest challenge for a democratic government is to refashion our institutions to bring the new workless class back into society and into useful work. Governments can all too easily institutionalise poverty rather than solve it, lock people into dependency rather than give them a means to be independent.
>
> —Tony Blair in his first speech as prime minister of Britain, London,
> June 2, 1997

Welfare reform is one of the central planks of the New Labour policy of the British government.[1] Tony Blair indicated this centrality by dedicating his first keynote speech as prime minister to the "problem" of Britain's "workless classes" and the danger of government institutions hindering rather than helping their cause by "locking them into dependency." Of course, this is not the first time "worklessness" has been problematized nor public assistance criticized. As long as there has been public assistance for poor people there have been concerns about its potentially morally damaging effects. In Britain, public welfare systems have repeatedly been castigated as part of the problem of "worklessness," from the Poor Relief Act of 1601, with its aim "to provide aid to the deserving and to deter wandering beggars and vagabonds" (Department of Health and Social Security 1985: 59), through the Poor Law of 1834 and its concern that assistance is "a bounty on indolence and vice" (Webb and Webb 1929, quoted in Ditch 1991: 25), to Conservative government concerns in the 1980s that, in the words of John Moore, secretary of state for Social Security at the 1987 Conservative Party conference, "welfare measures . . . must be aimed ultimately at encouraging independence, not dependence." The attempts of the New Labour government to reform the current public welfare system, together with the discursive construction of a particular benefit claimant subjectivity, are the focus of this chapter.

My theoretical approach draws on what has been called the "new economic geography," that is, an economic geography that has been influenced by feminist and cultural geographies (Lee and Wills 1997). In contrast to the Marxian political economy that dominated economic geography in the 1970s, the new economic geography encompasses questions of social construction, discourse, and subjectivity, questions at the heart of this chapter. Further, feminist work on "demystifying dependency" (Fraser and Gordon 1994) and the politics of need interpretation (Astor 1996) are sources of theoretical inspiration on the substantive topic of welfare reform and the construction of dependency. This chapter draws especially on the work of J. K. Gibson-Graham (1996), who advances a feminist critique of political economy and the construction of capitalism as dominant, all-powerful, and inevitable. Gibson-Graham argues that the *representation* of capitalism as hegemonic is constitutive of capitalism's seeming inevitability; that noncapitalist and anticapitalist projects remain largely hidden and silent because of the way capitalism is constructed. Gibson-Graham criticizes "discourses of capitalist hegemony" and attempts to "clear a discursive space for the emergence and development of hitherto suppressed discourses of economic diversity, in the hope of contributing to an anti-capitalist politics of economic invention" (Gibson-Graham 1996: xi).

Poststructuralist analyses of public policy, such as welfare reform, which focus on discourses, social constructions, and subjectivities, are increasingly common (for example, Leonard 1997; Fraser and Gordon 1994; Levitas 1998; Fairclough 2000). Language, in these writings, is regarded as constitutive, rather than merely descriptive of political policy, and it is through language that a particular, narrow subjectivity of "the benefit claimant" is constructed, which then becomes the focus of policies of welfare reform. These policies have enormous material effects on individuals, not least through the reduced income that follows benefit cuts. Examining social welfare policy in terms of constructions of subjectivity enables us to critique the "taken-for-grantedness" and underlying assumptions of the "workfare offensive" (Theodore and Peck 2001) in the United States and the United Kingdom. As Leonard (1997: 50) argues, "Perhaps most important for the constructing of subjectivity within the area of state welfare has been the discursive division between the subject as dependent or independent."

Acknowledging the contribution of Michel Foucault to critical linguistics, critical discourse analyst Norman Fairclough discusses the "major role of discourse in the constitution of social subjects" (1992: 44). Sara Mills (1997: 133–134) expands on this point:

[L]anguage is a central vehicle in the process whereby people are constituted as individuals and as social subjects, and because language and ideology are closely imbricated, the close systematic analysis of the language of texts can expose some of the workings of texts and, by extension, the way that people are oppressed within current social structures.

Further, as Fairclough (2000: 6) has argued, because of the New Labour government's concern with media "spin" and control over their public perception, "a focus on the language of New Labour can enhance our understanding, as well as analysis, of the politics of New Labour." The first part of this chapter draws on these ideas to analyze current political discourse in the United Kingdom, which I argue constructs the "dependent, passive benefit claimant."

In the second half of the chapter I discuss the lived experiences of benefit claiming, drawing on interviews with forty long-term claimants, defined as people who have claimed social security benefits for a period of more than six months. Following Gibson-Graham (1996), I argue that the dominance of a particular construction of claimant subjectivity "crowds out" contesting discourses, such as those produced by the claimants themselves. The critical analysis of political welfare reform discourse in the first half of this chapter is thus juxtaposed with excerpts from the transcripts of interviews with claimants in an attempt to "clear a discursive space." Further, Gibson-Graham (1997b: 95) writes:

> Research, the activity that most economic geographers are engaged in, involves the production of knowledge and knowledge is performative as well as powerful. Alternative knowledges interpellate (in the Althuserian sense of calling into being) alternative political subjectivities and thereby enable new forms of agency.

This approach, and especially the desire to highlight alternative political subjectivities, guides the research discussed in the second half of the chapter.

The interviewees are from a medium-size town in central Scotland that has, like all places tend to, a spatially uneven distribution of wealth and employment opportunities. Respondents were recruited primarily from those areas of town that, as one respondent put it, have "all the usual indicators that the Scottish Office says are used to define deprivation."[2] All but three of the respondents live in areas with high levels of unemployment and significant proportion of families on low incomes.[3] It is these areas that are targeted in political discourse as showing all the signs of a "dependency culture." But these interviewees contest the constructions of passivity and dependency, of work-shyness and work-detachment, dominant in political discourse.

THE CONSTRUCTION OF THE PASSIVE, DEPENDENT BENEFIT CLAIMANT

The phrase that Blair used in his first speech as prime minister, the "workless classes," hints at a dichotomy that has characterized New Labour policy and its discourse throughout its first four years in power: the dichotomy between paid work and welfare benefits. This dichotomy associates financial dependence on the labor market in the form of paid work with independence, "activeness," and well-being, while income from benefits is associated with dependence, passivity, and unhappiness. The "problem" with the benefits system is that it rewards "non-work," and so "the Government's aim is to rebuild the welfare state around work" (Department of Social Security 1998: 23).

New Labour welfare policy has been informed by, and reproduces, what can be described as the work detachment perspective. According to this perspective, long-term benefit claimants have almost completely lost contact with, or become detached from, the world of work and employment. People who are long-term unemployed, it is argued, lose the habits of work, have less structure in their day-to-day lives, tend to socialize with other unemployed people, lose motivation in their search for work, and are less likely than other job seekers to be considered favorably by employers. They are not aware of job opportunities around them. People who are on benefits for too long, the argument goes, become unsocialized in the ways of work, they lose *employability*, and are resocialized into the "benefits dependency culture."

One element of this discursive production of the dependent claimant is the notion that certain areas and certain people have lost their work ethic, that is, they have lost the belief in the value and importance of paid work. In a speech to the British Chamber of Commerce in April 2000, the chancellor of the exchequer[4] Gordon Brown, for example, asserted that one of the preconditions for increased productivity in Britain is "reinvigorating the work ethic in every community of our country." He continued:

> For too long too many people had become accustomed to not working and to a benefits system that failed to make work pay and led to the "why work" syndrome at a cost to the work ethic. For too long historic British virtues—hard work and self improvement—had been drowned out.

While the benefits system is linked with an alleged decline of the work ethic, work is linked with virtue and self-improvement. Speaking at a conference held in May 2000 titled Creating the Entrepreneurial Economy, Stephen Timms, financial secretary to the Treasury, was similarly concerned with what he termed "entrenched cultural barriers to enterprise," asserting "the work ethic [must] be reinvigorated in every community in Britain." Again, work is associated with vigor, and the work ethic is described nostalgically, as something once present, now lost, and in need of renewal. Benefits are repeatedly associated with passivity and inactivity. For example, Richard Layard (1997a: 191), economist and adviser to the government's welfare-to-work initiative, writes that "unemployment benefits are a subsidy to inactivity and it should not be surprising if they lead to a rise in inactivity." Layard continues: "after a period of a disheartening job search, unemployed individuals often adjust to unemployment as a different lifestyle." The picture painted is one where long-term benefit claimants fail to subscribe to "mainstream" values about the intrinsic worth of paid work.

The explanation for this alleged decline in work ethic is claimants' supposed detachment from the world of work, which constitutes a second element in the discursive production of the dependent claimant. In Layard's terms, long-term benefit claimants "adjust" to unemployment as a "different" lifestyle, different, one assumes, from the lifestyle of workers. The world of work and the world of benefits are thus constructed as distinct and separate, rather than as overlapping, intermingling, and mutually pervious. Government minister Peter Mandelson argued in the *Observer*

Newspaper (August 17, 1997) that "many of them [the socially excluded] are so dis-tanced from the labour market that they have very many bridges to cross just to bring them back into any sort of mainstream living." Likewise, Layard (1997b: 57) writes:

> Once people have been unemployed that long, their chances of finding work have been largely destroyed. The very fact of failure makes failure more likely, and many employ-ers will not even look at someone who has been out of work for a long time.

In these statements, work is narrowly constructed as *paid* work, and long-term claimants are assumed to be detached from this world. Another New Labour minis-ter has expressed the concern that "they [the socially excluded] and their families are trapped in dependency. They inhabit a parallel world where income is derived from benefits, not work. . . . These are whole communities which are completely discon-nected from the world of work."[5] This language evokes a picture of claimants *trapped* in dependency, and not even inhabiting this world, but a parallel one in which ben-efits are the only currency. The explanation of this threatening foreignness of this parallel world is its distance from the world of work.

A symptom of the "detachment from the world of work" is argued to be claimants' lack of awareness of job opportunities in their areas. Employment Secretary David Blunkett said, at the launch of a national Jobs Hotline telephone initiative in No-vember 1998, "the fact is that there are lots of jobs available at the moment that em-ployers cannot fill."[6] It is because, the construct goes, long-term claimants are pas-sively sitting at home, removed from the world of work that it is deemed necessary, according to Gordon Brown, to "take action to visit, telephone and coach long-term unemployed men and women back into the jobs on offer."[7]

One policy solution to the uneven geography of unemployment under the New Labour government has been the development of ActionTeams. At their launch in July 2000, government minister Tessa Jowell stated:

> The Action Teams will have a free hand to come up with imaginative, flexible ideas to overcome personal and community barriers to work. It's about finding local solutions to local problems. This jobs boost focuses on matching people to jobs, tackling postcode discrimination, building confidence, training in basic skills and dealing with public transport problems. Some examples of what Action Teams will do include:
> - run bus services to collect and deliver children to and from childcarers
> - provide vouchers for work clothing, tools, haircuts
> - support clients with driving lessons, and help with taxing/insuring their cars
> - provide local freephone services to link employers with jobseekers
> - fund people on benefits other than Job Seekers Allowance to go on New Deal options

The notion that certain areas suffer high rates of unemployment because the labor market is depressed, for example because of the collapse of manufacturing indus-tries, is completely missing from this picture. What Employment Secretary David Blunkett called "communities blighted by long-term unemployment" are, by the logic of the Action Teams, more in need of driving lessons and haircuts than job creation policies.

To sum up, the subjectivities of long-term benefit claimants are discursively produced as passive and dependent, in contrast to the discursive construction of paid workers. Paid work becomes the salvation for claimant: work is active, virtuous, self-improving, the source of independence, and distant from the parallel world of benefits and benefit claiming. According to a major policy document on welfare reform, "Work provides people with social networks and a sense of purpose" (Department of Social Security 1998: 31), and "paid work is the most secure means of averting poverty and dependence" (23). The dominant political discourse of benefits is the opposite of all this—benefits are passive, morally hazardous, self-damaging, synonymous with dependency and much detached from the parallel world of work. A "comprehensive welfare-to-work programme" is therefore necessary to "break the mould of the old, passive benefit system" (24). Welcoming a report of the Organization for Economic Cooperation and Development, which praised the success of the welfare-to-work program "in helping people move from dependence to independence," the British government promised that "everyone [would be] given the means and opportunity to tackle any barriers to independence" (Department for Education and Employment press release, November 19, 1999). Benefits are constructed in relation to passivity every time the prime minister decries the "something-for-nothing" welfare state. Describing the government's welfare reform program in the center-right national newspaper, the *Daily Mail*, Blair (February 10, 1999: 10) declares:

> Individuals . . . have a responsibility to accept work, train themselves for jobs, be flexible in the jobs they take and avoid dependency where they can. It marks the end of the something-for-nothing welfare state. The days of an automatic right to benefit will go. It's tough, but the right thing to do.

In a similar attack on the something-for-nothing welfare state, in a speech on social reform delivered in November 1999 to Demos (a left-leaning think-tank), Employment Secretary David Blunkett proposed that, by contrast, "something for something gives people a stake" and "where we seek to extend cash benefits, we should debate the idea of adding some conditions—such as a commitment to training or self-improvement." The subject that claims benefits is assumed to be in particular need of such improvement.

LIVED EXPERIENCES OF BENEFIT CLAIMING

As I have argued, New Labour political discourse constructs benefit claimants as dependent, passive, getting something for doing nothing, work-shy, work-detached, and work-poor. But during a qualitative study of lived experiences of benefit claiming I heard very few stories that resonate with this dependent, passive subject, and it is to these alternative stories that I now turn, drawing on the accounts of benefit claiming related by forty long-term benefit claimants in a series of group and individual interviews. These stories conflict with those told in the previous section: respondents often subscribe to dominant values about work, have various and multiple connections to the world of work, and display in-depth knowledge of their local labor markets and the "opportunities" therein.

Attitudes toward Work

Table 10.1 highlights key elements of the argument made in this section. The left column of the table offers examples of the language and images about benefit claiming discussed in the previous section. The picture evoked is this: claimants are never "actively" claiming, but always "on" benefits; they are never "up and about" but always "sitting down"; they spend all day at home and so the special Action Teams have been created to persuade them out to work; they are not enjoying an active life but are "chained to passive dependency." The quotations in the right column illustrate that claimants are aware of this stereotype, but that it is far removed from the reality of their everyday lives. The quotations trouble the notion that claimants have somehow lost the work ethic, or lost their belief in the importance of work. The majority of respondents said that they enjoy work, miss full-time employment, and

Table 10.1. Political Constructions of "Passivity" versus Respondent Reports of "Activity"

Constructions of "Passivity"	Examples of "Activity"
We expect everyone who can work to go to work and not sit at home on benefits. (speech by Gordon Brown, July 2000)	I'm a community councilor, I'm on the sports council management committee, I coach for the council in schools, and I'm doing an Open University degree as well, just to keep going, rather than sitting around doing nothing. (Noel)
[We will] take action to visit, telephone, and coach long-term unemployed men and women back into the jobs on offer. (speech by Gordon Brown, July 2000)	I've been in that Job Center today again, I go in regular anyway and I've applied for at least, mebbie, three jobs a week. (Ian)
[The welfare system] chains people to passive dependency instead of helping them to realize their full potential. (Department of Social Security, 1998)	I need new challenges, I have usually got more than one thing going at a time, so you don't get rusty. (Malcolm)
The public will not support a social security system that appears to tell people they can sit in bed all day watching television and drawing benefit. (unnamed cabinet minister quoted in Powel, 2000: 45)	I'm not sitting at home all day watching the TV, I'm doing things, fixing Land Rovers or signing on or doing courses. (Larry)

want to get back into reasonably paid, full-time jobs.

The perceived advantages of work, reported by respondents, include the potential for higher income and increases in self-esteem and self-confidence. For example, Gary[8] said

> I think the pluses of paid work are just in the sense of society being like that, it gives you self-esteem, to be in paid work. "What do you do?" "Oh, I'm a train driver." You know, something like that, just the very fact of being paid is a huge psychological boost in a way, it means that somebody really appreciates what you do.

Similar views emerged in other interviews as the following excerpt illustrates.

Rose: Pluses are self-esteem, self-respect, um, conformity . . . right, acceptance by others who work.
Niamh: That's interesting that you said self-esteem first. Do you think that's important?
Rose: I think it is aye, because you feel you've done something, and contributed, not just for yourself but for society.[9]

These remarks reflect the dominance of ideas and discourses about work being good for one and part of one's contribution to society. Crucially, they also show that these respondents accept such ideas and subscribe to these discourses. The comments were all responses to questions about the *positive* aspects of work; they suggest that respondents believe that work is good because it provides a route to conformity and acceptance in society. These responses do not fit in with the construction of a benefit dependency culture of people who fail to subscribe to dominant discourses around the importance of work. I found no evidence of a separate dependency culture among benefit claimants; instead I found evidence that claimants understood the rules of the game, and, in the Foucaultian sense, internalized these rules and norms and the gaze of society (Foucault 1970).

Gender stereotypes embedded in dominant discourses of family are also evident in respondents' attitudes toward work. Male respondents often expressed anxiety about the difficulties experienced in fulfilling the role of "breadwinner" within their families, as well as more general concerns of not "contributing to society." One male respondent who said his self-confidence had declined since being out of work linked this feeling to the fact that it compromised his ability to fulfill the breadwinner role:

Niamh: Why do you think it dents your confidence not being in work?
Ron: It's the whole thing of just providing, eh, providing for your family . . . there's all that stigma attached to it . . . you know, you cannae fend for yirsel sort of thing . . . it makes me feel bad.[10]

The same respondent had recently expressed interest in a job, only to find out that he would have been financially worse off than he is on benefits. He spoke of a real desire to get back into full-time work and mixed emotions at being unable to take up the job opportunity:

Niamh: How would you have been worse off doing that job?
Ron: I'd have probably felt better, but the family would have been suffering, the wife would have been worse off . . . and I think she's worried that I'd just jump into work and end up wi' less money, which at the end of the day won't pay your bills . . . but you dinnae want to get caught on benefit, I mean I don't want to sit on benefit to be honest, this is the longest I've been unemployed over the last three year, and before that from the age of 16 to 29 I'd never ever signed on.[11]

Ron admits that his self-confidence would have improved had he taken this job, but the family's financial situation would have worsened. He links the lack of confidence from not being in work with inability to provide for his family, but then explains how he could not apply for a job because it would have further compromised his ability to provide for his family. This respondent is not prevented from getting a job by lack of desire to work, or by any lack of knowledge of job opportunities available to him. He knows that the opportunities open to him in his trade of paving are so poorly paid and insecure that his family would be worse off if he took a job of this kind, and it is for these reasons that he is still unemployed.

There are many stories from other respondents expressing their enjoyment of previous jobs and acknowledging the benefits they experience from paid work. It is difficult to reconcile this picture of respondents who hold overwhelmingly positive attitudes toward work, with the picture of benefits as part of a dependency culture in which claimants fail to appreciate the benefits of work. Enjoyment of work is also evident in the numerous connections to work the claimants maintained, to which I now turn.

Connections to the Worlds of Work

The respondents interviewed have many and varied connections to the worlds of work and could even be described as work-rich. I am not using work-rich in the traditional sense of describing double-income professional households, but borrowing it to show how those conceived of as work-shy are actually often work-rich, in terms of connections to work, if not income from work.

One respondent expressed surprise at the amount of work done by people on his "back-to-work" training course, saying: "when I came here, I thought everyone would have not worked at all for six months, or whatever it was it had to be, but there's quite a lot of people that actually still work just now, and it's legal sometimes!" (Nick).

Of the forty people interviewed, twenty-nine were working to some extent, most of this work being legal rather than undeclared.[12] The types of work undertaken fell into five categories: therapeutic work (that is unpaid work done for health reasons), voluntary work, caring work in the home, undeclared paid work "on the side," and declared part-time work. Respondents reported maintaining connections to work despite obstacles such as employer's prejudice and institutional bureaucracy. Two women with whom I spoke in a group interview, both of whom had mental health difficulties, had eight different voluntary and therapeutic work commitments between them, including committee work, development work, catering work, and funding allocation work. Both, however, expressed the feeling that employers in the formal labor market do not appreciate their skills:

> Evelyn: Oot in the community naybody really wants you to work for them, you know what I mean? Because you've got a mental health problem.
> Fiona: [You are] classed as useless
> Evelyn: And it's sad, the types of things that get done up here is unreal, the skills that people have got, a lot of people out there havenae got any skills, compared to what we've got. But we get classed as "well, they're no able to work." That really annoys me. The way I feel the noo, I feel like I cannae move on, I'm stuck, I cannae move on to a job, naybody'll have me.[13]

Another respondent complained that the Benefits Agency discourages claimants from doing voluntary work, or at least from declaring all the voluntary work they do because incapacity or disability benefits may be taken away if claimants show they are capable of voluntary work. The fear is that questions may be raised about why such claimants continue to be considered mentally or physically unfit for work. This may be seen as reasonable questioning on the part of the Department of Social Security, but is insensitive because the voluntary work is often very different from paid work for an employer. Some respondents do just two hours of work every week or two and are free to turn down work. In this sense it is the voluntary sector that is flexible in relation to the needs of its workers, in contrast to the formal paid labor market. Similarly, the Benefits Agency fails to be flexible in relation to the needs of its "clients."

Another example of respondents' strong connections to the world of work was unusual in that the interviewee was doing undeclared work but was typical in that he was doing some work:

> OK, my last job I had was Thursday night working behind the bar, a little fly one, um, but at present I'm employed on a casual basis driving a wagon for a guy who doesn't use me all the time but if he's got a job, a pick-up from Dundee or something, he'll get me to do that on a casual basis. Plus I've got my own ghost tours company, and we do banquets over a weekend, Fridays and Saturdays, so that keeps me ticking over.

At the time of the interview this respondent was running his own business and working for two employers on a semi-casual basis, illustrating that he was very far from being detached from work.

Knowledges of Local Labor Markets

The construction of claimants as so far detached from the world of work that they are unaware of the opportunities around them is another construction that falls apart when claimants' reports are considered. Respondents often held in-depth knowledge of their local labor markets and of the reality of the "flexible labor market." Flexible labor is often used in descriptions of the "top" of the labor market, where the dominant image is of executives changing jobs regularly, developing their human capital, and selling their skills to the highest bidder, a scenario that can benefit the worker. At the bottom of the labor market, however, flexible labor means short-term temporary contracts, part-time work, poor in-work conditions, no pensions, and low pay (see table 10.2). The benefit claimants interviewed are more aware of this type of work than many precisely because they have done these jobs in the past and are currently being encouraged or compelled to do them again.

Table 10.2. Respondents' Knowledge and Experience of Their Local Labor Markets

Lack of severance pay	I was there [at last job] four years, but every Christmas . . . they paid you off . . . you'd be guaranteed to get paid off for three, four weeks and then they sent for you again, just to make sure they werenae giving you your redundancy. (Andy)
Unsociable, long hours	I was a security guard. It's not very well paid, I was coming oot wi' about 200 pound a week, I was working from half four at night till nine the next morning . . . on a Friday I worked from half three till Monday morning at nine without sleeping. They expected me to do that. I admit it I slept, but the first couple o' months I was on the site I stayed awake, chased people off the land an that, till I thought it was reasonable ok, I could get ma head doon for a few hours. (Billy)
Short-term/ temporary work	More and more work is becoming very short term, short-term contracts, you get a lot more work put onto you then you really ought to have. (Craig)
Part-time work	If you go into shops and stuff it's usually part time that they want, which is not always good for you but is better for them obviously . . . because we don't have the same rights as the full-time employees, we don't have the same holiday, sick pay . . . it's just better for them in the long run. (Freda)
Poor prospects	All these training facilities, how to do CVs, interview techniques . . . and at the end of the day, "Oh, Wicks are opening a new store! Get down there, you might get a job!" Need all this to go get a job at Wicks? You need all this to get a proper job, a long-lasting job, a career type job, not to . . . stack shelves in Tesco's. (Keith)
Low pay	I'm no' wanting to work as a security guard for eighty hours a week for 140 pound, it's just not on. (Kevin)

The combination of poor conditions and low pay makes it very difficult for claimants to find entry-level jobs that generate income greater than benefits.[14] As one respondent put it:

It all depends if you're making a living oot o' it, you know, they're advertising jobs for £3.60 an oor [the minimum wage], which is just . . . well some people can do that, some people cannae, and the majority o people that are looking for jobs just couldnae possibly dae it, you couldnae do forty oors at £3.60 an oor and have a hoose and a wife and weans and a dug and a car, it's just impossible, you just couldnae dae it, you couldnae pay a mortgage or pay the rent or, you just couldnae have things like that at £3.60 an oor . . . so having a job is all right as long as you're living off it. I mean there's nae point in me gaun oot and gaun aff the broo and gaun to dae a job as a security guard or something in a shopping centre and working 60 oors a week for £3.60 an oor, you know, you just couldnae dae it! Then again, if you go get a job as a delivery driver or something, or working in a store room or something, you know, and getting £5.50 an oor, it's an easy enough job to do, it's sensible money, and you'd have a wee bit o' money at the end of the week.[15]

Respondents are not living in ignorance of job opportunities in their local labor markets because of their supposed detachment from the world of work. They know that there are few opportunities in depressed local labor markets, and those "opportunities" that do occasionally arise are so poorly paid as to be hardly worth their while.

Another respondent showed awareness of the effects of gender, geography, and insecurity of tenure, which are often missing from government accounts of the causes of unemployment.

Niamh: Do you think it's hard to find work around here?
Gaynor: Oh aye, "X" is bad for trying to . . . you know it's OK for the likes o' catering or hotels or something like that, but if you've got qualifications in something else it's quite difficult, especially for men I think, I think it's a lot mair difficult for men than it is for women, at the moment.
Niamh: How's that?
Gaynor: There's no really a lot o men's jobs as such, like labourers or tar-men or builders, you know they're building the big supermarket, but it's limited, you know they're only in work for so long and then they end up losing their job, I think it's a limited thing, whereas women can go into shops or cleaning and different things, waitressing and things like that . . . you see men doin' some o' that but no' very much. . . . I think there's a lot mair limitations to a man than there is to a woman. . . . I think it all depends on where you're actually situated, in Glasgow there'd be a lot mair work for a man, but in the likes o this area, it's no . . . cos there's no all that many jobs gaun aboot for men. You know they're building that supermarket at the moment, but that's no a permanent thing, that only gies them employment for nine month, a year and then they're back on the dole again, whereas the women that is going for cashiers or whatever,

there's going to be some men that get the job but the biggest majority is gaun to be women, but that's gaun to be permanent, if they want it, ken.

Niamh: Is that the big one up the back?

Gaynor: Yep, men are OK for building it, but to keep it going it needs the women (laughter).[16]

Gaynor is obviously aware of job opportunities in her area; she displays knowledge of current and future opportunities and whom these opportunities will suit. The problem is that the only jobs available are poorly paid and insecure, and these jobs rarely compensate fully for the benefits forgone by taking them. And yet despite both past experiences and what respondents know about their local labor markets, they generally remain determined in their job searches (see table 10.1).

CONCLUSION: ACCOUNTING FOR THE POPULARITY OF THE DEPENDENCY DISCOURSE

If claimants' experiences on the edges of the formal labor market are so removed from their subjectivities as produced by political discourse, how can we explain the continuing popularity of these discourses? One explanation may be that discourses of the work-shy and work-detached, the passive and dependent can be used as a justification for particular kinds of policy intervention. If benefit claiming is constructed as a problem of benefit claimants and their alleged "culture" and behavior, then the policy "solution" is to focus on claimants. If the problems are defined as claimants' passivity and dependence, then the solutions are training, coaching, and cajoling claimants back to the civilizing effects of work. The problems of uneven geographies of economic well-being and labor market buoyancy are rarely discussed in relation to welfare reform or unemployment. Even when this spatial unevenness of unemployment is acknowledged, the problem is still defined as lying with the people who find themselves unemployed, as shown by the discourse surrounding Actions Teams. What all the welfare reform and unemployment policies have in common is that they focus on labor supply to the exclusion of labor demand, and this is a reflection of the prevailing economic ideology. As Theodore and Peck (2001: 89) argue, "workfare strategies may represent social policy complements to neo-liberal or 'deregulationist' labour market policies, working actively on the supply side of the labour market to prepare the workforce for a life of 'flexible' jobs."

With the New Labour government we have seen the continuing construction of globalization as inevitable and the market as the defining framework for all social welfare policy. Gibson-Graham (1996) argues that capitalism is constructed not only as the economy, but as society too. That "we live in a capitalist society" is repeated so often that to question this "fact" becomes almost absurd. And yet, as Gibson-Graham (1996) shows, so much of what is "economic" is noncapitalist, so many of our daily economic transactions are nonmarket transactions. Writing about Marxist analyses of capitalism Gibson-Graham argues that "the project of understanding the beast has itself produced a beast" (1), and it is this constructed beast (capitalism) that is profoundly limiting for the noncapitalist and anticapitalist imagination. Similarly, the construction of capitalism and globalization as inevitable givens is a profoundly limiting position for public policy.

The welfare state, especially benefit claiming, is increasingly seen as the opposite of what the modern economy is about and is a threat to Britain's international competitiveness. Bringing people back into useful work (read paid work) is Blair's greatest challenge. Whether the work is there in the first place is something that is insufficiently addressed. What it certainly does is construct a benefit-claiming subject that eclipses important aspects of the lives of benefit claimants. Clearing discursive spaces in which claimants can construct alternatives is vitally important if dominant political rhetoric in the United Kingdom and elsewhere is to be challenged.

NOTES

1. The British Labour Party began to use the term "New Labour" in 1995 in a discursive strategy designed to distinguish itself from the old, business-unfriendly, socialist and supposedly unelectable Labour Party of the previous fifteen years.

2. The Scottish Office was the branch of the UK government in charge of Scottish affairs before the establishment of the Scottish Parliament.

3. Some respondents were recruited from an agency hired to deliver the New Deal welfare-to-work program in the region. I was dependent on people to volunteer to be interviewed, and three of those who did lived in middle-class areas with lower levels of unemployment.

4. The Chancellor of the Exchequer is the British title for the government minister in charge of the Treasury.

5. Harriet Harman in a speech at the launch of the Centre for Analysis of Social Exclusion, London School of Economics, November 1997.

6. Gordon Brown also frequently bemoans the thousands of job vacancies nationwide.

7. In a speech to the Royal Economic Society, St. Andrews, in July 2000.

8. All respondents have been given pseudonyms.

9. I preserve, as far as possible, the interviewees' patterns of speech. In this quotation, aye = yes.

10. Cannae = cannot, yirsel = yourself.

11. Dinnae = do not.

12. Only four respondents reported current involvement with undeclared work.

13. Oot = out, naybody = nobody, havenae = have not, the noo = now.

14. Part of the government's approach to dealing with this "poverty trap" problem is the introduction of a system of tax credits, including the Working Families Tax Credit (WFTC). These tax credits have been introduced under the government mission of "making work pay." While I welcome any policy that gives low-income families greater take-home pay, I would question the long-term viability of what amounts to the effective subsidization of employer's low wage levels by the government.

15. O' = of, oor = hour, dae = do, hoose = house, weans = children, dug = dog, nae = not, gaun = going, aff = off, broo = unemployment benefit.

16. Mair = more, gie = give.

11

Hot Gossip: Rumor as Politics

Rosaleen Duffy

This chapter examines the role and importance of rumor and gossip in the research process. It draws on my experience of interviewing government officials, representatives of nongovernmental organizations (NGOs), academics, journalists, and community groups about the politics of conservation in Belize and Zimbabwe.[1] The chapter shows how rumor and gossip assist both relatively powerful and relatively powerless interest groups to spread their ideas and to influence political processes, and how research interviews may be used to such ends. It also shows how gossip creates, sustains, and supports certain political networks. Drawing on analyses of these processes the chapter elucidates the interplay between knowledge claims and subjectivities in particular political contexts. I begin by discussing the place of oral evidence in research, and then I investigate the role of rumor both as a political instrument for powerful interest groups and as a means of political resistance through particular examples. Finally I discuss how such material can be prepared for broader academic audiences.

The issue of what constitutes knowledge has a critical bearing on the ways in which academic research is conducted and prepared for publication. When research relies on information that is passed through oral networks, it is always open to criticism that the stories people tell about people, places, and events do not constitute "data" but are merely unsubstantiated rumors or gossip. Moreover, the term "gossip" is usually used pejoratively to undermine the importance or credibility of information passed through oral networks and is typically construed as a feminine practice operating outside the domain of rational discourse (for an introduction to wider debates surrounding gender and communication see Cameron 1990; Spender 1980).

The social values embedded in dictionary definitions of gossip reflect the way that oral networks, and the substance they convey, have been constructed as unimportant, marginal, irrational, feminine, and unreliable. For example, the *Oxford English*

Dictionary defines a "gossip" as "a person, mostly a woman, of light and trifling character, especially one who delights in idle talk; a newsmonger; a tattler"; "gossip" is characterized as "idle talk; groundless rumour; tittle-tattle; . . . especially about persons and social incidents"; and "rumour" is defined as "general talk, report, or hearsay not based on definite knowledge." For the purposes of this chapter I make no distinction between rumor and gossip, the important differences lying in the ways different people and social groups talk about issues of interest to them.

In light of such definitions it would seem that gossip and rumor should have no place in academic research, which is supposed to be carried out according to strict methodological rules that specifically exclude unreliable evidence. However, as feminists have long argued, conventional definitions of scientific knowledge as rational and objective produce and rely upon the exclusion of forms of knowledge that are devalued, in part, through their association with femininity (Antony and Witt 1993; Harding 1986; Hekman 1992; Lloyd 1984; Rose 1993). This not only perpetuates gendered patterns of inclusion and exclusion from the world of academic research, it also excludes many important topics from research. Consequently, feminist critiques of science validate new areas for research, including issues of national and international political sensitivity and unrecorded or illicit social, economic, and political phenomena, which can only be accessed by listening to gossip and rumor (Kanter et al. 1984; Rich 1980; Spender 1986).

Boden and Zimmerman (1991) argue that talk is at the center of everyday existence and is pervasive in every setting of human affairs, providing a fundamental framework for social interaction and social institutions. Part of this talking takes the form of gossip and rumor. The truth status of information passed through oral networks is often much less important than the various social and political effects of its passage. Moreover, talk provides a record of particular narratives on particular topics, and the subjectivities produced and mobilized by different narratives underpin competing analyses of political events and processes. Further, by focusing on gossip and rumor the researcher can illuminate the production of particular knowledges and subjectivities. For example, the accusation that information is mere rumor or gossip is often indicative of efforts by interest groups to claim authority on a particular topic and to exclude or undermine other knowledges, information networks, and social groups.

The idea that gossip is women's talk and does not constitute an accurate record of an event or political process is vitally important and is often used to exclude and undermine certain kinds of contributions to political debates. Although gossip has been feminized, numerous actors, including many men, engage in and utilize gossip, not least in attempts to exercise political power (Cameron 1985, 1990). Marginalized groups are excluded from political debates in part by depicting their contributions as meaningless chatter, thus ensuring that they are prevented from engaging effectively in political discussions (compare Russ 1984). The feminization of gossip is also linked to its representation as highly personal and personalized and as outside rational discourse.

In the course of various research projects with which I have been involved it has become clear that there are vitally important oral cultures that pervade and constitute politics; for example, many of those I have interviewed use gossip and rumor to engage with, describe, and participate in political processes in the conservation sector. While the research has been primarily concerned with environmental politics, my work has led me through these gossip networks into studying parallel economies centered on the illicit trade in drugs and wildlife products. Likewise, my research on the environment has become closely intertwined with various political interest groups that have used rumor to undermine opposing factions, while also claiming that the rumor-based resistance strategies of marginalized groups represent knowledge that is value-laden and therefore value-less.

The ways in which people talk about one another provide vital evidence that may be more informative than written sources and that, at the very least, indicate how people construct the world around them. As Wickham (1998) points out, most people tap into gossip networks, and in universities, for example, an examination of the minutes of departmental meetings will only provide an institutional history of the organization, when what really matters is missing from the minutes. The key information for many members of a department is the coffee room gossip about who made the good points, who had a tense moment with whom, who got in the way of which proposals, but none of this evidence about the tensions and politics of the institution appears in the official minutes (Wickham 1998). Gossip can be used to build political constituencies in order to ensure that the key supporters of a particular political position have a broader base from which to lobby for their interests; controversial items are often discussed in advance with sympathetic colleagues to float ideas, listen to feedback, and build supportive political alliances.

Clearly, rumor is an important political instrument, and this is especially the case in societies where newsprint and other forms of media are strictly controlled by single interest groups. Under such conditions, the best sources of information about current political issues, corruption, and illicit trading networks are often found in spoken form, and interviews can provide a researcher with unrivaled insight into these social, economic, and political processes. Ellis (1989) argues that an important source of political information in sub-Saharan Africa is *radio trottoir*, literally "pavement radio." Pavement radio is broadcast via oral networks and often discusses matters of political importance in the absence of official announcements. Pavement radio advances causes, details the number and nature of casualties, which may be at odds with government figures, spreads salacious gossip about top level government ministers, and so on. While politicians and news managers make strenuous efforts to control the circulation of political ideas and perspectives, the African public reserves the right to decide what is important and interesting (Ellis 1989). Pavement radio also indicates that in sub-Saharan Africa (and elsewhere) particular forms of knowledge are valued in very different ways from in the West; in particular information that is passed through oral networks is often more trusted than in Western societies, which cling to the idea that "real news" is found in newsprint. Unlike newspapers, radio, and television, rumor cannot be banned, closed down, or manipulated in order to serve the supposed interests of the state. Instead, it can provide one of the few unregulated forms of political communication in societies where the media is strictly controlled (Ellis 1989).

White (2000) argues that gossip focuses primarily on people in positions of power. It therefore shows how fragile political reputations can be because it discloses weakness, rendering the powerful vulnerable. Interest groups sometimes successfully spread stories across enormous geographical and social distances precisely because they are considered interesting enough to repeat to others within particular networks. Since such oral networks are often keen to discuss the politically powerful and their various activities (including wrongdoing and scandals), they create an important role for themselves within domestic politics. Thus, Scott (1985) argues that marginalized social groups use oral networks as a means of political resistance. In Scott's terminology, talking is one of the "weapons of the weak." For example, in Kenya, where politics is very strongly dominated by one party, political rumors are often deemed to be critically important by the political leadership. As a result, President Daniel Arap Moi periodically endeavors to bring national debate or gossip to a halt by declaring that a particular issue or incident cannot to be discussed anymore (Mwangi 1997).

Despite its role as a means of political communication, gossip has a bad press, and there is a long history of telling people, especially women, not to gossip because it is idle and trivial. However, gossip is not idle, it is not necessarily malicious, it is not necessarily untrue; indeed gossip is often most effective when it is "true." Moreover, even when it is not, it can provide an accurate representation of the attitudes of a particular social group, and it structures the relationship between the group of gossipers and those being gossiped about (Wickham 1998). White (2000), in her study of the stories of *mumiani* (blood suckers or vampires) in eastern and central Africa, suggests that these stories should not be viewed as "truth" in a positivist sense, which is precisely why academics have often ignored them. Rather the stories of bloodsuckers indicate the negotiation of meanings through hearsay, which generates the kind of truths in which people believe. Gossip of this kind does not deliver information but discusses it in ways that "correct" and amend stories with every retelling. In a similar way, some certain social and political worlds can only be revealed by investigating rumors that illuminate aspects of daily life and thought that elude written evidence. For this reason, listening to gossip can be a vitally important source of information in the research process. This is especially the case when researching illegal activities that necessarily go unrecorded or underrecorded in official sources. Listening to gossip is equally important when researching in contexts where free association is impossible and a free press nonexistent. In a repressive political climate, oral networks often provide the best source of news and evidence of resistance to dominant groups or organizations.

However, listening to gossip and rumor is far from straightforward. By its very nature rumor and gossip are generally passed through trusted networks that are constituted by politically sympathetic individuals. Entry into such networks may pose major problems for researchers. If entry is gained, researchers necessarily enter into complex power relationships with informants and are liable to become active participants in the political process, rather than being discreet or detached observers. Issues of confidentiality and the protection of interviewees, vitally important in all forms of social research, may become especially significant, for example in politically charged situations where interviewees may have genuine and well-grounded fears for their safety if they were to criticize powerful people or groups. Some interviewees may ask to have their comments kept off the record and strictly confidential for many reasons, including fear of reprisals from powerful opponents, which may even include threats of assassination or violent attacks on family members. As a result, much of the material contained in this chapter comes from sources who must remain anonymous in order to protect the informants. A number of interviewees in Zimbabwe and Belize took significant personal risks to provide information about the complexities of environmental politics. The issues they discussed in interviews included allegations of criminal activity by high-profile political figures who had previously been accused of silencing opponents through the use of violence.

While in some circumstances it is very important to be aware of the vulnerability of the researched in relation to whom the researcher may wield great power, in other situations informants wield power over researchers (Warwick 1993). Thus, interviewing government ministers demands different interviewing techniques from those required when interviewing journalists or members of community groups. All may have their own axes to grind, but they occupy very different positions in relation to the researcher. There have been moments in interviews when I have been too quick to impose my own categories on information offered to me, but on other occasions, when interviewing powerful individuals, I have sometimes felt utterly powerless, not only unable to influence the agenda, but actively drawn into processes through which the powerful sustain themselves.

Qualitative interviews provide a means of gaining access to ways in which people construct their everyday lives and justify and legitimate their opinions and actions. While these methods do not necessarily lack the rigor that some critics suggest (Baxter and Eyles 1997), researchers have to be aware of a number of issues affecting the nature of evidence generated by interviewees. This is especially the case when interviewing key informants about politically sensitive topics.

Interviewees are always self-selecting, since researchers can only interview those who agree to participate, and representing the views of those who refuse to participate is impossible. Some interviewees insist on defining how long the interview will take, while others can require a list of sample questions or summary of the topics to be discussed in advance. Each interview is different because it is an interaction between two people. When I begin an interview I do not know if the interviewee has had a good day or a stressful day, whether he or she is concerned about the purpose of the interview or if he or she considers it to be a routine matter of providing a description of the official position of his or her particular organization. Interviewers need to be sufficiently adaptable to cope with such uncertainties, as well as being ready to manage the tensions that arise when discussing politically controversial topics.

As Chambers (1988) argues, informants have the capacity to provide researchers with false or misleading information both intentionally and unintentionally, and it is often difficult to filter out (mis)information presented to the interviewer with the intention of propagating a fiction, from the interviewee's genuine beliefs about people, places, and events. Since gossip and rumor are political instruments designed to support particular agendas or to detract from the reputation of opponents, interviewers should expect research interviews to be used in this way. One of the problems for researchers is how to differentiate between rumors already circulating within the respondent's networks and those created opportunistically within the interview itself. Thus, the motives underlying disclosures are often at least as important as the content.

Competing depictions of a political event or process provide clear evidence that knowledges and "truths" are produced. Gaps between different interpretations of the same issue or event demonstrate that notions of truth are intimately bound with the positions and identities of those who circulate rumor and gossip. Consequently, gossip and rumor are as much about the production of subjectivities as the production of knowledges. With this in mind I now turn to discussion of particular examples.

RUMOR AS A POLITICAL INSTRUMENT

In 1994 and 1995, while conducting fieldwork in Zimbabwe on the controversial topic of wildlife utilization, a series of politically charged rumors rocked the Department of National Parks and Wildlife Management (DNPWLM, more commonly referred to as the Parks Department). These rumors were discussed in everyday conversations and were reported in the local press, primarily because they raised wider concerns about corruption, governance, and the ruling party in Zimbabwe.

The rumors centered on an alleged power struggle within the Parks Department, which is the primary agency in Zimbabwe responsible for wildlife conservation. The allegations and counter-allegations of corruption and mismanagement resulted in the suspension of the director and deputy director of the Parks Department, who became the subjects of a public service tribunal and then a full-scale criminal investigation.[2] The two factions involved used the local press, local gossip networks, and my own interviews to support and spread their own versions of events. Through these instruments they provided evidence of how conflicting interest groups use rumors and gossip, in this case as part of their internal power struggle over positions of influence within a government department with access to lucrative tourism deals, to ivory and rhinoceros horn, to the prosperous wildlife ranching industry, and other financially attractive wildlife schemes. The following account necessarily draws on stories that are not independently verifiable. However, the use of rumor by the different factions as an instrument of political communication is very significant in itself, delineating conflicts that proved to be very influential politically. NGOs and donors within Zimbabwe believed some of these rumors, and the external donor community formulated aid policy on the basis of information passed through gossip networks, thereby demonstrating the importance of political accusations within Zimbabwean politics.[3]

The power struggle within the Parks Department was indicative of wider divisions in Zimbabwean politics. It illustrated lines of patronage in the ruling party (ZANU-PF) and attempts by two key alliances to gain control over resources. The two groups involved in the power struggle in the Parks Department can be characterized as the conservationist alliance and the patronage alliance. The conservationist alliance included the former minister of Environment and Tourism, Herbert Murerwa, deputy director of Parks Rowan Martin, and director of Parks Willie Nduku and their supporters within the Parks Department. This group was highly respected in the international community and among local conservation NGOs. They were all qualified professionals with long records of commitment to wildlife conservation in Zimbabwe. Their domestic and international standing meant that they were able to attract donor funding for wildlife programs and represent Zimbabwe's case at international fora concerned with conservation issues.

Those opposed to the conservationist faction formed an influential alliance that included the permanent secretary to the Ministry of Environment and Tourism, Tichafa Mundangepfupfu, Willis Makombe in the Parks Department, and their allies in ZANU-PF.[4] The ability of this alliance to exert influence within the Parks Department was derived from its domestic political position. Wildlife conservation is one of the most racially controversial areas of public policy in Zimbabwe because it is widely perceived as a white domain, and its demands for large areas of land mean that it is in direct conflict with aspirations for land redistribution. Superficially, the patronage faction used the issue of indigenization and black empowerment to justify its actions against the conservationist faction, which was largely identified (though not exclusively) with the white settler community, and this proved particularly effective in the campaign for the 1995 and 1996 presidential elections.[5] Its influence was also derived from the support it received from Vice President Joshua Nkomo (Makumbe 1994).

The power struggle in the Parks Department had its roots in a series of resignations and retirements of several senior Parks officers in the late 1980s. In the post-independence period the public sector has been undergoing a process of indigenization, meaning that black employees have had new opportunities to secure promotion and experience in the context of efforts to redress the racial imbalance in employment caused by the settler regime (Lopes 1996: 25–26). The posts vacated in the Parks Departments were difficult to fill with suitably qualified personnel, and the recruitment drive and promotions that followed the late 1980s' "brain drain" acquired a racial overtone.

Indigenization is highly controversial, and the conservationist faction spread rumors in oral networks and the local press to the effect that, while addressing racial balance was perfectly legitimate, the indigenization strategy had been subverted and was being used as a screen for patronage and corruption. In addition, the conservationist faction spread gossip indicating that white Parks officers were being squeezed out to make way for those allied to particular elements in the ruling party under the guise of black empowerment. These rumors and gossip circulated easily not least because many people believed that the "brain drain" had already resulted in the rapid promotion of people who lacked the appropriate qualifications. For example, the appointment of Willis Makombe as one of the deputy directors was viewed by those sympathetic to rumors spread by the conservationist faction as exemplifying the inappropriate promotion of the politically favored over the suitably qualified. The rumors raised concerns that without suitably qualified personnel the Parks Department would not be able to carry out its most basic functions.[6]

Conversely, rumors were spread by those interested in greater party control of the Parks Department to the effect that proposals for privatization and commercialization were designed to empower the white community once again. Again, these rumors were readily believed by those sympathetic to the patronage faction because there were very few prominent black figures involved in the new privately owned and financially lucrative wildlife conservancies. The growth of wildlife utilization had resulted in white commercial farmers obtaining large stocks of wildlife from the Parks and Wildlife Estate, and so when white officers left the Parks Department to enter the private sector, those supporting the patronage faction spread rumors that these officers were stocking private conservancies and game farms in their own interests and in the interests of their friends.[7]

Although the whispering campaign acquired a racial theme, conservationists, donors, and a number of Parks Department employees agreed that it was not really about racism or about black empowerment. Rather, they acknowledged that talk about indigenization was used as a smokescreen behind which the patronage alliance could maneuver its way into positions of power. The power struggle was primarily about a political fight between rival groups in conservation and in ZANU-PF. One commentator suggested that Willie Nduku (part of the conservationist alliance) had been harassed because of political affiliations dating back to the 1970s when he was closely linked to Reverend Sithole, who had been an outspoken critic of the Mugabe regime and head of ZANU-Ndonga, a small opposition movement.[8]

The social and political networks involved in rumor mongering developed their constituencies and built their power in part through gossiping. This particularly empowered the patronage alliance, putting the conservationist alliance on the defensive, although by no means rendering it powerless. The rumors surrounding key Parks Department personnel became so public that members of the patronage alliance were able to insist on criminal investigations. For example, Deputy Director of Parks Rowan Martin was subject to three different corruption charges: the first related to his acceptance of a vehicle in return for allowing Zimbabwean black rhinoceros to be exported to international breeding programs in Australia and the United States[9]; the second, again relating to acceptance of vehicles, resulted in Martin being sacked; the third was for the misappropriation of funds arising from a business transaction between the Parks Department, a private company, Wildlife Management Services, and a privately owned game reserve in Bophutatswana, involving the removal of live elephants from national parks in Zimbabwe to the game reserve.[10] The power struggle reached its height in 1995 after Deputy Director of Parks Rowan

Martin, as well as Director Willie Nduku, were suspended, prompting several professional conservationists within the department to resign.[11]

The charges leveled against key members of the conservationist faction were never proven, but they were sufficient to tie up key figures in the Parks Department in the Zimbabwean legal process for over two years. During that period the patronage alliance secured positions of influence within the Parks Department, which it still retains. The use of rumor and counter-rumor reveals how gossip functions to create and mobilize social and political networks. For example, friends of Rowan Martin in the wider Zimbabwean conservation community used rumors to support him and his claims of innocence.[12] Thus, the power struggle in the Parks Department built solidarity in the two factions, through which wider political debates in Zimbabwean society were articulated in the campaign for the 1995 general elections. The gossip about political maneuverings in the Parks Department clearly helped to build and sustain social networks on both sides of the divide. In this sense, talking created two communities that were broadly characterized as pro-ZANU-PF and anti-ZANU-PF.

RUMOR AS POLITICAL RESISTANCE

While the Zimbabwean example illustrates how powerful interests use gossip and rumor, similar strategies may also be deployed by marginalized and relatively powerless groups as tools of resistance. Hahn (1997), for example, suggests that in societies with great disparities of wealth and high levels of repression, rumors may be one of the few means by which subordinate groups can enter the terrain of public discourse. Rumors provide opportunities for anonymous communication and may therefore serve as a vehicle for anxieties and aspirations that cannot be openly expressed (Hahn 1997; Scott 1985). This was suggested in the course of interviews I conducted with people who occupied marginal positions in relation to proposals for a Maya Eco Park on the Belize-Guatemala border, where several interest groups used rumors and gossip to bolster their bargaining positions in relation to the government of Belize and a Malaysian logging firm, Atlantic Industries Ltd.

During fieldwork in Belize conducted in the late 1990s, interviewees from various organizations sought to present their own political interpretations of the ecotourism industry. One of the most politically fractious and controversial issues was the future development of a Maya Eco Park in the Toledo district in southern Belize. The indigenous peoples of Latin America, including the Maya, have experienced a long history of persecution from Latino- and Mestizo-dominated governments in the region. During the 1990s Mayan communities began to lobby internationally for recognition of their rights to land, and for social, political, and economic benefits that are available to other ethnic groups in the region. The broader regional pressure for fairer treatment of indigenous peoples had a critical bearing on the responses of the government of Belize and other interest groups in relation to proposals for a Maya Eco Park. A number of organizations in Toledo district were pressing for land on the southern border with Guatemala to be declared a protected area (Williams 1993a,

1993b).[13] The intention was that the Maya Eco Park would eventually connect with protected areas on the Guatemalan side, creating a cross-border area controlled by indigenous Mayan communities. The political implication was that this would confer tacit recognition of pre-colonial and pre-Columbian indigenous land rights in the region, and that the Mayan villages in the area would control the revenues from tourism in the Eco Park.

The issue of ecotourism development in the Toledo district was debated in the local press, and links were made to broader questions of political corruption in the country. Rumor and counter-rumor were used to present opposition to the Eco Park as part of a political conspiracy designed to prevent the region from being opened to tourism. The gossip networks provided a possible explanation by linking political interests opposed to tourism with the abuse of logging concessions in the Columbia Forest Reserve. For example, a local newspaper, *Amandala*, carried an article that suggested that local Mopan and Kekchi communities were enraged by the decision to grant a concession to log the Columbia Forest Reserve to the Malaysian logging company Atlantic Industries Ltd. The anger stemmed from the Mayan belief that the logging concession was detrimental to their way of life, that logging was unsustainable, and that there had been extensive abuses of the license.[14] The logging issue was also linked to broader allegations of political corruption surrounding the way that the concession was supported by the minister of Natural Resources and the local MP for Toledo.

Chet Schmidt of the Toledo Ecotourism Association (TEA) was one of the main proponents of the Eco Park. He claimed that the government of Belize was frustrating the development of the Eco Park because of old-fashioned anti-Mayan racism, because the Maya in the area had consistently opposed the government, regardless of the political party in power, and because success in this economically impoverished region would highlight the political corruption that had previously swallowed up funds destined for development. He also argued that efforts to prevent ecotourism development in the Toledo district were supported by tour operators, hotels, and bars in the north and west of the country, where well-developed tourism infrastructures already existed, because they wanted to retain control over the flow of tourists in Belize.[15]

The case of the Maya Eco Park became inseparable from allegations about the death of Mayan leader Julian Cho. Cho's family claimed in local newspapers that he had been murdered for his vocal stance on Mayan land rights, his support for the Eco Park, and outspokenness in the campaign against logging by Atlantic Industries Ltd. Cho was found face up in a pool of blood, having died from a blow to the back of the head. In local newspapers, such as *Amandala*, he was initially presented as a hero of the Maya people, who had made personal sacrifices in order to fight for his people.[16] However, once the police pathologist ruled Cho's death an accident, his opponents placed stories and letters in the local press that presented Cho as an alcoholic who liked to fight in bars, arguing that his death was a consequence of his drinking and violent temper rather than as a result of an elaborate political conspiracy.[17]

Regardless of the accuracy of allegations of murder and corruption, interviews and newspaper reports certainly provided insight into how key figures involved in the Eco Park, logging and the Mayan rights movements perceived processes of governance. The strategy of placing rumors that originated in close-knit oral networks in the local press also meant that those rumors could be spread further afield: instead of circulating only within trusted oral communities, they became available to potentially influential political interest groups elsewhere.

How the Toledo Ecotourism Association perceived government maneuverings influenced how it lobbied for the Eco Park, how it mourned the death of its leader, and how its members responded to researchers such as myself. For the purposes of publication it is impossible to refer to most of the interviewees by name or by the name of the organizations they represented because of their (often justifiable) fears about the possible consequences meted out by government and private industry. Interviewees were unwilling to have their names linked to specific statements about the minister of Natural Resources, Atlantic Industries Ltd., or to motives for the murder of Cho. Nevertheless, despite the risks, many still felt it was vitally important to get their views into the public arena, albeit anonymously. As Power (1998) suggests, rumors cannot prove the facts of the case, but they do reveal contested terrains and tensions that may not be evident in the documentary record.

RUMOR AND THE RESEARCHER

Rumor is an important source of information for the researcher, but as with all data sources it needs to be handled carefully and sensitively. Ellis and MacGaffey (1996) argue that anthropological methods are suited to research on clandestine trade, political corruption, and other unrecorded processes because of the need for the researcher to gain trust and rapport with potential informants. However, there are considerable ethical problems associated with research on activities that are outside the law, not least because the safety and well-being of both the researcher and the researched may be placed in jeopardy. A major problem concerns protection for the informant, and this may preclude research on some topics. Another problem is that the researcher may be caught between law enforcement and those engaged in illegal activities, sometimes arousing suspicions, and occasionally violence, against the researcher (Kleymeyer and Betrand 1993).

In this context it is not surprising that rumors affect the behavior of researchers. For example, during my fieldwork in Zimbabwe it was rumored that the Central Intelligence Agency routinely tapped phone calls and opened personal mail for evidence of antigovernment activity. There were strong indications that this practice had been widespread during the years of white rule, especially during the period of the Unilateral Declaration of Independence (UDI) (from 1967 to 1980), and in the mid-1990s rumors purported that the secret intelligence apparatus inherited by the black majority government of Robert Mugabe was not dismantled but was used against antigovernment groups within Zimbabwe. This directly impacted my own behavior. For example, I received a phone call from a family member in Britain who made some highly critical remarks about President Mugabe's handling of opposition groups. Fearing a visit from Intelligence, I tried in vain to change the subject to my forthcoming week off in Victoria Falls. This may seem unduly dramatic and paranoid, but I was researching the illegal trade in rhinoceros and ivory, including possible government involvement in wildlife poaching. In addition, Amnesty International, along with a number of conservation NGOs, had published lists of people who had died in suspicious circumstances after investigating military involvement in poaching and the wildlife trade in South Africa (Amnesty International 1992; also see Duffy 1999). Members of my household in Harare had already been interrogated by the police and the Central Intelligence Agency over a birthday party we had held during the campaign for the presidential elections, which was suspected of being a political gathering.

When researching topics such as smuggling, poaching, and political corruption, researchers are confronted with further difficulties in preparing the material for academic consumption. Academic journals and publishers are not newspapers and are often very nervous about publishing politically controversial work. Difficulties are compounded if the material contains negative conclusions about organizations or individuals regarded as particularly litigious. While some evidence can be presented in terms of perceptions or opinions, interviewees may insist on such a high degree of anonymity that important aspects of the context are lost, leaving the validity and authenticity of the evidence open to question. I sometimes hear the same allegations from different people, each of whom forbid me from using the material, or I am often given documents containing evidence supporting such allegations marked "confidential." This may make it impossible to substantiate important arguments.

Sometimes material from interviewees and confidential documents can be supplemented with documentary evidence already in the public domain. This arose in my research in Belize, which generated evidence about the links between offshore banking and drug smuggling in the Caribbean/Central America region. Numerous agencies produce reports about the drugs trade, the most useful of which are from the United States, especially those produced by the Drug Enforcement Administration and the Bureau for International Narcotics and Law Enforcement Affairs (1998a, 1998b, 1998c). These can be supported and contextualized with studies that touch on related issues, such as Steiner's (1998) study of Colombia's income from the drugs trade, published in *World Development*. However, as with all forms of documentary evidence, it is important to acknowledge the political context in which the documents are produced.

Material about the drugs trade in Latin America has to be considered in relation to the politically controversial U.S. "war on drugs" policy. In the late 1990s the government of Belize was criticized for failing to curb the use of the country as an entrepôt state, and this directly affected relations between the two countries. The United States assesses thirty-two major drug producing and drug transit countries annually, judging each in terms of the steps taken to enforce the goals of the 1988 UN Convention against Illicit Traffic in Narcotic Drugs and Psychotropic Substances.

This process is used as a diplomatic tool by the U.S. government to focus attention on producing and trafficking states rather than consumer states. There are three categories: full certification, decertification, and vital national interest certification. In the late 1990s Belize was decertified by the United States for failing to be active in the war against drugs. However, U.S. government documents indicate that Belize was swiftly granted the position of vital national interests, which meant that U.S. aid was not suspended, and that the United States would not vote against loans to Belize from the multilateral development banks (Bureau for International Narcotics and Law Enforcement Affairs 1998a).[18]

Belize is a major offshore banking center. Hampton (1996) argues that the deregulation of international banking during the 1980s was one of the key determinants of the rise of offshore banking centers willing to accept deposits derived from illicit sources.[19] According to Gelbard (1996, 1997), criminal organizations are well placed to take advantage of the relaxation of border controls and trade barriers, and as a result these organizations have been able to create highly effective illegal financial and drug smuggling networks that advance their interests in the context of a world keen to reduce economic barriers. Moreover, increasingly advanced computer technologies have facilitated electronic transfer systems that allow vast amounts of money to be moved around the globe in a matter of seconds (Grove 1995; Bureau for International Narcotics and Law Enforcement Affairs 1998b, 1998c). This means that key figures have access to financial resources with which to underwrite their positions in criminal syndicates and within legitimate government agencies or private sector organizations.

A legal framework that provides for total discretion about the sources of investment capital and the names of the investors has assisted the involvement of legitimate and illegitimate sources of foreign investment in tourism developments. For example, Maria Vega of the Vega Inn and Belize Tourism Industry Association stated that an increasing number of absentee foreign investors are the ultimate owners of restaurants, hotels, and bars in the tourist areas, but that these businesses are leased on long-term contracts of up to thirty years with a Belizean as the local manager.[20] Belize is also the site of a number of holding companies that are not required to disclose who the investors are or from where the financing originated (Bureau for International Narcotics and Law Enforcement Affairs 1998b, 1998c; Hampton 1996).

The Caribbean and Central American regions have been targeted as trafficking routes by Colombian drug cartels, and Belize has not been immune from the development of illegal international trade in narcotics. The position and geography of Belize marks it as an ideal route for smugglers since Belize lies between the producing countries of South America and the consumer countries of Europe and North America, and the Cayes—chains of hundreds of small islands—provide points to drop off and pick up consignments of drugs. In the local press, the increase in trafficking of so-called hard drugs has been partially blamed on Colombian drug cartels using the old trafficking routes for marijuana through Belize to Mexico and ultimately to the United States in order to reach U.S. markets for cocaine and heroin (Nietschmann 1997).[21] Indeed, it was reported in the Belizean press that when officers from the

U.S. Counter Narcotics Cocaine Unit visited customs at the port of Belize, drug-sniffing dogs were so overwhelmed by the smell of drugs they suffered sensory over-load and were unable to function.[22]

One of the striking features of the drugs trade is the way that growers, traffickers, and dealers are increasingly paid in drugs rather than cash. This means that trans-shipment countries are subject to an expansion in the availability of drugs and the attendant problems of narcotic abuse and rising crime (Calvani, Guia, and Lemahieu 1997). Belize certainly provides an example of this. The interrelationship between drug trafficking and money laundering through offshore banking and the construc-tion of hotels has also impacted the growing ecotourism industry. For example, it was reported that cocaine trafficking brought a new spurt of wealth to the local economy in Placentia, California, where the local press noted the appearance of new speedboats and the beginnings of a construction boom.[23] Similarly, there was local speculation, from critics of the involvement of foreign interests and possible crimi-nal elements, that entire resorts were bought with millions of dollars in cash derived from the drug trade.[24]

It is clear that, on the one hand, authorities in Belize have been overwhelmed by the extent of trafficking, and that, on the other hand, elements in the formal state apparatus have been complicit. For example, the U.S. State Department argued in a report for the Bureau for International Narcotics and Law Enforcement Affairs (1998c) that the ability of the government of Belize to combat trafficking was se-verely undermined by deeply entrenched corruption that reached into senior levels of government. While the United States insists that local militaries and law enforce-ment agencies are involved in internal drug enforcement missions, this may serve to increase the potential for corruption and human rights abuses. A number of inter-viewees remarked that they believed elements in the Fisheries Department, the Be-lize Defence Force, and the police to be engaged in the drugs trade.[25] One intervie-wee, who was formerly involved with the Fisheries Department, explained how it was possible and that the relevant authorities would not know if a few bales of co-caine, recovered when a drug transshipment was intercepted, were not handed in, and that these would be sold by the officers themselves. Finding and selling bales of cocaine washed up on the shores of Belize's various Cayes was referred to locally as winning the sea lotto (Andreas 1996).[26]

For the researcher it is important to listen to local gossip and rumor and to ana-lyze stories in relation to published documents and newspaper reports. In interviews related to the drugs trade, interviewees articulated particular political agendas: they were either opposed to the government of the day and blamed them for failing to address smuggling and money laundering; or they were keen to deflect blame from themselves and accused others of being responsible for illicit activities; or they wanted to distinguish themselves as campaigners against the growing drugs trade in the region. Researchers have to consider why a member of a particular gossip net-work is allowing an outsider access to their community. Interviewees use interviews to express political resistance, to identify scapegoats, to blame individuals or insti-tutions, to undermine the political opposition and other competitors, and so on.

Moreover, interviewees often take enormous risks to expose what they see as injustices and wrong-doing to outsiders in the hope that their versions of events will be made public.

CONCLUSION

Although gossip and rumor have a bad press, they can provide researchers with vital information that is not available by any other means. At the very least gossip and rumor provide evidence of how particular interest groups perceive a particular situation or issue and how they present it to outsiders. For the researcher, as with published documentary evidence, it is important to be aware of who is imparting information and why, since the political context in which information is passed to outsiders affects the type of material presented in interviews. Equally, interview settings affect what is said. For example, interviewees are likely to offer different opinions if they are interviewed in their workplaces, in the knowledge of colleagues, than if they are interviewed at home or in a neutral venue away from prying eyes and curious ears. This is critically important when researching in countries where freedom of association or press freedom is curtailed, and in researching politically controversial topics such as drug smuggling and political corruption. Gossip helps to build and sustain existing political and social networks of the powerful and the powerless. The ways that political rumors are spread across space and time through social networks indicate that members of particular networks believe that the information is important enough to be worth repeating. Gossip can be used in this way by the powerful to marginalize opposing social networks and undermine their version of events. Conversely, rumor can be used by excluded social groups to criticize powerful networks, thereby becoming a form of political resistance. The ways that gossip is used reveals contested terrains of knowledge and raises questions about what counts as knowledge.

NOTES

1. The choice of Zimbabwe and Belize arose out of doctoral research on wildlife politics in Zimbabwe (1993–1996), post-doctoral research on ecotourism, and coral reef management in Belize (1997–1999) (ESRC grant L320253245) and a research project comparing the politics of cross-border conservation in Belize and Zimbabwe for which I was principal investigator (1999–2000) (ESRC grant R000223013).

2. "Two National Parks Bosses Suspended," *Financial Gazette*, July 6, 1995; "Minister Suspends Two Parks Bosses," *Herald*, July 6, 1995; and "Jumbo Sale Tribunal Resumes," *Herald*, March 21, 1995.

3. Interview with Stephen T. Bracken, second secretary, U.S. Embassy, March 21, 1995, Harare; and interview with Caroline Plastow, third secretary (aid), British High Commission, March 27, 1995, Harare.

4. Anonymous interviewee.

5. "Suspicion and Distrust Sadly the Order of the Day at Parks Department" (letter from "depressed former ranger"), *Financial Gazette*, December 18, 1987; and "National Parks No Longer Capable," *Financial Gazette*, December 9, 1993.

6. "Suspicion and Distrust Sadly the Order of the Day at Parks Department" (letter from "depressed former ranger"), *Financial Gazette*, December 18, 1987; and "National Parks No Longer Capable," *Financial Gazette*, December 9, 1993.

7. Interview with Tom Taylor, chief executive of the Save Valley Conservancy, May 10, 1996, Harare.

8. Personal communication from anonymous source.

9. Interview with Stephen T. Bracken, second secretary, U.S. Embassy, March 21, 1995, Harare; and also see "Parks Director Accused of Protecting Deputy," *Herald*, September 28, 1994; "Nduku Backed Accord on Rhinoceros Relocation," *Daily Gazette*, September 28, 1994; and "Murerwa Denies Being Lobbied," *Daily Gazette*, September 27, 1994.

10. Anonymous interviewees; "Parks to Come Under Scrutiny," *Herald*, February 7, 1996; "Elephant Export Scandal," *Financial Gazette*, December 23, 1993; "Murerwa Probes Elephant Exports," *Herald*, December 25, 1993; and "Probe into Elephant Deal Launched," *Financial Gazette*, January 13, 1994.

11. "Two National Parks Bosses Suspended," *Financial Gazette*, July 6, 1995; "Minister Suspends Two Parks Bosses," *Herald*, July 6, 1995; and "Jumbo Sale Tribunal Resumes," *Herald*, March 21, 1995.

12. Interviews with Willie Nduku, July 7, 1995, Harare; Rowan Martin, May 29, 1995, Harare; and Brian Child, head of the Campfire Coordination Unit, DNPWLM, May 16, 1995, Harare. It is significant that none of these key staff members who I interviewed in their capacity as experts in the field of conservation remained in the Parks Department after 1996.

13. Also see "Rural Belizean 'Toledoans' Want to Address the House of Representatives," *Amandala*, October 11, 1998.

14. "Erosion of Democracy: The Malaysian Logging Concession," *Amandala*, March 29, 1998; "Maya Lawsuit against GoB," *Amandala*, April 5, 1998; and "Toledo Maya Take Government before Inter-American Commission on Human Rights," *Amandala*, August 16, 1998.

15. Interview with Chet Schmidt, Toledo Ecotourism Association, Punta Gorda, January 8, 1999, Belize. Other informants also talked about how they perceived the government's response to the Maya Eco Park, but requested that their remarks remain anonymous.

16. "Respect Julian Cho RIP," *Amandala*, December 6, 1998; "Funeral Homily for Julian Cho, by Fr. Dick Perl," *Amandala*, December 13, 1998; "Julian Cho May Have Been Murdered," *Amandala*, December 20, 1998.

17. "Friend Who Last Saw Mayan Leader Alive," *Amandala*, December 13, 1998; and "Mayan Leader Dies Alone!," *Amandala*, December 6, 1998.

18. Also see "Defendants in Belize's Biggest Cocaine Bust Walk," *Amandala*, September 27, 1997; "Colombian Drug Trafficker Pays Fine, Exits Prison," *Amandala*, October 5, 1997; and "Bad Baby Belize Says US," *Amandala*, March 9, 1997.

19. Also see *Offshore Times* (Winter 1997, Belize issue), published by the Offshore Association of Central America and the Caribbean, based in Panama; and the Belize Offshore Centre Brochure, produced by Cititrust International.

20. Interview with Maria Vega, January 21, 1998, Caye Caulker.

21. See "Whose Colony Is This Anyway?," *Guardian* (London, UK) June 17, 1997; "US Pressure in Drug Fight Rankles Some," *Amandala*, January 19, 1997; "Colombia and Mexico Sign Agreement to Cooperate in Anti Drug Fight," *Amandala*, February 9, 1997; "Drug Traffic Increasing in the Caribbean," *San Pedro Sun*, December 12, 1997; and "Belize Caught in the

Middle of a Drug War," *Amandala*, August 3, 1997. For further discussion of the global nature of the drugs trade see Stares (1996) and Nietschmann (1997).

22. "Belize by Sea: Much Coast Little Guard," *Amandala*, September 26, 1997; and anonymous interviewees.

23. "Belize by Sea: Much Coast Little Guard," *Amandala*, September 26, 1997. This was confirmed by several anonymous interviewees.

24. Anonymous interviewees.

25. Anonymous interviewees.

26. Confirmed by anonymous interviewees.

IV
INTERSUBJECTIVITIES IN RESEARCH PRACTICE

12

Whose Voice Is That? Making Space for Subjectivities in Interviews

Hannah Avis

ACT ONE: STARTING OUT

In a pub on the outskirts of Edinburgh. Two women sit having lunch with a tape recorder on the table beside them. They are friends but this particular lunch-time they are also engaged in being something other: one is a pilot interviewee, the other is a researcher.

Researcher: I should say before we start this will be confidential and if I do want to use any of it I will check it out with you first.

Elizabeth[1]: Oh that's all right I can't think that anything I have to say will be all that incriminating—or interesting!

Researcher: Well . . . I wouldn't say that necessarily! Anyway, some of the questions might seem a little strange, or maybe obvious because we know each other and I might already really know the answer, but they will hopefully make the interview as a whole make more sense because it might mean there are less gaps in what you tell me.

Elizabeth: No problem, it is an INTERVIEW after all . . .

Researcher: OK, well if you could begin by describing your home.

Both women are engaged in an act of juggling their familiarity with each other as friends and this new, research relationship. Elizabeth is weighing the desire to fit what she thinks her friend is looking for in an interview about her home and how it might impact her identity, and the assurances that her friend has given that being herself and considering her own experience is what is "wanted." The researcher—feeling flustered because, despite valiant efforts to be professional, and to be the collected researcher in whose hands her friend will feel safe, she has cut things exceptionally fine on the time front (this is usual for her), and because she still feels she has a little running to do before she catches up to where she has arrived—is playing, for the first time, the game of constructing the character of the researcher. They order lunch and have some chat about what is going on around them in the pub and in their lives generally—they are about to be in a performance in the Edinburgh Fringe and so have plenty to discuss—and yet it is easy to discern that something else is going on. There is something pressing upon them: there is an interview to be done. The friends are about to cease to be that and become something other? But what?

Over the course of the summer in which this encounter occurred this question arose for the researcher several times. She was setting out on an exploration of what it is to be a researcher, an interviewer, and in order to do this she had coopted five friends to give of their time and themselves—or at least some version of themselves—in an interview. The friendship element of this work came to be important in a variety of ways; at the outset friends would be people who were forgiving, who would more easily accommodate the faltering stammers of someone unpracticed. However, the interviewees' multiple statuses and positions—just as they were friends they were also interviewees, and homeowners, and professionals, and women, and so on—served to highlight the manner in which the position of the researcher was also constructed in the interviews. Thinking through the variety of positions that the interviewees occupied meant that as the researcher—and I'll come clean and reveal the researcher to be me—I was prompted to consider my own subjectivity in the establishing of research relationships; to think about the variety of positions that I occupy during, and after, research interviews; to reflect upon the subject that I am and that I might claim to be, want to be, or try to avoid being in the process of doing research.

Consideration of the five pilot interviews that began my fieldwork has meant recognizing the *me* in the process. It has also meant recognizing the multiplicity of that *me*. I do not only mean the me that is classed, gendered, and racialized, the me that is in and of the academy, that must be reflexively encompassed, that is (re)scripted, in the course of my work, but also the me that is a friend to my friends, that sings with them, drinks in the pub with them, goes to the cinema with them, and now, the me that interviews them. From the very start of the process there were signs that considering myself would be an important part of my research project: as one of my friends joked, I was researching middle-class, home-owning women because that is what I am! But the idea of self, of me as part of the process, was a more embedded and complex issue. I was aware that working with feminist theory, and wanting to be involved in what could be considered a feminist project, I would have to address issues surrounding the (re)presentation of self in the research process. So I grappled with calls for multiple positioning (Katz 1994), renewed notions of reflexivity (Rose 1997b), warnings of betrayal (Stacey 1988), and the problematics of (re)presentation (Gibson-Graham 1994). However, reading those calls and listening to the tapes of my pilot interviews made me think not only about the me that is in the process in terms of unzipping the interviewer/interviewee boundaries—in order to facilitate a more honest construction of researched knowledges—but also raised the issue of the story of me that is in those recorded exchanges. I am in the tapes of those interviews, I reveal as much of a tale as any of my friends: they tell of their homes and the impact they have on who they understand themselves to be, and I tell of who I understand the interviewer to be and how I see, and manage, the me that is a part of the interviewer.

But is that alright? Is it okay to be me? Is it appropriate to hear, appreciate, and consider my very personal presence on those tapes? Exactly which subject position is it acceptable to acknowledge as being involved in the interview process: can I be me or do I need to frame—perhaps obscure or subsume—myself within the interviewer that carries out an interview? Calls may have been made by feminists, and others, to appreciate the influence that researchers have on knowledges that are produced through interviews—and other research interactions—but to stand up and say that I am in there, that it is me who is asking, and laughing, and listening, and telling, could that be acceptable practice? Should the material that I write on recognizing mutuality in the research process and the idea of shared discourses contain insights about me, or should they be abstracted from the personalized researcher, recognizing her or his presence but marginalizing, or minimizing the details of that personality?

There were two events that proved to be influential in answering these questions and in seeking ways to be comfortable with the amount of me I could see and hear in the interviews that I was carrying out. The first was a session at a conference where three women spoke eloquently of the problems of their position as researchers, considering in turn their gender, sexuality, class, race, and the dynamics of the relations they (re)formulated (Bennett 1999; Mitchell 1999; Goudge 1999). In some ways the themes of their papers were not new. However, one in particular spoke of her subjectivity and self on slightly different terms than I had read anywhere in academic literature. Research, Bennett (1999) purported, is as much about allowing for the exploration of self as it is the exploration of the self of others: a reworking of the boundedness of self is a necessary process and is both problematic and adventurous. She spoke of herself, of the "me" that she found running through her research, and of the ways in which she came to terms with herself within the parameters of her academic project. What a relief to hear someone talk of their really personal self in an academic setting, to listen to a writer who addressed the problematics of subject positions within the research process in a way that kept the personality of the personal alive in the discussion.

The second of these events happened approximately one month later when, as part of the reading group from which this book develops, I took part in a discussion about Suzanna Fleischman's (1998) article on the inclusion of the personal in scholarly work. Championing a rich and layered sense of the personal—the I, the me—in scholarly work, the article was extremely heartening. It made me think that, perhaps, being aware of myself in those interviews was potentially fruitful for my research; that hearing myself, and recognizing it to be me, on those tapes was alright; and that writing about the processes of hearing and using some personalized sense of me was a positive project rather than one to apologize for. I began to read the literature on methodologies in a new way: I began to see that all sorts of pieces were about ways of including the idea of self in written work, ways that invested the idea of the personal with a "real" personality. Works by people such as Bondi (1999), Kelly (1988), Keith (1992), Kirkwood (1993), Valentine (1998), and Widdowfield (2000) (also see other chapters in this volume, especially in this section) discuss openly a sense of their personal selves in their work; indeed, they move beyond a sense of personal self in that they offer a retelling of the embodied experiences of their selves in their research. Such work, read afresh, appeared to highlight the possibilities for including the personal in research and showed a keen sense of the ways in which, as researchers, they/we/I am immersed in the process of constructing those relationships that make research. I also began to see the presence of emotional and embodied (re)actions to the experience of research in literary criticism, finding further ways in which a sense of the personal and the personality of the author/researcher can be written and told. I had a wobbly voice that wanted to make itself heard but was unsure whether the something I held to be so personal could, or rather should, have a place within the academic research I undertook.

This chapter offers an exploration of some of these concerns. It plays with the idea and process of the pilot interviews I carried out and observes my role—or the various roles/characters/cameos played out by me—in those interviews. It seeks to hear, acknowledge, and understand the wobbly voice that I had in those pilot interviews—the rambling questions, the coughs, the changes of subject, the laughter, and much more are there in the tapes to be heard as proof that I was part of the experience as it unfolded. It considers the process of balance that I strove for in advance of my pilot interviews, turning over feminist discussions on method and methodology to find the way through the character of the "old-style" researcher I knew I did not want to be, to the me as/within/infused through the researcher that I eventually heard. The chapter then moves on to consider how my voice actually turned out in the interviews. Alongside listening to my voice I will consider the impact hearing that voice had, on both the women I interviewed and myself, as I came to terms with the new roles I was trying out. As Mary Maynard (1994: 12) states, "at its heart the tenet of feminist research must begin with an open-ended exploration of women's experiences"; the exploration that unfolds, that is played out in this chapter is of me and my experience.

ACT TWO: SETTING UP THE SELF AS THE INTERVIEWER—THE FEARFUL PREPARATION

A flashback that moves between a number of different places—offices, midmorning cups of coffee in living rooms, bars, late evening rehearsals. Hannah considers the manner in which interviews should be carried out and, in particular, the role that she must play in them. There is much angst.

Kitty: So what is it that we are going to be up to?

Hannah: Well, I'll ask you some questions about your home and stuff, and you will . . . well, you'll answer them, well answer what you feel comfortable, or feel free to ask stuff yourself if you don't understand or anything . . . we're kind of just going to have a chat about things . . . no need to be anxious.

Kitty: That's OK, I trust you.

Lydia: Oh, having children has completely changed everything . . . it must sound clichéd, someone who doesn't have, like you, not having children . . . you'll never know until you are in there with them . . . er . . . I'm not sure how to explain it to you so you really get the picture.

As fieldwork became ever closer on the horizon I turned to many texts looking for advice on who to be in an interview. There were the tie-wearing, clipboard wielding interviewers put into perspective by Oakley's (1981) much cited chapter on interviewing women, but they seemed to be too far away from anything plausible to spend much time considering or emulating. Then there were extensive feminist debates on the problems of fieldwork, especially the power brokerage that is involved in the interviewing practice undertaken by academics. Engaging with these debates was, in practical terms, not an easy one—as I was heard to wail at a research training seminar, "But how do I do that?"—and in many ways reading those debates left me feeling so unrooted that I was unsure of who or why I should be whatever it was they were calling for. What seemed to be clear was that being reflexive, and flexible, and alert to the power imbalances in the practice of academic research was not about being a silent voice or presence holding the tape machine, but what sort of voice or presence should a researcher be?

It is all too apparent that discourses promoting the distant and objective researcher—the researcher who strives to follow the rules and carry out the perfect interview—remain persuasive and persistent, even for those who seek alternative ways to carry out research. Their persistence is evident in my seeking of a persona: "the interviewer" was a character, somebody other than my usual, everyday self. Even as I was looking to move beyond the distant and disembodied experience of being an interviewer, what I understood to be contained in the feminist calls for embodiment and connectedness was still nothing to do with me and myself, rather it referred to yet another kind of self. What seemed to be required was a construction of character that conveyed confidence and credibility while being involved and coopted into both the process and the product of research. That seemed a lot to achieve, particularly when there was also the issue of creating and maintaining the stimuli for disclosure to be considered.

These troublesome issues seemed to stem from concerns about my credibility—presentation and persona do abound in this discussion. Why would people tell me, Hannah Avis, anything, and then how would I disseminate things that I was told in a manner that would be acceptable? I was concerned about my age, my inexperience—both as an interviewer and researcher but also in terms of my own experiences of home, family, work, and so on—my voice and the way it would sound in asking questions. Would people recognize it as mine, would they relate to it? These and many other questions crowded my thoughts, making me doubt my ability to proceed. It seemed as though the only way to proceed was to assume a role, to become something for the purposes of the interviews, somebody that I would not normally be. To engage in persona and character playing seemed to be somewhat dishonest: it seemed to be acting in accordance with the calls for the distant and detached research practice, but it seemed, in advance of doing any interviews, the easiest way to proceed.

And so I decided I should be "the researcher," a character beyond that which was me. But what is the researcher to be? The researcher exposed, and rejected, in Oakley's 1981 piece is the person who strives to follow the rules and carry out the perfect interview; who aims for an interaction that effectively banishes the people practicing from the practice (examples of writings that are challenged by Oakley and other feminist researchers include Hyman et al. 1954; Denzin 1978; Selltiz et al. 1981). Involvement is to be guarded against lest it taint the data extracted from the interviewee; within a traditional paradigm of (false) objectivity, detachment, and hierarchy, there seems to be little room for the idea of uniqueness and the particularities that interpersonal involvement can bring about. The validity of the process seems to lie in the construction of an empty vessel through which an unbiased flow of material passes from discrete informer to abstract text. Words such as detachment, distance, observer, and professional echo around this packaging of the interview, forming as they do neat and seemingly impenetrable boundaries through which the emotional and embodied self cannot travel. Within such a version of the research process the researcher is a blank space, an unobtrusive collector, a recorder of data. The process is sanitized, it is neat and tidy, it is controlled and manageable.

However, the packaging was a little too tight; it was too neat for me to feel comfortable with. These were my friends; I had asked them if I could do an interview with them and that was what they were expecting—me. To enter their homes, or in one case to have lunch in a pub, and offer them a distanced, empty vessel who would collect material but not allow us to engage in the relationship that we had seemed wholly inappropriate. Why would they tell me anything at all if I was unrecognizable to them? How would being something other than the person for whom they were doing a favor—to be contained within the body of their friend but somehow not their friend—make them feel comfortable with the interview? I began to wonder whether it was a mistake to be interviewing people with whom I shared an existing relationship. Maybe it was the complexities of our relationships and the alterations that would occur during—and perhaps after—the interview process that were causing my confusion and anxiety. I was caught between wanting to position, and mobilize, interpersonal engagement as central to the research process, and a concern that too much personalized involvement would be disruptive of my efforts to collect and disseminate research data.

Perhaps then the issue was one of rapport and how to manage that rapport. The idea of rapport is discussed in both the more traditional school of interviewing and by those seeking to challenge such approaches, and it can be understood to offer a point of progression from an impersonal to an interpersonal interaction. Rapport is about finding some sort of shared understanding between the interviewer and the interviewee; it involves ideas of trust and some sort of likeability in order to create an atmosphere in which the person who is being interviewed feels sufficiently comfortable to make what may be sensitive disclosures. This I understood to be important, but how was this to be achieved when I, as the interviewer, was maintaining a depersonalized distance? The difficulties of creating and sustaining what I understood at that time to be opposing subject positions of researcher and of the more personal and embodied me began to mount.

I am not distanced from my friends; we weave complex webs of shared identities that are forged during the many social occasions we talk, laugh, discuss, and sing our way through. What the idea of rapport led me to rethink was the ways in which, during an interview, I would be engaged in a conscious process of locating and using the points on those webs that would unlock the "data" I was interested in for the purposes of my research project. If rapport encourages some level of sharing then it requires of an interviewer a certain amount of give in order that she or he can take. In other words, the building of rapport necessitates some disclosure by the person initiating the interview so that disclosure from the person responding can follow. The importance of building rapport means that we have to move away from casting the respondent as actively giving and the interviewer as receiving information in the manner of a "sponge" (Maynard 1994: 15). Instead the relationship necessitates a reciprocal arrangement in which information flows in both directions. This reciprocal disclosure punctures the boundary surrounding the researcher, effectively reducing the distance at which the researcher can hold her- or himself from personal presence and/or investment in the process of the interview. The process is necessarily a shared one, and in this sharing there may be space for understanding a subject position beyond the researcher-me dichotomy that I had at first thought to be the way forward.

The sharing involved in research processes, and the way I recognized that sharing to trouble the boundaries that had been holding the subject position of "the researcher" distinct from the subject position of me, does not, however, mean that there are no boundaries in the practice of fieldwork. Indeed Katz (1994) suggests that fieldwork is by its very nature a process of creating boundaries; we delineate what and where it is that we will carry out research and in so doing mark out boundaries between that which is of "the field" and that which is outside the field of study. Such delineation is useful because it helps to displace subjects and subjectivities from the relative obscurity of the everyday and in so doing potentially positions them under the spotlight of the research process. However, the problem with such displacement is that it also serves to fracture the "reality" that we might wish to find in the everyday. The construction of a "field" may serve to define a sense of time and place for a research project, and it may highlight particular subjectivities, but it also fractures them, creating something that is abstract rather then contextualized. The challenge, as Katz sees it, is to appreciate a sense of "the field" containing multiple subjectivities, and, further, to conceive of fieldwork as a kind of mapping of the many links between those various subjectivities so that the webs of meaning that they collectively create can be understood.

There is necessarily a tension involved in the displacement that we undertake during fieldwork, which serves both to highlight and to obscure those subject positions and spaces that as researchers we may seek to better understand. This is not to suggest that the problems of displacement render the project of fieldwork ineffective, but they do need to be carefully considered, not only in terms of the impacts on those on whom the research focuses, but also in terms of what this displacement means for those conducting the research. As Miller and Glassner (1997) suggest, to ignore displacement is to ignore the informing role that a contextualizing "reality" can play in shaping the experience, and the knowledge such experience comprises, which is created during the process of fieldwork. Obscuring the outside reality of the researcher is to ignore the interactive nature of the interview—the sharing that is the inevitable result of building rapport—and to bestow narrative with a power that it cannot hold without the support of other experiences: "to assume that realities beyond the interview context cannot be tapped into and explored is to grant narrative omnipotence" (Miller and Glassner 1997: 102; also see Reay 1996). I understand this in terms of my concern about my subject positions in the practice of fieldwork and take from it the need to encompass the web of friendship that surrounded, and flowed through, the pilot interviews I carried out. The relationships I already had with the women whom I interviewed at this stage in my fieldwork were central in that they facilitated the interviews and shaped the shared meanings that resulted.

The context provided by the *me* that is found in the relationships I have with those friends who agreed to take a role in my pilot interviews would seem to be important in the process of those interviews. Indeed, recognizing the presence of that particular position of me might serve to highlight the relative lack of power that any alternative narrative of self can hold in the process of interviewing. To seek an alternate story of self for presentation in an interview situation, or indeed in the dissemination of work that results from interviews, is to suggest that the alternative narrative itself holds the key to the product of the interviews. It accords power to the attempt to construct a "researcher self" that is discrete from any other subject position. Recognition of the ways that webs of self, and of subjectivity, are co-constructed during the interview process makes space for, indeed promotes the inclusion of, the me that lies beyond—or perhaps within—the researcher, because it is the me that is partly responsible for the interviews occurring in the way that they do.

Of course what this means is that what was previously thought of as invisible—or was made invisible—starts coming into view. The context of both the interviewee and the interviewer comes to be spoken and positioned within the research process; the marking of boundaries and acknowledgment of the points at which those boundaries are stretched and/or transgressed become, in themselves, explanatory. In her discussion of the self, Morwenna Griffiths (1995) highlights the way that senses of self are spoken or left unvoiced, exploring what this means for the assumptions lying behind the decision to speak of self or to stay silent. In particular, Griffiths examines the gendered nature of voicing the self, suggesting that the "invisible me" advocated in traditional research guidance is a very masculine construction. To stay silent on the subject of self implies a certain surety in the subject position that you occupy and a security in the knowledge that other people are appreciative of that position; and so those who use "we" are sure in the knowledge that they are known and understood without having to declare their presence and position.

I was not so sure, and my visibility before and during those interviews speaks of that lack of sureness. This lack of certainty was definitely part of trying out, for the first time, the voice and body of a researcher and of being uncertain whether I could successfully conduct research. However, it also speaks of my uncertainty about whether I belonged to that group of researchers who seek to make themselves invisible or believe that they are invisible. Griffiths (1995) writes of the problematic of wanting and not wanting to belong, and of seeking a subject position, a place for self, that lies between other, more acknowledged, positions. And in many ways this is where I understand myself to have been: I was not happy with the idea of invisibility and depersonalization nor was I comfortable with the idea of myself in those interviews, giving myself away by the very fact that I was present and easily seen as being present. Griffiths suggests there is potential liberation to be found in those in-between spaces in that they offer opportunities to construct subjectivities or senses of self that are transgressive and that stretch what is meant by visibility and invisibility, personalized and depersonalized, intersubjective and discrete (also see Rose 1996; Smith 1996; Nast 1994; Katz 1992). I think it is easier to write about such in-between spaces than it is to realize them in practice. To exist and move about these spaces is always to be aware of myself and to know that other people are likewise aware; it is a state of hyper-consciousness, which while admirable, may come at the cost of heightened vulnerability. However, the space of the in-between does offer the chance to speak and explore my own sense of autobiography, and in this there might be an increased chance of finding those points in the web of co-constructed meaning that facilitate the process of an interview.

Encompassing the idea of a personally constructed interviewer necessitates a working of the power hierarchies permeating an interview relationship. Power was something that I felt I had very little of; I felt that my youth was not on my side, and that inexperience would get the better of me. To be in control of the process I needed a sense of authority and the idea of being myself and allowing the interview to develop through personalized connections between myself and those I would be interviewing did not seem to provide a space of authority. Understanding the knowledge constructed in an interview to be a collaborative venture was one thing; to actually upset the power boundaries was quite another. After all, when you feel you have very little of something you cling to it all the harder; the personal was not something that I could fully accept as authoritative and so I found myself wanting to pull away from it despite all my intentions to move toward it. I was not sure who I was in those interviews, and assuming a role as "expert" potentially offered a route out of that uncertainty even if it meant positioning myself "above" the process of interviewing and the friends who had agreed to be part of that process.

What I was searching for was some way to achieve a sense of collaborative research that recognizes the mutually and co-constructed nature of any knowledge produced in an interview. As Mishler (1986) argues, any "story" that is created during the course of research is necessarily a joint production in that both the interviewer and the interviewee are actively engaged in creating the context and content of the interview. Crick (1992) also places great emphasis on this idea of collaborative knowledge as a means of encompassing the constantly shifting boundaries of mutual dependence— in Crick's work between himself and a street trader—characteristic of ethnography. It allows for those complex webs of shared experience that surround, and create, any given research situation to be grounded in a way that understands them as equal, and perhaps even integral, to the disclosures that occur in an interview. Hale (1991) writes of her frustration at being cast as a "mere listener" in interviews she carried out with prominent Sudanese women, suggesting that the work she did in creating and sustaining an atmosphere in which the women had space to articulate themselves was substantial and yet largely silent. For Hale, interviewing is about trying to find ways of working through the processes of personal, emotional, and bodily reinvention she as the researcher was going through. She suggests that mediation of selves is central to interview-based research; this means understanding the interview process to be a negotiation of authority, self-disclosure/disclosure of self, and honesty both on the part of herself and the women who she interviewed (also see Nast 1998).

The notion of collaborative subjectivities, of associated ideas of intersubjectivity, and the part that acknowledging the role such ideas play in interview processes emerge from the frustration of which Hale (1991) writes. The concept of collaborative subjectivities allows for the rethinking of power differentials, or hierarchies, and makes an analytical space for the webs of shared meaning that evolve. In this context, Smith (1993) suggests that the distance between the researcher and the researched is reduced because there is an understanding that both parties in any interview give as well as take. There can be no fixed subject positions within such a framework because there is constant movement around instances of self in order that the web of shared meaning can be realized. Perhaps what this offers is many spaces in which representations of self can be made during an interview: there is room to realize the me that I understand to lie beyond the interviewer, the me that is within the interviewer, and the various other representations of me that lie between these two positions. This offers answers to some of my concerns, but the idea of a substantial engagement with the ideas of mutuality and collaborative senses of self still seemed a big leap from that which I thought of as safe.

And so there I was, on the brink between "insider" and "outsider," unsure of how to really be either. The personal I, the academic I, and all the pieces that overlap were rushing around, not in a web of intersubjective and reflexive experience but in a web of confusion. I could not be a stranger to these women nor could I really be me, bare to the world with no disguise, or characterization, at all. What was also clear was that reading, and worrying, from the relative comfort of my office was not going to yield any answers. I had to step over the brink, take myself into those interviews, and see what happened.

ACT THREE: THE HEARING

In her study at home Hannah takes from its box a transcriber, reads the instructions, sets it up, listens and slowly begins to type.

Kitty: Yeah, I like to decorate, like having pictures and stuff, I suppose you'd call it . . . accessorizing your home.
Hannah: That sounds a bit trendy, a bit like Changing Rooms [both laugh].
Kitty: But you know what I mean . . . like I really like that print over there 'cos it has lots of really nice color in it which give off warmth, makes people feel at home and it has a girl playing the flute on it which is kind of appropriate for me, so it's personal as well you know, corny but I like it.
Hannah: . . . er, er no I know what you mean, urm . . . I, I, I have a couple of prints by the same woman, Rosie Watchmann, is that her name?
Kitty: Yeah, yeah it's something like that, R . . . something . . .
Hannah: Yeah well they're nice to look at but they have relevance too because one is of girls singing and the other has a cow on it.
Kitty: A cow? Relevant how exactly?
Hannah: Oh it's a family thing, er . . . it's, it's to do with me, well me and my, and my sister when we were young, kids and strangely mutated names, yeah it's sort of a family thing . . .

Oh my voice is wobbly, if it is my voice at all, for the tapes played at the speed needed to stand any chance of transcribing them brings about all sorts of distortions; my voice is slow and low. But wait, there, that sounds like the kind of thing that I would say and that little story, I recognize that. So there is no doubt about it, that is me on the tapes. And I am stuttering. It is like I am unsure of what I want to say, but I seem to carry on anyway, with rambling stories that seem to sweep aside that notion that it is just the interviewee who talks. Oh, but that one is embarrassing: how could that be right in an interview for my research? Not that sharing the fact that I have Rosina Watchmeister prints hanging in my house is embarrassing in and of itself, but to hear that on the tape of an interview? And to hint at old family nicknames? I am cringing now and surely Kitty could not have been interested?

That was what it was like listening to the tapes on which the interviews were stored; it was embarrassing. I had to hear my own voice and hear the way that I put together sentences and shared little bits of information about myself and hear when I was making no real sense. I suppose I just sounded more human than I had expected; I recognized the woman who has prints by Rosina Watchmeister hanging on her walls and was unprepared for the way in which this identified the interviewer as being me. I seemed to be doing what Jane Tompkins (1989) does in her discussion of the personal in academic work: I was taking the woman who owns those pictures, and has feelings about them, and making her part of academic work. The boundaries around myself as a theoretically situated researcher and myself as personally understood were being blurred just as Tompkins blurs them in her desire to take the girl who sits on the window ledge into her writing. So why was it embarrassing? Gradually reading through theoretical work on methodology had introduced me to the idea that attempting to make myself invisible as the interviewer—both in terms of what I thought of as me and in terms of the interviewer's presence—is not ideal, but to be so visible? As Tompkins suggests, I found myself trapped by a dichotomy between epistemology and the personal. I wanted the personal to be commensurable with the idea of knowledge, but at the root of my construction of a researcher still lay the conditioning that distanced me and privileged distance, depersonalization, and discernment. These were practice interviews and as an apprentice it seemed a difficult task to bend the convention and establishment to quite the extent that I could hear myself doing in those interviews.

Inextricably bound to this were my continuing concerns with the idea of being credible and appearing to be sufficiently in control of *myself*—or to sufficiently contain *myself*—so that the interview could be carried out and the interviewee could trust that I knew what I was doing. I was confused about the extent to which the boundaries around researcher and *me* had to be respected; I had begun to realize that moving toward a recognition of the complex overlapping of selves involved in the process of an interview was good practice, but to hear myself so starkly on the tapes reawoke my concerns about containment and the role that discretely packaged senses of self might be easier, even more appropriate, to deal with. This tension came through perhaps most strongly in the interview I carried out with Lydia, the oldest of the five women and the only one who was married with children. During the interview itself there were several points at which I found myself feeling embarrassed about the things I was asking or telling Lydia. An extract from my research notes is demonstrative:

> Interview with Lydia: HARD!
> Had to deal with children, both being there and the fact that she has them and I don't. Did she take my questions seriously? A tension between her lived reality and my hidden awayness in "academia." Much less personal—couldn't be without blushing as to share my life with hers seemed silly. Tried to become serious academic, didn't like that and it made me blush more, could hear the discomfort in my voice.
> Links hard to find and then maintain . . . aaaaah . . . last one and I feel a bit lost again.

We are friends and yet our lives are very different and I was concerned that she would interpret my questions as being rooted in the carefree, frivolous life of a woman who is unmarried, childless, and in her mid-twenties, and conclude both the questions and the questioner had no real bearing on the reality of her life. Here the glimpses of myself, the construction of my own personal narrative, were the most hard to listen to; they seemed to flounder and created few of the connections suggested by the extract from Kitty's interview. What seemed to be happening was that rather than finding shared webs of meaning that led to a collaborative sense of experience, the parts of my narrative of self seemed an imposition of me upon the situation. I was in some way forcing Lydia to listen to things about me and then construct her experience along similar, and what might be inappropriate, lines. My embarrassment at the time, and my subsequent discomfort listening to the tape, gives a strong indication that investing myself in the process and actively making a sense of me visible—or audible—in the interviews was not easy to do or to listen to, and perhaps not always successful. In this instance what I felt was that, rather than having a less hierarchical situation in the interview, my subject positions overwhelmed Lydia's subject positions. The person whose voice I had wanted to embrace as the expert of her own experience seemed to become lost behind my voice and my experience.

I listened on. Embarrassing as it was to hear myself, I felt it was important to continue. I wanted to be able to sort out my position even if that meant coming to terms with the inherent messiness of the process. For as much as listening to all those stories about myself was embarrassing, I was equally uncomfortable listening to a voice that attempted to hide myself behind that mask of a researcher. The voice that I/I thought would give me credibility and validity actually made me sound pompous and self-important. Tensions in the interview with Lydia aside, I found that allowing some sense of *my* own personal narrative to develop made me feel comfortable about being the interviewer and also helped to present a framework that I and whomever I was interviewing could use to good effect. Mbilinyi (1989) discusses the way in which the use of personal narratives can provide a frame of understanding by offering bridges between experience and theory. She writes from the point of view of collecting the narratives spoken by others, but I found her points also useful in relation to using my own narrative to access the experiences of others. Thus in the interview with Kitty, talk about my wall hangings and the relevance they held for me facilitated further discussion about the importance for her of choosing the décor of her home. Here are the webs of mutuality: in part my giving encouraged Kitty to give, but it also made for a sense of shared experience through which shared understanding could be discussed, which in turn provided a bridge to other meanings.

The way in which my own stories often unlocked the interviewee's stories came as a great relief to me, and, even though this was problematic in the interview with Lydia, my observation went a long way toward easing my issues with credibility. I found that my voice did work, albeit in a wobbly way. What I came to realize was that my voice was that of a facilitator and what was at issue with Lydia was that I had yet to become sufficiently comfortable to allow voices to tell stories with which I could not engage personally. It was not that I was unprepared for people to have different stories, rather it was about realizing that the difference did not invalidate the stories I told in my voice, either as stories in their own right or as stories that facilitated other people's stories and voices. It seemed to be a process of moving from constructing my credibility toward recognizing the credible in me.

Listening to the tapes of interviews I gradually came to feel more comfortable with the voice I heard on the tapes as mine and began to be able to hear the effect that differing speech had upon the exchange that was taking place. Take, for example, a question I asked Jane in the second of my pilot interviews:

> So do you think that you like to construct a boundary between your private self and the one that can be seen at work and on the street and in other sort of places . . . erm . . .

and do you think that boundary, er, sort of er, coincides with the physical boundary that is the walls of your flat?

I understand that question and used it to move on to questions about the permeability of those boundaries, but did Jane? She tried very hard to understand it and thought carefully about the answer she wanted to give; she almost asked for clarification but was kind and struggled on. That was probably not the only point in the interview at which she experienced difficulty. The questions I asked often clattered along with the language of the academic uncomfortably pinned to them. What I realized listening to this, and to tapes of the other pilot interviews, was that the points at which I was not as cloaked in the language of a researcher bore as much, if not more, fruit than when I was. I was making my friends work very hard to be interviewees, and it was increasingly obvious that this did not have to happen for me to feel comfortable in the interview and to listen to what was on the tape and perceive it as successful.

To allow myself to speak without the clatter of academic language came as a relief, and it also meant that I did not have to work so hard in interviews. The penultimate results of my pilot interviews made this clear: it was the longest, yet the most enjoyable to do, and listening to the tape provoked the least embarrassment in me. It was as if I understood better the person who I wanted to be. I connected easily with much of what Mary said, I found some of it funny, and I was able to display this in my voice and speech. Take for example the exchange we shared about curtains:

Mary: . . . like, take the curtains in this room . . . my mum wanted me to have really bright, well colorful and . . . busy, yeah that is what she called it, 'cos the walls are so plain and the floor is wooden, to brighten the place up, you know and she wanted to put in big tie backs and stuff, puff them up.
Hannah: And you wanted to have something completely different?
Mary: Exactly [both laughing] and can you believe that we actually fought quite hard about it?
Hannah: Yes, my mother would exclaim in the material shop, so that all could hear, she thought the material I thought was a possibility was foul and in some ways it was kind of like she kind of felt that she should have a considerable say because she was going to make them, and pay for them!
Mary: Oh that is what it came down to too, she paid, had rights over taste and things like that.
Hannah: Difficult thing to resolve without hurting her feelings . . . or cutting off your nose to spite your face!
Mary: Worse still, having to pay for the curtains! [both laugh].

This felt comfortable and listening to it I easily understood the way in which the curtains were a means of introducing and discussing the complex role that parents have in the construction of a home as well as the shift from being a child home-dweller to an adult homeowner. Like Marjorie Devault (1990), I found that talk about routine and everyday experiences was a way of opening the boundary between theory and experience. I found ways in which the complexity of theory could be articulated in more everyday conversation about mundane experiences, without the underlying academic purpose of the conversation being lost. Through the discussion of what Devault terms standard topics of conversation, my interviewees and I found ways to talk of, and understand, the processes of establishing ourselves as adult homeowners. Thus there is no awkwardness in the exchange with Mary. What is also pertinent is that we were sharing an experience and creating a mutual understanding of the process under discussion: just as Mary tells of her curtains and her relationship with her mother while establishing her own home, so too do I. I am within that conversation, engaging and sharing my experience of my mother and my curtains.

I am immersed in that conversation, for I am immersed within the researcher. Listening to the tape of the interview with Mary I am strangely aware and unaware of this: I can hear that on one level I am talking about my curtains, but at the same time I am holding a position that is more distanced because I am aware of what it represents within my research. It is as if there were two senses of self working through the exchange; there is the distanced, observational self—the me that is the researcher—and there is also a more involved and intimate self that is actually experiencing the conversation. What is also apparent is that these two senses of self are not discrete or mutually exclusive; rather they are interwoven in a complex mesh that draws together the me that I understand to be academic and that which I feel exists beyond it. The effect of interweaving is of course that while I may present a singular subject position and think of it in terms of two positions, there are actually many positions that are encompassed or enveloped within that mesh. It is here, in this conversation about curtains, that I began to accept the multiplicity of subject positions I claim and occupy in the interview process, and to work with the idea that those positions overlap to create a mesh, which, while not always completely comfortable, facilitates the research process.

Perhaps this is simply the stuff of reflexivity? The practice of reflexivity is one that attempts explicitly to link the idea of self to the process of knowledge construction. It is about seeking that fusion of the subjective and the objective that might enable an embodied (re)telling of what is shared in an interview, and demands reflection on the ways in which I am embedded and coopted into the process of research (Rose 1997b; Nast 1994; Moss 1993; McDowell 1992; Thompson 1992; Allen and Farnsworth 1993). Well yes it is about that, but it is also more than reflexivity. It is not only about realizing the ways in which I who am doing the research am embedded within the knowledge that is constructed during that research, it is also about the variety of that subject I. It is about realizing the spaces that need to be created in order for that which I understand to be *myself*, to have some room within the process of interviewing and the subjective spaces of the interview. It is about more fully realizing the variety of subject positions that are possible, indeed necessary, for a researcher to be able to carry out research. It is about realizing that I am working within, presenting through, and performing from a mesh of subjectivities rather than traveling a singular line that has "the researcher" at one end and me at the other.

There is a certain in-between quality in this: it is a space in which there is enough latitude for me to make a mesh of my own varied subjectivities and see that mesh moving and reforming during the interviews I carried out. The in-between quality of that space has been enabling in that it has allowed me to have a dialogue with myself, with the idea of the researcher I carried with me into the project, and with the me that I found to be within the researcher that was carrying out the work (compare Rose 1996). In the dialogue that occurs in these discursive, in-between spaces I have been able to more fully realize what it is that I am capable of doing and of being. I understand better the ways in which I am consciously the protagonist of the conversation, shaping it for my own particular ends, but that this protagonist is also lost within those conversations with Kitty, Mary, Elizabeth, whoever, and me. I hear those tapes now, some months later, and I hear me talking with women who are my friends, and we are talking about the experiences that are the stuff of my research. We are having a conversation; it may not be one that we would have everyday, but it is not all that unusual or alien. I can hear the pub, the singing, and the cinema in the background, and yet it does not obscure the research that is the reason for the conversation.

It is as if I am able to bear witness to *myself*, the *me*, that is taking part in the conversation, while also appreciating that the conversation is strategic and directed toward the stuff of my research. There is a greater sense of complexity in the subject positions that I occupy than I initially thought there would, should, or ever could be. I am in a sort of movement, maybe a dance, that involves oscillating between immersion and observation and many other places that lie between or to the side of that supposed binary. The conversations that I had about curtains and pictures, about kitchens, beds, bread-making, mortgage payments, neighbors, boyfriends, husbands, children, pets, the list goes on and on, all come from everyday experience, much of which is mine as well as being that of the friends I was interviewing. I had not thought there would be room for such a personal narrative, but there it was and still is. That which I thought would be the personal and private me, the me that lies outside of the work that I do, punctures through the role of researcher that I was playing. It is messy and lies in those in-between spaces that are difficult to articulate but seem so important to use.

AN AFTERWORD

There is a knock at the door of Hannah's office and a head pops round the door.

Sally: Could I come and have a chat with you some time later today or sometime about method stuff and doing some interviews?

Hannah: Well yeah, I'm not sure I could be all that much help but you'd be more than welcome.

Sally: But you've got through all yours haven't you and it seems like you got some really interesting stuff and like I was told that you really enjoyed doing it like.

Hannah: Well, I've got some time this afternoon.

She is right: I have done all my interviews for this project now and I did enjoy doing them. It is not that I want to conclude this chapter by suggesting that I have become an expert; the tapes of the interviews that make up the bulk of my fieldwork are as messy as those five pilot interviews. But there is something satisfying about hearing my voice on them; there is something that feels good listening to the way that I weave the mesh that is me through all of the interviews; and it is great to hear that I am in control, not of the people who I interview or necessarily the direction the interview takes, but of myself and the many ways that I put in an appearance. I put in an appearance because I am the researcher; my narrative, my voice, myself is that narrative, voice, and self that the researcher uses. It is not necessarily a perfect match or reflection because overlapping the multiplicity of my selves means that there are pieces that stick out in different ways depending on the circumstances, but the mesh that results is dense enough for me to appreciate myself within the interviews and the way that I am central in facilitating the collaborative experience that is an interview.

So, I have found spaces for subjectivities in the interview process and most important I have found a way of realizing and accommodating the multiplicity of my subjectivity in research. I have found the in-between spaces that open up the possibilities for creating a mesh of collaborative identities—between myself as researcher and those I research and in so doing have become better at working out, and through, webs of shared meanings that create their own further webs of meaning for my research project. I wondered at the outset of this project if it was alright to hear so much of myself in the interviews that I was carrying out and I have realized that there is no other way to go about interviewing. If I am to attempt to realize the complex, embedded, and mutual nature of the knowledge that is created as a result of those interviews, the spaces in which the multiplicity of me—and of those I interview—have to be seen, understood, and used. It is not so much that I am confident about drawing conclusions, rather it is that this play with/on interviewing does seem to work and, although still difficult at times, I am beginning to like it.

NOTE

1. Pseudonyms have been used for all those referred to in this chapter, except for myself.

13

Research Ethics in Practice

Amanda Bingley

Entering the world of qualitative research, I arrived with more than two decades of experience of psychotherapy, some personal and some as a practicing psychotherapist. I intended to interview people individually and to run practical group workshops. I hoped that the kind of humanistic psychotherapy skills for which I had been trained—working with both individuals and groups—would transfer across the divide between the practice of therapy and the pursuit of academic research. My proposed methodology, although strongly supported by supervisors and peers, was greeted with some skepticism in certain quarters, for example, during formal departmental review sessions. In particular, my request for specialist psychotherapy supervision, which I knew I would require at certain points in the research in order to follow the kind of ethical protocol in which I had been trained, was considered highly unusual. Although the request was granted and additional funding provided, the reactions it provoked confirmed that there was some way to go before psychotherapeutic methodologies would be either reconciled with, or become widely used within, human geography (Bondi 1999). The purpose of this chapter is to point out the advantages, of which there are many, the potential, of which there is a great deal, and the problems, of which there are a few and most of which are easily avoidable, of incorporating some basic psychotherapeutic theory into qualitative research methods, and to demystify some of the processes involved. The methodologies discussed in this chapter are not necessarily appropriate for all qualitative research; rather, they are aimed at research in which personal issues are explored in detail.

The chapter is divided into three sections. First I discuss why and when psychotherapeutic methodologies are appropriate in qualitative research, and I address the ethics of working with participants where the research aims to facilitate access to early and/or unconscious material. Second I draw on my doctoral research, which is informed by the theories of psychoanalyst D. W. Winnicott (1965, 1971, 1986,

1988), to outline some key skills required for such in-depth research. In the third section I argue that researchers undertaking this type of project (and their participants) may benefit from specialist psychotherapeutic supervision. Throughout the chapter I focus on ethical dimensions of this methodology, with a view to encouraging more researchers to engage in this type of work, while at the same time promulgating awareness of the need for great care in the practice of in-depth qualitative research.

WHY USE PSYCHOTHERAPEUTIC
APPROACHES IN QUALITATIVE RESEARCH?

Although texts on qualitative research methods address ethical issues such as confidentiality, informed consent, problems associated with publication, and the prevention of exploitation or damage to the researched or the researcher, there is very little debate about the development of the relational and interactive skills required (also see chapter 12 in this volume). For example, qualitative research based on interviews is usually presented as involving nothing more than talking with individuals or groups for an hour or two on one occasion, or perhaps two or three times. Conducting interviews is typically presented as fairly effortless: the researcher "guides" the conversation (Rubin and Rubin 1995: 122); participants are "drawn out" on certain topics. The absence of comment on what happens to them afterward seems to imply that they will probably forget about the whole thing. David Morgan (1988), for example, encourages the idea of qualitative research (with focus groups) as conversations lasting an hour or two; intense and concentrated maybe, but nonetheless, just a conversation, just talking. Any conversation requires an extraordinary range of communication and social skills, and researchers are typically assumed to be able to apply these unproblematically. The qualitative interview "simply" calls on our abilities to put people at ease and to encourage them to talk. Women in particular are often deemed to be "highly skilled at listening" able to "more easily co-operate in understanding each other" (Devault 1990: 101; see also Spender 1980). All you need is a topic, a tape recorder, and enthusiastic determination to extract as much as possible in as short a time as possible from your willing victims. The rest—transcribing, analyzing, writing-up—is what is "really difficult": fieldwork is typically presented as "no problem" and as "the exciting bit."

Ethnographers, Martyn Hammersley and Paul Atkinson (1983) likewise observe that fieldwork is generally seen as "easy," and inexperienced graduate students are expected to "get out and do it" with very little training or advice, almost as a rite of passage. But, as they note, conducting research may, in practice, prove to be something of an ethical minefield, the results of which can be damaging for participants and researchers alike (Finch 1984; Olesen 1994; Stacey 1988). Similarly Maurice Punch (1994: 83) remarks that qualitative fieldwork is often assumed to be "fun," and "easy; anyone can do it," but that in practice it risks "bringing turbulence into the field, fostering personal traumas (for both researcher and the researched) and even causing damage to the discipline." Punch (1986) writes with feeling, having suffered serious ethical problems during and following his doctoral research, encountering difficulties not only with personal stress and fatigue, but also problems over access to his field site, intimidation, and contractual issues with his sponsors.

The difficulties of qualitative research arise directly from the methods employed, which entail the deliberate use of personal interactions and relationships with other people in order to explore behavior, ideas, experience, memories, and so on. To ask people to take part in research interviews is to request them to open themselves up to the researcher's questions and queries. The conversations that ensue are a form of social interaction like many others, but are also distinctive, sometimes in subtle ways. The difference lies in both the purpose of the interaction—the research interview is not a social chat—and the "depth" of the interaction, which will vary according to the nature of the topic and the means by which that topic is explored (Rubin and Rubin 1995: 125). But the qualitative research interview is frequently described as "in-depth," and researchers actively encourage interviewees to explore issues in ways that go beyond what is typical of many everyday forms of social interaction, and to share thoughts, ideas, and reflections in a way that is commonly perceived as going "down" into the "depths."

Some topics invite participants to delve deeper than others. My own research sought deeply personal reflections on individuals' childhoods, early relationships, and identities. Not all research topics will make the same demands of the participant, but during any "in-depth" interviewing, in which people are asked for their personal thoughts or responses, participants may move rapidly from familiar forms of conversation typical of ordinary social interactions into much deeper and more personal disclosures. Smith (1995: 482), for example, points out how the "synergistic effect" of a group, or feelings of safety in an individual interview, can result in even apparently undemanding topics becoming a forum for participants to talk "in depth" about themselves, their lives, and their problems. Such shifts may be more sudden and unexpected if researchers are working with people from backgrounds with which they are unfamiliar, or in another language, or another country. Any and every conversation can delve deeply in a very short time. From the first moment they meet, researcher and participant are involved in a dynamic interaction, and no such interaction is completely neutral, however apparently superficial, inconsequential, or predictable. Thus the power relations between, and the vulnerabilities of, both researcher and participant within the in-depth interview are important ethical concerns for qualitative researchers.

The bulk of qualitative research is written in ways that pay little attention to such concerns, and suggests an image of researchers blithely "plumbing the depths" with their interviewees, to whom they are usually total strangers. The image is persistent, despite attempts by several authors, most notably feminists, to open up ethical issues in qualitative research (Finch 1984; Maynard 1994; Mason 1996; Ramsey 1996). But in such encounters, complex feelings are evoked in both the researcher and the participant. From the perspective of the researcher, we may choose to ignore invitations to enter our participants' inner worlds if we feel such exploration to be unnecessary or inappropriate. But we may become "hooked in" unwittingly, fascinated, or seduced by their invitations, or we may unintentionally hurl ourselves in uninvited, and one way or another what began as "just" an interview, or "just" a conversation, can quickly develop in unexpected and deeply troubling ways. For example, we may end up with an uncomfortable sense of having pushed too hard for information, or that we have been sidetracked into irrelevancies, or that we have been "fed" stuff or "fobbed off." We may leave feeling insulted, embarrassed, hurt, angry, or carrying heavy burdens (see for example chapter 14 in this volume).

Human interaction is a multifaceted, many-layered affair, and researchers are no more immune from fears and anxieties than anyone else when entering new situations or meeting strangers. Can we maintain our inner sense of authority with this person or group? Will they cooperate with us? Will we like them? Will they like us? Will either of us get bored? Will the participant criticize us or ask awkward questions about the research? How will we react if they get upset or angry or challenge us? In her study of the emotional expectations of adult students and their tutors, Isca Saltzberger-Wittenberg (1983) suggests that people entering a new class often experience feelings similar to those they experienced as children starting school. The interpersonal dynamics of research are very similar. For instance, the participant typically looks to the researcher to structure the encounter, to provide cues, and invests in them the authority to conduct the research. Researchers hope to maintain professionalism, but some conversations with some people push that professionalism to the limit. The "deeper" we go in the interactions that constitute our research, the greater the demands on ourselves and our participants, and the more likely the researcher and participant will find themselves caught up in complex dynamics. Some interactions pose no threat to us, some challenge us, some excite or delight us, some set us on guard and require vigilance, or at the very least a protective suit. As researchers we are responsible for protecting our participants and protecting ourselves. This responsibility is the baseline of research ethics and a compelling reason to consider the use of psychotherapeutic skills to support this kind of research methodology.

Qualitative researchers conducting individual interviews or group sessions have several options available to them. They can take their existing skills for granted, hoping to negotiate their participants' and their own sensitivities in ways that enable them to obtain their data without undue damage. This means relying implicitly on their participants to defend themselves if necessary by refusing to be questioned beyond a certain point. At best this approach entails the fairly shameless "extraction" of data; at worst it entails the use of insensitive, "interrogative" questioning that fails to generate the material desired and is a very uncomfortable experience for both parties. Another option is to retreat at the first sign of difficulty, relinquishing any hope of eliciting valuable material. Many researchers no doubt compromise between these two, muddling through with some sensitivity toward their participants, but feeling so anxious about the risk of probing too deeply that perfectly valid opportunities to uncover and explore important concerns are missed. Many times researchers get most of what they want, but these approaches are necessarily less reliable than taking steps to develop interactive skills for research purposes (Mason 1996; Denzin and Lincoln 1994).

A rare example of research in which the development of such skills was considered is the work by Jacquelin Burgess, Melanie Limb, and Carolyn Harrison (1988a, 1988b), who sought to explore "environmental values which are deeply held and which clearly reflect a complex interpenetration of individual experiences and collective beliefs about nature, landscape, and society" (1988a: 311). They considered working with participants in a once-only group, but felt that this would enable people to offer only "superficial impressions and attitudes" (1988a: 311). They wanted to facilitate participants into deeper self-exploration and decided to work with small groups meeting several times at weekly intervals. This decision was informed by the knowledge and experience of psychoanalytic group work already gained by the researchers (Burgess, Goldsmith, and Harrison 1990; Burgess 1996). This background ensured that the research was conducted in a manner sensitive and responsive to the ethical issues involved in asking people to take part in research that invited them to open themselves up in such ways.

I am not suggesting that every qualitative researcher or every qualitative research project either needs, or will find it appropriate, to use psychotherapeutic skills. However, a considerable amount of sociocultural and feminist research does involve working with vulnerable people. Examples include Robert Burgess's (1984) study of teacher-pupil relationships in an inner city school, Hester Parr's (1998) study of people's experiences of mental health services, Tamar Rothenberg's (1995) research on New York City's lesbian community, as well as Jacquelin Burgess et al.'s (1988a, 1988b) study of environmental values. All these studies involve asking people to tell the researcher about their feelings, ideas, opinions either in unusual detail or on a subject that may be highly evocative, emotional, or even dangerous.

An individual's sense of self, personality, or, as psychoanalyst Christopher Bollas (1989) describes it, his or her "idiom," is expressed through a welter of conscious and unconscious actions, body language, sensory engagements, thoughts, and emotions. All of this is territory that qualitative researchers may hope to explore in relation to their particular topics. Skillful facilitation enables researchers to do this in ways that generate insight but do not unduly disturb the participants, so that both researcher and participant are left with more rather than less at the end of the fieldwork.

GOING IN THERE: PRACTICAL APPLICATIONS

In this section, I discuss my doctoral research in order to highlight the potential relevance of particular psychotherapeutic skills in qualitative research. A total of twelve people took part in my research, which explored in depth the influence of gender on landscape perception. Participants were each interviewed individually on two occasions, once before and once after a series of three full-day practical workshops held at fortnightly intervals. During the interviews they were asked about memories and experiences of landscape from earliest childhood to the present, as well as about their family histories. The workshops were designed to elicit participants' sensory experiences of landscapes, especially through the use of modeling materials before and after visits to different places on each of the three workshop days. During the workshops, participants were also encouraged to connect with, and reflect upon, childhood memories and experiences, and upon feelings and images that generally remain hidden at the edges of everyday awareness. I was seeking to go beyond the ordinarily "known" and to engage participants in ways that would make unknown or unconsciously held ideas and beliefs available. I therefore offered participants opportunities to move away from their rational, cognitive processes to engage with emotions and senses that only occasionally emerge in conscious thought, in many cases originating from, and echoing, early experiences.

The participants responded to my questions and to the practical work in all kinds of ways. I was often pushed to the limits of my skills, and I made some salutary mistakes, which without skilled support could have jeopardized the continuing data collection. Psychotherapeutic skills were essential for two main reasons. First, without sufficient experience of these skills designing the research would have been impossible: psychotherapeutic ideas were integral to the framing of the project. Second, the project encouraged people to enter sensitive personal territories in which they might feel vulnerable, and psychotherapeutic skills were essential in order to conduct the data collection (and analysis) with sensitivity and integrity; that is, in an ethically responsible way.

I drew particularly on the ideas of object relations psychoanalyst D. W. Winnicott (1965, 1971, 1986, 1988), who wrote extensively on experiences of early infancy and whose ideas have been very influential in the field of psychotherapy. Winnicott (1971) concludes from his extensive psychoanalytic work with children and adults that people experience their relationships with others in what he called the "potential space" or "intermediate area of experience." This "space" or gap between self and "other" or "not-self" (which may be a person, a group of people, an object, a landscape, and so on) has a mediating, relational function where, from infancy onward, inner and outer realities coexist and are explored. It is a place of "transition" between what we know to be ourselves and that which constitutes external reality. The transitional qualities of this space may be represented by what Winnicott (1971) calls "transitional objects": infants commonly make use of a teddy bear or a comfort blanket in this way. From infancy into adulthood the potential space and the objects with which we furnish it (increasing in sophistication during our development from childhood to adulthood) is the in-between space from which arise play, creativity, art, imagination, and, Winnicott (1971) suggests, our cultural experience in general.

Drawing on these ideas I designed the research to encourage the participants to enter into a relationship or "potential space" between themselves and landscapes (real and imagined), as well as between themselves and me. In this way I sought to examine the interfaces between self and "other," exploring the influence of primary relationships (primary caregivers) on relationships that develop beyond these, especially with the environment or landscape. I viewed the research as a two-way process, in which researcher and participants understand and acknowledge each other's roles and learn from each other within that context (compare Maynard 1994). While I provided the structure and the initial ideas, participants brought to bear their own particular ways of working within this framework. Thus, I needed to create an environment that was sufficiently secure and safe, but which was also creative and dynamic. This kind of environment has a good deal in common with that required for psychotherapy, hence the relevance of psychotherapeutic skills. At the same time these skills are "ordinary" elements of human communication, typically employed unselfconsciously. By naming and examining the skills I discuss in the rest of this section, it becomes possible to develop and refine them considerably, as well as to use greater awareness of them to good effect.

Facilitation refers to a group of interactive skills that have been theorized and developed in psychotherapy. Facilitation includes such things as providing the "structure" of an interview or workshop, and simultaneously enabling participants to engage with the task at hand and to use the framework provided in ways expressive of themselves. Winnicott (1965) describes successful facilitative communication as respecting the person's profoundest sense of self, by enabling three strands of communication to arise spontaneously, namely, silence, explicit communication, and exchange within the potential space. In the research context facilitators need to remain alert to both the overall framework within which they and their participants are working and to the moment-by-moment concerns of their participants individually, and, if relevant, collectively. In this context they need to be able to allow silences, receive communications, and enter into exchanges, choosing between particular responses in sensitive ways. This requires researchers to be finely attuned to the interactions of which they are part and capable of sustaining awareness of both their participants and themselves.

Successful facilitation requires the researcher to make appropriate interventions or comments, which may highlight, summarize, and/or support the participant's experience and feelings about an event or an idea. In psychotherapy, intervention is an important skill that a good therapist uses with great care in order to facilitate or encourage the client toward insights and self-awareness. Winnicott (1965) emphasizes the enormous benefits of appropriate intervention, but warns of the dangers of inappropriate, hasty or excessive intervention, which can block clients' progress or even damage them. In much the same way a researcher may intervene facilitatively or obstructively, the latter occurring when comments or actions serve to stifle conversation or impede the engagement of participants.

Facilitation may simply require the researcher to "follow" the conversation, picking up threads from the participant's previous comments to encourage the flow, as illustrated in the following excerpt from an interview transcript.

Amanda: So, when you played in the garden and so on, you played a lot of imaginative games, that was mostly what was happening?

Sarah[1]: Hmm, we played house, we used to dress up a lot, I can remember leaning out of my bedroom window, and throwing everything out, the blankets, the pillows, all sorts of things that we could sort of drape and make caves, and tents and things and . . .

Amanda: So, you'd take things out from the house and play with them?

Sarah: Hmm, hmm, just in the garden, or down into the, what . . . we used to call our house, 'cos "wendy" house is a fairly modern thing I know. . . . but I forget what we used to call it, we had just . . . our house perhaps.

Amanda: So, really that, that was quite, when you said local, it was quite a local area for you actually as a child.

Sarah: Hmm.

Amanda: It was quite a confined area in fact?

So far the facilitation was working well and the exchange was flowing smoothly. I indicated my interest and attention by my interventions, which acted to encourage Sarah along her own line of thought and perhaps elaborate or explore it more deeply. If, however, the researcher suddenly diverts the participant from his or her thread, confusion may result, and the process of deepening engagement is broken. Such a break was threatened by my next intervention.

Sarah: Yes, yes. Except that, for a little person, the gardens were very long, you know those sort of strips that you get near London, and when you have four strips in a row it gets to be quite large, and also, I was encouraged to look up, as it were, because when we'd not been there very long, they'd put electricity pylons through, we hated it, it, luckily wasn't in our garden. . . .

Amanda: So it was a bit like a Giles cartoon or something?

Sarah: It, dominated, you see, in all the photographs of the back garden, and of course nowadays they've decided it's not a very good thing to be living under isn't it?

My comment about the Giles cartoon cut across Sarah's line of thought. Comments like this arise from temporary lapses in concentration or personal associations on the part of the researcher. In this case, I was suddenly and powerfully reminded of a cartoon image from the 1960s, the era of my own childhood. Alongside the memory came a desire to share the image with Sarah, as if to emphasize myself as ally in a shared space. Such associations or memories are common in social interaction, for example in exchanges between friends. But in a research interview the purpose is different and the researcher needs to consider what will support the participant to deepen their own line of thought. Although an associative comment may turn out to be facilitative, it may also prove disruptive, and so a judgment must be made about its "appropriateness." In this instance, Sarah was sufficiently involved in her own memories to ignore my remark and continue with her own line of thought, as her comment immediately following my intervention reveals.

Sometimes, however, inappropriate interventions can have more damaging consequences. This can be illustrated by examining the impact of an intervention I made during the final session of the first workshop. I asked participants to move to the model with which they felt most affinity. All but one of them did as they were asked. Conversation stopped, people seemed disgruntled, and I felt that the energy in the room had dropped dramatically. After the workshop I reflected on what had happened in ways that were confirmed in subsequent interviews, when some people described how they had felt torn between following my direction, which entailed choosing one person's model as their favorite, and their reluctance to select one model in this way because it entailed not choosing (and implicitly rejecting) other people's models. They partially resisted my untimely and inappropriate intervention by withdrawing into themselves and going silent. One participant did not attend the remaining workshops and reported that the incident, which had made him feel very uncomfortable, may have been a factor (among others) in his decision not to attend the other workshops.

By contrast, appropriate interventions can greatly assist participants. For example, during one of the workshops, exchanges occurred about a model Keith had made to represent the sounds and scents of a woodland we had visited:

Keith: It's not the noise but it's . . . the smells I've brought back, I've concentrated in (he gestures to a clay "cave" full of leaves in the center of his model)
Evelyn: Sniff place (laughing).
Keith: Yes, yes,
(Several participants are laughing)
Amanda: Oh, you call it a "sniff-cave"
Keith: Yes
Teresa: Sniff-cave
Pamela: Grotto
Teresa: Grotto
Amanda: So we should know to go and have a sniff at it
Keith: It's earth and rotting and er growing, new things
Nancy: Great
(People start to sniff at it)
Keith: It's actually getting quite concentrated.
Wendy: Wow!
Amanda: What feels good about this bit for you then?
Keith: Erm, I, to be honest the most, the image in my mind that I was most pleased with was the jagged bit (he moves it to make the noise), that's nice, the, the strongest sense of the bit, and I do like this (crunching material in his hand) I like crunching it, crunching through the undergrowth.
Amanda: Hmm, that's the bit that gives you the most sense of the place?
Keith: Oh, yeah, I think so, yeah
Amanda: Sort of very much the sound bit, hmm?
Keith: Yeah
Amanda: Tractor, the sort of artificial and the?
Keith: Yeah, that was kind of, that was today's impression, could, might not have been on a different day and it didn't really stop though anyway, hmm

Amanda: Hmm, well I feel invited to sniff, I mean you could bottle that couldn't you?

In this exchange a combination of the researcher's and other participants' interventions, such as calling the cave-like part of Keith's model a "sniff place," a "sniff cave," and a "grotto," encouraged Keith to talk about it and to interact with the other group members. Likewise, the suggestion that the crunchy material gave Keith a sense of the place enabled him to elaborate his experience in more depth.

The art of successful facilitation, then, may be thought of as being like spinning wool: individual strands of various lengths are taken up and spun around each other in sequence to make up a single continuous thread. If the spinner is working well the strands spin smoothly together, and the breaks between strands are imperceptible. If the spinner loses concentration the thread can be erratic and uneven and may break altogether.

Transcripts only convey part of the facilitation process. Along with pauses and nonverbal sounds (such as "uhuh"), body language, the quality of laughter or lack of laughter, eye contact, and facial expression are all important. These actions are a vital though sometimes intangible part of facilitation. In my research, for example, my verbal facilitation lessened substantially as the workshops progressed, with my physical presence and occasional very brief reminders and encouragement being enough to enable the participants to continue with their tasks, and the group to flow and interact. Amanda Coffey and Paul Atkinson (1996: 77) outline some of the nonverbal strategies that can enhance facilitation and note the difficulty of analyzing the "performance" that occurs between researcher and participant, which "is as much about 'how things are said' as about what is said."

Effective interventions are outcomes of, and that enhance, trust; and the building of trust between people depends to a considerable degree on empathy. By empathy I mean the ability to be attuned to another person's situation or viewpoint and to imagine oneself in their position, while remaining clearly aware that it is their position and not one's own. Sympathy, by contrast, means identifying with the other person's experience in a way that collapses this distinction. Thus, empathy implies distance from the other person at the same time as compassionate recognition and appreciation of their position. Empathy is a powerful form of communication and has been refined and honed into a key psychotherapeutic skill. There are two reasons why empathy is important in qualitative research. First, by building up trust and empathy participants are encouraged to share ideas and thoughts, to "open up" emotionally and so to explore issues in depth. Second, ethical research practice requires the capacity to understand and empathize with participants; the researcher who engages empathically with participants is also able to treat them with respect, sensitivity, and responsibility (Grafanaki 1996).

Ideally, empathy and trust combine to create what Winnicott (1965) terms a "facilitative environment." This is a secure place in which the researcher and the participant can work together creatively. For Winnicott (1965, 1986, 1988) the facilitative environment is crucial to the earliest experiences of infancy and continues to be important throughout a person's life. He observed that the "holding and handling" of an infant by the mother (or primary caregiver) is essential to its successful development, together with the mother's role in introducing the infant to the ("not-me") world beyond itself, which he terms "object-presentation," and he described all of this as the "facilitative environment." Successful development, Winnicott argues, depends on the empathy and sensitivity of the mother to adapt to the infant's needs, safely contain disappointments and disillusionments, survive the infant's destructive fantasies, and thereby provide an environment in which the infant can develop from a state of complete dependency to become an autonomous individual.

Powerful echoes of such experiences and processes operate across childhood into adult life. Such echoes are the stuff of psychoanalytic and psychotherapeutic theory and practice: adults in therapeutic settings have provided much evidence of the ways in which infant experience informs subsequent emotions, ways of being, and life events (Winnicott 1965; Bollas 1992). Adam Phillips (1988: 11) maintains that the "holding environment" or "congenial milieu" is the "first and foremost . . . provision" of psychoanalytic treatment, and Christopher Bollas (1987) expands Winnicott's original thesis in his emphasis on the transformative potential of the facilitative environment in adult lives. He contends that, as adults, we constantly seek experiences that have the potential to transform us. Although tapping into "existential memory," such experiences are also new and creative (Bollas 1987: 39). This transformative potential requires a facilitative environment in which we feel safely "held," and from which, rather than being locked into old ways of being, we may instead experience the present moment as informed simultaneously by past patterns and future possibilities. Creating a facilitative environment is a difficult task and if either past patterns or future possibilities are denied, the environment is impoverished, potential space reduced, and creativity lost.

In my research I was working with participants in ways that parallel therapeutic processes, creating an environment sufficiently facilitative to enable people to tap into feelings and experiences that underlie adult life. The design of my fieldwork therefore drew extensively on the concept of the facilitative environment and the "holding" process, through which I sought to address the psychological and ethical needs of participants and researcher. This began with such basic but vital considerations as finding suitable venues for the work—places where participants would feel secure and comfortable, and which would be accessible to them. For one-to-one interviews I gave people choices about where to meet with me, the majority choosing to be interviewed in their own homes, where they probably felt most safe and secure. The venue used for the first workshop was on a university campus, but was found to be less than ideal in that the participants felt it to be too impersonal and too distant from the places we were due to visit. Another venue was found thereafter—one that seemed friendlier and was closer to the places to be visited. My observations of group dynamics, together with feedback from participants, indicated that the move was seen as a positive response to participants' needs.

The relationships between each participant and myself, among members of the group, and between all of us and the volunteer assistants who helped with video recording the workshops also required careful attention. My attentiveness was expressed, for example, in the structure I gave to each workshop through such things as preparing tasks or exercises, timetabling workshop sessions and breaks, and offering opportunities for feedback. I ensured that the basic structure and the instructions for each activity were clear and, as far as possible, acceptable, to all members of the group. During workshop exercises I kept in aural contact by reiterating instructions at intervals, noting the time remaining as a time boundary approached, acknowledging and, if appropriate, reassuring those who either had or had not yet completed a task. I was also available to help find tools or materials if needed. At the same time I remained unobtrusive in terms of the task in progress, never commenting on the models as they were being made, and not entering into unnecessary conversation with individual participants. By these means I endeavored to "hold" the group, and the individuals within the group, in a similar way to the caregiver or parent providing a secure environment for the child, thereby allowing the development of potential space within which creativity is possible. In this case, the aim was to facilitate adults to engage with their feelings and experience on the edges of awareness that seldom rise to consciousness.

While I endeavored to provide a good-enough environment for participants there was no way of predicting what might happen. There were, probably inevitably, points at which my capacity to "hold" the group was challenged and came under threat. In such moments, as facilitator of the group, I needed to respond in ways that averted the risk of the group disintegrating. During the second workshop, there were at least two separate occasions when I was challenged during feedback sessions. On the first occasion two participants referred to being "guinea pigs" for my fieldwork. Later in the same session another participant expressed great satisfaction that the ways in which she and one of the male participants had constructed their models of landscape demonstrated that my thesis about gender was incorrect. (I had not, in practice, discussed what, if any, thesis I had about gender with any of the participants.) Whatever underlay such challenges, they certainly provoked powerful responses in me: I felt angry, hurt, even betrayed. But had I reacted by expressing such feelings directly, for example, by defensively dismissing such comments, the potential space available for creative engagement would have been reduced, and the group might have fallen apart completely. In psychotherapeutic work, the therapist symbolically "holds" the client as he or she experiences current feelings or relives old events. It is crucially important that the therapist does not break down under the impact of the client's intense emotions, whether of anger, rage, acute distress, or madness, for example, through responses that imply that such feelings are unacceptable or intolerable. Instead the therapist empathizes with the client's experience while withstanding his or her powerful emotions. This process gradually enables the client to experience his or her feelings as survivable. Drawing on such skills in the face of challenges, I acknowledged and empathized with the discontent expressed, thereby indicating that I was able to tolerate their feelings without withdrawing from them or retaliating. If I had "lost it," the creative potential of the group would have been undermined or even destroyed. By not "losing it" the group not only survived, but thereafter appeared stronger and more committed to the task (Winnicott 1971).

THE USE AND VALUE OF
PSYCHOTHERAPEUTIC SUPERVISION

I turn now to consider the relevance of psychotherapeutic supervision. Supervision is used in many contexts including management, education, and the various caring professions. Gunnar Handal and Per Lauvås (1987) distinguish between supervision designed to "oversee" or "manage" less experienced, less qualified, or subordinate staff, and supervision designed to promote reflective practice; that is discussion and analysis of the actions, processes, and feelings constituting practice. They argue that reflective practice is typical of supervision in teaching and learning: for example, student and supervisor reflect on the student's learning in ways designed to enhance the student's learning skills. Research on doctoral supervision endorses this view (Delamont, Atkinson, and Parry 1997; Phillips and Pugh 1987). Supervision in the caring professions, and most especially in psychotherapy, also uses reflective practice, but there are some important differences between supervision in educational and psychotherapeutic contexts. In psychotherapy, supervision aims to explore the dynamics operating within relationships between practitioners and clients, and to support practitioners to develop effective and sensitive ways of working with clients (Bond 1993). Moreover, as Peter Hawkins and Robin Shohet (1989: 5) maintain, this type of supervision is "a very important part of taking care of oneself, staying open to new learning, and an indispensable part of . . . ongoing self-development, self-awareness and commitment to learning." Thus, psychotherapeutic supervision is concerned with supporting and protecting both therapist and client.

As I have argued, qualitative fieldwork often requires the intentional development of deep and complex relationships between researchers and their participants. I have also illustrated how these dynamic relationships can have a decisive impact on the quality of the evidence gathered during fieldwork. In this context specialist psychotherapeutic supervision can enhance the data collection and their interpretation, as well as helping to develop the researcher's interactive and relational skills (compare Carroll 1996). A supervision session of this kind involves the researcher and the supervisor engaging in a reflective process, where, for example, the researcher might bring an account of an episode in an interview, group discussion, workshop, or participant observation. This episode is likely to be experienced as problematic or troubling in some way for the researcher: examples include incidents I have described earlier in this chapter, such as the moment toward the end of the first workshop when my intervention was followed by silence and disgruntlement, and the challenges with which I was faced during the second workshop. Exploring these with my supervisor helped me to understand what had happened both for myself and for the participants. Moreover, these explorations enabled me to return to the fieldwork with new resources on which to draw.

In relation to the challenges during the second workshop, it was especially important for me to be able to acknowledge and explore the anger and resentment I felt toward several participants. Had I not been able to "process" this safely, away from the fieldwork, it would probably have interfered with my capacity to continue to work effectively (empathically) with these people and might generally have soured relations. Since the participants had already opened themselves up emotionally in ways that rendered them vulnerable, the consequences could certainly have been negative and potentially damaging. Such consequences would be regarded by many as indicative of unethical research practice.

Codes of ethics and practice in teaching and in research typically encompass such issues as confidentiality, the incompatibility of sexual and professional relationships, and any relevant legal issues arising, for example, under data protection legislation (Delamont, Atkinson, and Parry 1997). While such codes establish clear boundaries, they do not address issues arising in the relational practice between, say, supervisor and student or researcher and interviewee. They are therefore of limited use to researchers in navigating their way around the interpersonal complexities of fieldwork of the kind I have described. Research supervision is generally a requirement only for "apprentice" researchers engaged in research up to the doctoral level and typically entails guidance in relation to theoretical issues, research design, methodological decisions, writing of the thesis, and so on. It does not usually involve supervisors in more detailed reflections on students' dynamic relationships with research participants. Indeed, this is likely to lie beyond the skills of academic supervisors in disciplines such as human geography.

If a research student requires specialist support in a particular area beyond the supervisor's expertise, it is common practice for the supervisor to direct the student to seek expert advice elsewhere. Exploring the dynamics of relationships is the domain of a specialist discipline—that of psychotherapy—and I would therefore argue that to seek psychotherapeutic supervision is not very different from seeking advice from an academic specialist. I would also suggest that psychotherapeutic supervision during fieldwork can operate effectively alongside "conventional" academic supervision. Moreover, it is likely to be valuable for "experienced" researchers conducting in-depth qualitative work as well as for those less experienced.

CONCLUSION

I have demonstrated a number of advantages of drawing on psychotherapeutic skills in qualitative research. There are, however, some pitfalls to consider. These are primarily concerned with the risks of embarking on in-depth research without adequate training or supervision. Confusion about the difference between research and therapeutic work, together with a failure to be aware of one's limits, are particular dangers. Researchers are not psychotherapists, and while we may borrow from psychotherapeutic theory and practice, it is important to remember that we are using psychotherapeutic skills for different ends. Self-awareness is essential, and its development is one of the central themes of training in psychotherapy and psychotherapeutic skills. Without self-awareness, relational skills such as the use of empathy are liable to become confused with offering sympathy, or may become dependent on personal likes or dislikes.

Despite such dangers, in this chapter I have argued that qualitative researchers could benefit personally, professionally, and ethically from closer consideration of psychotherapeutic skills (compare McLeod [1996] and Rennie [1996], who discuss the use of qualitative methods in research on counseling and psychotherapy). In particular I have demonstrated the potential of such skills for enhancing the creation of facilitative environments in which trust is built through the use of empathy and appropriate intervention. I have also argued that specialist psychotherapeutic supervision can prove invaluable to researchers engaging with people in deeply personal ways: by supporting the researcher and fostering deeper insight it can substantially enhance the quality of the data collected and ensure research practice that is fully ethical in the sense of incorporating careful and sensitive consideration of relationships (also see chapter 15 in this volume).

Not every qualitative research project sets out to explore sensitive issues or to engage with people in great depth. However, even apparently "safe" topics and methods can generate complex interpersonal dynamics among those involved. I would therefore suggest that much wider acknowledgment of the benefits of both introductory training in psychotherapeutic skills and psychotherapeutic supervision would be valuable for qualitative research in general.

NOTE

1. Pseudonyms are used for all research participants.

14

Telling Stories, Making Selves

Victoria Ingrid Einagel

This chapter was inspired by researching the personal narratives of Sarajevan people who lived through the Bosnian war of 1992 to 1995 whom I met while conducting ethnographic fieldwork in Sarajevo between February and September 1998. My research began as a study about how Sarajevans are making sense of their lives and (re)constructing their identities in the aftermath of a war in which "ethnic cleansing" was a key weapon. I hoped to contribute to understandings of the formation of ethno-national identities through consideration of the consequences on everyday lives of violent conflict around issues of ethnic belonging. But as a result of the profound impact of my ethnographic fieldwork on my own sense of self and belonging, my research developed a "doubleness," which informs this chapter. Reflecting on my experience of fieldwork, I argue that subjectivities are mutually (re)constructed in ethnographic research relationships, and that, at moments, the task of (re)making selves must take priority over other aspects of research.

The doubled quality of my research arose directly from the "ordinary" practices of social research, which construct knowledge through interactions between researchers and those they research (also see chapter 12). It was not something decided upon and "designed" in advance, but it ensued from the methods I used, in the context in which I used them. Central to these methods was my use of myself as a means of gathering evidence in a particular place, which I had chosen in part because of its personal significance. My parents had left Yugoslavia when I was a young child, and in Sarajevo I was ambiguously (and doubly) positioned between the categories of "outsider" and "insider." Such ambiguities and doublings are not unusual in ethnographic research. For example, Judith Okely (1996: 25) refers to the "double knowledge" of the researcher who "has connections by birth or from an earlier life experience" of the culture in which fieldwork is conducted, and Helen Callaway (1992: 32–33) describes a "double frame of reflexivity" that operates in such contexts.

Expositions of certain kinds of doubleness appear to be a growing industry in a genre of belles lettres, most often written by historians (Applebaum 1994; Garton Ash 1997; Ignatieff 1993; Kapuscinski 1994; Schama 1995). These authors write about countries, places, and landscapes—mainly in central and Eastern Europe—by revisiting the lands and territories of their ancestors or childhoods. Explorations of "other" cultures are thus presented as deeply personal journeys into apparently un-known places and pasts in searches for roots, belonging, or memories. They there-fore constitute trajectories of "re-membering" relationships to other worlds in ways that reconstruct distinctions between self and other and (re)write autobiographies (compare chapter 8; also see Behar 1996; Casey 1987; Feld and Basso 1996; Massey 1994).

My task is different from these kinds of tellings. With the aim of deepening our understandings of the processes through which ethno-national identities are forged, I am concerned with the reshaping of ethno-national identities in the aftermath of a war fought around questions of ethnic and religious belonging. In the existing liter-ature on nations and nationalism, and on the formation of ethnic and national iden-tities, little attention has been paid to the impact of violent conflicts, which disrupt and often destroy the lives of ordinary people (Anderson 1991; Horowitz 1985; Smith 1991; compare Lofving and Macek 2000; Nordstrom and Robben 1995). Memory is a major element in the construction of identities and is often also a site of political struggle since it is used to legitimate authority or to provoke conflict and violence (Antze and Lambek 1996). Those who survive war do not forget their ex-periences; rather, in one way or another, memories of the war are passed on to gen-erations that follow, partly by what is told, but also by what is denied, left out, or "forgotten." Silences remain and remind subsequent generations of unknown di-mensions of past events. Closer examination of the experiences of survivors are of great importance because they generate the memories through which histories and identities are constructed.

The importance of people's personal experiences within my research required an openness on my part to deeply traumatic accounts. The impact of such accounts was profound and doubtless contributed to difficulties I experienced in writing about the tape recordings and field notes I had collected in, and took with me when I left, Sara-jevo. I found it extremely hard to write about the life stories I had gathered without writing about myself, but I found it equally hard to write about myself. Feelings of despair, guilt, fear, and powerlessness overwhelmed me, and I doubted my ability to do justice to my research subjects or to represent the complexity of my research. This chapter arises from these difficulties. I seek to illuminate the experience of mutual self-making through narrative, and in so doing I seek to find a place from which to voice my thoughts and feelings (compare Behar 1996; Rosaldo 1989). I begin by in-troducing the place in which I did my fieldwork, drawing on a transcript of one of the ethnographic interviews I conducted. I then discuss my complex positioning within the field, before turning to the intersubjective dynamics of telling and listen-ing to stories, in the context of which I link my use of one Sarajevan's narrative ac-count to the wider significance of self-narration in my research.

RECONSTRUCTING SARAJEVO

In 1991 the Socialist Federal Republic of Yugoslavia dissolved into six constitutive republics. The integrity of one of these, namely Bosnia-Herzegovina, was immediately threatened. The war that ensued resulted in approximately 250,000 recorded deaths, the exodus of a million people to more than twenty-five different countries around the world, and the internal displacement of more than another million people through ethnicization, that is the division of the population on the basis of ethno-national identity belonging. The Dayton Peace Agreement, which was signed in December 1995, brought the fighting to an end, and was also supposed to prevent any further ethnicization of the Bosnian population.

Prior to the war Sarajevo (and other urban areas in Bosnia) was characterized by a flourishing secular pluralistic culture. According to the 1991 census the population of Sarajevo was half a million, consisting of approximately 50 percent Bosnian Muslim, 28 percent Bosnian Serb, 7 percent Bosnian Croat, and 15 percent drawn from various other groups. Different ethno-religious groups (Bosnian Muslims, Orthodox Serbs, Catholic Croats, and Bosnian Jews) lived and worked in mixed communities. A high percentage of marriages were "mixed," with spouses drawn from different ethno-religious groups. In almost all of the city's places and spaces—private homes, apartment buildings, neighborhoods, city quarters, and workplaces—Sarajevans of different backgrounds lived and worked together. Sarajevo was thus a symbol of Yugoslavian "Brotherhood and Unity" and it embodied Yugoslavian multiculturalism. At the end of the war, the population of Sarajevo had fallen to approximately 350,000, of whom 87 percent were Bosnian Muslim, 5 percent Bosnian Serb, 6 percent Bosnian Croat, and only 2 percent drawn from other groups (United Nations High Commission for Refugees 1998). Such stark changes mean that at least in numerical terms Sarajevo is no longer a multiethnic city. Kemal Kurspahic (1997: 115–116) captured the almost unthinkable nature of what had happened in his book *As Long as Sarajevo Exists*, where he records his efforts to speak to various international audiences about the war.[1]

> "Look at any of the Sarajevo residential areas, streets, apartment buildings," I said. "In every one of them there are Muslims, Serbs, Croats, and Jews living together. You can not shoot at 'the others' there without shooting at your own people!" The fear of what the war would bring to a land of such interwoven people and fates such as Bosnia would be a sufficient deterrent. . . . I understood then that Sarajevo and all that it symbolized was being attacked by barbarians, as it were, who had not been touched by the civilizing, life-affirming cosmopolitanism that had flourished in Bosnia's urban centers and shaped the social ethos of its people. (For further accounts of everyday life in Sarajevo and elsewhere in Yugoslavia both during and prior to the war also see Ali and Lifschultz 1993; David and Kovac 1998; Drakulic 1993; Karahasan 1994; Macek 2000a; Mertus et al. 1997; Ugresic 1996, 1998.)

My research is concerned with the impact of these changes on the lives, memories, and identities of Sarajevans.

Bosnia is a post-war society learning to live with the destruction wrought by a protracted and brutal war, in which efforts were made to eradicate all traces of the multiethnic fabric of prewar life by means of ethnic expulsion and ethnic genocide. After some three and a half years of being a society-in-war, characterized by the dramatic collapse of order, it has become a society struggling to become ordered and "normal." It is a society undergoing reconstruction after the war, and, to a considerable extent, its reconstruction is in the hands of the international community through agencies such as the Office of the High Representative (established by the Dayton Peace Agreement), the Organization for Security and Cooperation in Europe, and the United Nations High Commission for Refugees, to name only the most prominent. Bosnia is therefore currently a semiprotectorate, and domestic efforts join those of the international community with a view to achieving the normalization and stabilization of Bosnia-Herzegovina and of the larger Balkan region. This is how Senada, a twenty-two-year-old woman working for an international agency, described the situation.[2]

> Well, as I say, it is thanks to the international community that the country is still together. . . . And, all the new things that are happening with the flag, the coat of arms, the number plates and with passports. All these sound like stupid things but they really change something in the mind-set of people. When all of a sudden new possibilities open up, you can begin slowly to overcome certain resistances you have. I mean it's the normalization process, something that would not have happened if the international community were not present, even if they are still too slow and still too uncoordinated. And, sometimes they should be more thoughtful of what the real interests of this country are.

The most obvious effects of war are the destruction of the physical environment, the loss of hundreds of thousands of lives, and the displacement of hundreds of thousands more. But war is also about its survivors, whose experiences include living through protracted life-threatening chaos and uncertainty. In this context war is about brutality and evil, the betrayal of friends, the shattering of hopes, beliefs, and illusions, the dramatic loss of trust, the inexorable growth of mistrust, incalculable loss, and deep sorrow. It should be noted that in Bosnia, explicit public debate about trauma only began to emerge in early 1998, almost two years after the war drew to an end. Senada described the psychological horrors of war very vividly:

> One of my best friends got killed . . . then like, it wasn't even the dead body. I mean I had seen many dead bodies and people getting killed but this was like walking over a human brain and having the reaction twenty-four hours later. You know? . . . three minutes later, I was sitting at home having lunch or whatever! And only the next morning when I passed the same spot I started vomiting and shaking, realizing only then what it was that I really saw. And also once, when I was very close to an explosion and had done like all the other people who either threw themselves on the street or whatever. Later when they were trying to hide from the next one possibly coming . . . I just continued to sit in the middle of the street, . . . I just sat! I didn't want to move and everyone was yelling at me, you know, to come and stand behind the wood

or whatever! And then I figured . . . It can't go on like this. And that was when I knew that it was time for me to leave. . . . [But while I was in Zagreb] some radical changes took place, like another big massacre in Sarajevo and then the NATO air strikes, something I will never forgive myself for missing. . . . When I got out of Sarajevo . . . even the wish for something normal was killed. In Sarajevo all I was dreaming of was for the silence, to sleep without fear and to know that I am safe and that there is not going to be another explosion that is going to wake me up. And in Zagreb, I lived in this very quiet neighborhood, and I hated the silence! And, you know, the only thing I wished for was another explosion! And it took me two weeks to get out of the apartment because I didn't want to go out. I didn't want to go out to the supermarket only five minutes away. I felt very bad with having everything, with the water, with the electricity and with the food.

As Senada's account indicates, the effects of the war were intensified by the siege of Sarajevo, which lasted for three and a half years. During this period those who remained were subjected to bombardment by artillery fire from the surrounding hills and sniper fire within the city itself, as well as suffering desperate food and other shortages. In such circumstances the once-familiar world transforms into something strange and profoundly frightening (Malkki 1995). In Senada's words:

[there is] not much that I can mentally relate to or refer to as my home . . . like everything else that happened there, the loss of our house made the loss bigger. . . . I don't know, at least for my parents, it is unacceptable to go back to live there. It is too painful for me as well. . . . It used to be . . . (silence, sigh) a nice little neighborhood. Many people were killed there, people we knew, people that were our neighbors.

Living through war and living in a city under siege fundamentally changes people's senses of belonging, possibly forever. War is therefore about the subtle as well as dramatic shifts that take place within individuals and in their understandings of self and other, which reverberate from one generation to the next (Cockburn 1998; Hirsch 1998; Macek 2000a).

In the wake of the war, different groups in Sarajevo have all been affected by the enormously difficult social, material, and economic conditions they faced, including very high rates of unemployment, very low and unreliable salaries, poor housing, poor health care, rising crime, and increasing levels of domestic violence. In certain respects relations between ethno-religious groups appeared to continue much as before. Thus, one of the most common refrains I heard during my fieldwork was "*zajedno smo uvjek zivjeli*" ("we have always lived together"). Senada illustrated the persistence of a sense of multiculturalism alongside ethno-religious difference as she talked about her own sense of identity:

I do not feel comfortable . . . to say that I am a Muslim. I am Muslim in the sense . . . that I am a religious person. But, in the sense of a kind of inter-country nationality, I am a Bosnjak. That is the historical name as I see it of the inhabitants of this region, of those who converted to Islam. And, the most unjust thing done in the Communist system, was actually to play this very dirty trick with the Bosnjaks, with Muslims as a nation, to grant them the right to call themselves Muslims with a capital "M." Because if I was to accept that as my national name, then I would call Serbs and Croats, Bosnian Catholics and Bosnian Orthodox. I really feel the need to express myself as a Bosnjak. It is not only belonging or respecting one religion but, you know, having something more than that, which is something all three nationalities have. People of Muslim faith have the same experiences and the same history as people of Catholic faith and people of Orthodox faith who lived in Bosnia for centuries. So, it is not a clear-cut boundary. . . . Being Yugoslav was the same as being Bosnian for me now. It is nationality in the sense of citizenship, and it is a nationality for me when I am abroad. In the same sense that I had of being a Yugoslav, I have strong feelings about being Bosnian.

However, the country is de facto divided into three entities, with three educational systems, three languages, and three armies, and nationalist parties still obstructing efforts to reunify. As Senada put it "the country is still together in one, two, three pieces." Individual lives are therefore burdened by divisive and discriminatory policies affecting all aspects of daily life. Moreover, peace is fragile, dependent on the presence of the international community, prompting fears about renewed outbreaks of violence whether in Bosnia-Herzegovina or in the larger Balkan region. Indeed barely six months after I left Sarajevo, conflict in Kosovo erupted into a war of international proportions.

An urban and cosmopolitan sense of identity has long been paramount to Sarajevans, and despite ethnic cleansing, the most significant marker in Sarajevo remains the prewar, one that divides urban from rural, separating the population between the "civilized" and the "primitives" or "peasants." It is not uncommon to hear Sarajevans pining over their "lost city," bemoaning the deterioration caused by the influx of peasants who are described as not knowing how to conduct themselves according to norms of urban life. This was hinted at by Senada when she spoke about the impossibility of returning to the neighborhood in which she and her family had once lived: "Many [of the original inhabitants] won't go back for different reasons, and the people who are there now . . . I mean, it just isn't possible!" Many Sarajevans would like to see their city emptied of the people displaced from other areas, both urban and rural, within Bosnia-Herzegovina as a result of ethnic cleansing, most of whom are Bosnian Muslims.

Sarajevans also distinguish between those who remained during the siege and returnees who abandoned the city at or soon after the start of the war, many of whom went abroad. Resentment between these groups persists. In one way or another Sarajevans who stayed have been scarred by the war. They live with the memories of protracted periods of hunger, of lack of heating, electricity, and running water, of intense fear and uncertainty, and of the terror of sniper fire and grenades. They are continually reminded of the loss of loved ones killed in the fighting and the loss of friends who fled. Those returning to rebuild their lives express enormous ambivalence, happy to be back home, but disturbed by the changed landscape, including the absence of familiar people and the presence of strangers, as well as the stress that results from the hardships of daily life.

IN-BETWEEN POSITIONS

Researchers never enter the field as neutral or impartial observers but arrive with extensive "baggage" and immediately negotiate complex issues about their positions (Callaway 1992; Hastrup and Hervik 1994; Katz 1994; Miles and Crush 1993; Smith 1998). My own experience of being in Sarajevo was influenced by repeatedly finding myself in "in-between" positions. Two aspects of this in-betweenness merit particular comment, namely my ambiguous positioning between "stranger" and "homecomer" (Schutz 1971a, 1971b; Smith 1998), and my position between international and local communities. I discuss each in turn.

I had grown up as an immigrant child of Yugoslav and Croat origin who arrived in Montreal, Canada, in the early 1960s. My family of origin thus belonged to a Yugoslavian diaspora, and this heritage was strongly felt throughout my upbringing. I had visited Yugoslavia on many occasions during my childhood and as an adult, and in 1996 I had been in Sarajevo as a member of an international team observing the postwar elections in Bosnia-Herzegovina. These connections meant that I was not an "insider" indigenous to the city and society I was researching, but neither was I an "outsider" marked by unambiguous "foreignness."

I arrived in the field with a strong and highly ambivalent relationship to the country. In field notes written while I was in Sarajevo, I observed:

> Since childhood the country represented for me an enormous bundle of tensions, of paradoxes, of contradictions, of a wealth of culture as well as a wealth of authoritarianism, suppression, and constraint. In particular, I strongly disliked the authority and hierarchy prevalent in everything . . . ; the apparent distinctions between what I would have called "class," but which "they" spoke of as being differences between the so-called "educated" and the so-called "peasants" or "uncivilized" people; the chauvinistic attitude towards women; the well of "taboo" subjects. . . . Early on I realized how many "silences" were being imposed, were being reinforced and re-created. There were so many things concerning the past my parents did not talk about. There are still so many things that remain "unspoken." . . . While my parents had chosen to stay out of politics, it managed to infiltrate into our home and into our lives in the most subtle forms and ways. Over time, I came to understand that much of what was "left behind" had to do with difficult struggles, with pain, with loss, and with trauma. While for many of my parent's generation it was best to leave parts of that past behind, I felt inclined "to know" and "to understand."

As my notes suggest, I was aware of my personal history throughout my research. I found the confrontation between my preexisting ideas and my experiences in the field profoundly painful. In particular I needed to untangle myself from preconceived notions of being Yugoslav, to unlearn Titoist versions of history (Harasym 1990), and to address critically taken-for-granted notions of ethno-national identity and belonging (Calhoun 1995).

As an ethnographer I was in some senses privileged by my fluency in the local language, by my status as Yugoslavian-born, and by my familiarity with local social norms and customs. Many times each day I was aware that Sarajevans accepted me into their lives on the basis of a shared Yugoslav identity. Several people underlined our shared history in terms of coming from the "crazy Balkans." But the ease of my acceptance also generated disadvantages. People sometimes assumed that I knew or understood more than I did in ways that were difficult to counter. Many people confided in me because they defined me as an "insider" ("one of us") rather than as an "outsider" ("one of them"), and I experienced a profound sense of responsibility toward them. As well as the longer-term impact of this it meant that I was sometimes drawn into situations in Sarajevo that left me feeling overextended and emotionally exhausted.

My sense of being neither an insider nor an outsider was also connected to my position between international and local communities. Because of the involvement of the international community in post-Dayton peacekeeping and reconstruction, there were many "internationals" in Sarajevo; indeed, I had been one of them during the 1996 and 1997 elections. I therefore had the capacity to interact easily with "international" as well as local people. However, before arriving in Sarajevo in 1998 I had decided to keep a distance from the international community because if local people perceived me to be "one of them," I feared that I would lose the advantages of my partial insider status. This was a factor influencing my choice of accommodation. Many of the internationals earn what by local standards are extremely high salaries, and the well-furnished, self-contained flats with functioning kitchens and bathroom facilities in which they live command the high rentals typical of many Western European cities.[3] Despite a fieldwork grant from the Norwegian Research Council, I could not afford such accommodation. Moreover, I felt that my capacity to research the everyday lives of Sarajevans would be enhanced by living in the same way as they did, especially if I was also able to observe and interact with their lives at close quarters. During my stay I lived in two different flats, each time renting a room from a widow who lived alone. Each of these women had an extra room, which offered me the peace, quiet, and space that I needed to record field notes and to rest. Both of them were in need of the extra income, one to help her two children now living in Croatia, and the other to help her two granddaughters now living in Montenegro. In relation to each of them I was invited into, and became, something of a surrogate daughter.

Living in this way, I was able to participate in activities like listening to the daily news, watching soap operas, drinking coffee, sharing homemade cakes with the neighbors, and talking with friends. Common topics of conversation included the difficulties of making ends meet on miserly wages and pensions, which were often paid late; the health and ill-health of friends and relatives; and, in hushed voices, local politics, in relation to which great frustrations built up because of the frequent postponement or obstruction of the implementation of policy decisions.

But despite these ways of participating in the lives of local people, I was always acutely aware that I did not really "belong." Ironically, many Sarajevans (especially the young and middle-aged) interacted a great deal with the international community: many of those with foreign language skills were employed by international agencies, others rented accommodations to international visitors, and most mixed with them in one way or another, for example in workplaces, shops, restaurants, or clubs. Indeed, despite points of tension, their presence was widely appreciated not only for the sense of stability and security they brought, but also because of a more general widening of horizons, which Senada described thus: "for me personally their presence gives me this feeling of globalization; . . . they make me feel somehow connected with things that are going on in the world." But, unlike local people, I always had the possibility of repositioning myself within the world of international agencies, and I knew that I would leave Sarajevo in due course.

Moreover, as well as keeping my distance from the international community, I had to avoid becoming overidentified with a particular group in Sarajevo because I needed to be able to interact with members of different Sarajevan communities. It was partly because of this that I moved during my time in Sarajevo: in the first flat in which I lived, I felt that the "space" available for me to maintain my independence was eroded to a degree that jeopardized my capacity to continue my fieldwork effectively. More generally, despite forging relationships that were in some sense "close," I never felt able to relax into friendship, and I frequently experienced an intense sense of "being apart" (compare Marcus and Fisher 1986).

I also felt very uncomfortable about the fact that I was "using" the evidence Sarajevans gave me and the trust they showed in me for my research, which I was conducting for a Ph.D. and, therefore, for my own career advantage. It would not help Sarajevans out of their misery, nor could it, in any way, change what had taken place in Bosnia-Herzegovina. On one occasion I was told that "they" were fed up with being the West's "guinea-pigs." I sometimes felt weighed down by guilt.

I could understand the resentment of Sarajevans toward the images that informed both the Western media and most of the key "international" actors. I thus began my research highly critical of much of the media coverage of the Bosnian war, which tended to promote one of two overly simplistic and therefore distorting explanations of the underlying causes of the war, seeing it either as a perpetuation of "ancient ethnic hatreds" or presenting a utopian Bosnian multiethnic society betrayed both by Serbian and Croatian nationalists and the international community (Cushman and Mestrovic 1996; International Commission on the Balkans 1996; Ó Tuathail 1996). I regarded both as very partial truths that I wished to unsettle and counter with a more nuanced account. But, while I wanted to contribute to debates about current affairs in Sarajevo and in Bosnia-Herzegovina more generally, I was also aware that many Sarajevans had too often heard "internationals" or "foreigners" telling them how to run their country. Consequently, at times I felt I must refrain from voicing my criticisms of their views or of their politicians and policymakers.

Overall my position can perhaps best be described as one of liminality: I was at the margins of various worlds. While this was appropriate to my role as ethnographer, it also generated in me a sense of living "suspended" between different worlds and anchored in none. It contributed to the stressful impact of my fieldwork.

BEARING WITNESS

During my time in Sarajevo, I encouraged people to tell stories about themselves and to reflect on the impact of past events, especially during the war, on their lives. I felt this to be the least intrusive method available to me for doing social research in a war-torn society. In telling their stories and remembering their pasts, people actively construct their senses of self, other, and place. Narrative redefinition is profoundly important for the rebuilding of lives in the aftermath of trauma (Brison 1997), including the trauma of a war that killed and displaced people because of ethnic and/or religious differences. According to the literary scholar Geoffrey H. Hartman (cited in Weine 1999: xi) "listening facilitates a 'welling-up of memories' (1996: 145) that carry a unique knowing, whereby 'the immediacy of these first-person accounts burns through the cold storage of history'" (138). Life stories, therefore, not only provide valuable insights about how people (re)shape their identities in such contexts, but their telling may also provide welcome opportunities for those reconstructing their lives in the aftermath of trauma.

Listening to individuals telling stories had been a favorite pastime of mine since childhood and so I felt strongly drawn to this form of data collection. During my time in Sarajevo I supplemented numerous spontaneous conversations with ethnographic interviews about people's life stories. As a listener I attempted to be "engaged but unobtrusive, nondirective but committed" (Weine 1999: xi). I identified increasingly with a characterization of the "listener" offered by psychoanalyst and holocaust survivor Dori Laub[4] (Felman and Laub 1992: 59), namely "a companion in a journey onto an uncharted land, a journey the survivor cannot traverse or return from alone."

There were many indications that my willingness to listen was valued by those around me. Almost all of those who entrusted me with their stories thanked me explicitly for taking the time to listen. Some who had initially claimed to have nothing much to tell me found, on the contrary, how much they had been holding back: for these people, telling and being listened to enabled them to articulate memories of which they were not even aware, and in so doing, to integrate more fully harrowing experiences into their senses of themselves (compare Brison 1997). Several people described feeling "lighter" after sharing their stories with me, as if relieved of a heavy burden. Indeed, many expressed concern about burdening other Sarajevans with their problems, all of whom were perceived to be heavily weighed down already by the impact of the war. It was therefore a relief to be able to speak to a "stranger," who had not suffered the trauma associated with the war.

While these observations indicate that my research methods were appropriate to the context and contributed positively to the remaking of lives and selves by the people of Sarajevo, listening to "stories about lives darkened by the nightmare of ethnic cleansing" (Weine 1999: x) is never a straightforward matter. I have already indicated that I felt a heavy burden of responsibility to those who helped me with my fieldwork. While I was in Sarajevo I was acutely aware that I had not shared directly in the suffering of which others spoke. Perhaps because of this I tended to underestimate the value of my own listening to those whose testimony I heard: I was far more aware of my indebtedness to them, and the enormous responsibility that I felt flowed from their willingness to tell me about their lives. Only much later did I begin to realize how my listening had facilitated tellings that were very active contributions to the re-making of selves after the trauma of the Bosnian war and the siege of Sarajevo.

In making sense of the impact on me of the testimony of survivors, I found Stevan Weine's (1999: ix) reflections a useful point of departure:

> I'm often asked, "What led you to do all this work with Bosnians? Are you Bosnian?" When I answer that I am an American Jew, I'm then asked, "But does your family come from there?" No, my grandparents immigrated to the United States early in this century from several other places in East Europe. But there is a connection between my life and my work that comes alive when I am sitting with a Bosnian refugee. Sometimes my mind drifts and I feel as if my grandmother Kate—once an immigrant child full of dreams of life in a strange, new country—is sitting and talking with me. "Do not ever forget who you are," she said to me one of the last times we were together. I was twenty-three, a medical student, and could not really know what she meant. In listening to the Bosnians struggling over memories and identity, sometimes I feel I am listening to her. I expected that my work with Bosnians would be difficult; what I didn't anticipate was that it would engage this question and nurture a connection with memories that are so central to the history that has shaped my life and the life of my family.

In my case, the connections were more direct and harder to tolerate. The stories I heard resonated with stories from my own childhood, recounted by my mother and my aunt. They too had told of grief and loss resulting from war (the Second World War) and dislocation. However, I was barely aware of this while I was in Sarajevo: it was on my move to the University of Edinburgh as a visiting scholar that the impact became apparent. Away from the immediacy of the traumatic stories to which I had listened, I became aware of the emotional burden of my research. For many months I felt deeply distressed and very vulnerable, and I found it impossible to write in the way in which I had intended.

WRITING SELVES

Psychiatrist Stevan Weine (1999: x, 4) also found the genre in which he had trained unsuitable for writing about the impact of the Bosnian war:

> The challenges of knowing this genocide are far too great to be contained within conventional psychiatric paradigms. Writing this text has been part of my search to find a new way of being professional in relation to mass political violence, its survivors and its witnesses—a way of being professional that takes into account both the moral engagement and the life involvement familiar to many who work with trauma survivors. Also, like other scholars, I wanted to find a way to understand traumatization not just of individuals, but of a whole society and its culture. To this end I use stories and a biographical approach. The narrative voice and the biographical structure are capable of supporting a reality, a complexity, and a truth often lost in the more analytical forms of

discourse common to my profession. . . . I have not yet gained enough distance from the Bosnian experience to accommodate such a project, and it is not possible for me to impose that distance right now. I am aiming to create a different kind of experience and understanding for readers, one that sticks closer to the words and meanings in the stories of those whose lives are marked by the historical nightmare of ethnic cleansing.

I too have found it impossible to subject my respondents' narratives to forms of analysis that cut across the thread of biographical telling. Even Senada's account, on which this chapter draws, began as a continuous story and was disrupted by "my" textual voice only through the editorial intervention of this book's lead author, Liz Bondi. And so it is because of the continuing imperative to preserve biographical integrity that I have drawn explicitly on only one person's story, to quote from several would feel for me like a violation of their selves.

This sense of the self's fragility in the wake of trauma is as much mine as theirs (compare Macek 2000b). My research certainly challenged me in ways I never dreamed possible. Stories of loss and displacement were familiar from my upbringing and doubtless drew me to bear witness to the trauma of others through my research. As Amanda Bingley argues in chapter 13, the personal impacts of fieldwork are certainly unpredictable. Moreover, for me it was the period after my fieldwork that was the most problematic. As Edward Said (1996: xviii) states, "there is something fundamentally unsettling about intellectuals who have neither offices to protect nor territory to consolidate and guard." I have since heard several people talk of the pain of leaving "the field" and of readjusting to life "elsewhere," typically lived within the orbit of the Western academy. In my own case, the eruption of war in Kosovo and Serbia shortly after I left Sarajevo intensified the pain and challenged my work anew, not least because I had by this time befriended a Sarajevan family of Serb origin living in Edinburgh.

As these comments indicate, bearing witness to the trauma of others had a major impact on my own sense of self. My need to preserve the biographical integrity of their testimony is in part a symptom of my own immersion in a process of remaking and rewriting myself. In this task I take inspiration from Edward Said (1996: xvii) once more when he writes of the (troubled and lonely) condition of intellectuals being "a better one than a gregarious tolerance for the way things are."

Subjectivities are mutually reshaped through encounters between researchers and those with whom they conduct their research. In my own case, because of the trauma experienced by the people of Sarajevo, together with my openness to their trauma, this reshaping has been profound. In other cases it may be less so. However, whether presented through life stories or in other ways, I would argue that somewhere, maybe deeply buried, social research is very often about the telling of stories and (re)making of selves.

NOTES

I am grateful to Liz Bondi and Nina Witoszek, both of whom have on various occasions pointed to the link between the distress I subsequently experienced and the genre within which I was trying to write. I also wish to note that this chapter began as an essay submitted for a doctoral course at the University of Oslo, but has been substantially reshaped thanks to the editorial work of Liz Bondi.

1. Kemal Kurspahic was the editor-in-chief of *Oslobodjenje*, an independent daily newspaper in Sarajevo and also the main newspaper in Bosnia-Herzegovina, from 1988 to 1994. *Oslobodjenje* missed only one day of publication throughout the war, and, according to Kurspahic, it acted as the voice of multiethnic Bosnia throughout that time. Kurspahic has received numerous awards for his journalism, including being honored by the International Press Institute in Vienna as one of fifty heroes of the free press over the past fifty years since the end of the Second World War.

2. Senada is a pseudonym for one of my research subjects. My research was conducted in accordance with the Institutional Ethics Guide at the University of Oslo.

3. These prices reflect aspects of the postwar economy of Sarajevo: one of the main sources of income for many Sarajevan families comes from renting their own flats and living with other family members.

4. Dori Laub is one of a group of psychotherapists and scholars who have, since 1979, undertaken video testimony interviews with holocaust survivors generating the Fortunoff Video Archive for Holocaust Testimonies at Yale University (Weine 1999: xi).

15

Situated Ethics
and Feminist Ethnography
in a West of Scotland Hospice

Bella Vivat

Between February 1998 and April 1999 I conducted an ethnographic study of St. Z's, a hospice in the west of Scotland. Building on feminist and postcolonial perspectives on the social shaping of knowledge (or, as Sandra Harding [1998] puts it, the co-evolution of cultures/societies and knowledges), I was seeking to investigate the claim of hospices to provide "total care" and the relation between this and allopathic medical practice, including the increased medicalization of hospices over the past thirty years. In particular, I sought to explore the spiritual aspects of hospice care.

Before embarking on my fieldwork, I had considered ethical issues that were likely to arise primarily in terms of establishing a framework for negotiating informed consent. But, as my fieldwork progressed, I became aware of the pervasiveness and relevance of questions about ethics to my research questions and my research practice. This chapter explores some of these issues, arguing that ethics are situated and, therefore, advocating a contextualized and situated approach to ethical research practice. In the remainder of this section I introduce the context informing my argument. I then proceed to outline the ideas and debates on which I have drawn to make sense of the numerous ethical concerns I engaged with during my time in St. Z's, and then end the chapter with a discussion of some of these concerns, focusing particularly on ethical issues that arose in the relationship between myself as a researcher and the people in my research site.

On one level it is obvious that ethical questions were present in my research from the beginning, since in daily life we are constantly making decisions, to a more or less conscious extent, concerning which actions are right or wrong. But, on another level, I have had to make specific ethical choices throughout my research, that is, make decisions concerning what I felt I should or should not do, and these decisions have in turn shaped the directions I followed. For example, ethical issues arose when

I was choosing a hospice in which to do my fieldwork and when I was considering whether to conduct tape-recorded interviews with hospice patients. I was aware that I thought about these choices in terms of right and wrong, but I had not consciously thought through, nor theorized, my own ethical position.

As my fieldwork progressed, I also became aware of disagreements between people in the hospice, which they often framed in ethical terms (that is, using words such as "should," "ought," "right/wrong," "fair/unfair"). Some of these disagreements were openly discussed. So, for example, there was some debate over staff interactions with, and attitudes toward, patients, especially when workers perceived particular patients as being "difficult to get on with." There were also less open tensions within hospice workers' relationships, especially between managers and staff, and also concerning how relationships among staff affected relationships between staff and patients. Some hospice workers explicitly referred to what they perceived as contradictions between managers' professed spiritual beliefs and their relationships with workers.

As a result of my increasing awareness of the tensions between people in the hospice, I began to consider how ethical issues arose in the relations between the people I was studying and their differing perceptions of the right and wrong ways of behaving toward others, particularly coworkers. I also began to work out the characteristics of my own moral position, to make sense of my own discomfort with the lack of fit of canonical ethical theories to my own ethical beliefs, to attempt to understand some of the disagreements between people in the hospice, and to link these to wider questions of knowledge and subjectivity.

My thinking is informed by feminist and postcolonial philosophies of knowledge, which, through concepts such as "situated knowledge" (Haraway 1988), "strong objectivity" (Harding 1986) and "neo-rationality" (Lazreg 1994) attempt to dislodge "pure" reason from its canonical status as the sole arbiter of what counts as knowledge (and which people count as knowers) without rejecting it completely. Linked to this, Susan Hekman (1995: 69) argues that "what we know and who we are cannot be neatly separated," and other feminist philosophers of knowledge such as Lorraine Code (1991) and Patricia Hill Collins (1996) argue that epistemology, subjectivity, agency, and morality are interwoven. Some discussions of spirituality, including Daphne Hampson's (1996) account of post-Christian morality, and Steve Wright and Jean Sayre-Adams's (2000) analysis of spirituality in health care as a "right relation" between caregivers and those for whom they care, similarly link subjectivity, morality, and spirituality.

In the context of these ideas this chapter examines the relevance of Carol Gilligan's work to my study. Gilligan's "ethic of care" (Gilligan 1993) is often equated with feminist ethics, but feminist ethics addresses many themes, of which the ethic of care is only one. Indeed, many feminist ethicists argue against the version of the ethic of care that is most prominent. Further, although this version of the ethic of care is based on the work of Gilligan, I will argue that it is an incomplete representation of her position. In the next section of this chapter I outline my understanding of Gilligan's work and argue for a shift away from her opposed "ethic of care" and "ethic of justice" to the notions of "situated ethics" and "detached ethics." In the light of this shift, I then consider my findings and experiences at St. Z's.

FROM AN ETHIC OF CARE TO SITUATED ETHICS

Carol Gilligan's (1993) landmark text *In a Different Voice* was conceived and written in response to Lawrence Kohlberg's (1981) argument that "mature," "advanced," or "post-conventional" morality is characterized by abstraction and detachment from concrete situations in favor of producing generalized rules and laws, and that women tend not to reach this stage of moral development. By contrast Gilligan argued that there are two different moralities and that these are gendered, such that men tend to adhere to what she calls an ethic of justice, or "morality of rights," which has fairness and equality as its primary values, while women tend to adhere to what she calls an ethic of care, or "morality of responsibility," which has inclusion and protection from harm as its primary values.

Echoing Kohlberg, Gilligan claims that both of these moralities have three levels: pre-conventional, at which the agent is self-centered; conventional, at which the agent conforms to social norms; and post-conventional, at which the agent questions and reflects upon these norms. At Kohlberg's post-conventional level of morality, agents produce abstract, detached ethical principles; but Gilligan argues that, since social norms differ for men and women, women at the post-conventional level of her ethic of care do not seek to detach themselves from relationships, and so women's post-conventional morality can appear conventional in Kohlberg's terms.[1]

Gertrud Nunner-Winkler (1993) argues that the difference between Gilligan's two moralities is one of orientation rather than of content, and I think that, despite her claim that the distinction between her two moralities lies in their primary values, Gilligan's work actually suggests that the values of inclusion and protection from harm do not replace, but rather coexist with values of equality and fairness. Similarly her ethic of justice may also include values associated with care. Indeed, Gilligan (1993: 74) explicitly states that at the post-conventional level of her ethic of care, "Care becomes the self-chosen principle of a judgement that remains psychological in concern with relationships and response but *becomes universal in its condemnation of exploitation and hurt*" (my emphasis). Thus, I would argue that this morality contextualizes and amplifies, rather than replaces, the principles of fairness and justice, so that the post-conventional level of Gilligan's ethic of care is both universal (condemning exploitation) and particular (concerned with context). In other words, at the post-conventional level of Gilligan's ethic of care, the agent applies abstract, universal rules contextually, emphasizing and seeking to preserve relationships between people.

Following from this, for Gilligan, the resolution of Kohlberg's "Heinz dilemma" (whether Heinz should steal a drug or allow his wife to die) is achieved for boys by establishing a hierarchy between wrongs, and for girls by weighing up the social and personal consequences of each wrong for the people involved. That is, for girls, as for boys, both stealing and allowing someone to die are (absolutely/universally) wrong, but when girls are asked to choose between these two actions, they attend to the context within which the choice is being made, rather than seeking to produce an absolute rule that applies regardless of the situation.

Nunner-Winkler claims that Kohlberg's "correct" solution to his Heinz dilemma demonstrates that his claim that his post-conventional morality is detached does not hold, but rather shows that a detached morality is impossible. It is not irrelevant that it is Heinz's wife around whom the dilemma revolves, since the solution to the dilemma is not that one should steal in order to prevent *all* people from dying, only a particular person. Thus, even at the post-conventional level of Kohlberg's ethic of justice, the agent pays attention to the situation. The difference is that this approach claims *not* to consider the context in which the ethical choice is made and extends this context-free claim to suggest that contextual judgments are flawed, immature, and inferior because of their subjective character.

In summary, the distinction between Gilligan's "ethic of care" and "ethic of justice" lies in how the agent applies universal ethical rules, that is, whether or not the agent explicitly acknowledges and takes account of the situation in which the moral choice is to be made, or claims it is irrelevant. Thus, Gilligan's ethic of care is overtly relational, as opposed to her ethic of justice, which claims to be individualistic, isolated, and detached from a situation or relationship.

Gilligan's works subsequent to *In a Different Voice* (Brown and Gilligan 1992; Gilligan et al. 1988) are richer, more complex, and more subtle. In contrast to her initial assumption of a unidirectional movement through the levels of her ethic of care, from pre-conventional through conventional to post-conventional, her later work shows women progressing and regressing between these levels. In her collaborative work with Lyn Mikel Brown (Brown and Gilligan 1992), they highlight the struggles and tensions adolescent girls experience in relation to the self-sacrificial nature of the conventional level of morality (thus also in relation to the conventional female self-sacrificial role), observing these girls' sense of having to "give themselves up" by prioritizing care for others over care for themselves, in order to (continue to) have relationships.

Gilligan has had a wide influence, and she has also been widely criticized. Some criticisms do not apply to the whole of her ethic of care, but rather to developments of its conventional level by writers such as Nel Noddings (1984) and Sara Ruddick (1989). So, Noddings argues that the ethic of care is modeled on *agape* in the mother-child relationship, that is, unidirectional caring from the caregiver (mother) to the cared-for (child). This is, however, only equivalent to the conventional level of Gilligan's ethic of care; at her post-conventional level the agent reflects on and rejects the inequity of this conventional level of morality. Other criticisms of Gilligan have greater validity, in particular those that challenge her methodology, her sweeping generalizations about "women," and the dichotomies she sets up. Linked to this, her interchangeable use of terms, such as morality and ethics, responsibility, and care, is also confusing and problematic.

Nevertheless, I agree with commentators such as Alison Jaggar (1991) and Michele Moody-Adams (1991), who argue that, even if Gilligan's work is flawed and overgeneralized, it remains extremely important. By suggesting that there is a way of reasoning ethically, which is profoundly different from that prized by the canonical tradition, and that, contra the canonical tradition, this other way of reasoning is neither immature nor inferior, Gilligan brought to light questions about morality in fundamental ways, and I have used Gilligan's work as my starting point. However, there are two important ways in which my analysis departs from Gilligan's framework. The first concerns conflicts among women and the second concerns a shift in terminology related to the question of dichotomies.

First, Brown and Gilligan's (1992) analysis of moral reasoning by adolescent girls emphasizes that girls allow rules to be broken or will abandon a game rather than disagree with one another or exclude someone. They also highlight how girls silence themselves in order to maintain relationships with other girls who would ostracize them if they did not conform. However, they fail to discuss the ostracizing of nonconformists from the perspective of those ostracizing or threatening to ostracize others. Such behavior, which contradicts their first claim above and can hardly be characterized as caring, points to potentially important conflicts among women and to limits to women's caring. As Elizabeth Spelman (1991) and María Lugones (1991) argue, women's uncaring behavior toward one another is a key issue for feminist ethics to examine, and I return to this point later in this chapter.

Second, Gilligan's terms are problematic for several reasons. The term "ethic of care" implies that "caring ethicists" do not pay attention to considerations of justice, yet, as I have argued, the distinctive characteristic of this morality is that the agent pays attention to the context within which he or she applies considerations of *both* care *and* justice, and applies them with care for that context, including relationships between people, immediately and into the future. Thus, too, the term "ethic of justice" similarly supports a false dichotomy between justice and care. In addition to this problem, "care" itself is a word with multiple meanings and definitions,[2] while "justice" also has multiple-layered meanings. Users of these terms therefore need to be clear about how they are using them, but Gilligan never clarifies her meanings.

In this context I have coined the term "situated ethics," which I use to explore issues and debates prompted by Gilligan's notion of an ethic of care. This term parallels Haraway's "situated knowledge," which counters the claim that knowledge is impartial and context-free or context-independent, arguing instead that knowledge is inevitably, unavoidably produced within a social and cultural context, and that all knowers should therefore acknowledge the context within which they produce knowledge (Haraway 1988). I understand situated ethics to be characterized by the agent paying explicit attention to the particular situation and to the consequences for the relations between those involved, and by an absence of interest in making universal claims, although the agent may still appeal to abstract principles of both justice and care. Such an approach to ethics can only be considered to be (solely) gendered from a narrow Western/northern perspective, since cultures that are more collective and less individualistic than those of the West/north may also have more contextual approaches to ethics (Kleinman 1995, on Chinese ethics; Kondo 1990, on Japanese ethics; and Collins 1996, on African American ethics).

Conversely, I use the term "detached ethics" to describe a morality that is characterized by the agent's attempt or claim to abstract universal principles from specific ethical decisions made in particular contexts (or to explain those decisions in terms of abstract principles). The same ideology—that a detached position is both possible and desirable—underpins both detached ethics and detached knowledge, as opposed to the claim made by proponents of both situated knowledges and situated ethics that pure detachment and "objectivity" are impossible.

I could seem to be contradicting myself here, since I am criticizing Gilligan for her use of dichotomies, yet using them myself. But the distinction between seeking detachment and accepting and acknowledging situatedness seems to me a more useful and fundamental dichotomy than the ones Gilligan uses. In the context of this reframing I now turn to issues arising in my research at St. Z's.

SITUATED ETHICS IN ST. Z'S

St. Z's was run by an order of nuns from Ireland, and a convent was attached to the side of the hospice. However, it was situated on the outskirts of a strongly Protestant town, which had resulted in some tension when the hospice and convent were first built in 1987. Other than one black British GP who attended the hospice to visit patients, the workers in St. Z's were all white, Western, and to a greater or lesser extent Christian. Most were women.

There are three main things from Gilligan's work that I applied to my fieldwork. First, in my records of conversations (field notes) and in my interview tapes and transcripts, I looked and listened for markers of moral reasoning such as "should," "ought," "good," "bad," "better," and also "fair," "unfair," "right," "wrong," "love," "care" (that is, considerations of both "justice" and "care"). I looked for these markers in what people said to me and to each other, in my own thoughts and feelings, and in the notes I took about these. Second, by listening for phrases such as "I mean," "you know," "I don't know," I listened for any difficulties people had in articulating their ethical positions. Third, I explored hospice workers' evaluations of care as self-sacrifice in relation to the three levels Gilligan uses to describe moral reasoning. I draw on these to examine some key aspects of my research practice including the negotiation of access, informed consent, reciprocity, and issues of representation.

Negotiating Access

Gaining access to a research site raised issues that illustrate significant differences between situated and detached ethics. In the decisions I made I was, on the one hand, inclined to do things that a proponent of detached ethics might consider unethical, but, on the other hand, I also placed greater restrictions on my actions than I would have had I adhered to detached ethics.

I had been volunteering at a hospice in Edinburgh for about eighteen months when I applied for access to do my fieldwork there, which was refused by the medical director. His refusal came in response to a letter I had written to the hospice's board of management, in which I had asked if it would be possible for me to meet and talk with them about my proposed research. I had given no details of what I hoped to do, nor was I given the opportunity to discuss it, but the medical director nevertheless said that it would be disruptive to the patients. What I had hoped to seek was permission primarily to do more of what I was doing anyway—talking to patients—although I intended to use this in a different way. In the role of volunteer, my talking to patients was seen as positive, useful, helpful, and certainly not disruptive. Indeed, at the same time as refusing me access to do my fieldwork, the medical director explicitly encouraged me to continue my work as a volunteer.

In refusing me access and arguing that research was disruptive to patients, the medical director appealed to considerations of care, and he applied general, universal rules of care and protection from harm along the following lines: research is disruptive; disruption is harmful; it is wrong to harm patients; therefore, it is wrong to do research with them. This is a very clear illustration of detached ethics, and it also illustrates that considerations of justice and considerations of care do not constitute a dichotomy in the way Gilligan suggests.

The medical director had not considered (indeed, was not aware of) the specific nature of my proposed research, nor the wider context of my relationships with patients and staff. He did not consider the consequences of his actions for these relationships, neither for me nor for those people with whom I had established relationships.[3] Even if, having gained access to do my research elsewhere, I had continued volunteering at this Edinburgh hospice, it would have been difficult for me to volunteer there and *not* think about what I was doing ethnographically, both in its own terms and also in relation to my experiences elsewhere. This meant that the refusal of access had consequences for my volunteering, and, given that some of the people with whom I had established relationships over a significant length of time were patients and therefore terminally ill, it was very likely that my relationships with them could not be continued, even if I returned to the hospice after conducting my fieldwork elsewhere.

In the event, I gained access elsewhere, and, although I visited the Edinburgh hospice a few times after completing my fieldwork at St. Z's, my connection with it and with the people there had been broken, not least because several of the people I had known had died since I had stopped volunteering there. Although we said goodbye to each other when I left, we lost time together as a consequence. I did not return to the Edinburgh hospice as a volunteer after completing my fieldwork, partly because my connection with the people there had been broken, but also partly because I did not want to create overlap or confusion with analyzing and writing about my findings from St. Z's. Thus, not gaining access to the Edinburgh hospice put an end to my voluntary relationship with the people there.

For a while after being refused access, I considered the possibility of continuing to volunteer at this hospice and doing covert research. I did not feel that this would necessarily be unethical for two reasons. First, I did not believe that my research would be harmful to patients or indeed to staff, and, second, my interpretation of care for the patients differed radically from that of the medical director.[4] In the end, however, I decided against conducting covert research, not because I considered that this would be unethical, but because I was concerned that I would find the covertness too exhausting. I was also concerned that if I did covert research, I would ultimately have to justify myself within the dominant view of ethics, that is, in terms of detached ethics, when I came to submit my thesis, and if I were subsequently to seek publication in academic journals.

Reflecting on all this now, I think that I felt able to justify doing covert research at least partly because I felt that the medical director had shown a lack of trust in me and caring for me, and also, therefore, that he had been unfair to me, that is, that he had been neither caring nor just. For him, the context, including the relationships between me and other people, within which I had approached him to ask for access to do my research appeared to be irrelevant. However, it is possible that context *did* matter implicitly. Some years earlier another doctoral student had conducted research in this hospice, and her thesis had been quite critical (Mazer 1994). So her research—at least the written version of it—could indeed have been disruptive, although to staff rather than patients, and the medical director's refusal of access for my research could possibly have been related to that. However, I never discovered whether this was the case, and after I gained access elsewhere I did not think the question was worth pursuing.

While I was considering the question of whether to do covert research in the Edinburgh hospice, I applied to several other hospices for research access, eventually choosing St. Z's. I was not asked by St. Z's to seek formal approval to conduct my fieldwork, and I was given unrestricted access (at least ostensibly, although obviously tacit limitations would be in place). From a detached ethical position this could be taken to mean that I could speak to whomever I wanted and use the resulting material, together with that gained through my observations, as I wanted. However, for me, context, including relationships, mattered, and having unlimited access intensified my sense of responsibility and concern for the people there.

It can perhaps be taken as given that I felt a sense of responsibility and concern toward the patients in St. Z's; in any case, I will focus here on my sense of responsibility and concern for the workers. This operated partly on a general level: the managers of St. Z's did not know (any more than the medical director of the Edinburgh hospice) what my research involved, and I was concerned that they did not really understand the potential hazards of ethnography.[5] However, at least the managers, as "gatekeepers," had the option of granting or refusing me access, unlike the staff, who had no control over this. Yet the consequences of my research were less likely to be problematic for the managers than for the staff, who might not only find my fieldwork or my thesis upsetting, but might also find their jobs threatened as a result of my findings. I therefore felt an even greater sense of responsibility and concern for the staff of St. Z's, and will now move on to discuss how this affected my decisions concerning who to study and also raised questions for me concerning the meaning of the term "informed consent."

Informed Consent

In the early stages of my fieldwork, I hypothesized that the spiritual aspects of hospice care were to be found in the manner in which care was delivered, that is, the way in which caregivers provided care, rather than in the content of that care. However, as I spent more time in the hospice, I began to find this hypothesis more problematic and began to focus more on the content of care. Although it seemed to me that staff were generally very caring, I found it difficult to identify anything that seemed to me particularly spiritual as opposed to emotional or psychological. I wondered whether this was because the more spiritual aspects of care would necessarily be very intimate, for example, given on a one-to-one basis when the caregiver and patient were alone together, such as in the bathroom, and so I would be unlikely to witness them. I also felt that the taboo around open discussion of spirituality (evident even in this explicitly Christian hospice) meant that it was more likely that people would talk to me on a one-to-one basis than in the public spaces of the hospice.

I therefore decided to conduct individual taped ethnographic interviews in order to explore people's understandings of spirituality and the spiritual aspects of care in depth. However, since I was in some doubt as to whether patients were receiving more than very limited spiritual care, I felt that it would be wrong for me to raise the question of spiritual needs with them if I felt that neither I nor hospice workers were likely to meet such needs.[6] So I conducted tape-recorded interviews only with hospice staff. If patients raised spiritual or religious issues in (untaped) conversations with me, I followed this interest, but the decision I made not to tape-record interviews with patients means that my material on patients' perceptions is limited, and my thesis focuses more on hospice workers' understandings of the spiritual aspects of care.

This decision also illustrates the practice of situated ethics: I considered not only whether I had access, but also the consequences of my research for people in the present and the future. However, while my focusing primarily on staff resolved one ethical issue—concerning patients—it raised others concerning staff.

In the United Kingdom, when prospective Ph.D. students submit a research proposal to the Economic and Social Research Council, they are asked to discuss "any ethical issues" relating to their project. The same is true of applications to most funding bodies as well as for research on health services. This, of course, refers to ethics within the generally understood ethical framework, that is, the framework of detached ethics, which is how the dominant idea of informed consent is framed (Engelhardt 1996; Kleinman 1995). At the time of submitting my proposal, I duly discussed ethical issues within this framework, but, as I have indicated, I subsequently realized that for me abstract ethical considerations are *not enough*, and that situated ethics effectively subsume detached ethics.

Before going to St. Z's, and once there, I was careful to tell staff and volunteers what my research involved, as far as this was possible, given that ethnographic research evolves in the interaction between researcher/s and "researchee/s." After I arrived I was repeatedly asked (sometimes several times by the same person) "What is it you're doing again?," a question I always tried to answer as fully and honestly as I could. I asked all the people with whom I conducted taped interviews to sign consent forms, so I was "covered" ethically, that is, in terms of detached ethics. Nevertheless, I was very uncomfortable with whether I could really say that I had obtained *informed* consent from my "researchees."

In terms of detached ethics, it is enough to give an information sheet and have the consent form signed. If the person gives consent and if no deception takes place, it is, in effect, irrelevant whether the person "really"—that is, fully and completely — understands what is going to happen. The repeated question "What is it you're doing?" suggests that, although my "researchees" had read the information sheet on which I detailed the aims of my research, had had the opportunity to ask questions about it, and had signed the consent forms, they did not really understand what they had agreed to. I would argue that participants in—"subjects" of—ethnographic research do not (indeed, cannot) ever really understand the consequences of what they agree to since it is impossible to fully anticipate what one will reveal or how the researcher will use it. Indeed, when I first started my fieldwork, for much of the time *I* did not fully understand what I was doing or trying to do, in practice as opposed to theory, and if this was true for me then it was all the more so for those whose consent I sought. Having conducted this ethnography, and, as a result, being more aware of the potential of such research to misrepresent people, despite using their "own words," I am not at all sure that I would agree to participate in an anthropological study of my work situation, certainly not without having a great deal of trust in the researcher.

With those members of staff with whom I did not conduct interviews, issues of this kind were in some ways even more pronounced. Although I told people that I was there to do fieldwork and explained to them what my research involved, many of those with whom I interacted appeared to find it very difficult to recognize my presence as that of a researcher/ethnographer, not least because ethnographic research does not fit with the usual allopathic medical understanding of research. Indeed, it emerged that many staff made sense of me by thinking of me as a kind of volunteer, which was a recognizable role within the hospice. So, for example, when I was in the palliative care ward one Friday afternoon, and planning to stay there into the evening, one of the auxiliary nurses suggested that I help at the children's drop-in in the early evening, since she had signed up to help after she finished her shift, but she had realized that she was unable to go after all and the drop-in would be short of helpers.

Staff's repeated questioning of me concerning what I was doing could be interpreted as stemming from their distrust of me, but generally I felt that their actions implied a great deal of trust. At times I felt they trusted me or confided in me too much, and I was uncomfortably aware of the potential for this trust to be abused, at least within the framework of detached ethics, which makes it possible to claim that, having been given access and possessing signed consent forms, I can ethically use everything that I observed and was told.

Reciprocity

In practice, the care and trust I received from people at St. Z's generated in me a sense of reciprocal care. Sarah Hoagland (1988) argues against Noddings' (1984) unidirectional caring, or *agape*, as a model for caring relationships, arguing instead for *philia*, reciprocal care between equals. The professional caregiver-patient relationship is unequal, like that between parent/caregiver and child: in neither of these relationships will the cared-for reciprocate equally, if at all, nor can he or she be expected to.[7] Nevertheless, the caregivers in these asymmetric relationships still need to be cared for by someone else, and I would suggest that care between caregivers (that is, when a community of caregivers cares for one another, rather than the cared-for reciprocating for the care they receive) could be called indirect reciprocity.

Thus, in the Edinburgh hospice where I volunteered I felt cared for by the volunteer coordinator and the day hospice staff, in return for the care I gave to the patients, and I felt that the medical director did not care for me in this way.[8] At St. Z's, where I also felt cared for by many of the staff, I felt a reciprocal sense of responsibility. I cared about them, and I felt that I owed them something in return for their trust in, and caring for, me. My role as ethnographer prompted me to set limits to my research, and, in order to address my own discomfort with what sometimes felt to me their extreme openness, I deliberately attempted to draw attention to the fact that I was a researcher by taking out my notebook and pen and visibly taking notes while sitting in the nursing station, rather than going and sitting in the bathroom to do so (which I had been doing initially, so as *not* to make staff aware and self-conscious that I was taking notes on what was happening).

Some of the care I received highlighted broader issues about my position within the hospice. In her study of service industries, such as the airlines, Arlie Hochschild (1983) suggests that employers specifically seek out employees (frequently women, in the case of cabin crew) who already have the required (gendered) characteristics and then set out to develop these characteristics as work assets. This was something that clearly happened in St. Z's, and I was aware of it early on, using the phrase "talent-spotting" as a shorthand for it. Many student nurses came to the hospice on six-week placements toward the end of their training. At an early stage of their placement, managers seemed to make a decision as to whether they were the kind of nurses who would "fit" in to the hospice. Those who were identified as such were often approached at the end of their placement and asked to apply for posts in the hospice after their training was completed. Several of the nurses working there during the period of my fieldwork had been approached in this way, and St. Z's was their first (and only) job since training.

"Talent-spotting" also happened to me. I was repeatedly validated by both staff and managers in remarks such as: "What are you going to do next? You should work with people," or "You could be a counselor," or "Would you like to sit with D? I know you've built up a good relationship with her." This was both disconcerting, in that it drew my attention to how I too was being observed in my interactions with people (in ethnography, the researcher-researchee relationship is often two-way), and ironic, because it was important to me that my interactions with patients were noted and valued. I therefore felt reciprocal care toward those people (including managers) who validated me, yet at the same time I knew that the managers did not (explicitly) validate workers who, I also knew, would have liked to have been acknowledged.

The cynical interpretation of such comments is that managers were trying to "keep me sweet." But if that were the case, why me and not staff? Why did the managers not feel that it was necessary to validate their workers? Alternatively, they could have perceived validation of me as appropriate precisely because I was not a waged worker, and my presence there was not seen as my work (again, blurring the boundary between volunteer and ethnographer). But, whatever the reason, the point is that how I was and what I did, particularly with patients, that is, the "emotional work" (Hochschild 1983; James 1992) that I was doing, was not seen as *work*, but as innate, as "just how I am." This paralleled managers' perceptions of the emotional work of those nurses who managers characterized as people who "just have that gift," and who "gave without expecting to get back." Yet what was taken as "just how I am," was something I worked at; I was well aware of the emotional work involved in not being entirely myself. This is not to say that I was being false, but I was deliberately suppressing parts of myself, for example, by listening to people's opinions and, while possibly questioning them, not challenging them, and that took *work* (Treweek 1996; Young and Lee 1996).

Issues of reciprocity became more complicated because of tensions among hospice staff. In the early months of my fieldwork, I was not aware of tensions in relations between staff and management, and, even when I became aware of these, I chose not to explicitly focus on this area, thinking of it to some extent as background, which did not significantly impact upon spiritual issues for patients. It was only relatively late in my fieldwork, when people who were particularly unhappy began to express their unhappiness to me, that I began to think about the connection between spirituality and ethics, and to think that, even apart from the consequences for patients if staff were unhappy, staff-management relations also raised important ethical issues, and that these were also (therefore) spiritual issues.[9]

I cannot claim to have paid equal attention to all the workers in the hospice: I had strong links with most of the paramedical staff, and with some nurses and volunteers, but by no means with all, and my connections with the administrative workers and domestics and kitchen staff were the most superficial. This was predominantly owing to where, and with whom, I spent most of my time, but toward the end of my fieldwork I began to wonder whether my lack of strong connections with some nurses was to some extent because of the staff-management relations and the resulting (unspoken) questioning on their part: Could they trust me? Was I a management spy?

Those who told me how they felt about staff-management relations tended to be people who were close to leaving or retiring and/or those whose unhappiness was considerable. The confidences these people chose to share with me raise questions about their motives: Did they trust me to keep their confidences to myself, or were they trusting me to represent them and their views to others? When I checked with the people who were the most critical about management, whether I could quote (represent) their words, they all said that they wanted me to do so. The ethical implications of this, however, were far from clear. By explicitly representing these people's positions in my thesis, I would be, on one level, being fair to them. But, while those who were planning to leave would be unaffected by me making their point for them retrospectively, there are potential risks for those working in the hospice if the managers read my thesis and determine who said what to me. I discuss this further in the next sub-section, but before doing so I want to comment briefly on another response to this dilemma.

At an all-female session of the workshop discussed in the introduction I presented an early version of this chapter and raised the question of how I was to represent staff criticisms of their managers in my thesis, bearing in mind the very real risk that, however circumspect I might be, within the hospice individuals would probably be recognizable to one another. Some of the women at the workshop suggested that staff might perceive me (and, by extension, my research) as a conduit to management and a way of indirectly expressing their concerns and put forward utilitarian arguments, along the lines of the greatest good for the greatest number, for why I should include all this material in my thesis. These women were expressing detached rather than situated ethics, again suggesting that these two moralities are not necessarily gendered but are themselves situated, with the dominance of detached ethical frameworks within academic contexts probably fostering this response (compare Nicholson 1993).

Representing Research

According to Jaggar (1991: 99), "on the metaethical level, the goal of feminist ethics is to develop theoretical understandings of the nature of morality that treat women's moral experience respectfully but not uncritically." She argues further that if moral philosophers are to abandon transcendental approaches to ethics, they have no alternative but to start from, and to describe, actual moral experience. However, she points out that "no critical ethical theory can be satisfied with convention," but instead, it "must find a way of moving from description to prescription," and that this means facing some of the deepest problems in moral epistemology.[10]

Thus, to some extent feminist ethics are prescriptive, since feminist ethicists are motivated by a political agenda and seek to challenge canonical ethical theory. Gilligan's work is partly descriptive and partly prescriptive: for her, women should aspire to the post-conventional level of her ethic of care. Since even post-conventional morality is at least partly formed at a deep level, I think that one experiences one's personal ethical position as being unavoidably absolute, prescriptive, although it may still be open to negotiation. To move forward one needs to accept that other people's ethical positions are similarly absolute, and, through open debate and discussion, revise, develop and/or adapt one's own position.

The possibility of negotiation and revision is crucial both methodologically and ethically and affirms the importance of approaching ethics descriptively.[11] Thus, while I have my own ethical position, which agrees to some extent with that of some of the people in the hospice, I am trying to understand all their positions and not to judge them, although this is at times difficult, since moral positions are deep rooted and therefore powerful.

In practice I related most strongly to those women who were trying to care for others, while refusing the symbolic gender associations with self-sacrifice, that is, to women who seemed to me to be struggling to resist the conventional level of situated ethics and to move to the post-conventional level. However, I am concerned to do justice to the positions of all parties and not to represent that with which I have most sympathy as the "right way." In other words, I do not want to judge as morally inadequate those people who seemed to me to operate at the conventional level of situated ethics. In addition, as I have already suggested, people's morality is not purely internally determined but is powerfully influenced by their circumstances. Further, if people are to negotiate and revise their moral positions through dialogue with others, that dialogue must enable a range of positions to be recognized and respected. I would argue that all the workers at St. Z's were well intentioned, but that they were struggling with conflicting perceptions of the world, including the influence of their own socialization and dominant (moral and gender) conventions. My concern to be fair and just toward these people is interwoven with my care and concern for them and my sense of responsibility toward relationships between people there, which could be damaged by what I chose to write about. This further illustrates the consequences of situated ethics for writing about fieldwork.

Feminist research methodologies hold that researchers should not use the words of research participants in isolation, that is, as raw material to support or illustrate the researcher's arguments, but should locate them within the context of the conversation or interview, and also within the wider context of the situation of the person who is speaking. This theoretical or methodological point is rooted in ethical considerations—to do justice, to avoid exploitation—but it can also lead to ethical conflicts.

In a small institution like St. Z's, contextualizing a quotation with details about the conversation, or about the institutional position or personal attributes of the speaker, would enable others within the institution to identify that person. The question of trust and confidentiality was already an issue in the hospice. For example, X talked to me about her discomfort, having confided in Y, at subsequently hearing her (X's) words repeated back to her by Z. If I were to give any details about X or about what she was talking about, she could easily be identified. So, although I have a signed consent form from X "covering" the taped conversation in which she talked about her discomfort, and although she repeated her consent for me to write about this in my thesis when I checked with her later, there remains a moral tension for me concerning how, and if, I represent such evidence, which relates to my sense that I have a wider, ongoing responsibility for the relationships between the people in the hospice.

A proponent of detached ethics would probably argue that a researcher has met her ethical obligations as long as she has done her best to disguise the particular research site (in this case, the hospice) and the particular individuals to whom she refers (by using pseudonyms). But this can only protect those people to a certain, limited extent, that is, from being identified by outsiders, and implies disregarding considerations of the impact of the written version of a study on future interactions between them.

It is also worth noting that the use of pseudonyms raises language-related problems, since names have meanings. In the west of Scotland names are markers of Catholicism and Protestantism, and people can almost always be placed by their surname, often by their forename. Moreover, several names (especially saints' names) were shared among several women in the hospice, and people therefore distinguished between these women by calling them by their first name and surname (for example, Betty Smith, Betty Jones). This use of full names happened frequently, since a particularly striking thing within the hospice was how all the workers and volunteers regularly used each other's names in conversation or greeting. Also, the hospice and the wards within it had saints' names, which had been chosen for their particular meanings, that is, the concerns for which particular saints are patrons, and using pseudonyms changes those meanings.

CONCLUSION

As my discussion shows, the moral orientations, expressed both by the people with whom I interacted in my fieldwork and within my own decision making, were broadly similar to those described by Gilligan in terms of (different levels of) an ethic of care and an ethic of justice. However, the distinction between these moral orientations was more subtle than her dichotomies between care and justice convey; indeed, considerations of care and considerations of justice were frequently inextricably intertwined. Consequently, the value of broadening concepts of morality in line with Gilligan's ideas is greatly enhanced by recasting her moral orientations in terms of what I have called detached ethics and (the various levels of) situated ethics. With this reframing Gilligan's work has proven helpful in reflecting on my own moral choices and also for thinking about tensions between people in St. Z's.

I have also argued that, although women may *tend* to adhere to one moral orientation and men to the other, these orientations do not map directly onto gender. They might be more usefully thought of as symbolically feminine and symbolically masculine and linked with associated perceptions of truth and knowledge. Combined with Gilligan's notion of three levels of moral reasoning, especially her collaborative reworking of movement between levels, and with the emphasis on context in the notion of situated ethics, this highlights how women's (and men's) struggles with moral issues also entail struggles with dominant social conventions. People's subjectivities and understandings of the world shape their various ethical positions, resulting in different perceptions of need, right, wrong, guilt, and blame.

NOTES

1. Drawing on Nancy Chodorow's (1978) theories concerning the consequences of woman-centered childrearing, Gilligan argues that her work illustrates how women tend to fear separation and abandonment, while men fear closeness, and she claims that men and women differ widely in how they delineate their selves. Gilligan claims that the male self is commonly constituted by difference and separation. Men see themselves as central and see the world as relating to them. Their goal is individual achievement, so involvement with others qualifies their identity, rather than leading to its realization. They therefore fear intimacy and seek to break out of situations they perceive as smothering. Conversely, Gilligan argues that women understand the self as constituted by connection, they fear isolation, describe themselves in terms of their relations with significant others, are more concerned with both sides of an interdependent relationship, and quicker to recognize their own interdependence. They believe that hierarchical relationships and isolation of the self lead to aggression. Thus, Gilligan claims, each sex perceives a danger in relations with others that the other sex does not: men in connection, women in separation. She concludes that, because of this, men and women have diametrically opposed tasks in their transition to adulthood (and/or moral maturity), that is, that, as Daphne Hampson (1996: 94) puts it, "men need to learn to be a self-*in-relation*; women . . . to be a *self*-in-relation" (her emphases). Arguably, also, Kohlberg's post-conventional men are *conforming* to social norms for men, by increasing their detachment.

2. In particular, the association between care and the "private" realm is not always questioned (see for example Noddings 1984). With its provision of intimate care for strangers, nursing straddles, and potentially challenges, the supposed public-private divide (see, for example, Bowden 1997).

3. This is not to say that if he had considered these issues he would necessarily have given me access; the point is that he did not see them as relevant to his decision.

4. It is interesting to note here that when discussing this question with my two Ph.D. supervisors, my female supervisor (a social scientist) was sympathetic with my position and my male supervisor (a nurse) sympathized with the medical director, although obviously it is not valid to generalize from this to all women and men.

5. I am thinking here of the risk of "hatchet jobs" that people who grant access for "fly-on-the-wall" documentaries sometimes experience; indeed, at one point one of the doctors commented that I was a "fly on the wall," and I tried to explain the distinction between my work and such documentaries but without much success.

6. I was not in a position to meet them, not only because of my lack of qualifications and experience, but also because of my intermittent presence in the hospice and the consequent lack of continuity.

7. Although patients, particularly female patients, may often care for their professional caregivers and/or indeed for their fellow patients.

8. Indeed, the voluntary sector well recognizes the need to care for volunteers, if only on the very pragmatic basis that such care is necessary to retain them.

9. I also then began explicitly to widen my exploration of "spiritual aspects of care" to consider caregivers' spiritual needs as well as those of patients.

10. Also see Hoagland's (1988) ethics for lesbians, and Hampson's (1996: 96) claim that recent feminist thinking is "not only descriptive . . . but . . . also legislative."

11. My approach closely parallels Bowden's (1997) study of caring.

Conclusion

Gillian Rose

The chapters in this book cover a wide range of research projects, and their topics are correspondingly diverse. However, as Liz Bondi demonstrated in the introduction, they share a number of themes that are part of a wider feminist project concerned with the politics of knowledge production. They were all written as part of what its participants characterized as a (particular kind of) feminist academic practice: a collaborative, reiterative, and supportive process of reading and writing that tempered the more conventional academic model of sole authorship (Feminist Geography Reading Group 2000). All these chapters also engage with a number of interpretive problematics concerned with the relations between knowledge and subjectivity. All assume that knowledge is embodied; that is, that knowledge is produced by corporealized subjectivities. All assume that those bodily subjects are positioned in extraordinarily complex articulations of identity, including gender. And all assume that those identities are relational; we are always located in relation to others, not least for academics to those we research. While each chapter can address only some aspects of these assumptions in any depth, it is their shared pertinence to all of them that also gives coherence to this volume.

The spatialized language with which these claims about knowledge production are made—talk of bodily boundaries, situated knowledges, and dis/connections—is now so familiar that it is perhaps difficult to remember that this has not always been the vocabulary with which feminist geographers have addressed the importance of spaces to the production of knowledge. Feminist geography first began to emerge into publication in the mid-1970s. That geography needed feminism was evidenced in two ways in this early work: first, geography to date had paid no attention to women, and, second, the discipline had paid no attention to what were perceived as "women's issues." In an important analysis of why this had been the case, Janice Monk and Susan Hanson (1982) drew on another spatial analytic: that of the distinction between public and private space. They argued that this distinction structured much of geography's conventional methodologies so that geographical knowledge was concerned only with what were seen as "public" issues; thus subdisciplines like economic geography and political geography were seen as central to geography as an academic discipline, and there was no such thing as "domestic geography." It seemed that geography assumed (wrongly of course) that women were somehow confined to the "private sphere," and even when the discipline paid some attention to questions such as household structure and location, it was the male head of household who was deemed to represent the whole household (also making children and elderly relatives in households invisible to this particular geographical imagination). Feminist geographers thus began to remedy geography's analytical masculinism in two ways. First, they explored women's participation in those spaces deemed "public," exploring women's participation in paid work and in urban spaces outside the home, for example. Second, they turned to domestic labor and explored the spaces of women's unpaid work (Women and Geography Study Group of the IBG 1984). There were also many discussions about why there were so few women in the discipline of geography as its practitioners. It seemed that the assumptions geographers made about what were the appropriate spaces and subjects for geographical study also extended to who were the appropriate kinds of work colleagues to have; hence the establishment of the Association of American Geographers' Committee on the Status of Women and the Women and Geography Study Group of the Institute of British Geographers mentioned in the introduction. The work culture that dominates the academy to this day, of individuals striving for authoritative, commanding knowledge by working long, long hours, can still be characterized as masculinist, as the introduction also made clear. (It is also inimical to the demands of parenting, of course.)

One result of this work by feminist geographers was to show just how difficult it is to map the distinction between "public" and "private" onto any particular built environment, as chapter 2 acknowledges. Moreover, what is deemed "public" or "private" varies between different cultures, places, and historical periods. But the importance of the distinction between public and private as a means of policing the boundaries between genders is evident in so many practices that it continues to be of concern to feminist geographers. Chapter 11 offers one example of the way the notion of the "private" continues to be associated with femininity, in Rosaleen Duffy's discussion of the legitimacy in the academy of knowledge characterized as "gossip." And in chapter 6 Shonagh McEwan makes the distinction between public and private her central problematic, examining several sorts of distinctions between masculine and feminine that boundaries between public and private spaces articulate in golf clubs (Bondi and Domosh 1998).

From the very beginning of feminist geography, then, what kinds of knowledge count as "geography" has been recognized as a central issue.[1] And one of the ways feminist geographers have examined what gets seen as appropriate geographical knowledge by the discipline and what is discounted as trivial, irrelevant, or banal is by thinking about the ways that knowledges themselves have a spatiality that structures their inclusions and exclusions. Thus for a long while geography was concerned only with a certain definition of the public; as Monk and Hanson (1982) argue, the distinction between public spaces (and people) and private spaces (and people) explained the absence of women as the objects of geographical investigation, and the absence of the spaces and things associated with them: homes, gardens, children, for example.

As feminist geography became more established, however—as more voices joined the discussions and the project came to feel a little less precarious than I imagine it did for its first advocates—the vocabulary available for understanding the relation between gender, space, and knowledge expanded. As geography participated in the so-called cultural turn taken by large parts of the social sciences, so the resources for diagnosing the discipline's silences were increased. One of the most important implications of the notion of "culture," which had such huge importance in the social sciences in the late 1980s and much of the 1990s, was that knowledges are produced by specific constellations of circumstances and remain marked by those specificities. As many geographers have noted, many of the conceptualizations of the ways identities, knowledges, and power relations were articulated through "culture" were replete with spatial terms. Identities were located, knowledges were situated and traveled, geographies imagined, and contact zones mapped. Feminists were central in developing this project, and their work provided some fresh possibilities for doing new kinds of geography in new kinds of ways (see, for example, my own dependence of the work of Michele Le Doueff and Teresa de Lauretis, among others, in Rose 1993). Feminist geographers like Geraldine Pratt (1992) and Cindi Katz (Smith and Katz 1993) sound a note of caution about the proliferation of what they termed "spatial metaphors" in much of this work, though. Both were concerned—although in rather different ways—that this newly spatialized culture was paying too little attention to some of the enduring power relations that structured spaces in systematic patterns of power. Feminist geographers have thus engaged with spatial vocabularies of more recent scholarship with some care. While all the research projects discussed in this volume take seriously the claim that knowledge is marked by the circumstances of its making, feminists in geography, like those in other social science disciplines, have pondered long and hard the implications of this claim for their own production of knowledge. Thus the connection between feminist theory and the methods adopted in order to carry out research remains clearly in focus, and the 1990s saw a flurry of debate about "feminist research methods" in geography. As the present volume bears witness, that connection remains the site of much thought, reflection, and careful practice.

Indeed, in parallel with a certain amount of skepticism about the cultural turn that has developed very recently among its once-advocates, it is not surprising that, in the work of this group of feminist scholars at least, the spatial analytics deployed to understand the relations between knowledge and subjectivity are, I would suggest, rather few, and are utilized in particular ways. As I read these chapters and remember our discussions, there is above all a concern for *boundaries*; for *situation*; and for *relationality*.

(1)   The concern for boundaries is best approached, I think, by thinking through the bodies evoked in these chapters. Several chapters in this book understand the body as flesh given form by various processes of spatial articulation. Of course, to say "the body" minimizes the diversity of possible embodiments and the possible differences between the bodies projected onto certain subjects by others and their own senses of corporealization. Chapter 9 contains an example of an imagined embodiment, in Anja-Maaike Green's discussion of how arts professionals in Edinburgh imagine those people who do not attend arts events: as lumpen, greedy, passive couch potatoes, slumped and vegetating in front of TVs, or loutish in football grounds, in working-class areas of the city. So too does Lynda Johnston's account in chapter 5 of how straight spectators see the gay bodies on display at pride carnivals as "abject," which also notes how some people refuse the body image offered to them by other gazes, such as the group of transgenders who chose to present themselves as pure and feminine to parade spectators. Chapters 5 and 9 are also about various kinds of boundaries. To begin with, there is the boundary being established between these fantasized bodies and the bodies of those fantasizing. Imagining the body of the arts nonattenders make (or at least, purport to make) a clear distinction between that nonattender and the arts professional who is engaged with art; in the case of gay pride parades there are the rather more complexly imagined boundaries between gay and straight and host and tourist. These two studies explore processes of categorization among bodies and the attempts made to segregate bodies thus imagined as different.

As well as boundaries between different sorts of bodies, there are the boundaries that constitute the individual body. These latter sorts of boundaries are a central theme of the two chapters on agoraphobia in the first part in this book. Chapter 1 offers another example of differentiation between bodies, this time between sufferers of agoraphobia and "experts" on it. More centrally, in chapters 1 and 3, Joyce Davidson and Ruth Bankey respectively argue that agoraphobia is not a fear of open spaces, but rather of the breakdown of the boundaries that a person imagines as containing their self. In their persuasive accounts, agoraphobia is a kind of panic about losing bodily integrity.

Boundaries then are an important problematic in this book. Boundaries are understood as dividing and are thus central to the abjection of certain kinds of embodied subjectivities: the uncultured, the gay, the agoraphobic. But boundaries of a kind are also necessary for the survival of subjectivity; hence, the horror of their feared dissolution in an agoraphobic panic attack. Moreover, boundaries intersect and diverge in complicated ways, as chapter 5 suggests. And chapter 5 also examines how these boundaries are policed—quite literally in the form of crowd control barriers and marshals in Johnston's example—and notes how the very insistence on the boundaries suggests that the divisions they mark are less clear-cut than they seem.

(2)   The phrase "situated knowledge" is common now, but the question of how the space through which that situatedness is to be imagined is less often asked (Rose 1997b). Yet this is a question that these discussions of boundaries raise in acute form. If we imagine our selves—and imagining our research selves is not necessar-

ily straightforward, as Hannah Avis makes clear in chapter 12, in her exploration of the boundary between her self and her role as researcher—if we imagine ourselves through a topography of boundaries, multiple, leaky, persistent, necessary, in what terms can we describe our "situation"? What is our position? That is, in relation to what boundaries do we chart our location and interpret those of others? The difficulty of this question is registered in several chapters. In chapters 8 and 14 Mona Marshy and Victoria Ingrid Einagel respectively explore the question in relation to their own connections with the people they are researching. Neither offer firm conclusions. Marshy's "Palestinianness" in chapter 8 is rendered elusive not only by her own family history and geography but also, as she notes, by the diversity of meanings being Palestinian has to the musicians she talks to; and in chapter 14 Einagel's Yugoslav-Croat links to Sarajevo are overwhelmed, it seems, by the emotional difficulty of dealing with the effects of another boundary, between those who experienced the war there and those who did not, and the guilt and the responsibility entailed in being a "researcher" and not a "survivor." Like Nichola Wood in chapter 4, Einagel confronts the emotional qualities of doing research. She also touches on the difficulties of articulating such emotions: the difficulty of living with them, the difficulty of writing them, even the difficulty of feeling them, in the repressions caused by too much pain and grief.

Situating a self in a space of boundaries, then, is an awkward process. It is awkward because these boundaries are imagined and experienced as highly complex: multiple, overlapping, diverging, articulated through various media, fleshy and psychic, emotional and analytical. They are also shifting, permeable, and to some degree unpredictable. They are also highly resistant to mapping in conventional ways, on a spatial plane from a commanding viewpoint. In chapter 7 Susan Lilley demonstrates the elusiveness of boundaries as she chases the figure of the "expert" software user. Her research is based in an institution that had only recently introduced a new computer software system to its staff, and many of them felt very incompetent with it, compared to these "super-users." But this boundary between incompetent and expert proved hard to find. Not only did no one claim to be an expert, the very notion of expertness was phrased not in technical terms but in terms of magic and wonder. Thus the registers through which boundaries are articulated can be surprising too.

The awkwardness of boundaries as a space for situating a researcher self is certainly amplified when the boundaries are intensely felt, producing the kinds of emotions described in chapter 14, for example. The exploration of boundaries so integral to feelings of self can be fraught with emotional and ethical dangers and thus demand the kind of care described by Amanda Bingley in chapter 13. The argument here is based firmly on the need, indeed the inevitability, of relationality. Bingley discusses the particular qualities of the research relationship when the research is interested directly in questions of self and identity: in this case, gendered selves and relations to landscape. As well as relations between her research participants and their landscapes, she examines the relationship between the participants and herself and her own need for a supportive supervisory relation with another in order to reflect on the research process. In chapter 15 Bella Vivat reflects further on notions of relationality and uses those reflections to understand the ethics of her research work. She frames her discussion of right and wrong not in universalizing terms—what she calls a "detached ethics"—but in terms of a situated ethics that takes account of the local situation when reaching a decision about how to act in relation to others. Hence her emphasis on reciprocity as a central element of an ethical relationship. (3) All the chapters in this volume address relationality in some form or another. Whether it be exploring the relation between researcher and researched, or examining relations between subjectivities, these chapters' authors assume that subjectivity is lived relationally. Indeed, chapter 10 could be read as an attempt to assert a relation where one is denied, in Niamh O'Connor's account of a shared work ethic between a government policy and a group of benefit claimants. The issue at stake in the chapters of this book is about what kind of relation should be aimed for, whether that be in research practice or government policy or urban planning practice or whatever. The parallel concern with boundaries and relationality in this collection is thus less paradoxical than it seems. After all, the kind of boundaries with which we are concerned unite as much as they divide. In making a distinction these boundaries can also suggest a connection. This ambivalent understanding of boundaries—as both dividing and connecting—is a complicated space within which to chart locations. But its complications are what all these chapters are working with. None rest particularly easy with these complexities. But then the vigilance with which their difficulties must be negotiated must be a necessary tactic for working in, and perhaps changing for the better, what is a messy, complex world.

NOTE

1. Feminist geographers have also examined the marginalization of women from the foundation of both the academic discipline of geography and from institutions such as the Royal Geographical Society in London. For just one example of this kind of work, see Domosh (1991).

References

Adorno, Theodore W. 1990."On Popular Music. (1941)." Pp. 301–315 in *On Record: Rock, Pop and the Written Word,* edited by Simon Frith and Andrew Goodwin. London: Routledge.

Adorno, Theodore W. 1991. "On the Fetish Character in Music and the Regression of Listening." Pp. 26–53 in *The Culture Industry: Selected Essays on Mass Culture,* edited by Jay M. Bernstein. London: Routledge.

Ahmed, Leila. 1982. "Western Ethnocentrism and Perceptions of the Harem." *Feminist Studies* 8, no. 3: 520–534.

Ainley, Rosa, ed. 1998. *New Frontiers of Space, Bodies and Gender.* London: Routledge.

Aisenberg, Nadya, and Mona Harrington. 1988. *Women of Academe: Outsiders in the Sacred Grove.* Amherst: University of Massachusetts Press.

Alcoff, Linda Martín. 1996. "Feminist Theory and Social Science: New Knowledges, New Epistemologies." Pp. 13–28 in *Bodyspace: Destabilizing Geographies of Gender and Sexuality,* edited by Nancy Duncan. London: Routledge.

Alcoff, Linda, and Elizabeth Potter. 1993. *Feminist Epistemologies.* London: Routledge.

Ali, Rabia, and Lawrence Lifschultz, eds. 1993. *Why Bosnia? Writings on the Balkan War.* Stony Creek, Conn.: Pamphleteer's Press.

Allen, Katherine, and Elizabeth Farnsworth. 1993. "Reflexivity in Teaching about Families." *Family Relations* 42: 351–356.

Allwood, Robin. 1996. "'I Have Depression, Don't I?': Discourses of Help and Self-Help Books." Pp. 17–36 in *Psychology, Discourse, Practice,* edited by Erica Burman. London: Taylor and Francis.

American Psychiatric Association. 1994. *Diagnostic and Statistical Manual of Mental Disorders,* 4th ed. Washington, D.C.: American Psychiatric Association.

Amnesty International. 1992. *Zimbabwe: Poaching and Unexplained Deaths: The Case of Captain Nleya.* London: Amnesty International.

Anderson, Benedict. 1991 (1983). *Imagined Communities: Reflections on the Origins and Spread of Nationalism,* 2nd ed. London: Verso.

Andreas, Peter. 1996. "In Focus: US Drug Control Policy." *US Foreign Policy in Focus*, vol. 1. Project of the Institute for Policy Studies and the Interhemispheric Resource Centre.

Ang, Ien. 1991. *Desperately Seeking the Audience*. London: Routledge and Kegan Paul.

Ang, Ien. 1996. *Living Room Wars*. London: Routledge.

Antony, Louise M., and Charlotte Witt, eds. 1993. *A Mind of One's Own: Feminist Essays on Reason and Objectivity*. Boulder, Colo.: Westview Press.

Antze, Paul, and Michael Lambek, eds. 1996. *Tense Past: Cultural Essays in Trauma and Memory*. New York: Routledge.

Anxiety Disorders Association of Ontario. 1999. *ADAO Educational Guide*. Ottawa: Anxiety Disorders Association of Ontario.

Applebaum, Anne. 1994. *Between East and West: Across the Borderlands of Europe*. London: Papermac.

Astor, Nancy. 1996. *Women, Politics and Welfare*. Marlborough: Adam Matthew Publications.

Attali, Jacques. 1985. *Noise: The Political Economy of Music*. Minneapolis: University of Minnesota Press.

Bankey, Ruth. 1999. "The Paradox of Panic: A Geographic Analysis of Agoraphobic Experiences." Unpublished MSc thesis, Carleton University, Ottawa.

Bankey, Ruth. 2001. "La Donna é Mobile: Constructing the Irrational Woman." *Gender, Place and Culture* 8, no. 1: 37–54.

Bardenstein, Carol B. 1999. "Trees, Forests, and the Shaping of Palestinian and Israeli Collective Memory." Pp. 148–168 in *Acts of Memory: Cultural Recall in the Present*, edited by Mieke Bal, Jonathan Crewe, and Leo Spitzer. Hanover, N.H.: Dartmouth College.

Barnes, Trevor, and James Duncan. 1992. "Introduction: Writing Worlds." Pp. 1–17 in *Writing Worlds: Discourse, Texts and Metaphors in the Representation of Landscape*, edited by Trevor Barnes and James Duncan. London: Routledge.

Bätschmann, Oskar. 1997. *The Artist in the Modern World: A Conflict between Market and Self Expression*. Cologne: Dumont.

Battersby, Christine. 1998. *The Phenomenal Woman: Feminist Metaphysics and the Patterns of Identity*. Cambridge: Polity Press.

Baxter, Jamie, and John Eyles. 1997. "Evaluating Qualitative Research in Social Geography: Establishing 'Rigour' in Interview Analysis." *Transactions of the Institute of British Geographers* 22: 505–525.

Beagles, John. 1997. "Under the Central Belt." *Variant* 2: 12–13

Behar, Ruth. 1996. *The Vulnerable Observer*. Boston: Beacon Press.

Bell, David, and Gill Valentine. 1997. *Consuming Geographies: You Are Where You Eat*. London: Routledge.

Bell, David, and Gill Valentine, eds. 1995. *Mapping Desires: Geographies of Sexualities*. London: Routledge.

Bell, David, Jon Binnie, Julia Cream, and Gill Valentine. 1994. "All Hyped Up and No Place to Go." *Gender, Place and Culture* 1: 31–47

Bennett, Katy. 1999. "Was Insider, Now Outsider (with no sign of hyphen)." Paper presented at RGS-IBG Annual Conference, University of Leicester, January.

Bennett, Tony. 1998. *Culture: A Reformers Science*. London: Sage.

Bissoondath, Neil. 1994. *Selling Illusions: The Cult of Multiculturalism in Canada*. Toronto: Penguin Books.

Boden, Deirdre, and Don H. Zimmerman. 1991. "Structure-in-Action: An Introduction." Pp. 3–22 in *Talk and Social Structure*, edited by Deirdre Boden and Don H. Zimmerman. Cambridge: Polity Press.

Bollas, Christopher. 1987. *The Shadow of the Object*. London: Free Association Books.
Bollas, Christopher. 1989. *Forces of Destiny: Psychoanalysis and Human Idiom*. London: Free Association Books.
Bollas, Christopher. 1992. *Being a Character: Psychoanalysis and Self Experience*. London: Routledge.
Bond, Tim. 1993. *Standards and Ethics for Counselling in Action*. Thousand Oaks, Calif.: Sage.
Bondi, Liz. 1990. "Feminism, Postmodernism, and Geography: Space for Women?" *Antipode* 22: 156–167.
Bondi, Liz. 1992. "Gender and Dichotomy." *Progress in Human Geography* 16: 98–104.
Bondi, Liz. 1997. "In Whose Words? On Gender Identities and Writing Practices." *Transactions of the Institute of British Geographers* 22: 245–258.
Bondi, Liz. 1998. "Gender, Class and Urban Space: Public and Private Space in Contemporary Urban Landscapes." *Urban Geography* 19: 160–185.
Bondi, Liz. 1999. "Stages on Journeys: Some Remarks about Human Geography and Psychotherapeutic Practice." *Professional Geographer* 51: 11–24.
Bondi, Liz. 2001. "'Gender, Place and Culture': Paradoxical Spaces?" Pp. 80–86 in *Feminist Geography in Practice*, edited by Pamela Moss. Oxford: Blackwell.
Bondi, Liz, and Mona Domosh. 1998. "On the Contours of Public Space: A Tale of Three Women." *Antipode* 30: 270–289.
Bonnemaison, Sarah. 1990. "City Policies and Cyclical Events." *Celebrations: Urban Spaces Transformed, Design Quarterly* 147. Cambridge, Mass.: MIT for the Walker Art Center.
Booth, Chris, Jane Darke, and Susan Yeandle. 1996. *Changing Places. Women's Lives in the City*. London: Paul Chapman.
Bordo, Susan. 1986. "The Cartesian Masculisation of Thought." *Signs: Journal of Women in Culture and Society* 11: 439–456.
Bordo, Susan. 1992. "Anorexia Nervosa: Psychopathology as the Crystallization of Culture." Pp. 90–109 in *Knowing Women: Feminism and Knowledge*, edited by Crowley Helen and Susan Himmelweit. Cambridge: Polity Press.
Bordo, Susan. 1993. *Unbearable Weight: Feminism, Western Culture, and the Body*. Berkeley: University of California Press.
Bordo, Susan, Bonnie Klein, and Marilyn K. Silverman. 1998. "Missing Kitchens." Pp. 72–92 in *Places through the Body*, edited by Heidi Nast and Steve Pile. London: Routledge.
Bottoms, Anthony E., and Paul Wiles. 1992. "Explanations of Crime and Place." Pp. 11–35 in *Crime, Policing and Place: Essays in Environmental Criminology*, edited by David J. Evans, Nicholas R. Fyfe, and David T. Herbert. London: Routledge.
Boullata, Kamal. 1993. "Facing the Forest: Israeli and Palestinian Artists." Pp. 65–79 in *For Palestine*, edited by Jay Murphy. New York: Writers and Readers.
Bourdieu, Pierre. 1996. *Distinction: A Social Critique of the Judgment of Taste*. London: Routledge.
Bowden, Peta. 1997. *Caring: Gender-Sensitive Ethics*. London Routledge.
Bowman, Glenn. 1994. "'A Country of Words': Conceiving the Palestinian Nation from the Position of Exile." Pp. 138–170 in *The Making of Political Identities*, edited by Ernesto Laclau. London: Verso.
Bragg, Melvin. 2001. "Watch with Amazement." *The Observer Newspaper*, Review Section, April 1: 1–2.
Brehony, K. A. 1983. "Women and Agoraphobia: A Case for the Etiological Significance of the Feminine Sex-Role Stereotype." Pp. 112–125 in *The Stereotyping of Women: Its Effects on Mental Health*, edited by Violet Franks and Esther Rothblum. New York: Springer.

Bricknell, Chris. 2000. "Heroes and Invaders: Gay and Lesbian Pride Parades and the Public/Private Distinction in New Zealand Media Accounts." *Gender, Place and Culture* 7, no. 2: 163–178.

Brison, Susan, J. 1997. "Outliving Oneself. Trauma, Memory and Personal Identity." Pp. 12–39 in *Feminists Rethink the Self*, edited by Diana Tietjens Meyers. Boulder, Colo.: Westview.

Brown, Gillian. 1987. "The Empire of Agoraphobia." *Representations* 20: 134–157.

Brown, Lyn Mikel, and Carol Gilligan. 1992. *Meeting at the Crossroads: Women's Psychology and Girls' Development*. Cambridge, Mass.: Harvard University Press.

Bureau for International Narcotics and Law Enforcement Affairs. 1998a. *Country Certifications*. Washington, D.C.: U.S. Department of State.

Bureau for International Narcotics and Law Enforcement Affairs. 1998b. *International Narcotics Control Strategy Report, 1997: Money Laundering and Financial Crimes*. Washington, D.C.: U.S. Department of State.

Bureau for International Narcotics and Law Enforcement Affairs. 1998c. *International Narcotics Control Strategy Report, 1997: Canada, Mexico and Central America*. Washington, D.C.: U.S. Department of State.

Burgess, Jacquelin. 1996. "Focusing on Fear: The Use of Focus Groups in a Project for the Community Forest Unit, Countryside Commission." *Area* 28: 130–135.

Burgess, Jacquelin. 1998. "'But Is It Worth Taking the Risk?' How Women Negotiate Access to Urban Woodland: A Case Study." Pp 115–128 in *New Frontiers of Space, Bodies and Gender*, edited by Rosa Ainley. London: Routledge.

Burgess, Jacquelin, F. B. Goldsmith, and Carolyn M. Harrison. 1990. "Pale Shadows for Policy: Reflections on the Greenwich Open Space Project." Pp. 141–167 in *Studies in Qualitative Methodology: Reflections on Field Experience*, vol. 2, edited by Robert G. Burgess. London: JAI Press.

Burgess, Jacquelin, Melanie Limb, and Carolyn M. Harrison. 1988a. "Exploring Environmental Values through the Medium of Small Groups 1: Theory and Practice." *Environment and Planning A* 20: 309–326.

Burgess, Jacquelin, Melanie Limb, and Carolyn M. Harrison. 1988b. "Exploring Environmental Values through the Medium of Small Groups 2: Illustrations of a Group at Work." *Environment and Planning A* 20: 57–476.

Burgess, Robert G. 1984. *In the Field: An Introduction to Field Research*. London: Unwin Hyman.

Burman, Erica, and Ian Parker, eds. 1993. *Discursive Analytic Research: Repertoires and Readings of Texts in Action*. London: Routledge.

Butler, Judith. 1990. *Gender Trouble: Feminism and the Subversion of Identity*. London: Routledge.

Butler, Judith. 1993. *Bodies that Matter: On the Discursive Limits of "Sex."* London: Routledge.

Butler, Ruth, and Hester Parr, eds. 1999. *Mind and Body Spaces: Geographies of Illness, Impairment and Disability*. London: Routledge.

Cahn, Susan. K. 1994. *Coming on Strong: Gender and Sexuality in Twentieth-Century Women's Sport*. New York: Free Press.

Calhoun, Craig. 1995. *Critical Social Theory*. Oxford, UK: Blackwell.

Callaway, Helen. 1992. "Ethnography and Experience: Gender Implications in Fieldwork and Texts." Pp. 29–49 in *Anthropology and Autobiography*, edited by Judith Okely and Helen Callaway. London: Routledge.

Calvani, Sandro, Elizabeth Guia, and Jean-Luc Lemahieu. 1997. "Drug Resistance Rating: An Innovative Approach for Measuring a Country's Capacity to Resist Illegal Drugs." *Third World Quarterly* 18: 659–672.

Cameron, Deborah. 1985. *Feminism and Linguistic Theory*. London: Macmillan.

Cameron, Deborah. 1990. *The Feminist Critique of Language*. London: Routledge.

Capps, Lisa, and Elinor Ochs. 1995. *Constructing Panic: The Discourse of Agoraphobia*. Cambridge, Mass.: Harvard University Press.

Carroll, Michael. 1996. *Counselling Supervision: Theory, Skills and Practice*. London: Cassell.

Carter, Erica, James Donald, and Judith Squire, eds. 1993. *Space and Place: Theories of Identity and Location*. London: Lawrence and Wishart.

Casey, Edward S. 1987. *Remembering*. Bloomington: Indiana University Press.

Cataldi, Anna. 1993. *Letters from Sarajevo: Voices of a Besieged City*. Shaftesbury, Dorset: Element Books Limited.

Chambers, Robert. 1988. "Sustainable Rural Livelihoods: A Key Strategy for People, Environment and Development." Pp. 1–18 in *The Greening of Aid*, edited by Czech Conroy and Miles Litvinoff. London: Earthscan.

Chambless, Dianne. 1982. "Characteristics of Agoraphobia." Pp. 1–18 in *Agoraphobia: Multiple Perspectives on Theory and Treatment*, edited by Dianne L. Chambless and Alan J. Goldstein. New York: John Wiley and Sons.

Chambless, Dianne L., and Alan J. Goldstein. 1992. "Anxieties: Agoraphobia and Hysteria." Pp.113–134 in *Women and Psychotherapy*, edited by Annette M. Brodsky and Rachael T. Hare-Mustin. New York: Guilford Press.

Chambless, Dianne L., and J. Mason. 1986. "Sex, Sex-Role Stereotyping and Agoraphobia." *Behaviour, Research and Therapy* 24: 231–235.

Chambless, Dianne L., and Alan J. Goldstein, eds. 1982. *Agoraphobia: Multiple Perspectives on Theory and Treatment*. New York: John Wiley and Sons.

Chodorow, Nancy J. 1978. *The Reproduction of Mothering: Psychoanalysis and the Sociology of Gender*. Berkeley: University of California Press.

Chow, Rey. 1992. "Postmodern Automatons." Pp. 101–120 in *Feminists Theorise the Political*, edited by Judith Butler and Joan W. Scott. New York: Routledge.

Clifford, James. 1997. *Travel and Translation in the Late Twentieth Century*. New Haven, Conn.: Harvard University Press.

Clum, G. A., and S. S. Knowles. 1991. "Why Do Some People with Panic Disorder Become Avoidant?: A Review." *Clinical Psychology Review* 11: 295–313.

Cockburn, Cynthia. 1998. *The Space between Us: Negotiating Gender and National Identities in Conflict*. London: Zed Books.

Code, Lorraine. 1991. *What Can She Know? Feminist Theory and the Constitution of Knowledge*. Ithaca, N.Y.: Cornell University Press.

Coffey, Amanda, and Paul Atkinson. 1996. *Making Sense of Qualitative Data: Complementary Research Strategies*. Thousand Oaks, Calif.: Sage.

Cohen, A. 1980. "Drama and Politics in the Development of a London Carnival." *Man* 15: 65–87.

Cohen, A. 1982. "A Polyethnic London Carnival as a Contested Cultural Performance." *Ethnic and Racial Studies* 5, no. 1: 23–41.

Cohen, Anthony. 1994. *Self-Consciousness: An Alternative Anthropology of Identity*. London: Routledge.

Cohen, Sara. 1994. "Identity, Place and the 'Liverpool Sound.'" Pp. 117–135 in *Ethnicity, Identity and Music*, edited by Martin Stokes. Oxford: Berg.

Cohen, Sara. 1995. "Sounding Out the City: Music and the Sensuous Production of Place." *Transactions of the Institute of British Geographers* 20: 434–446.

Collins, Patricia Hill. 1996. "The Social Construction of Black Feminist Thought." Pp. 222–248 in *Women, Knowledge and Reality: Explorations in Feminist Philosophy*, edited by Ann Garry and Marilyn Pearsall. New York: Routledge.

Connell, Robert W. 1995. *Masculinities*. Cambridge: Polity Press.

Connor, Walker. 1994. "Beyond Reason: The Nature of the Ethnonational Bond." Pp. 195–210 in *Ethnonationalism: The Quest for Understanding*, edited by Walker Connor. Princeton, N.J.: Princeton University Press.

Correll, S. 1995. "The Ethnography of an Electronic Bar: The Lesbian Café." *Journal of Contemporary Ethnography* 24: 270–298.

Crawford, Adam. 1998. *Crime Prevention and Community Safety. Politics, Policies and Practices.* Harlow: Longman.

Crawshaw, M. 1998. "HERO Worship." *Metro* (February): 30–35.

Cream, Julia. 1995. "Resolving Riddles: The Sexed Body." Pp. 31–40 in *Mapping Desire: Geographies of Sexualities*, edited by Gill Valentine and David Bell. London: Routledge.

Cresswell, Tim. 1996. *In Place/Out of Place: Geography, Ideology and Transgression*. Minneapolis: University of Minneapolis.

Crick, Michael. 1992. "Ali and Me. An Essay in Street-Corner Anthropology." Pp. 175–192 in *Anthropology and Autobiography*, edited by Judith Okely and Helen Callaway. London: Routledge.

Crosset, Todd W. 1995. *Outsiders in the Clubhouse: The World of Women's Professional Golf.* Albany: State University of New York Press.

Cushman, Thomas, and Stjepan G. Mestrovic, eds. 1996. *This Time We Knew*. New York: New York University Press.

Czarniawska-Joerges, Barbara. 1992. *Exploring Complex Organisations. A Cultural Perspective.* London: Sage.

da Costa Meyer, Esther. 1996. "La Donna é Mobile: Agoraphobia, Women, and Urban Space." Pp. 141–156 in *The Sex of Architecture*, edited by Diana Agrest, Patricia Conway, and Leslie Kanes Weisman. New York: Harry N. Abrams, 1996.

Daly, Kathleen, and Amy L. Chasteen. 1997. "Crime News, Crime Fear, and Women's Everyday Lives." Pp. 235–248 in *Feminism, Media and the Law*, edited by Martha Fineman and Martha McCluskey. Oxford: Oxford University Press.

David, Filip, and Mirko Kovac. 1998. *Kniga Pisama 1992–1995*. Split: Feral Tribune.

Davidson, Joyce. 2000a. "'. . . The World Was Getting Smaller': Women, Agoraphobia and Bodily Boundaries." *Area* 32, no. 1: 31–40.

Davidson, Joyce. 2000b. "A Phenomenology of Fear: Merleau Ponty and Agoraphobic Lifeworlds." *Sociology of Health and Illness* 22: 640–660.

Davidson, Joyce. 2001a. "'Joking Apart . . .': A 'Processual' Approach to Researching Self-help Groups." *Social and Cultural Geography* 2: 163–183.

Davidson, Joyce. 2001b. "Fear and Trembling in the Mall: Women, Agoraphobia and Body Boundaries." Pp. 213–230 in *Geographies of Women's Health*, edited by Isabel Dyck, Nancy Davis Lewis, and Sara McLafferty. London: Routledge.

Davidson, Joyce. 2001c. "Pregnant Pauses: Agoraphobic Embodiment and the Limits of (Im)pregnability." *Gender, Place and Culture* 8: 283–297.

Davidson, Joyce, and Mick Smith. 1999. "Wittgenstein and Irigaray: Gender and Philosophy in a Language (Game) of Difference." *Hypatia* 14, no. 2: 72–95.

Day, Kirsten. 1999. "Embassies and Sanctuaries: Women's Experiences of Race and Fear in Public Space." *Environment and Planning D: Society and Space* 17: 397–328.

de Beauvoir, Simone. 1997 (1949).*The Second Sex*. London: Vintage.

Delamont, Sara, Paul Atkinson, and Odette Parry. 1997. *Supervising the PhD: A Guide to Success.* Buckingham and Philadelphia: SRHE and Open University Press.

DeNora, Tia. 2000. *Music in Everyday Life.* Cambridge: Cambridge University Press.

Denzin, Norman. 1978. *Sociological Methods: A Source Book,* 2nd ed. London: Butterworth.

Denzin, Norman K., and Yvonna S. Lincoln, eds. 1994. *A Handbook of Qualitative Research.* Thousand Oaks, Calif.: Sage.

Department of Health and Social Security. 1985. *Reform of Social Security.* London: HMSO.

Department of Social Security. 1998. *New Ambitions for Our Country: A New Contract for Welfare.* London: HMSO.

Devault, Marjorie L. 1990. "Talking and Listening from Women's Standpoint: Feminist Strategies for Interviewing and Analysis." *Social Problems* 37, no. 1: 96–116.

Deveaux, M. 1994. "Feminism and Empowerment: A Critical Reading of Foucault." *Feminist Studies* 20: 223–247.

Ditch, John. 1991. "The Undeserving Poor: Unemployed People, Then and Now." Pp. 24–40 in *The State or the Market,* edited by M. Loney. London: Sage.

Domosh, Mona. 1991. "Towards a Feminist Historiography of Geography." *Transactions of the Institute of British Geographers* 16: 95–104.

Dovey, Kim. 1999. *Framing Places. Mediating Power in Built Form.* London: Routledge.

Dowling, Robyn. 1998. "Suburban Stories, Gendered Lives: Thinking through Difference." Pp. 69–88 in *Cities of Difference,* edited by Ruth Fincher and Jane Jacobs. London: Guilford Press.

Drakulic, Slavenka. 1993. *How We Survived Communism and Even Laughed.* New York: Norton.

Duffy, Michelle, Susan J. Smith, and Nichola Wood. 2001. "Musical Methodologies." Paper presented at the 97th annual meeting of the Association of American Geographers, New York, February 27–March 3.

Duffy, Rosaleen. 1999. "The Role and Limitations of State Coercion: Poaching and Anti-Poaching Policies in Zimbabwe." *Journal of Contemporary African Studies* 17: 97–121.

Duley, Bridget. 1997. "Authoring New Zealand: Media Representations of National Identity." Unpublished Ph.D. thesis, University of Waikato, Hamilton, New Zealand.

Duncan, Nancy, ed. 1996a. *BodySpace.* London: Routledge.

Duncan, Nancy. 1996b. "Renegotiating Gender and Sexuality in Public and Private Spaces." Pp. 127–145 in *BodySpace,* edited by Nancy Duncan. London: Routledge.

Durkheim, Emile. 1982. *The Rules of Sociological Method.* London: Macmillan.

Dyck, Isabel. 1995. "Hidden Geographies: The Changing Lifeworlds of Women with Multiple Sclerosis." *Social Science and Medicine* 40: 307–320.

Dyck, Isabel. 1999. "Body Troubles: Women, the Workplace and Negotiations of a Disabled Identity." Pp. 119–137 in *Mind and Body Spaces: Geographies of Illness, Impairment and Disability,* edited by Ruth Butler and Hester Parr. London: Routledge.

Eagleton, Terry. 1981. *Walter Benjamin: Towards a Revolutionary Criticism.* London: Verso.

Ellin, Nan, ed. 1997. *Architecture of Fear.* New York: Princeton Architectural Press.

Ellis, Stephen. 1989. "Tuning in to Pavement Radio." *African Affairs* 88: 321–330.

Ellis, Stephen, and Janet MacGaffey. 1996. "Research on Sub-Saharan Africa's Unrecorded International Trade: Some Methodological and Conceptual Problems." *African Studies Review* 39: 19–41.

Elmessiri, Nur, and Abdelwahab Elmessiri. 1996. "Introduction." Pp. 1–29 in *A Land of Stone and Thyme: An Anthology of Palestinian Short Stories,* edited by Nur Almessiri and Abdelwahab Elmessiri. London: Quartet Books.

Englehardt, H. Tristram. 1996. *Foundations of Bioethics,* 2nd ed. Oxford: Oxford University Press.

Fairclough, Norman. 1992. *Discourse and Social Change.* Cambridge: Polity Press.

Fairclough, Norman. 1995. *Media Discourse.* New York: Edward Arnold.

Fairclough, Norman. 2000. *New Labour, New Language?* London: Routledge.

Feld, Steven, and Keith H. Basso, eds. 1996. *Senses of Place.* Santa Fe, N.M.: School of American Research Press.

Felman, Shoshona, and Dori Laub. 1992. *Testimony: Crises of Witnessing in Literature, Psychoanalysis, and History.* New York: Routledge.

Feminist Geography Reading Group. 2000. "(Un)doing Academic Practice: Notes from a Feminist Geography Workshop. *Gender, Place and Culture* 7: 435–439.

Ferguson, K. E. 1989. "Knowledge, Politics and Persons in Feminist Theory." *Political Theory* 17: 302–314

Finch, Janet. 1984. "It's Great to Have Someone to Talk To." Pp. 70-87 in *Social Researching: Politics, Problems, Practice,* edited by Colin Bell and Helen Roberts. London: Routledge and Kegan Paul.

Fischer, Michael M. J. 1986. "Ethnicity and the Post-modern Arts of Memory." Pp. 194–233 in *Writing Culture: The Poetics and Politics of Ethnography,* edited by James Clifford and George E. Marcus. Berkeley: University of California Press.

Fisk, John. 1987. *Television Culture.* London: Methuen.

Fleischman, Suzanna. 1998. "Gender, the Personal, and the Voice of Scholarship: A Viewpoint." *Signs: Journal of Women in Culture and Society* 23: 975–1016.

Foucault, Michel.1970. *Discipline and Punish.* New York: Vintage Books.

Foucault, Michel. 1977. *Discipline and Punish: The Birth of the Prison.* Trans. by Alan Sheridan. London: Allen Press

Foucault, Michel. 1981. *The History of Sexuality, Volume One—An Introduction.* London: Penguin.

Foucault, Michel. 1984. "The Order of Discourse." Pp. 108–138 in *Language and Politics,* edited by Michael J. Shapiro. Oxford: Blackwell.

Foucault, Michel. 1991. "Governmentality." Pp. 87–104 in *The Foucault Effect: Studies in Governmentality,* edited by Graham Burchell, Colin Gordon, and Peter Miller. Hemel Hempstead: Harvester Wheatsheaf.

Fraser, Nancy, and Linda Gordon. 1994. "A Genealogy of Dependency—Tracing a Keyword of the United States Welfare State." *Signs: Journal of Women in Culture and Society* 19: 309–336.

Fraser, Nancy, and Linda Nicholson. 1990. "Social Criticism without Philosophy: An Encounter between Feminism and Postmodernism." Pp. 19–38 in *Postmodernism/Feminism,* edited by Linda Nicholson. London: Routledge.

Frith, Simon. 1991. "The Good, the Bad, and the Indifferent: Defending Popular Culture from the Populists." *Diacritics* 21: 112–115.

Frith, Simon. 1996. "Music and Identity." Pp.108–128 in *Questions of Cultural Identity,* edited by Stuart Hall and Paul du Gay. London: Sage.

Fuss, Diana. 1990. *Essentially Speaking.* New York: Routledge.

Gallop, Jane, ed. 1995. *Pedagogy: The Question of Impersonation.* Bloomington: Indiana University Press.

Gardener, Carol Brooks. 1994. "Out of Place: Gender, Public Places and Situational Disadvantage." Pp. 335–355 in *Now Here, Space Time and Modernity,* edited by Roger Friedland and Deidre Boden. Berkeley: University of California Press.

Gardener, Carol Brooks. 1996. *Passing By: Gender and Public Harassment*. Berkeley: University of California Press.

Garland, David. 1997. "'Governmentality' and the Problem of Crime: Foucault, Criminology, Sociology." *Theoretical Criminology* 1, no. 2: 173–214.

Garton Ash, Timothy. 1997. *The File: A Personal History*. New York: Random House.

Gatens, Moira. 1996. *Imaginary Bodies: Ethics, Power and Corporeality*. London: Routledge.

Gelbard, Robert S. 1996. "The Globalisation of the Drug Trade." Address at the John Jay College of Criminal Justice, Dublin, Ireland.

Gelbard, Robert S. 1997. "The Threat of Transnational Organised Crime and Illicit Narcotics." Statement before the UN General Assembly, New York City.

George, Jane. 1997. "Women and Golf in Scotland." *Oral History* 25: 46–50.

Gibson-Graham, J. K. 1994. "'Stuffed If I Know!': Reflections on Post-modernist Feminist Social Research." *Gender, Place and Culture* 1: 205–224.

Gibson-Graham, J. K. 1996. *The End of Capitalism (as We Knew It)*. Oxford: Blackwell.

Gibson-Graham, J. K. 1997a. "Postmodern Becomings: From the Space of Form to the Space of Potentiality." Pp 306–323 in *Space and Social Theory. Interpreting Modernity and Postmodernity*, edited by Georges Benko and Ulf S. Strohmayer. Oxford: Blackwell.

Gibson-Graham, J. K. 1997b. "Re-placing Class in Economic Geographies: Possibilities for a New Class Politics." Pp. 87–97 in *Geographies of Economies*, edited by Roger Lee and Jane Wills. London: Arnold.

Giddens, Anthony. 1991. *Modernity and Self-Identity: Self and Society in the Late Modern Age*. Cambridge: Polity Press.

Gilligan, Carol. 1993. *In a Different Voice: Psychological Theory and Women's Development*, 2nd ed. Cambridge, Mass.: Harvard University Press.

Gilligan, Carol, Janie Victoria Ward, and Jill McLean Taylor with Betty Bardige, eds. 1988. *Mapping the Moral Domain: A Contribution of Women's Thinking to Psychological Theory and Education*. Cambridge, Mass.: Harvard University Press.

Gilman, Sander. 1993. *Hysteria beyond Freud*. Berkeley: University of California Press.

Gilman, Sander. 1995. *Health and Illness: Images of Difference*. London: Reaktion Books.

Gordon, Colin. 1991. "Government Rationality: An Introduction." In *The Foucault Effect: Studies in Governmentality*, edited by Graham Burchell, Colin Gordon, and Peter Miller. Hemel Hempstead: Harvester Wheatsheaf.

Goudge, Paulette. 1999. "Resistance and Power: Acceptance or Challenge of the White, Western Expert Role in Development and Aid in Nicaragua." Paper presented at the RGS-IBG annual conference, University of Leicester, January.

Grafanaki, Soti. 1996. "How Research Can Change the Researcher: The Need for Sensitivity, Flexibility and Ethical Boundaries in Conducting Qualitative Research in Counselling/Psychotherapy." *British Journal of Guidance and Counselling* 24: 329–338.

Greenwood, David. 1989. "Culture by the Pound: An Anthropological Perspective on Tourism as Cultural Commodification." Pp. 171–186 in *Hosts and Guests. The Anthropology of Tourism*, 2nd ed., edited by Valerie Smith. Philadelphia: University of Pennsylvania Press.

Gregory, Derek. 1989. "Areal Differentiation and Post-modern Human Geography." Pp. 67–96 in *Horizons in Human Geography*, edited by Derek Gregory and Walford Rex. London: Macmillan.

Gregson, Nicky, and Gillian Rose. 2000. "Taking Butler Elsewhere: Performativities, Spatialities and Subjectivities." *Environment and Planning D: Society and Space* 18: 433–452.

Griffiths, Morwenna. 1995. *Feminisms and the Self. The Web of Identity*. New York: Routledge.

Grosz, Elizabeth. 1989. *Sexual Subversions: Three French Feminists*. Sydney: Allen and Unwin.

Grosz, Elizabeth. 1990. "The Body of Signification." Pp. 80–104 in *Abjection, Melancholia and Love: The Work of Julia Kristeva*, edited by John Fletcher and Andrew Benjamin. London: Routledge.

Grosz, Elizabeth. 1992. "Bodies-Cities." Pp. 241–253 in *Sexuality and Space*, edited by Beatriz Colomina. London: Routledge.

Grosz, Elizabeth. 1993. "Bodies and Knowledges: Feminism and the Crisis of Reason." Pp. 187–215 in *Feminist Epistemologies*, edited by Linda Alcoff and Elizabeth Potter. London: New York: Routledge.

Grosz, Elizabeth. 1994. *Volatile Bodies: Toward a Corporeal Feminism*. Bloomington: Indiana University Press.

Grosz, Elizabeth. 1997. "Inscriptions and Body Maps: Representations and the Corporeal." Pp. 236–261 in *Space, Gender and Knowledge*, edited by Linda McDowell and Joanne P. Sharp. London: Arnold.

Grove, William. 1995. "The Drug Trade as a National and International Security Threat." Paper presented at the Security 94 conference held at the Institute of Strategic Studies and the Security Association of South Africa, University of Pretoria, South Africa.

Hahn, Stephen. 1997. "Extravagant Expectation of Freedom: Rumour, Political Struggle, and the Christmas Insurrection Scare of 1865 in the American South." *Past and Present* 157: 122–158.

Haig-Muir, Marnie. 1998. "Skirting the Issue: Women, Gender and Sexuality in the Golfing World." Pp. 315–322 in *Science and Golf III: The Proceedings of the World Scientific Congress of Golf*, edited by Martin R. Farrally and Alastair J. Cochran. Leeds, UK: Human Kinetics.

Halbwachs, Maurice. 1992. *On Collective Memory*, translated by Lewis A. Coser. Chicago: University of Chicago Press.

Hale, Sondra. 1991. "Feminist Method, Process, and Self-Criticism: Interviewing Sudanese Women." Pp. 121–136 in *Women's Words. Feminist Practice of Oral History*, edited by Sherna Berger Gluck and Daphne Patai. London: Routledge.

Hall, Michael. 1992. *Hallmark Tourist Events: Impacts, Management and Planning*. London: Belhaven Press.

Hall, Stuart, and Paul du Gay, eds. 1996. *Questions of Cultural Identity*. London: Sage.

Hammersley, Martyn, and Paul Atkinson. 1983. *Ethnography: Principles in Practice*. London: Routledge.

Hampson, Daphne. 1996. *After Christianity*. London: SCM Press.

Hampton, Michael P. 1996. "Where Currents Meet: The Offshore Interface between Corruption, Offshore Finance Centres and Economic Development." *IDS Bulletin* 27: 78–87.

Handal, Gunnar, and Per Lauvås. 1987. *Promoting Reflective Teaching: Supervision in Action*. Milton Keynes, UK: SRHE and Open University Press.

Hanmer, Jalna, and Mary Maynard, eds. 1987. *Women, Violence and Social Control*. London: Macmillan.

Harasym, Sarah, ed. 1990. *The Post-colonial Critic. Interviews, Strategies, Dialogues/Gayatri Chakravorty Spivak*. London: Routledge.

Haraway, Donna. 1985. "A Manifesto for Cyborgs: Science, Technology and Socialist Feminist in the 1980s." *Socialist Review* 80: 65–107.

Haraway, Donna. 1988. "Situated Knowledges: The Science Question in Feminism and the Privilege of Partial Perspective." *Feminist Studies* 14: 575–599.

Haraway, Donna. 1992. "The Promises of Monsters: A Regenerative Politics for Inappropriate/d Others." Pp. 295–337 in *Cultural Studies*, edited by Lawrence Grossberg, Cary Nelson, and Paula Treichler. New York: Routledge.

Haraway, Donna. 1997. *Modest_Witness@Second_Millennium: FemaleMan meets OncoMouse*. New York: Routledge.

Harding, Sandra. 1986. *The Science Question in Feminism*. Milton Keynes, UK: Open University Press.

Harding, Sandra. 1991. *Whose Science, Whose Knowledge: Thinking from Women's Lives*. Milton Keynes, UK: Open University Press.

Harding, Sandra. 1994. "Feminism and Theories of Scientific Knowledge." Pp. 104–115 in *The Woman Question*, edited by Mary Evans, 2nd ed. London: Sage.

Harding, Sandra. 1998. *Is Science Multicultural? Postcolonialisms, Feminisms, and Epistemologies*. Bloomington: Indiana University Press.

Hargreaves, Jennifer. 1994. *Sporting Females*. London: Routledge.

Harley, Brian. 1992. "Deconstructing the Map." Pp. 231–247 in *Writing Worlds*, edited by Trevor Barnes and James Duncan. London: Routledge.

Harré, Rom. 1986. "An Outline of the Social Constructionist Viewpoint." Pp. 2–15 in *The Social Construction of Emotions*, edited by Rom Harré. Oxford: Basil Blackwell.

Hartman, Geoffrey, H. 1996. *The Longest Shadow: In the Aftermath of the Holocaust*. Bloomington: Indiana University Press.

Harvey, David. 1998. "The Body as Accumulation Strategy." *Environment and Planning D: Society and Space* 16: 401–421.

Hastrup, Kirsten, and Peter Hervik, eds. 1994. *Social Experience and Anthropological Knowledge*. London: Routledge.

Hawkesworth, Mary. 1988. "Knowers, Knowing, Known: Feminist Theory and Claims of Truth." *Signs: Journal of Women in Culture and Society* 14: 533–537.

Hawkins, Peter, and Robin Shohet. 1989. *Supervision in the Helping Professions: An Individual, Group and Organisational Approach*. Buckingham: Open University Press.

Health Canada. 1996. *Anxiety Disorders and Their Treatment: A Critical Review of the Evidence-Based Literature*. Ottawa: Health Canada Publications.

Hekman, Susan. 1992. *Gender and Knowledge: Elements of a Postmodern Feminism*. Cambridge: Polity Press.

Hekman, Susan J. 1995. *Moral Voices, Moral Selves: Carol Gilligan and Feminist Moral Theory*. Cambridge: Polity Press.

Hendershot, C. 1992. "Vampires and Replicants: The One Sex Body in a Two Sex World." *Science Fiction Studies* 22: 373–398.

Herbert, David T. 1989. "Crime and Place: An Introduction." Pp 1–15 in *The Geography of Crime*, edited by David J. Evans and David T. Herbert. London: Routledge.

Herbert, David T., and Judy Darwood. 1992. "Crime Awareness and Urban Neighbourhoods." Pp 145–163 in *Crime, Policing and Place: Essays in Environmental Criminology*, edited by David J. Evans, Nicholas R. Fyfe, and David T. Herbert. London: Routledge.

Hester, Marianne, Liz Kelly, and Jill Radford, eds. 1996. *Women, Violence and Male Power*. Buckingham: Open University Press.

Hillier, Bill. 1996. *Space Is the Machine*. Cambridge: Cambridge University Press.

Hirsch, Marianne. 1998. "Past Lives: Postmemories in Exile." Pp. 418–446 in *Exile and Creativity: Signposts, Travelers, Outsiders, Backward Glances*, edited by Susan Rubin Suleiman. Durham, N.C.: Duke University Press.

Hoagland, Sarah L. 1988. *Lesbian Ethics*. Palo Alto, Calif.: Institute of Lesbian Studies.

Hochschild, Arlie Russell. 1983. *The Managed Heart: Commercialization of Human Feeling.* Berkeley: University of California Press.

Hockenos, Paul. 1993. "Unhappily Ever After: Racial Tensions in Czechoslovakia." *New Statesman and Society* (February 5): 24–27.

Horowitz, Donald L. 1985. *Ethnic Groups in Conflict.* Berkeley: University of California Press.

Huysmann, A. 1988. *After the Great Divide: Modernism, Mass Culture, Post-modernism.* Basingstoke: Macmillan.

Hyman, Herbert, with William Cobb, Jacob Feldman, Clyde Hart, and Charles Stember. 1954. *Interviewing in Social Research.* Chicago: University of Chicago Press.

Ignatieff, Michael. 1993. *Blood and Belonging. Journeys into the New Nationalism.* Toronto: Penguin Books.

International Commission on the Balkans. 1996. *Unfinished Peace: Report of the International Commission on the Balkans.* Foreword by Leo Tindemans, Chairman. Washington, D.C.: Carnegie Endowment for International Peace and Aspen Institute Berlin.

Irigaray, Luce. 1985. *This Sex Which Is Not One.* Ithaca, N.Y.: Cornell University Press.

Jackson, Peter. 1988. "Street Life: The Politics of Carnival." *Environment and Planning D: Society and Space* 6, no. 2: 213–227.

Jackson, Peter. 1991. "The Cultural Politics of Masculinity: Towards a Social Geography." *Transactions of the Institute of British Geographers* 16: 199–213.

Jackson, Peter. 1992. "The Politics of the Streets: A Geography of Caribana." *Political Geography* 11: 1–22.

Jacobs, Jane. 1961. *The Death and Life of Great American Cities.* Harmondsworth: Penguin.

Jaggar, Alison. 1991. "Feminist Ethics: Projects, Problems, Prospects." Pp. 78–104 in *Feminist Ethics,* edited by Claudia Card. Lawrence: University Press of Kansas.

James, Nicky. 1992. "Care = Organisation + Physical Labour + Emotional Labour," *Sociology of Health and Illness* 14, no. 4: 488–509.

JanMohamed, Abdul R. 1992. "Worldliness-without-world, Homelessness-as-Home: Toward a Definition of the Specular Border Intellectual." Pp. 96–120 in *Edward Said: A Critical Reader,* edited by Michael Sprinker. Oxford: Blackwell.

Jay, Martin. 1993. *Downcast Eyes: The Denigration of Vision in Twentieth-Century French Thought.* Berkeley: University of California Press.

Johnson, James H. 1995. *Listening in Paris: A Cultural History.* Berkeley: University of California Press.

Johnston, Lynda. 1996. "Flexing Femininity: Female Body-builders Refiguring 'the Body.'" *Gender, Place and Culture* 3: 327–340.

Johnston, Lynda. 1997. "Queen(s') Street or Ponsonby Poofters? The Embodied HERO Parade Site." *New Zealand Geographer* 53, no. 2: 29–33.

Johnston, Lynda. 2001. "(Other) Bodies and Tourism Studies." *Annals of Tourism Research: A Social Science Journal* 28, no. 1: 180–201.

Jones, Colin, and Roy Porter, eds. 1998. *Reassessing Foucault: Power, Medicine and the Body.* London: Routledge.

Jones, John Paul, III, Heidi J. Nast, and Susan M. Roberts, eds. 1997. *Thresholds in Feminist Geography.* Lanham, Md.: Rowman & Littlefield.

Jowett, Benjamin. 1892. *The Dialogues of Plato.* Translated into English, with analyses and introductions, by Benjamin Jowett. Oxford: Clarendon Press.

Kabbani, Rana. 1986. *Europe's Myths of Orient.* Philadelphia: Temple University Press.

Kanter, Hannah, Sarah Lefanu, Shaila Shah, and Carole Spedding, eds. 1984. *Sweeping Statements.* London: Women's Press.

Kapuscinski, Ryszard. 1994. *Imperium*. New York: Alfred A. Knopf.

Karahasan, Dzevad. 1994. *Sarajevo, Exodus of a City*. New York: Kodansha Globe.

Katz, Cindi. 1992. "All the World Is Staged: Intellectuals and the Projects of Ethnography." *Environment and Planning D: Society and Space* 10: 495–510.

Katz, Cindi. 1994. "Playing the Field: Questions of Fieldwork in Geography." *Professional Geographer* 46: 67–72.

Kearns, Robin A. 1997. "Narrative and Metaphor in Health Geographies." *Progress in Human Geography* 21, no. 2: 269–277.

Keith, Michael. 1992. "Angry Writing: (Re)presenting the Unethical World of the Ethnographer." *Environment and Planning D: Society and Space* 10: 551–568.

Keller, Evelyn Fox. 1985. *Reflections on Gender and Science*. London: New Haven.

Keller, Evelyn Fox. 1992. "How Gender Matters, or Why It's So Hard for Us to Count Past Two." Pp. 42–56 in *Inventing Women: Science, Technology and Gender*, edited by Gill Kirkup and Laurie Smith Keller. Cambridge: Polity Press.

Kelly, Liz. 1988. *Surviving Sexual Violence*. Cambridge: Polity Press.

Kirby, Kathleen M. 1996. *Indifferent Boundaries: Spatial Concepts of Human Subjectivity*. New York: Guilford Press.

Kirkwood, Catherine. 1993. "Investing in Ourselves: Use of Researcher Personal Response in Feminist Methodology." Pp. 25–38 in *Perspectives on Women's Studies for the 1990s: Doing Things Differently?* edited by Joanna De Groot and Mary Maynard. London: Macmillan.

Kleinman, Arthur. 1995. *Writing at the Margin: Discourse between Anthropology and Medicine*. London: University of California Press.

Kleymeyer, Charles D., and Wendy E. Betrand. 1993. "Mis-Applied Cross Cultural Research: A Case Study of an Ill-fated Family Planning Research Project." Pp. 365–437 in *Social Research in Developing Countries*, edited by Martin Bulmer and Donald P. Warwick. London: UCL Press.

Kohlberg, Lawrence. 1981. "Indoctrination versus Relativity in Moral Education." Pp. 6–28 in *The Philosophy of Moral Development*, vol. 1. San Francisco: Harper and Row.

Kondo, Dorinne K. 1990. *Crafting Selves: Power, Gender and Discourses of Identity in a Japanese Workplace*. Chicago: University of Chicago Press.

Kong, Lily. 1995. "Popular Music in Geographical Analyses." *Progress in Human Geography* 19, no. 2: 183–198.

Koskela, Hille. 1997. "Bold Walk and Breakings: Women's Spatial Confidence versus Fear of Violence." *Gender, Place and Culture* 4, no. 3: 301–319.

Koskela, Hille. 1999. "Fear, Control and Space. Geographies of Gender, Fear of Violence, and Video Surveillance." Unpublished Ph.D. thesis, University of Helsinki.

Koskela, Hille, and Rachel Pain. 2000. "Revisiting Fear and Place: Women's Fear of Attack in the Built Environment." *Geoforum* 31: 269–280.

Kristeva, Julia. 1982. *Powers of Horror: An Essay on Abjection*, translated by Leon S. Roudiez. New York: Columbia University Press.

Kurspahic, Kemal. 1997. *As Long as Sarajevo Exists*. Stony Creek, Conn.: Pamphleteer's Press.

Latour, Bruno. 1993. *We Have Never Been Modern*. Hemel Hempstead, UK: Harvester Wheatsheaf.

Latour, Bruno. 1999. *Pandora's Hope: Essays on the Reality of Science Studies*. London: Harvard University Press.

Layard, Richard. 1997a. "Preventing Long-term Unemployment." Pp. 190–204 in *Working for Full Employment*, edited by John Philpott. London: Routledge.

Layard, Richard. 1997b. *What Labour Can Do*. London: Warner Books.

Lazreg, Marina. 1994. "Women's Experience and Feminist Epistemology: A Critical Neo-Rationalist Approach." Pp. 45–62 in Knowing the Difference: Feminist Perspectives in Epistemology, edited by Kathleen Lennon and Margaret Whitford. London: Routledge.

Lee, Roger, and Jane Wills, eds. 1997. Geographies of Economies. London: Arnold.

Lefebvre, Henri. 1990 (1974). The Production of Space. Oxford: Basil Blackwell.

Lehr, John. 1983. "'Texas When I Die': National Identity and Images of Place in Canadian Country Music Broadcasts." Canadian Geographer 27, no. 4: 361–370.

Leonard, Peter. 1997. Postmodern Welfare. London: Sage.

Levitas, Ruth. 1998. The Inclusive Society? Social Exclusion and New Labour. London: Macmillan.

Lewis, Claire, and Steve Pile. 1996. "Woman, Body, Space: Rio Carnival and the Politics of Performance." Gender, Place and Culture: A Journal of Feminist Geography 3, no. 1: 23–41.

Leyshon, Andrew, David Matless, and George Revill. 1995. "The Place of Music." Transactions of the Institute of British Geographers 20: 423–433.

Livingstone, David N. 1992. The Geographical Tradition. Oxford: Blackwell.

Lloyd, Genevieve. 1984. Man of Reason: Male and Female in Western Philosophy. London: Methuen.

Lofving, Staffan, and Ivana Macek, eds. 2000. "On War Revisted." Special issue, Antropologiska Studier 66/67.

Longhurst, Robyn. 1995. "Discursive Constraints on Pregnant Women's Participation in Sport." New Zealand Geographer 51: 13–15.

Longhurst, Robyn. 1996. "Refocusing Groups: Pregnant Women's Geographical Experiences of Hamilton, New Zealand/Aotearoa." Area 28: 143–149.

Longhurst, Robyn. 1997. "(Dis)embodied Geographies." Progress in Human Geography 21: 486–501

Longhurst, Robyn. 2001. Bodies. Exploring Fluid Boundaries. London: Routledge.

Lopes, Carlos. 1996. Balancing Rocks; Environment and Development in Zimbabwe. Harare: SAPES Books.

Lorraine, Tamsin. 1999. Irigaray and Deleuze: Experiments in Visceral Philosophy. Ithaca, N.Y.: Cornell University Press.

Lugones, María. 1991. "On the Logic of Pluralist Feminism." Pp. 35–44 in Feminist Ethics, edited by Claudia Card. Lawrence: University Press of Kansas.

Lupton, Deborah. 1994. Medicine as Culture: Illness, Disease and the Body in Western Societies. London: Sage.

Lupton, Deborah. 1995. "The Embodied Computer/User." Pp. 97–112 in Cyberspace/Cyberbodies/Cyberpunk: Cultures of Technology, edited by Mike Featherstone and Roger Burrows. London: Sage.

Lupton, Deborah. 1998. The Emotional Self. London: Sage.

Macek, Ivana. 2000a. "War Within: Everyday Life in Sarajevo under Siege." Unpublished Ph.D. thesis, Uppsala University, Uppsala, Sweden.

Macek, Ivana. 2000b. "Breaking the Silence." Antropologiska Studier 66/67: 34–49.

Makdisi, Jean Said. 1990. "Beirut Fragments." Raritan 9, no. 4 (Spring): 32–61.

Makumbe, John. 1994. "Bureaucratic Corruption in Zimbabwe: Causes and Magnitude of the Problem." Africa Development 19: 45–60.

Malkki, Liisa H. 1995. "Refugees and Exile: From 'Refugee Studies' to the National Order of Things." Annual Review of Anthropology 24: 495–523.

Malm, Ulf. 1997. Kriminalitet och trygghet i boendet. En studie i stadsdelen Hjällbo. Göteborg: Förvaltnings AB Framtiden.

Malm, Ulf. 1999. Kriminalitet och trygghet i Bergsjön. Göteborg: Förvaltnings AB Framtiden.

Malson, Helen. 1997. *The Thin Woman*. London: Routledge.

Manning, F. E. 1989. "Carnival in the City: The Carribeanization of Urban Landscapes." *Urban Resources* 5, no. 3: 3–43.

Marcus, George E., and Michael M. J. Fischer. 1986. *Anthropology as Cultural Critique*. Chicago: University of Chicago Press.

Marks, Isaac M. 1980. *Living with Fear: Understanding and Coping with Anxiety*. New York: McGraw Hill.

Marks, Isaac M. 1987. *Fears, Phobias and Rituals*. New York: Oxford University Press.

Marsden, J. 1996. "Virtual Sexes and Feminist Futures: The Philosophy of Cyberfeminism." *Radical Philosophy* 78: 6–16.

Marsh, Ian, and L. Galbraith. 1995. "The Political Impact of the Sydney Gay and Lesbian Mardi Gras." *Australian Journal of Political Science* 30, no. 2: 300–320.

Martin, David. 1991. *Geographic Information Systems and Their Socio-Economic Applications*. London: Routledge.

Mason, Jennifer. 1996. *Qualitative Researching*. Thousand Oaks, Calif.: Sage.

Massey, Doreen. 1993. "Power-Geometry and a Progressive Sense of Place." Pp. 59–69 in *Mapping the Futures: Local Cultures, Global Change*, edited by Jon Bird, Barry Curtis, Tim Putnam, George Robertson, and Lisa Tickner. London: Routledge.

Massey, Doreen. 1994. *Space, Place and Gender*. Cambridge: Polity Press.

Matrix Collective. 1984. *Making Space: Women and the Man-Made Environment*. London: Pluto Press.

Maynard, Mary. 1994. "Methods, Practice and Epistemology: The Debate about Feminism and Research." Pp. 10–26 in *Researching Women's Lives from a Feminist Perspective*, edited by Mary Maynard and June Purvis. London: Taylor and Francis.

Maynard, Mary, and June Purvis, eds. 1994. *Researching Women's Lives from a Feminist Perspective*. London: Taylor and Francis.

Mazer, Thérèse M. 1994. "Death and Dying in a Hospice: An Ethnographic Study." Unpublished Ph.D. thesis, University of Edinburgh.

Mbylinyi, Marjorie. 1989. "'I'd Have Been a Man.' Politics and the Labour Process in Producing Personal Narratives." Pp. 204–227 in *Interpreting Women's Lives*, edited by the Personal Narratives Group. Bloomington: Indiana University Press.

McClary, Susan. 1991. *Feminine Endings: Music, Gender and Sexuality*. Minneapolis: University of Minnesota Press.

McDowell, Linda. 1992. "Doing Gender: Feminism, Feminists and Research Methods in Human Geography." *Transactions of the Institute of British Geographers* 17: 399–416.

McDowell, Linda. 1995a. "Understanding Diversity: The Problem of/for 'Theory.'" Pp. 280–295 in *Geographies of Global Change: Remapping the World in the Late Twentieth Century*, edited by Ron J. Johnston, Peter J. Taylor, and Michael J. Watts. Oxford: Blackwell.

McDowell, Linda. 1995b. "Body Work: Heterosexual Gender Performances in City Workplaces." Pp. 75–95 in *Mapping Desire: Geographies of Sexualities*, edited by David Bell and Gill Valentine. London: Routledge.

McDowell, Linda, and Gill Court. 1994. "Performing Work: Bodily Representations in Merchant Banks." *Environment and Planning D: Society and Space* 12: 727–750.

McDowell, Linda, and Joanne P. Sharp, eds. 1997. *Space, Gender, Knowledge*. London: Arnold.

McLeay, Colin. 1997. "Popular Music and Expressions of National Identity." *New Zealand Journal of Geography* 103 (April): 12–17.

McLeod, John. 1996. "Qualitative Approaches to Research in Counselling and Psychotherapy: Issues and Challenges." *British Journal of Guidance and Counselling* 24: 309–316.

McNally, Richard J. 1994. *Panic Disorder: A Critical Analysis.* New York: Guilford.

McNay, Lois. 1992. *Feminism and Foucault.* Cambridge: Polity Press.

McQuail, Denis. 1997. *Audience Analysis.* London: Sage.

Mehta, Anna, and Liz Bondi. 1999. "Embodied Discourse: On Gender and Fear of Violence." *Gender, Place and Culture* 6: 67–84.

Mertus, Julie, Jasmina Tesanovic, Habiba Metikos, and Rada Boric, eds. 1997. *The Suitcase, Refugee Voices from Bosnia and Croatia.* Berkeley: University of California Press.

Metcalfe, Andrew. 1999. "Inspiration." *Canadian Review of Sociology and Anthropology* 36: 217–240.

Meyer, Leonard B. 1956. *Emotion and Meaning in Music.* Chicago: University of Chicago Press.

Miles, Miranda, and Jonathan Crush. 1993. "Personal Narratives as Interactive Texts: Collecting and Interpreting Migrant Life-Histories." *Professional Geographer* 45: 95–129.

Miller, Daniel. 1991. *Material Culture and Mass Consumption.* Oxford: Basil Blackwell.

Miller, Jody, and Barry Glassner. 1997. "The 'Inside' and 'Outside.' Finding Realities in Interviews." Pp. 99–112 in *Qualitative Research. Theory, Method and Practice*, edited by David Silverman. London: Sage.

Mills, Sara. 1997. *Discourse.* London: Routledge.

Mishler, Elliot. 1986. *Research Interviewing: Context and Narrative.* Cambridge, Mass.: Harvard University Press.

Mitchell, Allyson. 1999. "Lesbian Graffiti and Sub-Cultural Anxiety Attacks: Reading, Spraying and Methodology." Paper presented at IBG-RGS annual conference, University of Leicester, January.

Monk, Janice, and Susan Hanson. 1982. "On Not Excluding Half of the Human in Human Geography." *Professional Geographer* 34: 11–23.

Moody-Adams, Michele M. 1991. "Gender and the Complexity of Moral Voices." Pp. 195–212 in *Feminist Ethics,* edited by Claudia Card. Lawrence: University Press of Kansas.

Mooney, Jayne. 1997. "Violence, Space and Gender: The Social and Spatial Parameters of Violence against Women and Men." Pp. 100–115 in *Transforming Cities: Contested Governance and New Spatial Divisions,* edited by Nick Jewson and Suzanne MacGregor. London: Routledge.

Moores, Shaun. 1995. "Media, Modernity and Lived Experience." *Journal of Communication Inquiry* 9, no. 1: 5–19.

Morgan, David L. 1988. *Focus Groups as Qualitative Research.* London: Sage.

Morley, David. 1989. *Family Television, Cultural Power and Domestic Leisure.* New York: Routledge.

Morley, Louise, and Val Walsh. 1996. *Breaking Boundaries.* London: Taylor and Francis.

Morse, M. 1994. "What Do Cyborgs Eat? Oral Logic in an Information Society." Pp. 157–189 in *Culture on the Brink: Ideologies of Technology,* edited by G. Bender and T. Druckey. Seattle: Bay Press.

Moss, Pamela. 1993. "Focus: Feminism as Method." *Canadian Geographer* 37: 48–49.

Moss, Pamela, 1999. "Autobiographical Notes on Chronic Illness." Pp. 155–166 in *Mind and Body Spaces: Geographies of Illness, Impairment and Disability,* edited by Ruth Butler and Hester Parr. London: Routledge.

Moss, Pamela, and Isabel Dyck. 1996. "Inquiry into Environment and Body: Women, Work and Chronic Illness." *Environment and Planning D: Society and Space* 14: 737–753.

Moss, Pamela, and Isabel Dyck. 1999. "Body, Corporeal Space, and Legitimating Chronic Illness: Women Diagnosed with ME." *Antipode* 31, no. 4: 372–397.

Munt, Sally. 1995. "The Lesbian Flâneur." Pp. 114–125 in *Mapping Desire: Geographies of Sexualities*, edited by David Bell and Gill Valentine. London: Routledge.

Mwangi, Wangethi. 1997. "Expanding the Frontiers of Press Freedom in Kenya." Paper at the annual international conference "Running, Researching and Reporting Africa," University of Edinburgh, Centre for African Studies, October 21–22.

Namaste, Ki. 1996. "Genderbashing: Sexuality, Gender and the Regulation of Public Space." *Environment and Planning D: Society and Space* 14: 221–240.

Nash, Catherine. 1994. "Remapping the Body/Land: New Cartographies of Identity, Gender, and Landscape in Ireland." Pp. 227–250 in *Writing Women and Space: Colonial and Postcolonial Geographies*, edited by Alison Blunt and Gillian Rose. New York: Guilford Press.

Nast, Heidi. 1994. "Opening Remarks on 'Women in the Field.'" *Professional Geographer* 46: 54–66.

Nast, Heidi. 1998. "The Body as 'Place.' Reflexivity and Fieldwork in Kano, Nigeria." Pp. 93–116 in *Places through the Body*, edited by Heidi J. Nast and Steve Pile. London: Routledge.

Nast, Heidi J., and Steve Pile, eds. 1998a. *Places through the Body*. London: Routledge.

Nast, Heidi J., and Steve Pile. 1998b. "Introduction: MakingPlacesBodies." Pp.1–19 in *Places through the Body*, edited by Heidi J. Nast and Steve Pile. London: Routledge.

Negus, Keith. 1996. *Popular Music in Theory: An Introduction*. Cambridge: Polity Press.

Nicholson, Linda. 1993. "Women, Morality, and History." Pp. 87–101 in *An Ethic of Care: Feminist and Interdisciplinary Perspectives*, edited by Mary Larrabee. New York: Routledge.

Nielsen, Joyce M. 1990. *Feminist Research Methods*. Boulder, Colo.: Westview.

Nietschmann, Bernard. 1997. "Protecting Indigenous Coral Reefs and Sea Territories, Miskito Coast, RAAN, Nicaragua." Pp. 193–224 in *Conservation through Cultural Survival: Indigenous Peoples and Protected Areas,* edited by Stan Stevens. Washington, D.C.: Island Press.

Noddings, Nel. 1984. *Caring: A Feminine Approach to Ethics and Moral Education*. Berkeley: University of California Press.

Nora, Pierre. 1989. "Between Memory and History: *Les Lieux de mémoire*," trans. Marc Roudebush. *Representations* 26: 7–25.

Nordstrom, Carolyn, and Antonius C. G. Robben. 1995. *Fieldwork under Fire*. Berkeley: University of California Press.

Nunner-Winkler, Gertrud. 1993. "Two Moralities? A Critical Discussion of an Ethic of Care and Responsibility versus an Ethic of Rights and Justice." Pp. 143–156 in *An Ethic of Care: Feminist and Interdisciplinary Perspectives,* edited by Mary Larrabee. New York: Routledge.

Nylund, Katarina. 2000. "Place and Cultural Identity in the Segregated City." *Finnish Journal of Urban Studies (Yhteiskuntasuunnittelu)* 38: 6–16.

O'Docherty, Brian. 1999. *Inside the White Cube: The Ideology of the Gallery Space*. Santa Monica, Calif.: Lapis Press.

Oakley, Anne. 1981. "Interviewing Women: A Contradiction in Terms." Pp. 30–61 in *Doing Feminist Research*, edited by Helen Roberts. London: Routledge.

Okely, Judith. 1996. *Own or Other Culture*. London: Routledge.

Olesen, Virginia. 1994. "Feminisms and Models of Qualitative Research." Pp. 158–174 in *A Handbook of Qualitative Research,* edited by Norman K. Denzin and Yvonna S. Lincoln. London: Sage.

Oliver, Kelly. 1993. *Reading Kristeva: Unravelling the Double Bind*. Bloomington: Indiana University Press.

Ormrod, S. 1995. "Feminist Sociology and Methodology: Leaky Black Boxes in Gender/Technology Relations." Pp. 146–173 in *The Gender Technology Relation: Contemporary Theory and Research,* edited by Keith Grint and Rosalind Gill. London: Taylor and Francis.

Ó Tuathail, Gearóid. 1996. "An Anti-Geopolitical Eye: Maggie O'Kane in Bosnia, 1992–93." *Gender, Place and Culture* 3: 171–185.

Owens, Craig. 1997. "The Birth and Death of the Viewer: On the Public Function of Art." Pp. 16–23 in *Dia Art Foundation,* edited by Hal Foster. Seattle: Bay Press.

Pain, Rachel H. 1991. "Space, Sexual Violence and Social Control: Integrating Geographical and Feminist Analyses of Women's Fear of Crime." *Progress in Human Geography* 15: 415–431.

Pain, Rachel H. 1997. "Social Geographies of Women's Fear of Crime." *Transactions of the Institute of British Geographers* 22: 231–244.

Pain, Rachel. 2000. "Place, Social Relations and the Fear of Crime: A Review." *Progress in Human Geography* 24: 365–388.

Painter, Kate. 1992. "Different Worlds: The Spatial, Temporal and Social Dimensions of Female Victimization." Pp. 164–195 in *Crime, Policing and Place: Essays in Environmental Criminology,* edited by David J. Evans, Nicholas R. Fyfe, and David T. Herbert. London: Routledge.

Park, D. C., J. P. Radford, and M. H. Vickers. 1998. "Disability Studies in Human Geography." *Progress in Human Geography* 22, no. 2: 208–233.

Parr, Hester. 1998. "The Politics of Methodology in 'Post-Medical Geography': Mental Health Research and the Interview." *Health and Place* 4: 341–353.

Pateman, Carol. 1989. *The Disorder of Women.* Cambridge: Polity Press.

Peake, Linda, ed. 1989. "The Challenge of Feminist Geography." *Journal of Geography in Higher Education* 13: 85–121.

Penny, S. 1994. "Virtual Reality as Completion of the Enlightenment Project." Pp. 231–248 in *Culture on the Brink: Ideologies of Technology,* edited by G. Bender and T. Druckey. Seattle: Bay Press.

Penrose, Jan. 1994. "'Mon pays ce n'est pas un pays' Full Stop: The Concept of Nation as a Challenge to the Nationalist Aspirations of the Parti Québécois." *Political Geography* 13, 2: 161–181.

Petridis, Alexis. 1999. "The Cardigans in Japan." *Q* 152 (May): 70–74.

Phillips, Adam. 1988. *Winnicott.* London: Fontana.

Phillips, Estelle M., and D. S. Pugh. 1987. *How to Get a Ph.D.: A Handbook for Students and Their Supervisors.* Buckingham: Open University Press.

Pile, Steve, and Nigel Thrift, eds. 1995. *Mapping the Subject* London: Routledge.

Plumwood, Val. 1993. *Feminism and the Mastery of Nature.* London: Routledge.

Pocock, Douglas. 1989. "Sound and the Geographer." *Geography* 74: 193–200.

Pocock, Douglas. 1993. "The Senses in Focus." *Area* 25, no. 1: 11–16.

Porteous, J. Douglas. 1985. "Smellscape." *Progress in Human Geography* 9, no. 3: 356–378.

Poster, Mark. 1990. *The Mode of Information: Post-structuralism and Social Context.* Cambridge: Polity Press.

Powell, Martin. 2000. "New Labour and the Third Way in the British Welfare State: A New and Distinctive Approach?" *Critical Social Policy* 62: 39–60.

Power, Joey. 1998. "Remembering Du: An Episode in the Development of Malawian Political Culture." *African Affairs* 97: 369–396.

Pratt, Geraldine. 1992. "Spatial Metaphors and Speaking Positions." *Environment and Planning D: Society and Space* 10: 241–243.

Probyn, Elspeth. 1993. *Sexing the Self: Gendered Positions in Cultural Studies*. London: Routledge.

Punch, Maurice. 1986. *The Politics and Ethics of Fieldwork*. Beverley Hills, Calif.: Sage.

Punch, Maurice. 1994. "Politics and Ethics in Qualitative Research." Pp. 83–97 in *A Handbook of Qualitative Research*, edited by Norman K. Denzin and Yvonna S. Lincoln. London: Sage.

Radway, Janice. 1988. "Reception Study: Ethnography and the Problem of Dispersed Audiences and Nomadic Subjects." *Cultural Studies* 2, no. 3: 359–376.

Ramsay, Karen. 1996. "Emotional Labour and Qualitative Research: How I Learned Not to Laugh or Cry in the Field." Pp. 131–146 in *Methodological Imaginations*, edited by E. Stina Lyon and Joan Busfield. Basingstoke: Macmillan.

Reay, Diane. 1996. "Insider Perspectives or Stealing the Words Out of Women's Mouths: Interpretation in the Research Process." *Feminist Review* 53: 57–73.

Rennie, David L. 1996. "Fifteen Years of Doing Qualitative Research on Psychotherapy." *British Journal of Guidance and Counselling* 24: 317–327.

Revill, George. 2000. "Music and the Politics of Sound: Nationalism, Citizenship, and Auditory Space." *Environment and Planning D: Society and Space* 18: 597–613.

Rich, Adrienne. 1980. *On Lies, Secrets and Silence*. London: Virago.

Richards, Janet Radcliffe. 1980. *The Sceptical Feminist: A Philosophical Enquiry*. London: Routledge and Kegan Paul.

Roberts, John. 1996. "Notes on 90s Art." *Art Monthly* 200: 3–4.

Rodaway, Paul. 1994. *Sensuous Geographies: Body, Sense, Place*. London: Routledge.

Rogoff, Irit. 2000. *Terra Infirma: Geography's Visual Culture*. London: Routledge.

Rosaldo, Renato. 1989. *Culture and Truth. The Remaking of Social Analysis*. Boston: Beacon Press.

Rose, Gillian. 1993. *Feminism and Geography: The Limits of Geographical Knowledge*. Cambridge: Polity Press.

Rose, Gillian. 1996. "As If the Mirror Had Bled. Masculine Dwelling, Masculinist Theory and Feminist Masquerade." Pp. 56–74 in *Body Space. Destabilizing Geographies of Gender and Sexuality*, edited by Nancy Duncan. London: Routledge.

Rose, Gillian. 1997a. "Spatialities of 'Community,' Power and Change: The Imagined Geographies of Community Arts Projects." *Cultural Studies* 11, no. 1: 1–16.

Rose, Gillian. 1997b. "Situating Knowledges: Positionality, Reflexivities and Other Tactics." *Progress in Human Geography* 21: 305–320.

Rose, Gillian. 1999. "Performing the Body." Pp. 247–259 in *Human Geography Today*, edited by Doreen Massey, John Allen, and Philip Sarre. Cambridge: Polity Press.

Rose, Nikolas. 1992. "Political Power Beyond the State: Problematics of Government." *British Journal of Sociology* 43, no. 2: 172–205.

Rosler, Martha. 1999. "Lookers, Buyers, Dealers, and Makers: Thoughts on Audience." Pp. 311–339 in *Art after Modernism: Rethinking Representation*, edited by Brian Wallis and Marcia Tucker. New York: New Museum of Contemporary Art in association with Godine.

Ross, Andrew. 1991. *Strange Weather: Culture, Science and Technology in an Age of Limits*. London: Verso.

Rossel, Pierre, ed. 1988. *Manufacturing the Exotic*. Copenhagen: International Working Group for Indigenous Affairs.

Rothenberg, Tamar. 1995. "And She Told Two Friends: Lesbians Creating Urban Social Space." Pp. 165–181 in *Mapping Desire: Geographies of Sexualities*, edited by David Bell and Gill Valentine. London: Routledge.

Rubin, Herbert J., and Irene S. Rubin. 1995. *Qualitative Interviewing: The Art of Hearing Data*. Thousand Oaks, Calif.: Sage.

Ruddick, Sara. 1989. *Maternal Thinking: Toward a Politics of Peace*. Boston: Beacon.

Russ, Joanna. 1984. *How to Suppress Women's Writing*. London: Women's Press.

Said, Edward W. 1993. *Culture and Imperialism*. New York: Alfred A. Knopf.

Said, Edward, W. 1996. *Representations of the Intellectual*. New York: Vintage Books.

Said, Edward W. 1999a. "Palestine: Memory, Invention and Space." Pp. 3–20 in *The Landscape of Palestine: Equivocal Poetry*, edited by Ibrahim Abu-Lughod, Roger Heacock, and Khaled Nashef. Birzeit: Birzeit University Publications.

Said, Edward W. 1999b. "Farewell to Tahia." *Al-Ahram Weekly* (October 7–13).

Saltzberger-Wittenberg, Isca. 1983. *The Emotional Experience of Teaching and Learning*. London: Routledge and Kegan Paul.

Savage, Edna. 1987. *Overcoming Agoraphobia*. Rochdale, UK: Byron Press.

Sayigh, Rosemary. 1979. *Palestinians: From Peasants to Revolutionaries*. London: Zed.

Schama, Simon. 1995. *Landscape and Memory*. London: HarperCollins.

Schutz, Alfred. 1971a. "The Homecomer." Pp. 106–119 in *Collected Papers II. Studies in Social Theory*, edited by Arvid Brodersen. The Hague: Martinus Nijhoff.

Schutz, Alfred. 1971b. "The Stranger." Pp. 91–105 in *Collected Papers II. Studies in Social Theory*, edited by Arvid Brodersen. The Hague: Martinus Nijhoff.

Scott, James C. 1985. *Weapons of the Weak: Everyday Forms of Peasant Resistance*. New Haven, Conn.: Yale University Press.

Scott, James C. 1990. *Domination and the Arts of Resistance: Hidden Transcripts*. New Haven, Conn.: Yale University Press.

Seidenberg, Robert, and Karen DeCrow. 1983. *Women Who Marry Houses: Panic and Protest in Agoraphobia*. New York: McGraw Hill.

Selltiz, Claire, Lawrence Wrightsman, Stuart Cook, and Louise Kidder. 1981. *Research Methods in Social Relations*. New York: Holt, Rinehart and Winston.

Sennett, Richard. 1994. *Flesh and Stone. The Body and the City in Western Civilization*. London: Faber.

Shepherd, John. 1991. *Music as Social Text*. Cambridge: Polity.

Shore, Cris, and Susan Wright. 1997. "Policy: A New Field of Anthropology." Pp. 3–37 in *Anthropology of Policy: Critical Perspectives on Governance and Power*, edited by Cris Shore and Susan Wright. London: Routledge.

Showalter, Elaine. 1985. *The Female Malady*. New York: Pantheon.

Showalter, Elaine. 1997. *Hystories: Hysterical Epidemics and Modern Media*. New York: Columbia University Press.

Shuker, Roy, and Michael Pickering. 1994. "Kiwi Rock: Popular Music and Cultural Identity in New Zealand." *Popular Music* 13, no. 3: 261–278.

Sibley, David. 1995. *Geographies of Exclusion: Society and Difference in the West*. London: Routledge.

Skeggs, Beverley. 1997. *Formations of Class and Gender: Becoming Respectable*. London: Sage.

Slater, Don. 1995. "Photography and Modern Vision: The Spectacle of 'Natural Magic.'" Pp. 218–237 in *Visual Culture*, edited by Chris Jenks. London: Routledge.

Slyomovics, Susan. 1998. *The Object of Memory: Arab and Jew Narrate the Palestinian Village*. Philadelphia: University of Pennsylvania Press.

Smith, Anthony, D. 1991. *National Identity*. London: Penguin.

Smith, Fiona. 1996. "Problematizing Language: Limitations and Possibilities in 'Foreign Language' Research." *Area* 28: 160–166.

Smith, Mark J. 1998. *Social Science in Question*. London: Sage.

Smith, Michael J. 1995. "Ethics in Focus Groups: A Few Concerns." *Qualitative Health Research* 5: 478–486.

Smith, Neil, and Cindi Katz. 1993. "Grounding Metaphor: Towards a Spatialized Politics." Pp. 67–83 in *Place and the Politics of Identity,* edited by Michael Keith and Steve Pile. London: Routledge.

Smith, Sidonie. 1993. "Who's Talking/Who's Listening Back? The Subject of Personal Narrative." *Signs: Journal of Women in Culture and Society* 18: 392–407.

Smith, Susan. 1987. "Fear of Crime: Beyond a Geography of Deviance." *Progress in Human Geography* 11: 1–23.

Smith, Susan. 1989. "Social Relations, Neighbourhood Structure, and the Fear of Crime in Britain." Pp 193–227 in *The Geography of Crime,* edited by David J. Evans and David T. Herbert. London: Routledge.

Smith, Susan J. 1994. "Soundscape." *Area* 26, no. 3: 232–240.

Smith, Susan J. 1997. "Beyond Geography's Visible Worlds: A Cultural Politics of Music." *Progress in Human Geography* 21, no. 4: 502–529.

Smith, Susan J. 2000. "Performing the (Sound)World." *Environment and Planning D: Society and Space* 18: 615–637.

Spain, Daphne. 1992. *Gendered Spaces.* Chapel Hill: University of North Carolina Press.

Spelman, Elizabeth. 1991. "The Virtue of Feeling and the Feeling of Virtue." Pp. 213–232 in *Feminist Ethics,* edited by Claudia Card. Lawrence: University Press of Kansas.

Spender, Dale. 1980. *Man Made Language.* London: Routledge.

Spender, Dale. 1986. *For the Record: The Making and Meaning of Feminist Knowledge.* London: Women's Press.

Spooner, Rachel. 1996. "Contested Representations: Black Women and the St Paul's Carnival." *Gender, Place and Culture: A Journal of Feminist Geography* 3, no. 2: 187–203.

Stacey, Jackie. 1988. "Can There Be a Feminist Ethnography?" *Women's Studies International* 11: 21–27.

Stanko, Elizabeth. 1990. *Everyday Violence.* London: Virago.

Stanley, Liz, and Sue Wise. 1993. *Breaking Out Again: Feminist Ontology and Epistemology.* London: Routledge.

Stares, Paul B. 1996. *Global Habit: The Drug Problem in a Borderless World.* Washington, D.C.: Brookings Institution.

Stattin, Jochum. 1990. *Från gastkramning till gatuvåld—en etnologisk studie av svenska rädslor.* Stockholm: Carlsson.

Steffensen, Joanne. 1996. "Decoding Perversity: Queering Cyberspace." *Parallel Gallery and Journal* <http://www.va.com.au/parallel/>.

Steiner, Roberto. 1998. "Colombia's Income from the Drug Trade." *World Development* 26: 1013–1031.

Stokes, Martin, ed. 1994. *Ethnicity, Identity and Music.* Oxford: Berg.

Stone, Sandy. 1995a. "Sex and Death among the Disembodied: VR, Cyberspace and the Nature of Academic Discourse." Pp. 69–84 in *The Cultures of Computing,* edited by Susan Star. Oxford: Blackwell.

Stone, Sandy. 1995b. *The War of Desire and Technology at the Close of the Mechanical Age.* Cambridge, Mass.: MIT Press.

Storr, Anthony. 1992. *Music and the Mind.* London: HarperCollins.

Strinati, Dominic. 1995. *An Introduction to Theories of Popular Culture.* London: Routledge.

Swedenberg, Ted. 1995. *Memories of Revolt: The 1936–39 Rebellion and the Palestinian National Past.* Minneapolis: University of Minnesota Press.

Swedenberg, Ted. 1999. "Arab 'World Music' in the US." Paper presented at symposium on the Arts in Arab Societies: Culture in a Transnational Era, Georgetown University, April 7–8.

Symonds, Alexandra. 1973. "Phobias after Marriage: Women's Declaration of Dependence." Pp. 288–303 in *Psychoanalysis and Women*, edited by Jean Baker Miller. New York: Brunner/Mazel Publishers.

Synnott, Anthony, and David Howes. 1996. "Canada's Visible Minorities: Identity and Representation." Pp. 137–160 in *Re-situating Identities: The Politics of Race, Ethnicity, Culture*, edited by Vered Amit-Talai and Caroline Knowles. Peterborough, Ontario: Broadview Press.

Teather, Elizabeth Kenworthy, ed. 1999. *Embodied Geographies*. London: Routledge.

Theodore, Nik, and Jamie Peck. 2001. "Searching for Best Practice in Welfare-to-Work: The Means, the Method and the Message." *Policy and Politics* 29: 81–94.

Thompson, Linda. 1992. "Feminist Methodology for Family Studies." *Journal of Marriage and the Family* 54: 3–18.

Thrift, Nigel. 2000. "Afterwords." *Environment and Planning D: Society and Space* 18: 213–255.

Tian, P. S., K. Wanstall, and L. Evans. 1990. "Sex Differences in Panic Disorder with Agoraphobia." *Journal of Anxiety Disorders* 4: 317–324.

Tiby, Eva. 1991. "Kvinna och rädd?" Pp. 13–26 in *Rädslan för brott*, edited by Gunilla Wiklund. Stockholm: BRÅ-rapport.

Tiby, Eva. 1999. *Hatbrott?: homosexuella kvinnors och mäns berättelser om utsatthet för brott*. Stockholm: Stockholms Universitet.

Tompkins, Jane. 1989. "Me and My Shadow." Pp. 121–139 in *Gender and Theory. Dialogues on Feminist Criticism*, edited by Linda Kauffman. Oxford: Basil Blackwell.

Treweek, Geraldine Lee. 1996. "Emotion Work, Order, and Emotional Power in Care Assistant Work." Pp. 115–132 in *Health and the Sociology of Emotions*, edited by Veronica James and Jonathan Gabe. Oxford: Blackwell.

Turkle, Sherry. 1995. *Life on the Screen: Identity in the Age of the Internet*. New York: Simon and Schuster.

Ugresic, Dubravka. 1996. "The Confiscation of Memory." *New Left Review* 218: 26–39.

Ugresic, Dubravka. 1998. *The Culture of Lies*. London: Phoenix House.

United Nations High Commission for Refugees (UNHCR). 1998. *Statistics Package, March 1998*, Sarajevo, Bosnia: United Nations High Commission for Refugees.

Urry, John. 1990. *The Tourist Gaze: Leisure and Travel in Contemporary Societies*. London: Sage.

Valentine, Gill. 1989. "The Geography of Women's Fear." *Area* 21: 385–390.

Valentine, Gill. 1992. "Images of Danger: Women's Sources of Information about the Spatial Distribution of Male Violence." *Area* 24: 22–29.

Valentine, Gill. 1995. "Creating Transgressive Space: The Music of k.d. lang" *Transactions of the Institute of British Geographers* 20: 474–485.

Valentine, Gill. 1996. "(Re)Negotiating the 'Heterosexual Street': Lesbian Productions of Space." Pp. 146–155 in *BodySpace: Destablizing Geographies of Gender and Sexuality*, edited by Nancy Duncan. London: Routledge.

Valentine, Gill. 1998. "'Sticks and Stones May Break My Bones': A Personal Geography of Harassment." *Antipode* 30: 305–332.

Vines, Robyn. 1987. *Agoraphobia: The Fear of Panic*. London: Fontana Paperbacks.

Walby, Sylvia. 1996. "Woman and Nation." Pp. 235–254 in *Mapping the Nation*, edited by Gopal Balakrishnan. London: New Left Review.

Warr, Mark. 1985. "Fear of Rape among Urban Women." *Social Problems* 32: 238–250.

Warwick, Donald P. 1993. "The Politics and Ethics of Field Research." Pp. 315–330 in *Social Research in Developing Countries*, edited by Martin Bulmer and Donald P. Warwick. London: UCL Press.

Weber, Max. 1978. *Economy and Society: An Outline of Interpretive Sociology*. Berkeley: University of California Press.

Weil, Stephen. 1997. "The Museum and the Public." *Museum Management and Curatorship* 16: 257–271.

Weine, Stevan M. 1999. *When History Is a Nightmare: Lives and Memories of Ethnic Cleansing in Bosnia–Herzegovina*. New Brunswick, N.J.: Rutgers University Press.

Whatmore, Sarah. 1997. "Dissecting the Autonomous Self: Hybrid Cartographies for a Relational Ethics." *Environment and Planning D: Society and Space* 15: 37–54.

White, Luise. 2000. *Speaking with Vampires: Rumour and History in Colonial Africa*. Berkeley: University of California Press.

Wicke, Peter. 1985. "Sentimentality and High Pathos: Popular Music in Fascist Germany." *Popular Music* 5: 149–159.

Wickham, Chris. 1998. "Gossip and Resistance among the Medieval Peasantry." *Past and Present* 160: 3–24.

Widdowfield, Rebekah. 2000. "The Place of Emotions in Academic Research." *Area* 32, no. 2: 199–208.

Williams, Raymond. 1995. *Culture and Society 1780–1950*. Harmondsworth: Penguin.

Williams, Simon. 1998. "Modernity and the Emotions: Corporeal Reflections on the (Ir)rational." *Sociology* 32: 747–769.

Willams, Steven. 1993a. "Pushing the Boundaries of Tourism." *Belize Review*: 3–8.

Willams, Steven. 1993b. "Tourism on Their Own Terms: How the TEA Blends in with Village Ways." *Belize Review*: 9–20.

Willis, Paul. 1990. *Common Culture*. Milton Keynes, UK: Open University Press.

Wilson, Elizabeth. 1991. *The Sphinx in the City. Urban Life, the Control of Disorder, and Women.* Berkeley: University of California Press.

Winnicott, D. W. 1965. *The Maturational Process and the Facilitating Environment*. London: Karnac.

Winnicott, D. W. 1971. *Playing and Reality*. London: Tavistock.

Winnicott, D. W. 1986. *Home Is Where We Start From*. London: Penguin.

Winnicott, D. W. 1988. *Babies and Their Mothers*. London: Free Association Books.

Wolmark, J. 1993. *Aliens and Others: Science Fiction, Feminism and Postmodernism*. London: Harvester Wheatsheaf.

Women and Geography Study Group of the IBG. 1984. *Geography and Gender: An Introduction to Feminist Geography*. London: Hutchinson.

Women and Geography Study Group of the Royal Geographical Society with the Institute of British Geographers. 1997. *Feminist Geographies: Explorations in Diversity and Difference*. London: Longman.

Wright, Stephen G., and Jean Sayre-Adams. 2000. *Sacred Space: Right Relationship and Spirituality in Healthcare*. London: Churchill Livingstone.

Yardley, Lucy. 1994. *Vertigo and Dizziness*. London: Routledge.

Yardley, Lucy, ed. 1997. *Material Discourses of Health and Illness*. London: Routledge.

Young, Elizabeth H., and Raymond H. Lee. 1996. "Fieldworker Feelings as Data." Pp. 97–113 in *Health and the Sociology of Emotions*, edited by Veronica James and Jonathan Gabe. Oxford: Blackwell.

Young, Iris Marion. 1990. *Justice and the Politics of Difference*. Princeton, N.J.: Princeton University Press.

Yuval-Davis, Nira, and Floya Anthias, eds. 1989. *Woman-Nation-State*. London: Macmillan.

Zemon Davis, Natalie, and Randolph Starn. 1989. Introduction to coedited special issue on Memory and Counter-Memory. *Representations* 26: 1–6.

Index

abjection, 7, 75, 84–88, 256
abnormal, agoraphobics as, 50, 51, 53, 55
Action Teams, 162–63, 164, 170
ADAO. *See* Anxiety Disorders Association of Ontario
Adorno, Theodore, 67
advertisements, golf equipment, 92, *93*
Africa, sub-Saharan, 174–75
agape, 239, 246
agoraphobia: agoraphobics as abnormal, 50, 51, 53, 55; boundaries and, 21, 22–23, 48–49, 55, 256; causes and treatment of, 25, 28–29, 50, 52; experiences of, 15, 19–30, 33n14, 45, 47, 48–53; geographies of, 53–55, 256; Greek origin of the name, 19, 56n2; nonclinical definition, 47; production of space approach, 7, 40; self-help resources, 6, 15–16, 17, 19; subjectivities of, 50–53
AIDS/HIV, 86, 88n1
alienation, 127, 128
Allwood, Robin, 16
Amnesty International, 183
analysis, and self-help videos, 17–19
Anderson, Benedict, 68, 141
Ang, Ien, 146, 147
Anxiety Disorders Association of Ontario (ADAO), 45, 48

Aotearoa/New Zealand HERO parades, 75, 76–78, 81, 82, 83–84, 86, 88, 88n1
Arabic culture, 128–34, 135–36
architects, feminist, 41
ArcInfo, 115
ArcView, 111, 115
arousal, and musical emotions, 63–64
art: and authenticity, 149–51; moral authority of, 150; performance and identity, 9, 123, 125, 126–34; and popular culture, 141, 143–44, 147–50. *See also* audiences; culture
artist: and audience, 143–45, 148. *See also* Palestinian artists
arts workers, 141, 146, 147, 150–51, 151–52, 153, 157n2, 256
Association of American Geographers: Committee on the Status of Women, 1, 254; Geographic Perspectives on Women Specialty Group, 1
Atkinson, Paul, 209, 217
Atlantic Industries Ltd., 180, 181, 182
Auckland, HERO parades, 75, 76–78, 81, 82, 83–84, 86, 88, 88n1
audiences: and arts workers, 141, 146, 147, 150–51, 151–52, 153, 157n2, 256; attitudes to, 9, 140, 147; and class, 144, 148, 151–53; community and

About the Authors

Hannah Avis is a lecturer in geography at the University of Edinburgh, where she studied for her Ph.D. Her research examines meanings of home among young middle-class women.

Ruth Bankey studied for her Ph.D. in the Department of Geography at the University of Edinburgh. Her research examines community organizing by and for those suffering from anxiety, panic, and agoraphobia.

Amanda Bingley is a research associate at the Institute for Health Research at the University of Lancaster. She studied for her Ph.D. in the Department of Geography at the University of Edinburgh. Her research examines gender and landscape perception and draws on her prior training and practice as a psychotherapist.

Liz Bondi is professor of social geography at the University of Edinburgh, where she has been based since 1985. She was founding editor of *Gender, Place and Culture*. She has published widely on gender identities and on gender divisions and urban change. Her current research is about the growth and social meanings of counseling services.

Joyce Davidson is a research fellow at the Institute for Health Research at the University of Lancaster, a post she took after studying for her Ph.D. in the Department of Geography at the University of Edinburgh. She has published several articles and book chapters based on her research on meanings of agoraphobia.

Rosaleen Duffy is a lecturer in the Department of Politics and International Relations at the University of Lancaster. Between 1997 and 1999 she was a research fellow in the Department of Geography at the University of Edinburgh. Her research is about environmental politics in developing countries, especially in Central America and South Africa. She is author of *Killing for Conservation: Wildlife Policy in Zimbabwe* 2000) and has published several articles on the politics of wildlife conservation in South Africa.

Victoria Ingrid Einagel is a research fellow in geography at the University of Oslo, Norway, where she studied for her Ph.D. She spent 1998–99 as a visiting scholar in the Department of Geography at the University of Edinburgh. Her research is about ethnicity and identity in postwar Bosnia.

Anja-Maaike Green is senior policy officer at the Scottish Museums Council. Before taking up this post she studied for her Ph.D. in the Department of Geography and the Department of Sociology at the University of Edinburgh. Her research focuses on cultural development and the changing social function of art in Edinburgh.

Lynda Johnston is a lecturer in geography at the University of Waikato, New Zealand. Between 1998 and 2001 she was a lecturer in geography at the University of Edinburgh. Her main research interests include the intersections of feminist and poststructuralist thought, focusing particularly on gendered/sexed and sexualized embodiment and tourism.

Susan Lilley is a researcher in the Central Research Unit at the Scottish Executive. Prior to taking up her current post she was based in the Department of Geography where she completed her Ph.D. and a postdoctoral research project concerned with how spaces are produced through the use of digital technologies.

Carina Listerborn studied for her Ph.D. at the Department of Urban Design and Planning at Chalmers University of Technology in Göteborg, Sweden. She spent part of the year 2000–2001 as a visiting scholar in the Department of Geography at the University of Edinburgh. Her research focuses on gender aspects of safer cities and crime prevention programs.

Shonagh McEwan studied for her Ph.D. in the Department of Geography at the University of Edinburgh, where she also completed her first degree. As an under-graduate she wrote a dissertation examining gender issues in golf. Her doctoral research is about disability and inclusion/exclusion in the spaces of golf.

Mona Marshy studied for her Ph.D. in the Department of Geography at the University of Edinburgh. Her research is about constructions of identity and culture among Palestinians in the diaspora, with a focus on visual art and musical productions by artists of Palestinian origin in Canada.

Niamh O'Connor is a research fellow in the Department of Geography at the University of Edinburgh, where she studied for her Ph.D. Her research is about political discourses of welfare in the United Kingdom.

Gillian Rose is a senior lecturer at the Open University in the United Kingdom. Between 1993 and 1999 she was a lecturer then a senior lecturer in the Department of Geography at the University of Edinburgh. Her publications include *Feminism and Geography* (1993) and *Visual Methodologies* (2001).

Bella Vivat is a researcher on the Psychosocial Oncology Research Team at the Lynda Jackson Macmillan Centre, Mount Vernon Hospital, Middlesex. Prior to this she studied for her Ph.D. in the doctoral program on Social and Economic Perspectives on Technology at the University of Edinburgh. Her doctoral research is an ethnographic study of spiritual aspects of care in a Scotland hospice.

Nichola Wood is a lecturer in geography at the University of Bristol. She studied for her Ph.D. in the Department of Geography at the University of Edinburgh. Her research centers on musical performances and the negotiation of Scottish national identities.